Fitting & Pattern Alteration:
A Multi-Method Approach

Elizabeth G. Liechty
Assistant Professor
Clothing and Textiles
Brigham Young University

Della N. Pottberg
Assistant Professor
Clothing and Textiles
Brigham Young University

Judith A. Rasband
Home Economist in Business
Provo, Utah

Fairchild Fashion & Merchandising Group
New York

ACKNOWLEDGMENTS

The measurement procedure for comparing the body to the pattern and the pattern alterations are credited to Elizabeth G. Liechty. The fashion and figure illustrations are credited to Judith A. Rasband. The original theory for the seam method was developed by Della Pottberg and presented to her students at Brigham Young University in unpublished materials entitled "Improved Slash Method" and "Swing and Slide Method." Judith Rasband further tested and developed these procedures for her master's thesis, "Alternative Methods of Pattern Alteration" (Brigham Young University, 1978). Additional refinements as presented in this text result from the combined efforts of the three authors.

We wish to thank our colleagues and Brigham Young University for their encouragement and help. A special thanks to Phyllis Colona for the first editing of the manuscript. Sincere appreciation is expressed to Olga Kontzias, our present editor, and Fairchild Publications for the efficient and effective manner in which they have brought this complex project to fruition.

Book Design by Janet Solgaard

Standard Book Number: 87005-775-8
Library of Congress Catalog Card Number: 85-82047
Printed in the United States of America

PREFACE

If you desire beautifully fitted and comfortable clothing that communicates knowledge, poise, and a positive self-image, this book will be a source of satisfaction for your creative efforts. It presents innovative and tested methods of garment fitting and pattern alteration. We hope it will increase your insight, proficiency, and confidence and stimulate further creative experimentation. Teachers, students, seamstresses, fitters, and tailors agree that individualized fitting and pattern alteration are two of the most frustrating tasks in clothing construction. Our intent is to overcome the problems that contribute to these feelings. Our approach is to teach methods of fitting and alteration that are logical, accurate, consistent, efficient, complete, and satisfying. We have relied upon our own experience in the classroom and authentic experimental research. The resulting book may be used with confidence as a teaching/learning tool. There is still room for refinement in methods, explanations, and illustrations. We invite your comments and look forward to related research.

We desire to meet the needs of the seamstress, student, teacher, lecturer, demonstrator, fitter, and tailor on both the professional and lay level. To meet these needs adequately, we have developed the following features.

- Each figure and pattern is realistically illustrated; each illustration was first drawn to scale and then photographically reduced in size.
- Each alteration procedure is accompanied by meaningful identification of the figure variation causing the fitting problem. Understanding the *what* and the *why* of the procedure is incorporated into the explanation, thus reinforcing learning.
- Each alteration is logical and appropriate for the specific fitting problem. We have carefully incorporated consistency in approach.
- Alteration procedures are presented in a logical manner. A subsequent procedure does not cancel a previous alteration.
- Each procedure has been developed to keep necessary restorations to a minimum. Restorations do not introduce inaccuracies.
- Each alteration example was completed on an actual pattern to ensure the completeness, consistency, and accuracy of the reproduction.
- Each alteration procedure has been developed to eliminate distorted pattern pieces.
- A choice of methods is offered to allow for varying abilities, purposes, or desires.
- Our approach encourages use of the simplest methods for a particular alteration, thus increasing efficiency.
- Illustrations are generally self-explanatory.
- Specific alteration procedures are given for multiple variations occuring on the same figure, since most figures varying from standard require more than one alteration.
- Alteration directions are given for the asymmetrical figure.
- Alteration procedures for basic pattern pieces are also applied to fashion pattern pieces.
- Part Two is organized for use as a ready reference.

Experience is essential to the sharpening of perception and to the perfecting of any skill. As you apply the techniques set forth in this book, we are confident you will develop self-reliance and the satisfaction of knowing that you too can consistently achieve a fault-free, custom fit.

CONTENTS

PART ONE THEORY

1 **Using the Elements & Principles of Design 3**

The Elements of Design **4**
    Line **4**
    Shape **7**
    Color **8**
    Texture **11**

The Principles of Design **14**
    Balance **14**
    Proportion & Scale **15**
    Rhythm **15**
    Emphasis **17**
    Harmony **17**

2 **Selecting & Using Equipment 21**

Measuring Tools **21**
Metric Conversion Charts **22**
Marking Tools **24**
Cutting Tools **26**
Stitching Tools **27**
Fitting Supplies **29**
Pattern Alteration Supplies **30**

3 **Evaluating the Figure 33**

Alternative Methods of Figure Evaluation **33**
The Standard/Ideal/Symmetrical Figure **34**
Symmetrical Variations from the Standard Figure **36**
The Asymmetrical Figure **36**
Posture Evaluation **37**

4 **Selecting Patterns 41**

Pattern Size—Body Circumference **41**
Figure Type—Height & Build **41**
    Children **42**
    Developing & Mature Females **42**
    Developing & Mature Males **43**
    Pattern Company—Build & Posture **43**

5 **Learning from the Contents of A Pattern 47**

Pattern Companies **47**
The Pattern Catalogue **48**
The Pattern Envelope **49**
The Guide Sheet **50**
The Pattern Pieces **51**

6 **Recognizing Correct Fit 55**

Basic Fitting Standards **55**
    Using Grainline & Balance to Evaluate Fit **55**

Using Structural Line & Balance to Evaluate Fit **56**
Using Basic Ease to Evaluate Fit **57**
Standards for Fitting a Basic Garment **57**
Standards for Fitting Fashion Garments **57**
Flare **57**
Pleats, Tucks, Vents & Slits **59**
Gathers **59**
Drape **59**
Darts **60**
Collars **60**
Pockets **61**

7 **Learning to Fit A Garment 63**
Fitting Area **63**
Personal Appearance **63**
Efficiency & Accuracy **64**
Fitting Guidelines **65**
Fitting Procedure **66**
Figure Analysis **66**
Fitting Analysis **66**
Figure Requirement **67**
Garment Alteration **67**
Pattern Alteration **70**

8 **Methods of Fitting 71**
Pinned Pattern Method **71**
Preparing the Pattern for Fitting **72**
Fitting Procedure for Each Unit **73**
Trial Garment Method **74**
Preparing the Pattern **77**
Preparing the Fabric **77**
Joining the Fabric Pieces **78**
Fitting Trial Garments **78**
Measurement Method **80**
Marking the Figure for Measurements **80**
Taking & Recording Body Measurements **80**
Lower Torso (for skirt or pants) **80**
Optional Measurements (for close-fitting pants) **82**
Upper Torso (for the bodice) **82**
Arm (for the sleeve) **84**
Comparing Body Measurements to the Pattern **84**
Lower Torso (skirt) **84**
Lower Torso (pants) **85**
Close-fitting Pants **90**
Bodice Lengths **90**
Bodice Widths **91**
Sleeve Lengths **95**
Sleeve Widths **98**

9 **Methods of Pattern Alteration 99**
Alteration Procedures **99**
The Slash Method **100**
The Seam Method **103**
The Pivot Method **104**
Alterations for Asymmetrical Variations **107**

10 Personalized Patterns & Slopers 111

1. Even Length Changes **111**
2. Combined Even & Uneven Length Changes **112**
3. Combined Even & Uneven Width Changes **114**

Checking the Finished Patterns for Accuracy **116**
Preserving a Personalized Pattern **116**
Using a Basic Pattern or Sloper to Compare Fit &
   Determine Alterations **120**
Using a Basic Pattern or Sloper to Design New Patterns **122**

PART TWO ILLUSTRATED ALTERATION GUIDE

Hip Area **125**
1. Long Lower Torso **126**
2. Short Lower Torso **128**
3. Large Waist **130**
4. Small Waist **132**
5. Prominent Hip Bones **134**
6. Prominent Abdomen **136**
7. Flat Abdomen **138**
8. Sway Back **140**
9. Pelvis Tilts Towards Back **144**
10. Prominent Upper Hip Curve **146**
11. Sloping Upper Hip Curve **148**
12. Broad Hips **150**
13. Narrow Hips **154**
14. Cylindrical-shaped Torso (hip area) **158**
15. Flattened Oval-shaped Torso (hip area) **160**
16. High Buttocks Contour **162**
17. Drooped Buttocks **164**
18. Large Buttocks **166**
19. Flat Buttocks **170**
20. Prominent Pubic Area **174**
21. Recessed Pubic Area **176**

Legs **179**
22. Long Legs **180**
23. Short Legs **182**
24. Large Thighs at Inside **184**
25. Shallow Thighs at Inside **186**
26. Large Thighs at Front **188**
27. Large Thighs at Sides **190**
28. Outward Knee Rotation **192**
29. Inward Knee Rotation **194**
30. Hyperextended Calves **196**
31. Large Legs **198**
32. Thin Legs **200**

Neck **203**
33. High Neck Base at Sides **204**
34. Shallow Neck Base at Sides **208**
35. Large Neck **212**
36. Thin Neck **214**
37. Forward Head **216**
38. Dowager Hump **218**

Shoulders **221**
39. Broad Shoulders **222**

40. Narrow Shoulders **226**
41. Square Shoulders **230**
42. Sloping Shoulders **234**
43. Long Arm Joints (bodice) **238**
44. Short Arm Joints (bodice) **240**
45. Forward Arm Joints (bodice) **242**
46. Prominent Collar Bones **246**

Rib Cage 249
47. Prominent Sternum/Rounded Chest **250**
48. Hollow Chest **252**
49. Rounded Upper Back **254**
50. Erect Upper Back **256**
51. Prominent Shoulder Blades **258**
52. Flat Shoulder Blades **260**
53. Broad Chest/Upper Back **262**
54. Narrow Chest/Upper Back **264**
55. Wide Rib Cage **266**
56. Narrow Rib Cage **268**
57. Cylindrical-shaped Torso (rib cage) **270**
58. Oval-shaped Torso (rib cage) **272**
59. Long Upper Rib Cage **274**
60. Short Upper Rib Cage **276**
61. High Bust Position **278**
62. Low or Pendulous Bust Position **280**
63. Wide Bust Point Span **282**
64. Prominent Bust **284**
65. Large Bust **288**
66. Small Bust **292**
67. Flared Lower Ribs **296**
68. Long Midriff **298**
69. Short Midriff **300**
70. Large Waist **302**
71. Small Waist **304**

Arms 307
72. Arm Length Variations **308**
73. Long Arm Joints (sleeves) **314**
74. Short Arm Joints (sleeves) **316**
75. Large Shoulder Joints **318**
76. Small Shoulder Joints **320**
77. Forward Arm Joints (sleeves) **322**
78. Large Arms **324**
79. Thin Arms **326**
80. Large Upper Arms **328**
81. Large Elbows **330**
82. Large Forearms **332**
83. Inward Rotation of the Elbow **334**
84. Large Wrists **336**
85. Small Wrists **338**

PART THREE

Measurement Chart **341**
Adjustment Record **342**

part one

theory

CHAPTER 1

USING THE ELEMENTS & PRINCIPLES OF DESIGN

People seldom look for evidence of a figure fault or variation. Consciously or unconsciously they seek an attractive and appropriate appearance. Such an appearance can be achieved when all elements of clothing design are selected to present the individual harmoniously. The value judgments that determine what is attractive, appropriate, and harmonious are subject to social and cultural influences. They form the frame of reference through which the figure and the garment are evaluated.

On the following pages the effects of the elements of design are approached in terms of what you *can* do as opposed to what you *should* do. Too often it is assumed that the short person should appear taller and the larger person should appear smaller; this may not be true. Larger individuals may enjoy the sense of presence created by their size; they may choose to emphasize this presence with textured fabrics, bright colors, and bold lines. Small individuals, on the other hand, may choose to emphasize their petite figure through delicate fabrics in small-scale pastel prints.

Categorical generalizations, such as *Use* versus *Avoid* or *Do* versus *Don't*, dictate rather than instruct. The choice of how the elements of design will be used is left to the individual. This choice carries with it the responsibility of evaluating the design elements separately and in combination to achieve a total harmony.

The *elements* of design are the basic, essential components of the art of design. Traditionally, they include line, shape, color, and texture. Each element may be manipulated to help create the desired effect in any given garment on any specific figure.

The *principles* of design are those goals that have become accepted—even expected—over time. They act as guides for the selection and use of the elements of design. The principles of design include balance, proportion, scale, rhythm, emphasis, and harmony. Effective use of the elements and principles of design can alter visual perception to create good design on the individual figure.

The two most effective ways of controlling visual effects are *repetition* and *contrast. Repeating* an element in garment design may reinforce or emphasize a desired figure trait. For example, narrow vertical lines and spaces may be used to reinforce and emphasize height. *Contrasting* an element in garment design with an undesired trait may camouflage or minimize the trait. For example, slightly curved lines and shapes can be used to camouflage the angularity of a very thin figure. If carried to extreme, however, the effectiveness may be lost. *Basic differences become accentuated when the degree of contrast is too extreme.* For example, very thin legs will be emphasized by a wide, bouffant skirt.

Individuals with extremes of height, weight, or shape are wise to avoid exact repetition or complete contrast of a feature they consider undesirable, for they will emphasize rather than counteract. The very lightness of thin, clingy fabrics may emphasize the contrasting heaviness of a full figure while at the same time revealing the body contours. Conversely, the opposite extreme of heavy, bulky, or stiff fabrics emphasizes the heaviness of the full figure by repetition. An intermediate degree of a specific design element can create a more flattering effect.

Both repetition and contrast may be employed in a single garment to focus attention on the area where it is desired and away from the area where it is not desired. Wise selection of clothing design can minimize the need for alteration by creating illusion, diverting attention, or effectively camouflaging an undesired figure trait.

Each design element or principle is individual and can be studied separately, yet when incorporated into a design, each is interdependent on every other. For example, a traditionally feminine, floral print may become bold and assertive when seen in very bright colors on a dark background; large-scale pleats may cause a small figure to look unbalanced; a row of buttons down one

---

DESIGN ELEMENTS
Line
Shape
Color
Texture

are manipulated
to create

DESIGN PRINCIPLES
Balance
Proportion
Scale
Rhythm
Emphasis

to achieve

FINAL GOAL
Harmony

Figure 1-1 Very fitted garment

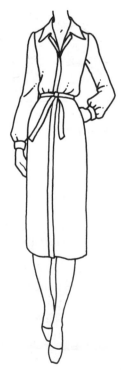

Figure 1-2 Slightly fitted garment

side of a garment may create asymmetrical balance; a rough texture may dull an otherwise intense color.

Because of the interrelationship of the elements and principles of design, traditionally hard and fast rules may not remain valid in all cases. Careful consideration must be given to selection, combination, and arrangement of each element; the figure on which the design elements are placed; and the setting in which they are viewed. Apparent height, weight, and shape are relative to each of the factors discussed above. No element or principle of design can be evaluated as an isolated entity. No matter how lovely any one part may be, the whole must also be considered in determining the end result.

The Elements of Design

LINE

Line is the most influential element of design in the presentation of the figure and in the fitting process. It measures the distance between two points, encloses and divides space, and defines shape. Line indicates direction and leads the eye throughout the design. Line may be seen in both the fabric and in the design of a garment.

Structural line in fabric is created by the position of the yarns as they cross each other at the right angles or as they loop vertically or horizontally. The directional lines thus formed may be observed and are commonly referred to as *grain*. The lengthwise fabric grain lies parallel to the selvage and perpendicular to the floor. The crosswise fabric grain lies between or at the right angles to the selvages and parallel to the floor. When the fabric grains lie at right angles to each other, the garment will hang evenly on both sides of the body. When the fabric grain is out of line, the garment will hang crooked, especially after it is washed. Always check the grain of the fabric prior to pattern layout. All natural fabrics without coated or heat-set finishes can be straightened very simply by pulling the weave into alignment. This is accomplished by cutting each end along one yarn, then pulling the fabric on the true bias in the direction of the shortest corners. Most synthetic fabrics can be straightened by pressing with a steam iron while the fabric is pinned to a porous or cork-top cutting table in a grain-perfect position.

The crosswise-grain tends to stretch more than the lengthwise grain; the lengthwise grain is more stable and durable. These are significant factors in garment design and fit because lengthwise areas of the garment placed on the crosswise grain may stretch or sag. During fitting and construction, check the grain for such distortions as bending, twisting, pulling, sagging, and wrinkling. If the grain is distorted due to poor garment construction, the garment will twist on the figure, causing poor fit. Grain distortions caused by figure variations can be corrected by alterations on the fitting garment and on the paper pattern (see **Part Three**).

Decorative lines in fabric can occur as stripes, plaids, and repeating motifs. The lines are created during fabric construction or added during printing and finishing processes. They should be considered in the layout of pattern pieces on the fabric and in relation to the body areas on which they will be seen.

Outline in garment design is established by the garment edges. Outside lines that enclose space and define the body or the garment shape are known as the *silhouette*. The garment silhouette should achieve vertical and horizontal balance and pleasing proportional relationships, and it should avoid emphasizing a figure variation considered undesirable. The garment silhouette may or may not define the body silhouette. Either the body or the garment silhouette will be dominant, depending on the closeness or looseness of fit. The closeness of fit may be categorized as very fitted, slightly fitted, slightly loose, or very loose.

A very fitted garment repeats body contours exactly (see **Figure 1-1**). It allows little ease for body movement. It is suitable only for photographic and stage purposes, and some evening wear. The body silhouette is dominant.

A slightly fitted garment repeats body contours but provides standard wearing ease; it should fit the body without constraint. The body silhouette is still dominant (see **Figure 1-2**).

A slightly loose garment only suggests body contours and stands slightly away from the body or flows loosely over it (see **Figure 1-3**). There is considerable added ease. The garment silhouette tends to become dominant.

A very loosely fit garment does not define body contour at all (see **Figure 1-4**). Fullness may begin at the shoulders. Fabric may stand away from the body or fall loosely around the body in folds. The garment silhouette is dominant.

A combination of these styles may be termed partially fitted. A partially fitted garment is fitted in specific areas, such as over the upper bodice, the midriff, or the upper hip area (see **Figure 1-5**). A looser degree of fit is incorporated into the styling of other areas. Either the body or the garment may become dominant in various areas, depending on the degree of fit. Such designs provide the greatest potential for creating effective illusion to minimize a figure variation.

Looseness in fit can be created by such construction techniques as released tucks, unpressed pleats, gathers, shirring, flare, or flared insets. No one need feel limited to tent-like styles to conceal the body silhouette but rather one may make use of controlled fullness in the areas of concern. For example, a fitted yoke in the shoulder area can be used to control gathered fullness in the bodice below. Varying degrees of close or loose fit can be used alone or in combination to meet an infinite variety of figure needs.

Wise selection of clothing silhouettes can reduce or even eliminate the effects a figure variation has on a garment and the resulting need for alteration. Slightly loose and partially fitted designs are generally advised for the fuller figure or for camouflaging a figure variation. Rather than revealing the body contours beneath, they allow the fabric to flow smoothly over the body or the area of concern; the garment silhouette is dominant. A dress that does not have a fitted waist is not likely to require alteration for the waist circumference; a flared skirt is less likely to need adjustment in the hip area.

Garment silhouettes are subject to shifts in fashion and can mirror social values and change. Regardless of fashion trends, however, when an artistically attractive appearance is desired we are well advised to select only those silhouettes that present the figure harmoniously.

During the fitting process, there is often an unintentional tendency for the beginner to overfit a garment—to increase the closeness of fit. This results in a loss of ease. *Ease* is the difference between actual body measurements and the measurements of the garment or pattern intended by the designer. The amount of ease may vary from style to style. Unless intentionally departing from the original design, maintain the degree of fit intended by the designer.

Improper amounts of ease affect the garment silhouette. Insufficient ease results in lengthwise, crosswise, or diagonal wrinkles in strained areas and reveals the body contours beneath. The garment will bind and pull in fitted areas, and normal body movement will be uncomfortable.

When a garment is too tight in any body area, fabric shifts to a smaller area and crosswise wrinkles are produced. Diagonal wrinkles occur where there is insufficient ease over a body bulge. The fabric will return to its proper position when sufficient ease has been introduced. On the other hand, too much ease will generally cause fabric to sag, puff, or form vertical folds. Excess ease must be removed to restore the fabric to its proper position. Fabric pulls or bows upward in the direction of a body contour that is too large and sags downward over an area where the body contour is small or shallow. (See **Chapter 7** and **Part Three** for further discussion of wrinkle correction.)

Interior design lines lie within the garment itself and can be either structural or decorative. They can divert attention away from the silhouette; they can be used to create vertical, horizontal, or diagonal eye movement; they

Figure 1-3 Slightly loose garment

Figure 1-4 Very loose garment

can divide the total area into pleasing proportional areas in scale with one another and with the wearer.

Structural interior lines are created by stitched darts and seams. Seamlines should intersect accurately in an appropriate position for the wearer. Dartlines should be directed toward the crown of the body bulge they are designed to fit. On a fashion garment, structural lines also may be created by gathers, pleats, or tucks.

Decorative interior lines can be created by the placement of buttons, pockets, and appropriate trim. Interior design lines that are well planned lead the eye throughout the garment with a smooth, rhythmic movement. They do not compete with one another for attention. Effective interior lines do not emphasize an undesired figure variation but rather divert attention to another area considered more acceptable and attractive.

Lines can be straight or curved. *Straight* lines oppose the curved lines of the body to varying degrees. *Curved* lines conform more harmoniously to the curves of the body. Lines that are only slightly rounded are referred to as restrained curves, while more circular lines are referred to as full-rounded curves.

Straight lines can indicate exact vertical, horizontal, or diagonal directions. Curved lines reflect the character of the direction they most closely resemble. Line direction can be created through the placement of grainline and fabric design lines, the silhouette, and interior design lines.

Vertical lines can be observed in a tubular silhouette. Interior design lines that may produce a vertical direction include finished edges, seamlines, necklines, pleats, panels, tucks, folds, slash pockets, center front and back plackets, button and zipper openings, a row of buttons, a soft or straight hanging tie, and so forth.

Horizontal lines can be seen in a bouffant silhouette. They occur in the interior of a garment as finished edges and seamlines such as yokeline, waistline, hipline, and hemline. They may be observed in necklines, patch or slash pockets, pocket flaps, cuffs, bow ties, belts, double-breasted closures, and so forth.

Diagonal lines can be observed in an A-line silhouette. They may occur on the interior of the garment as lapels, panels, inserts, seamlines and finished edges, or garment openings such as surplice.

Alone or in combination, straight lines generally have a slimming effect due to the flatness of the line. Curved lines can add visual weight because the line is rounded. How straight or how curved the garment lines should be will vary according to the desire to outline or camouflage the body silhouette or to create illusion in a particular area. The visual impact created by restrained curved lines is generally more subtle than that created by rigid straight lines.

Single vertical lines generally create the illusion of increased height and slimness in the area where they are used. This is because the eye is drawn inward toward the line then follows it upward and downward, mentally continuing the length of the line unless stopped by a horizontal intersection.

However, when several vertical lines are repeated at close intervals, they carry the eye *across* the body, thus creating the illusion of increased width and decreased height. Width is also created by the use of wide lines, widely spaced lines, and panel lines spaced far apart. The eye focuses on the one line, then moves across the body to the next line, thus measuring the width between.

When correctly fitted, a tubular silhouette with obviously greater height than width can create the effect of a vertical line and elongate the figure. Vertical wrinkles caused by poor fit produce the illusion of increased height and narrowness, emphasizing the too-big appearance of the garment. Asymmetrical vertical lines can visually alter the proportional areas of the body from side to side.

Single horizontal lines generally create the illusion of decreased height and increased width in the area where they are used. This is because the eye is drawn to the line and follows its path from side to side, until stopped by a

Figure 1-5 Partially fitted garment

vertical intersection. The total of the divided areas of the body appears shorter than the total height.

The greater the number of widely spaced horizontal divisions, the shorter the individual may appear. Depending on the placement of the horizontal line, proportional body lengths can be visually increased or decreased. For example, the dropped waistline at hip level visually lengthens the upper part of the body and shortens the lower part of the body. Such divisions are important considerations in the achievement of balance, proportion, and emphasis.

When several short, thin horizontal lines are repeated at close intervals, the illusion of increased height can be created as the eye is led up and down, from line to line. This is particularly true if a vertical line is also present in the center front, as with a center front opening. The narrower the vertical silhouette, the greater the effect. Fullness in the design creates a wide silhouette and the effects of a horizontal line occur at the area of greatest fullness. Horizontal wrinkles caused by poor fit produce the illusion of increased body width, emphasizing the too-little appearance of the garment.

Diagonal lines tend to increase length or width at their end points. This is because the end points are visually compared with the opposite edge point of the silhouette. The thickness, length, and degree of slant of the diagonal influence apparent height and width. A short diagonal line appears to increase width. A long diagonal line appears to increase height. A sharply angled diagonal, lying nearly horizontal, takes on the characteristics of a horizontal line and appears to increase width. A subtle diagonal, only slightly angled and lying nearly vertical, takes on the characteristics of a vertical line and tends to increase height and slimness. The combination of length and slant of the diagonal line must be considered to determine the final effect of the line. A diagonal line increases emphasis in the area where it is placed.

The actual length of a line can be measured; however, the impact or *visual strength* of a line is determined by the length of time the eye dwells on it. The longer the eye follows a line, the more effective the line becomes in creating an illusion. Lines can be exaggerated or reinforced by construction and decorative techniques, such as piping, ribbing, bands, panels, welt seams, lapped seams, top stitching, and other trims, particularly when they are set into a contrasting background. The ability of a line or lines in combination to create an illusion becomes a matter of length and strength factors, of long or short lines, of many or few lines, of raised or flat lines, and of the background on which they are placed.

Generally, the greatest amount of emphasis occurs when a line directly repeats a line on the figure. However, lines in direct and extreme contrast to a line on the figure also emphasize, due to the amount of difference between them. *Transitional* lines move smoothly from one direction to another without abrupt change in direction. They may be used to lead the eye to another part of the body.

When vertical and horizontal lines are used in combination, as in a plaid, the effect of increased body size is dependent on the spacing of the lines and contrast with the background. Generally, the wider the spacing of the lines and the greater the color contrast, the larger the apparent size. Conversely, decreased space between the lines and a similar-colored background minimize the effect of increased size. A greater sense of harmony is also achieved when the scale of the plaid is in proportion to the person wearing it—for example, when a petite figure wears a small- to medium-scale plaid. Always evaluate the interrelationship of all elements of design as they affect the appearance of the figure.

SHAPE

Shape is the element of design created by the enclosure of space and is usually restricted to a two-dimensional area having length and width. It can be seen as the silhouette of a garment or as the enclosed spaces that constitute the garment design. These interior shapes can be created by structural seamlines or may lie on the surface of the garment, as with pockets and collars. These shapes appear as the foreground, with background area or space between them. Printed or woven motifs create the shapes that constitute the fabric design.

Closely related to shape is *form*. Form generally refers to a three-dimensional object, such as the body. The shape of the garment encloses the form of the body. As is true of line, either body form or garment shape will dominate. If the form of the body and shape of the garment repeat each other, the body form will be accentuated. Fashion shapes do not always present the individual figure well. If harmony is desired between garment and figure, the body form must be respected. The closeness of fit appropriate for the body or its parts that was discussed under line applies here also. Body form can be camouflaged by a slightly loose fit in the garment shape.

Shapes *within* the garment design can repeat and reinforce the basic silhouette. The choice to repeat or contrast the shape of the silhouette will depend upon attitude toward the figure. Interior shapes can create illusions of increased or decreased height, width, and weight, depending on placement, size, and line direction. *Angular* shapes tend to emphasize the angularity of a figure by repetition. *Curved* shapes tend to soften angularity in the figure and repeat body curves. Because shapes are composed of straight and curved lines, the discussion under line applies.

Many shapes, or divided areas within a garment, tend to decrease height and increase width, depending on the manner of division and line direction. Foreground shapes tend to add visual weight in the area where they are placed; the size and form of the surface shapes should be in harmony with the area. The number and size of shapes are most pleasing when relative to the amount of background space determined by the garment shape and structural seamlines. Avoid the placement of too many shapes in a small place. The result is crowded and confusing, with conflicting points of interest. Match stripes, plaids, and motifs wherever possible to achieve a more harmonious appearance.

To keep all elements congruent, keep the size of interior shapes created in the garment in scale with the size of the wearer. Small shapes and motifs on a small person are congruent. To create illusions of increased or decreased height, width, and visual weight, use a gradual transition in the size of shapes—small with medium to increase, large with medium to decrease. Generally the jump from small to large or large to small is too extreme to be harmonious.

Interior shapes can serve several functions. They can add interest to a plain garment design, create a point of emphasis by attracting attention to a specific body area, or divert attention away from an undesired figure variation. If attention is not desired in a specific area, such as the bust or buttocks, the area is best left as background.

The illusory effects of shape can be modified by the interrelated elements of design: line, color, and texture. However, an evaluation of the effects of each element on the total composition is necessary. For example, the texture of the fabric affects the line and shape of the silhouette. A firm fabric holds a specific garment shape and causes the garment to become dominant, but a soft fabric falls closely about the figure, causing the body to become dominant. Because of these differences in texture, the same design lines can appear quite different made up in dissimilar fabrics.

COLOR

Color is the most complex and stimulating of the art elements. It refers to the components into which white light, or the full spectrum, may be separated. An object, such as fabric, absorbs or reflects light. When all light is absorbed, the eye perceives black. When all light is reflected, the eye perceives white.

The varying degrees to which light rays are absorbed or reflected accounts for the chromatic color perceived by the eye. Specific fabric dyes absorb specific light rays; the light rays that are reflected account for the color perceived. For example, when the dye absorbs all colored light rays except red, the fabric appears red.

There are three separate yet interrelated dimensions of color: hue, value, and intensity. Each has the ability to create illusions about visual size and weight. *Hue* is the name given to a particular color family. Warm hues—such as red, orange, and yellow—are mentally associated with fire. Because of longer wavelengths they appear to advance, thus causing shapes to appear closer, somewhat larger, and more important. Such cool colors as green, blue, and violet are mentally associated with the sky and water. Because of shorter wavelengths they appear to recede, thus causing shapes to appear farther away, somewhat smaller, and less important. Colors "with hue" are called *chromatic* colors.

A hue can be made to appear relatively warmer or cooler. Green pigment appears warmer when mixed with yellow and cooler when mixed with blue.

Value refers to the lightness or darkness of a hue that results when either white or black is added to the basic hue. Black, white and gray are "without hue" and are called *achromatic* colors. With the addition of a small amount of yellow or blue even achromatic colors can appear warmer or cooler. When white is added, the hue lightens to a higher value and is referred to as a *tint*. Very light, high-value tints reflect the light and appear to advance, causing shapes to appear closer, slightly larger, and less compact.

When black is added to a hue, the hue darkens to a lower value and is referred to as a *shade*. Very dark, low-value shades absorb light and appear to recede, causing shapes to appear smaller, farther away, and more compact. They tend to outline the silhouette in contrast to the background against which it is seen.

When a combination of black and white (gray) is added to a hue, it may remain the same in value or become lighter or darker, depending on the value of the original hue and the particular gray. The resulting color is also dulled and may be referred to as a *tone*. Generally the middle values and grayed tones are less obvious in their effects; although they tend to maintain apparent size and weight, they lean more toward reduction than magnification. The degree to which color creates an illusory effect depends on the background against which the value is observed. The greater the contrast, the greater the effect.

Intensity is often referred to as chroma. It is the degree of brightness or dullness of a hue and is determined by the strength, saturation, or purity of the basic hue. Bright, pure, strong, saturated hues are said to be of high intensity or full chroma. They appear to advance, causing shapes to appear nearer, slightly larger, and more emphatic. Dulled, weak, grayed hues are created by the addition of the complement of the basic hue or gray and are said to be of low intensity. Dulled hues are called tones. They appear to recede, causing shapes to appear farther away, smaller, less emphatic, or of less importance.

Perception of hue, value, and intensity varies among individuals. Color perception is dependent on the shape of the lens in the eye, the color of the lens and the iris, the ability of the retina to perceive color, the ability of the brain to interpret color, and on cultural and educational background as it influences color awareness, interpretation, and appreciation. While many people may agree that a particular hue is red, they may not agree on subtle differences between warm orange-red, red, and cool blue-red, light red and dark red, or bright red and dull red due to differences in perception. It is essential to increase color awareness and maintain objectivity in color evaluation and interpretation.

Colors are seldom seen in isolation; they are perceived in combination with other colors in the clothing, the body, and the background against which they are placed. Colors have an altering effect on one another. The apparent hue, value, and intensity of a color may be manipulated according to the combination of colors with which it is used or against which it is seen. A red-violet appears more violet next to a true red, more red next to a true violet. A medium-value orange appears lighter next to brown (dark orange) and darker next to beige (light orange). A medium intensity blue appears brighter when placed next to a dull blue and duller when placed next to a bright blue. The closer together the colors lie in the spectrum (color wheel), the more apparent their basic differences become.

A knowledge of the effects of color allows us to use a specific color in a specific area to create a specific illusion. The combined use of warm, light, bright hues causes the figure or body area to appear nearer, somewhat larger, and heavier. The combined use of cool, dark (but not to the point of black), dull hues causes the figure or body area to appear farther away, somewhat smaller, and less weighty. These effects are summarized in the following chart:

CHARACTERISTICS	EFFECTS
Warm Hues	Advance
Light Values	Enlarge
High Intensities	Excite
	Emphasize
Cool Hues	Recede
Dark Values	Reduce
Low Intensities	Calm
	Minimize

By controlling the hue, value, and intensity of the specific color, we control the effects of the color. For example, a warm red appears farther away, smaller, quieter, and less noticeable in a dark value of low, dull intensity. A cool blue appears closer, slightly larger, heavier, and more emphatic in a light value of a high, bright intensity.

The use of one solid hue in an outfit, or combinations of close values and intensities of the same hue, appears to decrease width and weight and increase height. The figure is not divided and the eye can travel freely up and down the entire length.

The use of contrasting hues, values, and intensities in large areas in an outfit causes the figure to appear larger and heavier. It also appears shorter. The figure is divided into shapes where the contrasting colors come into contact with each other. The body height is broken into comparative parts, thus creating proportional divisions. Body proportions can be altered at the line where a color change occurs. For example, a torso considered too long can be visually shortened by a belt matched to the color of the skirt or slacks. An upper torso considered too short can be visually lengthened by a belt matched to the color of the bodice. Vertical balance can be improved for the person with more weight in the lower portion of the figure by using light colors in the bodice and darker colors in the skirt or slacks. A combination of contrasting colors in the bodice area also increases the visual weight in the upper portion of the figure.

The appropriate use of color combinations in prints and patterns to create a desired illusion requires an evaluation of lines, shapes, and colors. To increase apparent height and slimness, for example, select small-scale patterns in cool hues with close values and intensities, in clothing styles that have vertical movement. To increase apparent width and weight, select large-scale patterns in bright, warm hues with strong value and intensity contrasts, in clothing styles that have horizontal eye movement.

Use a contrasting hue, value, or intensity to call attention to a desired point of emphasis, thus diverting the eye from an undesired figure variation. When two or more colors are used in unequal amounts, one color should dominate; otherwise confusion and conflict result.

Always evaluate the use of a specific hue, value, and intensity in relation to your purpose and to the other elements of design. For example, someone desiring not to emphasize a large figure might decide against wearing warm, bright colors (which emphasize the figure and its contours) in the daylight. However, the same colors often appear duller under artificial lighting. Made into a flattering style in a soft, matte-textured fabric, such colors could present a large figure very attractively.

Seldom does an individual correspond to a particular color type. Individuals possess an infinite variety of personal coloring patterns and combinations of apparently warm- and cool-based hues. In addition, personal coloring may change with age and exposure to the environment.

Colors in combination can be used to reinforce or counter undesirable effects on personal coloring. If a selected color is perceived to present skin, hair, or eye color poorly, wear it with another color near your face that will flatter and alter negative effects. For example, if navy blue is so dark that it absorbs a great deal of light and seems to drain color from your face, wear it in combination with a lighter color such as white, yellow, peach or sky blue to reflect more light and provide needed dark/light contrast.

If a selected color is so dull that you also appear dull and uninteresting, wear it in combination with a brighter color to enliven your looks. A color scheme in tan and taupe comes alive with the addition of red, rose, or teal blue. If a color has no relationship to your personal coloring, wear it in combination with one that does. You can quickly become an integral part of the color scheme you create with your clothes. For example, ivory and rose in combination with black may repeat hair and cheek color. Rust and teal in combination with gray may repeat hair highlights and eye color. The appropriate use of makeup, such as mascara and cheek blush, can introduce desirable color repetition or contrast and expand the variety of colors that can be worn beautifully.

TEXTURE

Texture is the element of design that describes the surface characteristics of fabric. These characteristics are perceived by the senses of sight, touch, and sound. The texture of a fabric is determined by the fiber, yarn, method of fabrication, and applied finishes.

Fibers can be natural (such as cotton, silk, linen, and wool) or they can be synthetic (such as nylon, polyester, and acetate). Short, rough fibers usually produce yarns and fabrics that absorb the light and appear dull. Long, smooth fibers usually produce yarns and fabrics that reflect the light and are shiny. Fibers may be stiff or pliable, which also affects the final fabric characteristics.

Yarns are created by twisting fibers together. Loosely twisted yarns have fewer twists per inch, therefore exposing longer segments of fiber surface to light. They reflect more light and appear shiny. This effect may be changed if loosely twisted yarns are brushed to create a fuzzy nap. Fiber slippage is greater in loosely twisted yarns, and bagginess may result. This affects fit adversely.

Tightly twisted or crepe yarns have a greater number of twists per inch, therefore exposing only short segments of fiber surface to the light. The yarn twists cast shadows and the yarns appear duller. Fiber slippage is reduced in tightly twisted yarns, resulting in a more stable yarn. The fit remains constant.

Fabrics are created by weaving, knitting, crocheting, felting, or braiding; still other fabrics are extruded in sheets. The final textural effect in a fabric is so dependent on the type of fiber and yarn used that an infinite variety is possible. For example, a silk crepe of tightly twisted yarns can be very fluid and drapable—also dull in appearance. Cotton fabric can be as delicate as dotted swiss or as sturdy as tent canvas. Wool fabric can be as lightweight as challis or as heavy as a blanket.

Applied finishes (such as flocked voile) can alter the physical properties of fabric, and ultimately the texture. If not permanent, some finishes relax or wear off, thus leaving a new set of textural characteristics.

Textural characteristics are expressed in terms of opposites. For example: shiny/dull, rough/smooth, crisp/limp, stiff/pliable, stable/stretchy, compact/porous, opaque/transparent, thick/thin, bristly/downy, heavy/light.

Such descriptive words help communicate the specific combination of characteristics belonging to a fabric. The effect of each characteristic is relative to its position on a continuum between extreme opposites. In other words, there are many degrees of softness, stiffness, sheerness, heaviness, and so forth. No characteristic should be considered intrinsically good or bad, but rather should be used as a clue to match fabric to function within the garment design and on the figure. To ignore these fabric characteristics is to invite fitting problems and a lack of harmony between fabric garment design, and figure.

The word *hand* refers to the tactile aspects of fabric; it describes the way fabric feels. *Drape* refers to the way the fabric hangs or falls into soft or crisp folds. *Scroop* refers to the audible characteristics of fabrics. For example, taffeta has a characteristic rustle when brushed against itself. Corduroy emits a swishing sound when rubbed against itself.

Textural characteristics determine the suitability of a fabric for a garment style or purpose. For example, a slippery, lightweight fabric may be very suitable as a lining but totally inappropriate as a dress. A tailored tubular design requires a firm fabric to hold the shape. A draped design requires soft, pliable fabric to fall into soft folds. Conversely, to stand away from the body, a bouffant design requires stiff, crisp fabric or under-stiffening.

Fabrics also influence the closeness of fit. For example, coat designs allow a greater amount of ease to accommodate the heavier, bulky fabrics needed for warmth. If such a coat is made of a lightweight fabric, it will be too large. On the other hand, designs intended for lightweight fabrics will be too tight if made from thick, heavy fabrics. Designs intended only for stretch fabrics have eliminated some of the usual ease; the same garment constructed in a woven fabric will be too tight and likely will not withstand the strain in bust, bicep, and hip areas. Recommended fabric names and weights for a particular design generally are listed on the pattern envelope (see **Chapter 4**).

Bulky or loosely woven fabrics require simple designs with few seams; flat, smooth, tightly woven fabrics may accommodate several seams and design details. The presence of each seam introduces the added bulk of seam allowances and the possibility of fraying and sagging. These factors influence the achievement of a well-fitted garment.

Often medium- and lightweight fabrics with opposing characteristics can be used interchangeably in the same design. However, the resulting silhouette and drape will be considerably different—as for example with crisp fabrics versus soft fabrics. The garment style must be appropriate to the fabric used so it does not appear too heavy or limp and without body. Quantity of fabric and placement of grain also may need adjustment to achieve the desired effect.

Textural characteristics influence the selection of appropriate fabric for a specific figure. The size, weight, bulk, firmness, light absorption or reflection, and degree of opaqueness of a fabric can reveal or camouflage the body through optical illusions. Soft, stretchy, clingy fabrics that are limp and drapable hug the body and reveal body contours. The effect is unattractive when they are overfitted or allowed to rest or hang on a body area such as the bust, prominent abdomen, buttocks, or thighs. Medium-weight, smooth, firm fabrics that hold their shape can conceal the figure without adding size and weight. Bulky, rough-textured fabrics conceal body silhouette and contours but increase size and weight. Transparent fabrics reveal the body shape and, if crisp, add visual bulk to the figure. The effect may be poor on a figure that is considered too thin or heavy.

The degree of luster in the fabric—shiny or dull—must also be evaluated. Shiny fabrics appear lighter and brighter. In illusion they tend to advance, thus increasing figure size and weight and attracting attention. The same hue in a dull-surfaced fabric will appear darker. Such fabrics tend to recede in illusion, thus decreasing figure size and weight and minimizing attention drawn to the figure. For example, compare the shiny face of a crepe-back satin with the dull back, or compare the apparent color differences in corduroy or velveteen that result from the direction of the pile.

The illusion of decreased height and increased size and weight can be created by using heavy, thick, stiff, napped, rough, nubby, or bonded fabrics; they add bulk to the body. Paradoxically, soft, flimsy, sheer, shiny, drapable fabrics can produce similar effects because they reveal body contours. Combining different textures can also have the effect of dividing the body into several shapes, each affected by the texture used in that area.

To create the illusion of increased height and decreased size and weight, use fabrics that are light to medium weight, flat to medium thick, opaque or dull, with firm, smooth, hard finishes. The use of one texture throughout the outfit also helps create the illusion of increased height.

All factors must be evaluated to determine the appropriateness of any fabric. For example the visual effect of size and weight produced by a dull or shiny fabric will be relative to its bulk, softness, and firmness. Whether to use a stiff, bulky fabric will depend on its relative thickness. Before purchasing a fabric, drape it over the body in approximately the same grain and style line and amount as will be required in the garment. Evaluate in a full-length mirror its potential affects on the garment design and on the figure.

Fabric textures—and therefore performance—can be altered by the use of interfacing, underlining, interlining, and lining. *Interfacing* provides body and increased stability to a fashion fabric. It is applied to areas of stress and wherever a firmer shape is desired. *Underlining* is cut from the same pattern as the garment pieces and is sewn as one with the fashion fabric during garment construction. It provides additional body to a fashion fabric and creates an opaque appearance. *Interlining* provides extra warmth in a garment. It is generally quite bulky and may interfere with the standard ease allowance. Often it is sewn as an underlining with the lining. *Lining* provides an interior finish to the garment. It is sewn as a separate unit, placed in the garment with wrong sides together, and attached at facings, neckline, waistline, and hemline. Lining fabrics are usually lightweight, soft, pliable, slippery, and opaque. They help absorb the stress of body movement and allow the garment to slide smoothly over the body or other fashion garments.

Each of these inner layers of fabric must be compatible with the fashion fabric. To determine appropriateness, layer the fabrics against each other prior to purchase. The innermost layer, such as lining, must fit the body with appropriate ease. *Each successive outer layer must be made slightly larger than the last inner layer.* This allows the layers to fit smoothly and comfortably over one another.

Fabric shrinkage also can alter correct fit. Natural fibers may require preshrinking according to the recommended method. If fabric is not preshrunk, it may shrink later due to laundering or steam pressing. Heat-sensitive fabrics also may shrink when overheated in a dryer.

All elements and principles must be considered in relation to one another and to the individual who will wear the clothing. For instance, skin and hair texture is fine, coarse, smooth, or rough. The selection of smooth, fine fabrics for someone with coarse, rough skin may be unflattering because of the extreme contrast.

Select fabric textures that are proportionally in scale to the wearer. Thick, heavy fabric on a large body will emphasize the largeness through repetition. On the other hand, thick, heavy fabric on a small body will overpower the wearer because of extreme contrast. Embossed patterns or the length of a nap also can influence the appropriateness of a fabric for a particular figure.

Textures can be used to divert attention away from an undesired figure variation and toward a flattering point of emphasis. For example a small amount of shiny fabric can be used as piping on a bodice yoke to draw attention away from large hips.

When combining textures for various effects, take care that textures combine harmoniously. For example, denim and chiffon in the same garment almost certainly conflict because of extreme differences in their characteristics, expected use, and care.

Fashion changes result in trends in textural preferences because the styles that are in fashion dictate the texture appropriate for use. However, the texture of a current fashion fabric may not be appropriate for a specific figure. For example, fake furs may be overpowering on a petite figure. Avoid fashionable textures that are inappropriate for a particular figure and focus attention on the use of fashionable colors, lines, and shapes instead.

The Principles of Design

BALANCE

Balance refers to the equal distribution of actual or visual weight about a central point. When there is balance there is a pleasing relationship of all the parts from side to side and from top to bottom. A sense of stability results.

Horizontal balance is achieved when the visual weight of one side of the body is equal to the other side. The standard horizontal balance is termed *symmetrical*. There is an even distribution of weight and contour over the body frame, and both sides of the body appear identical. When the body is *asymmetrical* or the two sides are unequal, it generally is considered desirable to bring the body closer to visual symmetry by manipulating the elements of design. Line, shape, color, and texture can be effectively used in clothing to create the illusion of increased or decreased height, width, or weight, and the dominance or subordinance of a particular area.

Every garment design has a real or imaginary center line from side to side. The eye mentally assigns a visual weight to each area of the design. Symmetrical horizontal balance is created when actual or imagined center front or center back lines divide the area into visually equal or nearly equal parts; both sides of the garment appear identical. Horizontal garment balance can also be asymmetrical. Asymmetrical styles do not compare body sides for identical size and shape, but they remain visually balanced. The elements of design can be manipulated to increase the visual weight and size of the smaller side, and garments can be selected that seem to contract or expand a particular area to achieve balance.

Vertical balance, sometimes referred to as *perpendicular* balance, is achieved when the upper part of the figure is balanced by the lower part. Generally, the heavier, solid torso or upper body should appear balanced by the longer hip and leg area or the lower body. This creates a sense of stability in the total figure.

Vertical or perpendicular balance is one of the goals in good garment design. Proper selection of clothing contributes to the achievement of perpendicular balance. For example, an individual with broad shoulders can balance the figure with width or fabric weight in the design of the skirt.

Once again, interrelationships must be carefully evaluated. Dark colors in low, dark values have a greater visual weight than lighter hues and values. A small area of dark color can balance a large area of light color. Large shapes and bulky textures also influence the balance of a garment by causing the figure areas where they are used to appear heavier.

PROPORTION & SCALE

Proportion is the size relationship of the areas of the body or garment design to one another and to the whole. The relationship between the areas can be defined in terms of numerical ratios. Generally, uneven ratios of 1:3, 2:3, and 3:5 are considered most interesting in clothing designs. They most nearly repeat the natural body proportions, and the divisions are interesting because they are not equal or readily discernible. For example, when the space division occurs at the waist, the average body ratio is two parts above the waist and three parts below. The sizes of the various garment areas are in proportion when they relate harmoniously to one another, to the whole garment, and to the figure of the wearer. Attractive garment proportions do not call attention to variations in body proportions caused by bone structure or the uneven distribution of weight on the body frame (see **Chapter 3**).

Comparative proportional areas are described in terms of *scale*: small, medium, or large. Bone structure can account for variation in the scale of different figures. When sizes are similar or related, they are said to be in scale: for example, small prints, pockets, and collars worn on a small frame.

The parts of the body may not be proportional to or in scale with other parts of the body or the whole. Each area may look normal when seen as an isolated unit, but out of proportion when viewed next to an adjoining area or as a whole. Structural or decorative lines create and shape the divisions in garment design. Body proportions can be visually altered by placing division lines at the shoulder for a yokeline, above the waist for a midriff line, and below the waist for a hip yokeline. All the various effects of design elements previously discussed can be used to bring body areas into better proportion. Shapes, colors, and textures in the design or in accessories can also visually increase or decrease the comparative height, weight, or dominance of a particular area.

The size of body areas can be emphasized by either repetition or extreme contrast in the scale of the garment details; therefore, shift no further than from small to medium or from medium to large within one design and in comparison to the figure. A shift into the medium range provides an illusory transition, reducing the comparative effect of exact repetition or extreme contrast.

Not all fashion trends are pleasingly proportional for all figures. Fashion illustrations show an unrealistic, elongated figure with increased length in the lower part of the body. This partially accounts for frequent disappointing differences between fashion drawings and the constructed garment on an actual figure.

RHYTHM

Rhythm is a sense of orderly movement. It is achieved in garment design when the design elements are arranged to lead the observer's eye directionally throughout the garment and to a point of emphasis. Rhythmic movement serves to unify the design, provide a transition between areas of the garment, avoid conflicting areas of interest, and identify the center of emphasis in a design. Rhythm may be either obvious or subtle.

Arrangement of the elements of design to produce rhythm can include repetition of lines, shapes, colors, or textures; alternation of lines, shapes, colors, or textures; gradation of lines, shapes, sizes, color values and intensities, and textures; continuous line of shapes, colors, or textural trims; or radiation of lines, shapes, colors, or textural folds (see **Figures 1–6** through **1–10**).

In each of these illustrations, the viewer visually follows a particular path throughout the design and feels satisfaction as the pathway continues to a pleasing and dominant point of emphasis. The elements of design can be

Figure 1-6 Repetition of lines, shapes, colors or textures

Figure 1-7 Alternation of lines, shapes, colors or textures

Figure 1-8 Progression of lines, shapes, sizes, colors or textures

Figure 1-9 Continuous line of shapes, colors or textural trims.

Figure 1-10 Radiation of lines, shapes, colors or textural folds

deliberately arranged to camouflage the figure, create an illusion, or divert the eye away from an undesired figure variation and toward an area considered more suitable to emphasize.

EMPHASIS

The principle of emphasis in design is the creation of a dominant point or center of interest. That point may be the facial area or another body area as defined by the garment design. There may or may not be subordinate points of emphasis; these points are smaller, less obvious, or less emphatic in their claim for attention. Nevertheless, to avoid a spotty appearance, one area should dominate. Conflicting areas of emphasis become confusing to the observer's eye.

Determine body areas you wish to emphasize through the figure evaluation process. This involves value judgments about what society deems attractive; such preferences may or may not be suited to the particular individual. Generally such elemental details as line, shape, color, and texture are used to camouflage or divert attention away from a figure variation; however, sometimes we see an unexpected figure characteristic emphasized to make a statement of individuality—for example a longer neck or broad shoulders.

Emphasis occurs at the point of the greatest visual interest or contrast. These points may be created in the following ways.

- A change or contrast in shape, color, or texture or in line direction or type of decorative detail
- Repetition or concentration of lines, shapes, or colors
- The reinforcement of a design detail by trim in that same area

The more attention claimed—or the more emphasis created—by one element, the less the others should claim. In other words, the more dominant one element, the more subordinate the others should be.

HARMONY

To achieve harmony, all design elements must be selected and arranged to create a unified idea, concept, or theme. This is the ultimate goal in any creative effort. It requires combining lines, shapes, colors, and textures in a way that is appropriate to the purpose; all individual details must relate to form a congruent whole.

Generally in pattern, fabric, or garment selection, and in fitting and alteration, the purpose is to present the figure as attractive, well balanced, and well proportioned. A garment design should be sought that is harmoniously unified among its various parts as well as with the figure on which it is to be worn. The interrelated aspects of the elements and principles of design become apparent as we evaluate the harmony of the whole, not just the parts.

As you attempt to camouflage or emphasize a particular part of the figure, there is danger of ruining the harmonious presentation of the whole. There is also danger of emphasizing one figure variation while attempting to camouflage another. Therefore, the illusory effects of the entire garment design must be evaluated in relation to the figure and the defined purpose. For instance, a woman might have a proportionally large bust, small waist, and large hips. The small waist may be considered the most attractive area of the figure and such clothing details as a cinch belt may be selected to emphasize that area. However, attention at the small waist emphasizes the largeness of the bust and hips by extreme contrast.

For each of the illustrations in **Figure 1-11**, evaluate the use and interrelated effect of lines, shapes, colors, and textures in achieving balance, proportion, scale, rhythm, emphasis, and—ultimately—a harmonious appearance.

Once you have gained an understanding of the elements and principles of design as they relate to an attractive appearance, you need not be limited to traditional selections or arrangements. The design elements can be manipulated to create a desired effect. In the final analysis, the dominance of a particular element is the most important. For example, a large-scale plaid generally is assumed to add visual size and weight to a figure; however, a large plaid appears smaller when presented in soft, grayed tones. Color becomes the dominant element controlling the effect of the lines and shapes in the plaid. To give another example, a small-scale floral print traditionally is thought to be delicate and to help the larger figure appear smaller; however, this print takes on increased size and visual weight when presented in strong, intense colors. Again, the element of color becomes dominant and overpowers the ultimate effect of the shapes.

To give additional examples, the visual weight of a heavier, thick fabric can be modified by a simple style with few structural lines and an absence of decoration. In this case, the style and shape of the garment become dominant and control the effects of the texture. A clingy fabric can be caused to stand slightly away from the body in a softly gathered/draped style worn over an undergarment treated with an antistatic finish. In this case, the style and shape of the garment are combined with another treated texture to control the effects of the clingy fabric. We must *always* examine and determine the dominance of the various elements of design in terms of the intended purpose.

As you finalize the selection and arrangement of the design elements most appropriate for the figure, you may feel unsatisfied or emotionally uncomfortable with the choices. Although correct in themselves, they may conflict with personal preferences based on values, attitudes and interests, geographic location, personality, mood, economic ability, or availability. In other words, you must also identify and evaluate the social and psychological interrelationships in terms of the individual and the individual's purpose.

Figure 1-11 Use of line, shape, color and texture to
achieve or disrupt harmony

Frequently you must adapt what is available to personal needs, adapt personal needs to preferences, or satisfy two conflicting needs at the same time. For example, if you value being in fashion but the current style does not present the figure well, you must determine how to modify the style lines or select from other fashion details, such as color or accessories. By carefully evaluating effects and the alternatives, you can usually arrive at an acceptable solution to personal needs in both home-sewn and ready-to-wear clothing.

- If a current fashion stresses square shoulders, which may accentuate shoulders that are already square, the shoulder pad can be eliminated. To give the firmness and smooth appearance desired in the area, use a layer of drapery heading or two layers of a crisp fabric.
- If puffed or extended sleeves are currently in vogue but will emphasize already broad shoulders, consider omitting the usual alteration for broad shoulders and allowing the shoulder to occupy some of the space created by the puff or extension.
- If necklines on currently popular patterns lie lower on the chest than you desire, raise the neckline by altering the pattern prior to cutting.
- If a ready-to-wear skirt has horizontal wrinkles at the back caused by a swayed back, alter the skirt and reset the waistband.

You can find solutions to fitting problems once the problem is recognized, the cause understood, and the alternatives carefully weighed. Many fitting problems can be solved by selecting appropriately styled clothing.

When a correct fit cannot be achieved by appropriate style selection alone, the ability to correctly fit and alter clothing and patterns is essential in presenting an attractive and harmonious appearance.

CHAPTER 2

SELECTING & USING EQUIPMENT

The quality of construction and potential for effective fit of the garment begins with correct selection and wise use of appropriate sewing tools. Tools that are clean, accurate, readily accessible and properly stored retain their usability and increase one's efficiency during the total sewing process. They also help eliminate the frustration that inevitably results when an essential tool is missing or does not function properly.

Many types of sewing tools are available. Some are necessities; others are helpful and make the task easier; still others are nothing more than superfluous gadgets. Be aware of new developments, but use logic in evaluating new products and their advertised usefulness. However clever, a tool is valuable only to the degree that it simplifies or improves and accomplishes the intended sewing task. Following is a list of useful equipment, including information on selection and proper use. Cleaning and storage suggestions are also given to ensure that the sewing tools continue to function in top condition.

Measuring Tools

Accurate sewing depends to a great extent on accurate measuring. The manner of measuring affects the finished size and shape of the garment and the harmony between various body areas and the corresponding fabric.

Learning to use metric measure may be necessary for everyone. Commercial patterns began to introduce metric measurements several years ago. Once the system is understood, it is surprisingly easy to use. Metric measurements are always designated with whole numbers. When divided into smaller units, the decimal is used rather than the fractional division common to the inch system. Wherever measurements are quoted throughout our text, we state amounts in inch measurements first followed by the metric equivalent in parentheses.

We suggest purchasing equipment with both metric and inch measurements to help relate the two systems.

YARDSTICK (Meter Stick)

A measuring stick is of great help when marking long, straight lines on the flat surfaces of a pattern or fabric. It is also useful when laying cloth smoothly on the cutting table. Sliding the stick between layers of napped or rough fabric helps the fibers, yarns, and bubbled areas adjust correctly during the grain-straightening and fabric-flattening processes.

The most durable types of measuring sticks are made of metal or waxed hardwood with metal end tips. The markings should be clearly printed in fractions and whole numbers. Smooth surfaces, edges, and corners prevent snags in fabric. Several plastic measuring devices similar to yardsticks are available. They usually combine a curved edge, a straight edge, and an L-square (90-degree angle). The curved edge is very helpful for designing areas with curved lines and for redrawing curves during pattern alteration.

Store metal or wooden measuring sticks in a hanging position in a cool dry place. This prevents warping, rusting, and other damage. Remove finger marks and other soil by wiping the sticks first with a cloth treated with furniture wax, then with a dry, soft cloth.

TAPE MEASURE

The flexibility of the tape measure makes it useful for measuring large curved or flat surfaces on the body, pattern, or fabric. The best tapes are made of fiberglass or cloth that has been specially treated to prevent stretching, tearing, and wrinkling. Paper tapes tear, fray, and wrinkle easily and do not retain their accuracy. Nearly all tape measures are 60 inches (1.5 m) long. This length has proven to be the most useful and efficient. Securely attached metal end tips increase the useful life of the tape and aid in taking accurate measurements.

Metric Conversion Charts

For Body Measurements

To determine your pattern size, compare your body measurements to the body measurements listed below. The chart lists measurements in both inches and centimeters.

MISSES'

Size	6		8		10		12		14		16		18		20	
	in	cm	in	cm	in	cm	in	cm	in	cm	in	cm	in	cm	in	cm
Bust	30½	78	31½	80	32½	83	34	87	36	92	38	97	40	102	42	107
Waist	23	58	24	61	25	64	26½	67	28	71	30	76	32	81	34	87
Hips	32½	83	33½	85	34½	88	36	92	38	97	40	102	42	107	44	112
Back waist length	15½	39.5	15¾	40	16	40.5	16¼	41.5	16½	42	16¾	42.5	17	43	17¼	44

MISS PETITE

Size	6 MP		8 MP		10 MP		12 MP		14 MP		16 MP	
	in	cm	in	cm	in	cm	in	cm	in	cm	in	cm
Bust	30½	78	31½	80	32½	83	34	87	36	92	38	97
Waist	23½	60	24½	62	25½	65	27	69	28½	73	30½	78
Hips	32½	83	33½	85	34½	88	36	92	38	97	40	102
Back waist length	14½	37	14¾	37.5	15	38	15¼	39	15½	39.5	15¾	40

WOMEN'S

Size	38		40		42		44	
	in	cm	in	cm	in	cm	in	cm
Bust	42	107	44	112	46	117	48	122
Waist	35	89	37	94	39	99	41½	105
Hips	44	112	46	117	48	122	50	127
Back waist length	17¼	44	17⅜	44	17½	44.5	17⅝	45

HALF-SIZE

Size	10½		12½		14½		16½		18½		20½		22½		24½	
	in	cm	in	cm	in	cm	in	cm	in	cm	in	cm	in	cm	in	cm
Bust	33	84	35	89	37	94	39	99	41	104	43	109	45	114	47	119
Waist	27	69	29	74	31	79	33	84	35	89	37½	96	40	102	42½	108
Hips	35	89	37	94	39	99	41	104	43	109	45½	116	48	122	50½	128
Back waist length	15	38	15¼	39	15½	39.5	15¾	40	15⅞	40.5	16	40.5	16⅛	41	16¼	41.5

For Fabrics

To convert fabric widths and yardages from inches and yards to centimeters and meters, compare what is listed in each yardage block to the chart below.

FABRIC WIDTHS	in 25	cm 65	in 27	cm 70	in 35	cm 90	in 39	cm 100	in 42	cm 107	in 45	cm 115	in 54	cm 140	in 60	cm 150
Yardage	Yd	m	Yd	m	Yd	m	Yd	m	Yd	m	Yd	m	Yd	m	Yd	m
	⅛	0.15	¼	0.25	⅜	0.35	½	0.50	⅝	0.60	¾	0.70	⅞	0.80	1	0.95
	1⅛	1.05	1¼	1.15	1⅜	1.30	1½	1.40	1⅝	1.50	1¾	1.60	1⅞	1.75	2	1.85
	2⅛	1.95	2¼	2.10	2⅜	2.20	2½	2.30	2⅝	2.40	2¾	2.55	2⅞	2.65	3	2.75
	3⅛	2.90	3¼	3.00	3⅜	3.10	3½	3.20	3⅝	3.35	3¾	3.45	3⅞	3.55	4	3.70
	4⅛	3.80	4¼	3.90	4⅜	4.00	4½	4.15	4⅝	4.25	4¾	4.35	4⅞	4.50	5	4.60
	5⅛	4.70	5¼	4.80	5⅜	4.95	5½	5.05	5⅝	5.15	5¾	5.30	5⅞	5.40	6	5.50
	6⅛	5.60	6¼	5.75	6⅜	5.85	6½	5.95	6⅝	6.10	6¾	6.20	6⅞	6.30	7	6.40

A tape with both inch and metric markings is especially useful. Efficiency is further increased if the tape is reversible (the inch and metric markings begin with the number *1* at opposite ends of the tape on opposite sides). A tailor's tape usually begins with the number *1* at the same end on both sides of the tape. This tape has a small, firm shield attached to the beginning of the tape that aids in taking the inseam length of pants. Other nonreversible tapes are more useful and efficient if the end beginning with 1 is marked for quick identification during use.

To maintain the temper in the tape material and prevent stretching and twisting, tapes should be loosely wrapped in a smooth coil when not in use. This will also keep the markings clear for a longer time. Fiberglass and treated cloth tapes may be cleaned with a damp cloth.

CLEAR PLASTIC RULER

Pattern and fabric markings are easily seen through a clear plastic ruler so that details can be measured or positioned accurately. A narrow, flexible ruler is useful for measuring small curved areas. Stand the ruler on its edge to measure or mark curved lines. The ruler can also be wrapped around the wrist or arm to measure the area and determine the ease desired. Wide plastic rulers [approximately 4 inches by 15 inches (10 by 37.5 cm)] are available but are too rigid to be bent. These wide rulers usually have several parallel slots that vary in distance apart. They are helpful for marking straight-of-grain lines, even amounts of change during pattern alteration, and so forth. However, the slotted areas break apart easily unless the ruler is used very carefully. Wide plastic rulers will also chip and break if dropped.

All plastic rulers should be stored in a hanging or flat position to prevent warping or breaking. Plastic is affected by extremes in temperature. These rulers must not be brought into contact with a hot iron. When cold the plastic is brittle; it will break or shatter if bent quickly or severely. Any plastic ruler is easily cleaned with a damp cloth. Chemical solvents—such as dry cleaning fluids—cause damage.

SEAM GAUGE

This simple but very useful device is usually 6 inches (15 cm) long. It has an adjustable marker to measure short or repeated distances during clothing construction, knitting, and so forth. A gauge with both inch and metric measurements is very useful. The marker should move easily, mark with precision, yet remain stable until deliberately changed.

A metal seam gauge is more durable than plastic, and the markings are usually easier to read. The metal marker is more pointed, therefore helping to produce more accurate measurements. A gauge that has a hole both in the marker and the end point (to accommodate a pencil and a pin, respectively) can be used as a simple compass to draw scallops and other curves.

A seam gauge should be kept flat during use and storage. Bending a metal gauge or using it as a screwdriver damages the smoothness and may cause the marker to move too loosely or tightly.

HEM MARKER

A level hem is one mark of professional fitting and sewing. An uneven hemline is usually an indication of a need for further fitting. Once proper fit has been incorporated above the hipline, leveling of the hem will be necessary only for skirt styles involving bias areas.

A hem marker is an upright measuring stick that is firmly attached to a base and is used to measure the skirt hem a given distance from the floor. An adjustable marker attached to the upper end of the stick allows simultaneous measuring and marking. Two types are available.

The marker on spray-types is a container of chalk with an air bulb attached. When the bulb is pressed, a short line of chalk sprays onto the garment. (The cutting line should be marked, not the foldline, because chalk remains in some fabrics and can leave a stain.) The chalk marker is very efficient; you can use it to mark your own skirt if you stand looking straight ahead with the body weight carefully balanced. Talcum powder can be used to refill an empty container or chalk refills can be purchased. The air tube and bulb deteriorate with use, and the tube will break or split if kinked.

The marker on pin-types is a hinged clamp that opens to allow the skirt to lie inside and be held firmly in place. When the clamp is closed, a pin is inserted into the fabric through a groove in the end of the clamp. The pins can be placed either at the trimming line or at the foldline. This hem marker requires a little more time to use than the spray-type. Time is saved later at the ironing board because the marking pins are accessible for reuse when turning the hem.

Both markers will remain more usable if stored hanging upside down. In this position the clamp on the pin-type is closed, thus preventing twisting or breaking, and the air tube on the spray-type extends straight from the nozzle on the container cap. Oversettling of the chalk, which occurs when it is kept in an upright position, will also be prevented.

Marking Tools

The accurate and neat transfer of pattern markings to the fabric counterparts is of paramount importance, both in fitting the fabric pieces together and in obtaining a fault-free finished product. The fit of the garment and its appearance on the figure are directly affected by the care used in this process. Markings should be permanent enough to be used effectively but temporary enough that they can be removed or remain totally inconspicuous on the garment.

TRACING WHEEL

Construction lines such as seam, dart, and trim lines are easily transferred from pattern to fabric using a tracing wheel and transfer paper. All types of tracing wheels function best over a solid surface. A square of masonite placed under the fabric helps ensure well-defined marks and prevents damage to the table top. A piece of thin, clear plastic or tissue paper may be placed between the pattern and cloth to prevent transfer of the printer's ink from the paper pattern.

Three types of wheels are available. The sawtoothed-edge type makes larger, more conspicuous dots, but it also may damage patterns. This tracing wheel is inexpensive and sells at all notion counters. The smooth edge type makes a solid line that is easily seen. It does not appreciably damage patterns. This type of wheel is also inexpensive, but it is less often available at notion counters. The needle-point tracing wheel is rarely sold on the retail market, possibly because of its higher cost. It is available through industrial notion catalogues. This tracing wheel is very desirable as it leaves only pin-dot marks on pattern tissue and fabric, and it does little damage to patterns. The points are extremely sharp and can be dangerous if not used and stored with care.

DRESSMAKER TRACING PAPER

This paper (to be used with a tracing wheel) is the easiest, most convenient method for transferring pattern marks to fabric. It is available in white and in several colors. Always choose a color that is lighter than the fabric. (White may be used on all colors of fabric including white.) Always mark the wrong side (back surface) of the fabric. When marking doubled layers of fabric, the single-coated paper can be used whether the face of the fabric is folded inward or outward. Double-coated paper can be used only when the back surfaces of the fabric are folded inward.

Disappointment and frustration result from inappropriate choice or incorrect use of tracing paper. Spongy or thick fabrics mark too heavy on the top layer and too light on the lower. Too much pressure results in conspicuous marks that may be forced through to the face of the fabric. When marking doubled layers of heavyweight fabric, mark each layer separately rather than applying extreme pressure. Rolling the wheel back and forth can make thick marks or two or more separate (and consequently inaccurate) lines. Colored marks show through thin or sheer fabrics; these fabrics should be marked by a different method. Paper in colors darker than the fabric will also make conspicuous marks. Polyester and nylon fibers absorb waxes. The coating on the waxed type of tracing paper may penetrate permanently into such fabrics. Marking dye can remain as a stain. If the marks are pressed, they cannot be removed by washing or dry cleaning—yet professional sewing cannot be done without pressing. Chalk-type coatings used on tracing paper brands such as

Saral seem to remain on the fabric surface. They loosen easily and disappear with slight brushing. The marks are not retained in the fabric when heat is applied. Other brands are available that advertise markings that disappear when moistened. All brands should be tested on the fashion fabric for the degree of clarity, show-through, and removal.

CHALK MARKERS

Clay and wax markers are very useful for marking sewing lines during the fitting and construction of a garment. When used with a ruler or curved guide, a very accurate line can be drawn. Clay chalk is available in brick, pencil and powder form. The powder form is white; bricks and pencils can be found in white, pink, and blue. The white and blue are less apt to stain. Clay chalk can be used on all fabrics except wool; the natural oil in wool absorbs the chalk and makes it difficult to remove. Synthetics absorb the oil in the wax markers.

The edge of the clay bricks and the pencil point glaze quickly during use, after which they mark poorly, if at all. Renew the marking surface on both frequently. Scrape both surfaces of the marking edge on the bricks to form a V-shape and maintain a sharp, usable marking tool. Sharpen the pencil with an ordinary pencil sharpener.

Clay bricks are often sold in a holder with an attached sharpening device and a brush for removing residue. The sharpener is of little value. It forms a rounded edge that makes a thick line lacking accuracy. The brush is stiff and may damage some fabrics. The bricks and pencil tips break if these tools are dropped.

Clay pencils are used in the same way as the bricks. If in the form of an ordinary pencil, the chalk can be sharpened to a fine point for making thin lines and small, accurate dots. The refillable marking pencils lack usefullness. They glaze easily, make thick marks, and are not easily sharpened.

Wax bricks are available in white, red, and black. White is usable on all colors of fabric, including white. This product does not glaze at all during use. Wax chalk is used only for marking wool. The wax disappears into wool fabric when pressed with a warm iron. When it is used on other fibers, a greasy stain may appear. The dye residue may remain in the fabric. The wax brick will melt if placed near heat.

A chalk marker is also available that dispenses powdered chalk. The product is very useful and efficient when a continuous line or extensive markings are necessary. The powder is held in a refillable, flattened container. The marking is made as a serrated wheel rotates through the chalk supply then along the fabric. The powder is easily removed with a light brushing or shaking of the fabric.

A thin sliver of light-colored or white hand soap is a good substitute for either clay or wax chalk if it has no added oils or cold cream. When the soap bar is worn too thin for cleaning the hands, it is the correct thickness for marking. Oilfree soap does not have any of the problems associated with clay or wax chalk. It disappears into all fabrics when pressed with a steam iron. The sliver may be kept sharp by scraping both surfaces of the edge.

ERASEABLE MARKING INKS

"Eraseable" ink is available in two forms of pens. The ink is a liquid in both pens. Very small dots can be made with a deft, quick touch. The lighter the mark is made, the easier it is to remove. The ink in the water-eraseable type is sky blue. It will disappear when a drop of water or a moistened cloth is placed on the markings before the product is touched with heat. The color neutralizes better on fabrics composed of synthetic fibers than it does on cotton or natural fibers. Do not use the product on fabrics that will water spot.

The air-eraseable type leaves a purple mark. Within 24–48 hours, the mark will neutralize and disappear if not touched with heat. The mark will disappear immediately if touched with water.

Cutting Tools

The quality of the cutting tool and the way it is used will directly affect the fit of the garment. Scissors that shred cloth and push or pull it out of line cause changes in the size and shape of fabric pieces. If these tools are to maintain a sharp cutting edge, they should be used only for cutting thread and fabric. High-quality shears or scissors are expensive, but with proper care and use they should last a lifetime. Buy the best quality available within your budget.

The best shears and scissors are made from hot-dropped, forged, surgical steel and have been coated with nickel or chrome to prevent rust. The screw should maintain blade tension, not allow it to loosen or tighten. The cutting action should be smooth, even, and clean for the full length of the blade. The tool should be easy to use and feel comfortable in your hand. Before purchasing, try several pairs on single and doubled layers of various fabrics. Cut the fabric using the full length of the blades. With the blades still closed, pull them away from the fabric. If they have rough edges or hooked points, they will not free the fabric. Dull areas on the blades leave poorly cut areas of fabric or will not cut at all. Also look for comfort and ease during the cutting process.

The weight and size of the selected tool should be compatible with the weight of the specific fabric. Lightweight scissors or shears will not cut heavyweight fabric accurately. Fabric that is too heavy can spring a tool that is too light, thereby damaging it for future use.

Dropping scissors or shears can break the tips or the screw holding the blades together; it can also spring the blades so they no longer have the proper tension to cut accurately. Cutting tools should be stored flat in a closed, dry place. Some are sold with a sheath to cover and protect the blades.

SHEARS

This tool is of heavy construction and is shaped with a smaller handle for the thumb and a larger handle to accommodate the last three fingers. Such a formation permits excellent control and the application of considerable pressure. Shears are used for extensive cutting tasks on thick fabric or multilayers of fabric. The most common sizes of shears are 7 inches (17.5 cm) and 8 inches (20 cm). The handles are shaped for either the right hand or the left hand. (It is almost impossible for a left-handed person to use right-handed shears or vice versa.)

The blades of straight shears extend outward between the two handles. The blades of bent shears are even with the lower (large ring) handle. Bent shears permit more accurate cutting because the angle allows the blades to lie more nearly parallel to the table. Shears with serrated blades prevent a fluid fabric from moving away from the pattern edges and the blades during cutting.

Lightweight shears are widely marketed; if they are made of good steel, they are serviceable for lightweight fabrics. However, with these shears heavier fabrics must be cut one layer at a time to maintain cutting accuracy and to prevent damaging the shears. Many cheap imitations of top-quality lightweight shears have flooded the market. They are not tempered, they dull easily, cut poorly, have riveted blades, and usually cannot be sharpened.

SCISSORS

Scissors are usually less than 6 inches (15 cm) long and are of lighter construction than shears. They are used for delicate jobs of snipping or for cutting light-to medium-weight fabric at the sewing machine, ironing board, or fitting area. The blade and handle are usually straight, but bent types are available. Frequently both handles have ring openings of the same size. To be effective, scissor tips must be very pointed and sharp.

CLIPPERS

The blades on clippers are either riveted together or connected with a loop of spring steel. Clippers do not have traditional handles. This tool should operate with a brisk, spring-hinge action. It permits quick snipping of thread ends and seam stitches during fitting and construction. Most brands are not heavy enough to snip fabric; to attempt to do so damages the blade tension. Some people hang the clippers on a loop of tape around the neck to keep them accessible while fitting or sewing.

SEAM RIPPER

This device aids rapid removal of unwanted stitching. Both large and small rippers are available. The point is usually protected with a cap. A large seam ripper has a more comfortable handle and a thick blade tip that is useful for cutting basting stitches during fitting. A small ripper has a very sharp point and can be used to remove fine stitching without damaging fabric. The cap fits over the end of the handle during use to extend the ripper and provide more control. Store the tool with the point covered.

To prevent damaging fabric with seam rippers, cut the stitches at close intervals on one side of the fabric, then quickly pull the unclipped thread. It will free itself in one continuous strand and will also loosen the clipped thread sections, which are then easily removed.

Stitching Tools

HAND-SEWING NEEDLES

Needles are sold according to type and size. The types most generally used are called *betweens*. These are short and can produce fine, accurate stitching. People with short fingers may use them more efficiently than people with long fingers. *Sharps* are medium length and should be used for longer stitches or for making several stitches at a time. *Milliners* are the longest needles and are excellent for basting long seams. *Crewels* (embroidery) have elongated eyes and are easier to thread, especially if embroidery floss or doubled strands of thread are being used for making tailor's tacks. The *calyx-eye* needle is self-threading and therefore efficient to use. It is particularly helpful for those people with vision problems.

Needle sizes are numbered from 1 (coarse) to 12 (fine). Select the correct size according to the texture of the fabric and the size of the thread. The needle eye should be large enough to be easily threaded yet small enough to prevent the thread from slipping out. Coarse needles are awkward to use on thin fabric and vice versa. A single yarn of a given fabric can be picked up if the needle size is correctly chosen. Store needles separate from pins. Store each in dry containers to prevent rust and corrosion.

MACHINE NEEDLES

The quality and type of sewing machine needle affects stitching and may determine whether alterations can be made after a garment is stitched. Machine needles can become unusable before they break. Sewing over pins ruins needles. Pins scrape the needle and dull, wear off, or scratch the blade surface. If the needle hits the pin directly, the needle tip can flatten, burr (chip), become hooked, or break. Sewing over pins also creates a wiggle in the stitching at each spot where a pin has been stitched across. Damaged needles cause permanent needle marks, skipped stitches, snags, runners, and other fabric damage. Needle points also become dulled or blunted simply from use, particularly when sewing polyester and other harsh or hard fabrics. To produce smooth, inconspicuous stitching, a machine needle should be changed often.

Machine needles should be compatible in size with the weight, texture, and yarn thickness in the fabric. Sizes vary from fine—size 70 (10)—to coarse—size 120 (19). The type of machine needle point should be chosen according to the type of fabric. Regular needle tips cut through yarns and can cause holes and runs in some knits. They should be used only on woven fabrics. Ballpoint tips push fabric yarns apart and therefore do not damage knits. They can be used for any woven or nonwoven fabric, but they do not function well on leather or vinyl.

A scarfed or bulged-eye needle has been developed to prevent overheating and to penetrate fabric more easily. Due to the strength and elasticity of polyester, especially knits, skipped stitches and overheating of the needle can occur. Skipped stitches can result from the bouncing of the fabric over the needle-plate opening or from the fiber forming a sticky residue on the needle. The deep scarf cut into the blade (at the eye area on the long-groove side of the needle) acts as an air cooler and slows the heating of the needle. A cooler needle picks up less lint residue. These needles are marketed under such trade names as the Coats and Clark Blue Needle (covered with silicone to help prevent skipped stitches), the Singer Yellow Band and the Schmetz LG SCARF.

THIMBLE

Although thimbles are a little awkward to learn to use, they can speed both temporary and permanent hand stitching. A thimble is also a piece of safety equipment. It protects the middle finger from the eye end of the needle and thus may prevent the blood from a pricked finger from spotting the fabric. The efficiency of a thimble depends on the depth of the thimble depressions; they should hold the needle securely while it is being pushed through the fabric.

A dressmaker's thimble has a closed end and should fit the finger snugly. Moistening the end of the finger will help the thimble stay in place. A tailor's thimble is open at each end and therefore, is used with a sideward motion. People with long fingernails may prefer to use this thimble or the new dressmaker thimble designed with an oval slit at the closed end to accommodate the nail.

Leather thimbles are made of soft, long-wearing deerskin. They fit the finger much like the conventional metal thimbles. A seam lies at each side and is purposely left unstitched at the closed end to form vents that permit breathing. The density of the leather prevents the needle from penetrating into the finger.

STRAIGHT PINS

Pins are sold by metal, diameter, and length. Brass will not rust. Nickel-plated steel will not tarnish. Stainless steel corrodes slightly, especially from chemicals in perspiration, and can leave a tarnish on light-colored fabrics. A magnet is effective for picking up pins made of stainless steel.

Dressmaker pins are of medium thickness and are more efficiently used on medium to coarse fabrics. Silk pins are finer in diameter and should be used for lightweight fabrics. You can substitute fine hand-sewing needles for pins to avoid marring delicate fabrics. Pins with colored glass or plastic heads are easier to see; they are usually longer than ordinary straight pins. Glass heads will not melt when touched by the iron.

A good supply of pins is essential during the processes of fitting and pattern alteration. For example, elastic, tapes, or bands are often used to define body lines. To maintain a flat, smooth surface over which to work, these must be overlapped and pinned, not tied. Pins are also used to define lines on the underclothing or the garment during fitting and when deciding on style changes.

Store pins in a pincushion. The pin heads are always upwards, easy to grasp, and ready for instant use. Some magnetic pin containers also dispense pins head first. Pins stored in a box become jumbled. They are difficult to pick up separately and with the point facing correctly for use. Pins inserted into paper are inefficient to use; both hands are needed to remove each pin. The paper absorbs moisture and allows the pins to rust or corrode. *Do not* store threaded needles in the same container with pins; the thread tangles badly around the pins.

Polish and smooth pins occasionally by pushing them back and forth through an emery bag. (This is the small, strawberry-shaped bag that is attached to some pincushions.) Do not use the emery bag to store pins or needles, as it allows rust to form on them.

PINCUSHION

A felt pad of wool or a bag filled with packed wool clippings, wool yarn, or clean hair permits needles to be inserted easily. The natural oil in wool and hair prevents rust from forming. Wrist pincushions are especially useful; they keep pins accessible during fitting. Weighted pincushions increase efficiency at the cutting table, sewing machine, or ironing board. Magnetic pin holders such as the Grabbit, Pintrapper or Needle Nabber hold pins securely and prevent loss. The holder also may be used to gather scattered pins or the retrieve those that have been dropped. Store any form of pin holder in a dry place.

THREAD

Sewing thread is sold by the twist, weight, and fiber. Loose twist is used for basting and for marking with tailor's tacks. Choose these threads in a white or contrasting pastel color to prevent color from fading or crocking onto the fabric. Regular twist is used for permanent hand and machine sewing.

Thread weight should be compatible with the fabric texture. Lightweight thread blends less noticeably into thin, sheer, or delicate fabrics. It is made in fewer colors and may be limited in availability. Regular-weight thread is used for medium- to heavyweight fabric and is readily available in a variety of colors. Top-stitching thread is for decorative use but may also be used as a gathering thread. It will not break easily when gathering excessive fullness.

Cotton thread is a universal fiber choice for all fabrics. It kinks very little during hand stitching and will not cause excessive wear on threaded parts of the sewing machine. Polyester thread is elastic and strong. Use care when removing polyester or silk thread. It can cut the fingers easily.

Polyester thread is sold in short staple and long staple. The short staple threads are fuzzy and therefore cause a build-up of lint on the threaded parts of the sewing machine. This lint can clog and wear the machine parts if it is not removed regularly. Long staple is more expensive, but its smooth surface is better quality. It stitches smoothly into the fabric. All polyester thread kinks badly during hand sewing. Cotton-wrapped polyester acts like cotton in the sewing or pressing process but retains the elasticity and strength of polyester.

Silk thread is compatible only with silk and wool. Although difficult to use for hand sewing, it makes an excellent basting thread. Its softness prevents thread marks in fabric.

Clear nylon thread is wiry. Machine tensions will require adjusting when nylon thread is used. Nylon thread kinks badly during hand sewing, and it will melt if pressed with an iron that is too warm. This thread is tougher than the fibers in the fabric and can damage the cloth. Such damage is often seen on commercial clothing sewn with clear nylon thread; holes occur along the stitching line where the thread penetrates the fabric. This damage limits fitting adjustment and shortens the wearability of the clothing.

Fitting Supplies

MEASURING TAPE

A flexible, accurate tape measure is a must in the fitting room. The numbers and the fractional markings should be clearly marked and easy to read. Tapes marked to begin with the number one at each end help to prevent annoyance occuring during the fitting and alteration processes.

PENCIL

Pencils with lead of a medium softness mark clearly on pattern tissue or fitting muslin and do not smear. Insoluble carmine red lead pencils are very useful for marking fitting changes on muslin. The markings do not bleed into the fabric when moisture is present.

CHART FOR RECORDING MEASUREMENTS

A chart can provide a systematic, orderly method for recording body measurements and for indicating the necessity and amount of ease for natural body movement. It can aid in the garment fitting and pattern alteration processes. The chart in **Part Three** organizes information in a concise, orderly manner. Space is also available for recording observations about body conformation and other information obtained during the figure evaluation.

SMALL-BEAD NECKLACE OR MEDIUM-WEIGHT CHAIN

Such a necklace or chain is very useful in fitting. Placed around the neck, it defines the position of the back neckline and width of the front neckline.

ELASTIC, TAPE, & BANDS

Elastic can be fitted around the body and used to define a line. Do not fit it so snugly that an indentation is formed. Choose a type that will not fold or roll. Use a ⅛ inch (3 mm) width for defining the armscyes and a ¼ inch (6 mm) width for defining the waistline.

Twill tape or woven hem tape can be used for defining the hipline and for placing across the body between the tips of the bust and the shoulder blades when measuring the center lengths of the upper torso.

Grosgrain ribbon 1 inch (2.5 cm) wide or nonstretch fabric doubled to a 1 inch (2.5 cm) width is firm enough to anchor a skirt or pair of pants firmly in place during fitting. The fastened band may then be marked and used to indicate the size of the waistband or waist stay-tape.

Pattern Alteration Supplies

PAPER SCISSORS

Do not use fabric shears and scissors for cutting paper. Paper and cardboard dull the blades so they will not cut fabric well—or at all. Any scissors are satisfactory for cutting paper as long as they cut evenly and are comfortable to use.

90-DEGREE TRIANGLE, L- OR T-SQUARE

This tool is used for truing the intersection of horizontal and vertical lines that must meet at right angles. A 90-degree angle is also used to maintain or establish the level of dart tips and pattern corners during alteration.

CURVED MARKERS

French curves and other commercially prepared devices are very useful for drawing smooth curved lines and restoring smooth curves on altered pattern edges. For an adaptation of the pivot method, use an appropriately curved marker to quickly reproduce and alter the pattern at its edge instead of tracing a curved edge of the pattern.

PENCILS

A pencil is often necessary for recording information, writing notes, and marking pattern alterations. Tracing the original pattern cutting line with a black-lead pencil is the initial process in the pivot method. Use a red pencil to mark the new cutting line. Medium soft black lead (no. 2), kept reasonably sharp, is easily seen on pattern tissue; a harder lead tears the pattern.

SOFT ERASER

Any recommended art eraser is satisfactory. These are of a soft composition and erase well with little pressure against the tissue. Pattern tissue is easily damaged by the hardness of pencil erasers and other firm compositions.

FROSTED CELLOPHANE TAPE

Frosted tape can be written on with pencil or pen and does not deteriorate as quickly as clear tape. A half-inch width is satisfactory for securing altered pattern areas to alteration tissue. Increase accuracy and efficiency while taping pattern areas by pinning the affected pattern area over corrugated cardboard or a cork board before adding the tape. Use short sections of tape and do not overlap. Long sections of tape tend to pucker the pattern tissue and shorten the pattern area.

GLUE

Rubber cement will neither shrivel nor harden paper. Pattern tissue is so thin, however, that this glue will pass through the paper. Altered pattern areas will stick together when the patterns are folded. A *glue stick* is very satisfactory on thin paper. This glue is in solid form and is placed in a storage device that operates like lipstick. The glue is wiped across the paper edge that is to be fastened; the glue sets immediately and permanently. Keep the container tightly capped following each use to prevent deterioration of the glue.

PUSH PINS

Push pins are easier to locate and to grasp than metal-head straight pins. They are very useful for securing pattern and alteration tissue in place prior to taping or gluing. A cardboard must be used underneath to protect the table top. Push pins may be used for all three methods of pattern alteration but are especially useful for the seam and pivot methods.

TISSUE PAPER

Tissue paper is the same weight as pattern tissue. It is easily obtainable and inexpensive. Select pastel-colored paper when it is necessary that the alteration be noticeable.

FUSIBLE PATTERN BACKING

Fusible pattern backing gives body and durability to pattern tissue. The back of entire pattern pieces can be covered for basic patterns that are intended for frequent reuse. A backed pattern is also much easier to alter. Strips of fusible backing can be used as alteration paper in place of tissue and tape or pins. Fusible pattern backing such as "Fash-on" and "Bak-a-Pattern" are available at notion counters and are sold either in a pre-packaged quantity or as yardage. Pattern backings look much like lightweight fusible interfacing. Fusible interfacing can be used for pattern backing, but *do not* use interfacing that shrinks with heat. The shrinkage will change the pattern measurements both in width and length. Plastic-coated freezer paper also may be used but it makes the pattern very stiff. The stiffness is useful, however, in making slopers (see **Chapter 10**).

CORRUGATED CARDBOARD

Use flat corrugated cardboard under patterns during alteration. Pins can be easily inserted to hold pattern areas securely to the alteration tissue. Using cardboard under the pattern helps ensure the accuracy of a flat, wrinkle-free altered pattern. The cardboard also protects the table top.

NOTE PAD

During fitting, alteration, and garment construction, many situations arise that necessitate making lists or other records of information. Using a note pad helps to prevent writing vital information on odd scraps of available paper or on pattern envelopes; notes written in such a manner are later unintelligible or lost entirely. An envelope, notebook, or small box will keep notes accessible and usable. A swatch of pertinent fabric attached to the note adds to its value; the note also can be pinned to the pertinent pattern envelope or garment in construction. Note pads composed of self-adhesive slips of paper are made in various sizes. The adhesive adheres to most surfaces and permits easy removal without leaving a residue or a stain.

CHAPTER 3

EVALUATING THE FIGURE

Clothing manufacturers and pattern companies design with a standard figure in mind. This established standard is based on the statistical average of many figures. It is often an "ideal" figure with proportions, contours, symmetry, and posture that are considered perfect. Standard figures vary according to the company of origin. An individual's figure is similar to a standard figure, but usually varies from the standard figure in one or more body areas in terms of height, width, depth, and circumference. Figure variations from the standard may be the result of heredity, ethnic origin, growth patterns, posture, disease, or accident. These variations cause fitting problems in both ready-to-wear and personally made clothing.

You can determine personal figure variations by conducting an objective evaluation of the entire figure. An awareness of major figure variations will aid in the selection of clothing styles to enhance the appearance of the figure. The awareness of figure variations should alert you to the need for possible pattern alteration and garment adjustment. An accurate evaluation should enable you to relate a fitting problem to its cause and to the resulting adjustment required.

Prior to an objective figure evaluation, most people assume a pleasingly proportioned and balanced figure. An effort must be made to see the figure as it is, not as you imagine or would like it to be. An inaccurate image of the body can lead to the selection of clothing styles or fit that exposes, calls attention to, or emphasizes an undesired variation.

To be effective, a figure evaluation must be realistic and objective; body assets as well as variations must be recognized. This is a surprisingly difficult task for some people who tend to feel dissatisfied with their individual body build, particularly in comparison to a statistical average or ideal. Self-consciousness and low self-esteem may result. Learning to recognize body areas that conform to the average and to create proportional balance is very important. Acceptance of the self is vital in developing the desire and ability to select styles and accomplish pattern alterations that will effectively and artfully camouflage or minimize figure variations.

Alternative Methods of Figure Evaluation

Methods of evaluating the figure vary according to the situation and equipment available. Wear appropriate clothing during the evaluation; form fitting underwear, swimsuit, leotard, or shorts and T-shirt. Possible methods of evaluation include the following techniques, using an assistant when necessary.

1. *Observe* front, side, and back views of the figure in a full-length mirror. Compare the figure to the standard figure illustrated and discussed on the following pages (see **Figure 3-1**). List variations to be considered in the fitting procedure and in the selection of clothing styles.
2. *Trace* the front and side views of the full-length silhouette on paper. Compare the traced figure with the illustrated standard figure (see **Figure 3-1**). List variations to be considered in the fitting procedure and in the selection of clothing styles.
3. *Photograph* the front, back, and side views of the full-length figure; 5-by-7-inch prints are ideal. Evaluate the figure as illustrated and discussed on the following pages.
4. Pin a basic *fitting pattern* together and try it on the figure. Evaluate the fit.
5. Construct a basic *fitting garment* and try it on the figure. Evaluate the fit.
6. *Measure* the figure and compare personal measurements to standard measurements (see **Chapter 8**).

When using **methods 1, 2,** or **3**, begin your visual observation of the figure at the head and move down the body. This allows the evaluation to proceed in a natural, continuous direction. The eye should not jump back and forth to various body areas, but should proceed smoothly down the figure. Observe front, back, and side views to detect all variations. When using **methods 4, 5,** or **6,** begin your observations at the waist as discussed in detail in **Chapter 8.**

Determine the general body frame or bone structure first. Body frame can be small, medium, or large. Determine the weight range considered standard for the size of the body frame. Then evaluate the proportional relationship of each area, front and back, to the previous area and to the whole. Identify figure areas that may be larger or smaller than the average or ideal (body length, arm length, hip width, and so forth).

Observe body conformation next; you can determine the degree of angularity or curving of the silhouette by the amount and distribution of body weight. Identify specific variations that may influence overall garment appearance: angular hip bones, protruding abdomen, hollow chest, and so forth. If you observe a variation in one area, examine other areas of the figure for a corresponding or related variation (such as rounded upper back and resulting hollow chest).

Each figure is unique. Establish an accurate mental image of the figure and posture. This will alert you to the need for fitting and alteration procedures and will aid you in the selection of appropriate clothing styles.

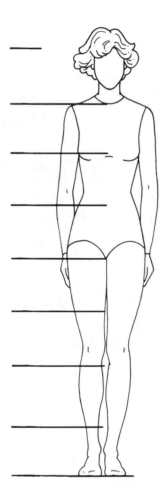

Figure 3-1 Standard 8-head fashion figure

The Standard/Ideal/ Symmetrical Figure

As you begin an evaluation of the figure, each half of the body, from side to center, is expected to appear symmetrical, or as mirror images. In other words, the figure is assumed to be balanced, side to side.

Body proportions may be expressed in fractional amounts, or head lengths. Standard, average, or ideal proportions generally suggest one-half the total body length is above the hip joint and one-half below. Arm length is divided into equal areas by the elbow, which is located at waist level. The wrist is approximately at crotch level. Length from the base of the neck to the waist at the center back is equal to or slightly less than the width across the shoulders. Ideally, hip width is equal to or slightly less than the width across the shoulders. The bust circumference is equal to the circumference of the hips, while waist circumference is generally ten inches smaller.

Body proportions are often expressed in head lengths; referring to the number of times the head length could fit into the total body length. The average individual—or standard—is seven and one half heads tall. The fashion figure is eight heads tall (see **Figure 3-1**). As you might expect, there are three head lengths above the waist and five head lengths below. Body widths and depths also may be expressed in head lengths.

Proportions for the "ideal" figure are the product of a particular culture and are subject to change according to the whims of fashion within that culture. Very few individuals conform to these standards. However, standards do concern us, as they are part of the basis for sizing ready-to-wear garments and commercial patterns. An awareness of personal variation from these standards is essential in selecting appropriate clothing for the individual figure and in identifying areas where alterations may be required. (**Chapter 4** discusses standards as adopted by the various commercial pattern companies.) As the fitting experience progresses, we will determine detailed variations from the standard used by the pattern company. At this point we are concerned with a general evaluation only.

The quantity and distribution of weight in relation to the size of the body frame determines the shape of the body and influences posture and fit in clothing. Traditionally, the bone structure or body frame size was determined by wrist circumference. Recently, however, the Metropolitan Life Insurance Company has published a new approach based on elbow breadth.

To discover your ideal weight range, first determine the elbow breadth. To do this, extend one arm in front of you, palm up. Bend it at the elbow, raising the forearm upward, the palm of the hand facing you. Place the thumb and index finger of the other hand on the two prominent bones on either side of the elbow. Using a ruler, measure the space between the fingers. Compare the elbow breadth measurement with the 1983 Metropolitan Life elbow breadth table below.

Next, find your height on the Metropolitan Life weight-range chart. Follow across to locate your body frame type. Your weight should fall somewhere between the ideal weight range given on the chart. If these weights seem a little heavy, realize they are based on women ages 25–29 wearing one-inch heels and three pounds of clothing, with muscles in top condition. Lower the range by five pounds if muscles are flacid.

FRAME SIZE

Height	Small Frame	Medium Frame	Large Frame
4'10"–5'3"	less than 2¼"	2¼"–2½"	more than 2½"
5'4"–5'11"	less than 2⅜"	2⅜"–2⅝"	more than 2⅝"
6'	less than 2½"	2½"–2¾"	more than 2¾"

IDEAL WEIGHTS

Height	Small Frame	Medium Frame	Large Frame
4'10"	102–111	109–121	118–131
4'11"	103–113	111–123	120–124
5'0"	104–115	113–136	122–137
5'1"	106–118	115–129	125–140
5'2"	108–121	118–132	128–143
5'3"	111–124	121–135	131–147
5'4"	114–127	124–138	134–151
5'5"	117–130	127–141	137–155
5'6"	120–133	130–144	140–159
5'7"	123–136	133–147	143–163
5'8"	126–139	136–150	146–167
5'9"	129–142	139–153	149–170
5'10"	132–145	142–156	152–173
5'11"	135–148	145–159	155–176
6'0"	138–151	148–162	158–179

(Courtesy of Metropolitan Life Insurance Company.)

If weight varies noticeably from standard, the underweight individual is generally less limited than the overweight individual in the selection of clothing. A thin figure is less obvious beneath attractive and well-fitted clothing. The variety of styles available is larger. There is also the possibility of layering clothing to provide the appearance of added weight. However, weight loss can be carried to an extreme, and a gaunt, emaciated appearance is generally considered unattractive—even unhealthy. In such cases, nutritional intake should be examined; health may be affected by poor nutrition, posture may become slumped or permanently impaired, and a poor fit in clothing will result.

Coupled with good muscle tone and posture, excess weight that is evenly distributed over the body frame may require only a change in garment or pattern size. Excess weight that is distributed unevenly may require several additional fitting adjustments and style selection becomes more limited. The strain from excess weight can lead to a breakdown of muscle tissue and support in the arms, chest, abdomen, buttocks, and thighs. Correct posture is difficult when the figure is overweight because of the increased effort required to maintain an erect alignment. The weight is not balanced over both feet from front to back. As the body parts are forced out of alignment, figure variations are introduced and fitting problems increase. Weight loss may eliminate some or all of these figure variations.

Symmetrical Variations from the Standard Figure

A careful evaluation of the figure may reveal one or more symmetrical figure variations from the standard figure. These variations occur identically on both sides of the body, front or back, and they can occur singly or in combination. Examples include narrow shoulders; full bust; broad upper back; long arms; small waist; high hips; sway-back; rounded upper back, hollow chest, and prominent abdomen; and long midriff, short legs, and high, full hips.

Symmetrical figure variations can cause clothing to fit poorly and uncomfortably when wearing certain clothing styles. Not every style will emphasize a variation or create discomfort. Care in the selection of styles can camouflage a variation or direct attention away from the area. Whenever clothing style selection can be used to minimize the variation, the need for alteration is reduced.

The Asymmetrical Figure

As the figure evaluation progresses, it may be determined that the halves of the figure, side to center, are not identical. In other words, the size and conformation of the right side of the figure may vary considerably from the size and conformation of the left side. When this happens the figure is termed *asymmetric*.

Asymmetric variations may or may not have been detected previously, depending on the degree of variation, the awareness level of the individual, and the style of clothing regularly worn. Although the discovery of an asymmetrical figure may come as a surprise, it should not be considered unusual. Variations may have been present at birth or they may have resulted from illness, poor posture, or some specific activity. A conscious effort to correct poor posture can minimize or eliminate the variation.

Akin to asymmetrical variations are variations that occur from front to back. They may be the result of disease, such as the rotation that occurs with scoliosis, or they may be postural attempts by the body to achieve a counterbalance, such as raising a shoulder to counter weight carried on the opposite hip.

Asymmetrical figure variations can occur anywhere on the body. Check for differences from side to side in the following areas:

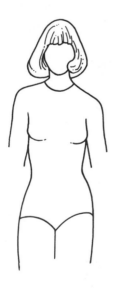

Figure 3-2 Single high hip and high shoulder on the same side of the body

Figure 3-3 Single high hip and high shoulder on opposite sides of the body

neck base slope	hip width
neck base width	hip height
shoulder length	armscye size
shoulder height	upper arm circumference
back width	upper arm length
back length	elbow circumference
blade size and contour	lower arm circumference
blade placement	lower arm length
chest width	wrist circumference
chest length	thigh circumference
bust size and contour	thigh length
bust placement	knee circumference
midriff width	calf circumference
midriff length	calf length
waist width	ankle circumference
waist placement	

Multiple asymmetrical figure variations are common and can include the following combinations:

- High shoulder, high breast, high hip, and long leg occurring on the same side of the body (see **Figure 3-2**)

- High shoulder and high breast, high hip and long leg occurring on the opposite side of the body (see **Figure 3-3**)
- Wide or full back, wide or full front occurring on the same side of the body
- Wide or full back, wide or full front occurring on opposite sides of the body (One shoulder blade protrudes while the other seems almost depressed; one breast is fuller than the other.)

Asymmetrical variations can account for fitting problems and for discomfort wearing certain clothing styles. Knowing the effects of various styles allows the individual to select those suited to the figure and thus eliminate time-consuming fitting and alteration procedures; however, dependence on these styles can be too limiting. Whenever other garment styles are selected, pattern alterations should be made to improve the fit and to create a balanced, more symmetrical appearance.

Posture Evaluation

Posture refers to the alignment of the body parts and to the manner in which the body frame is carried. It has a direct bearing on both physical and mental health. Posture can communicate an individual's self-image, personality, moods, and attitudes. It can influence physical attractiveness and the attractiveness of clothing.

Incorrect posture can introduce needless figure variations and fitting problems. Often improved posture—coupled with a weight change when needed—can eliminate many or all figure variations discovered in the evaluation of a figure. Therefore, evaluating posture is worthwhile even before becoming involved with fitting.

You can best evaluate your posture in front of a full-length, three-way mirror or with the aid of a photograph. Assume a normal, relaxed, but controlled stance; *do not* attempt to assume a corrected posture. (For an accurate evaluation, a realistic stance is required.) Stand without shoes; high heels affect body alignment by shifting the center of balance.

Your weight should be evenly distributed on both feet, from front to back and from side to side. A plumb line, a weighted string that hangs perpendicular to the floor, can be used to evaluate body alignment. Hang the line from the top of the mirror or draw it on the photograph. The edge of a door can also function as a plumb line. When viewing the body profile the line should extend from the ear to the floor. On the standard figure it will bisect the ear, neck, shoulder joint, and elbow, pass just to the back of the wrist, bisect the hip joint and knee, and finally pass in front of the ankle (see **Figure 3-4**).

Moving from the head downward, proper body alignment requires the following:

- The head and neck are centered over the shoulders, with the chin parallel to the floor
- The shoulders are pulled slightly back and down
- The chest is slightly lifted
- Buttock muscles are contracted slightly and tucked under, both sides parallel to the floor
- Abdominal muscles are taut
- The arms hang relaxed at the sides, the elbows bent slightly forward
- The knees are straight but relaxed, neither flexed (bent) nor hyperextended (locked)
- The feet are parallel and somewhat apart, with toes pointing straight ahead and the ankles joining the feet at right angles

Incorrect alignment causes the body to counterbalance itself in order to remain erect. *Overly erect posture* can be recognized by an exaggerated lift of the chest, which in turn creates an arch in the upper back (see **Figure 3-6**). The head may

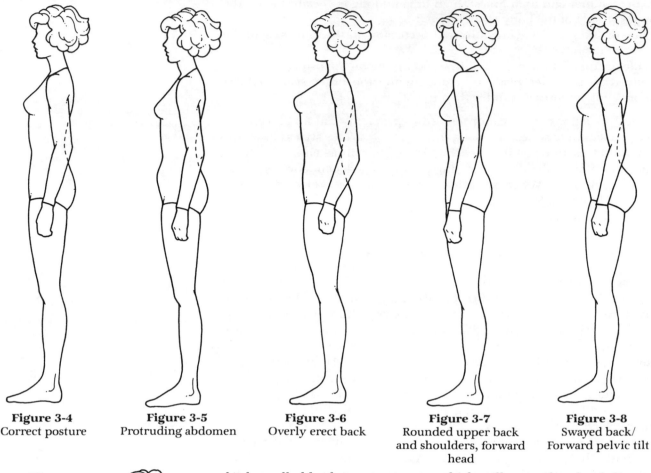

Figure 3-4
Correct posture

Figure 3-5
Protruding abdomen

Figure 3-6
Overly erect back

Figure 3-7
Rounded upper back
and shoulders, forward
head

Figure 3-8
Swayed back/
Forward pelvic tilt

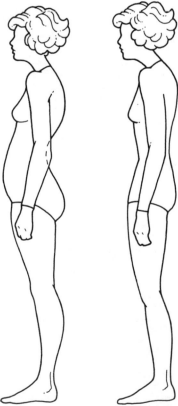

Figure 3-9
Slumped posture

Figure 3-10
Rounded shoulders,
forward head and
backward pelvic tilt

also be pulled back to an extreme, which will cause the plumb line to pass in front of the ear. The knees are often hyperextended to the back and locked into place. Such a stance places stress on the back and legs. A prominent bust, shortened upper back length, and an increased chest length from neck base to bust tip may result. Other possible results are squared shoulders, widened chest, and a narrowed back. The position of the shoulders is particularly important in fitting, as clothing hangs from the shoulders. If shoulders are incorrectly positioned, all garment areas below will drape or fit incorrectly.

Rounded back posture can be recognized by an overly curved upper back, a forward curve in the shoulders, a hollow chest, and a forward-tilted head (see **Figure 3-7**). The plumb line will pass behind the ear. Breathing may be hampered because of pressure on the lungs; the oxygen supply to the body will be reduced, and chronic fatigue may result. Among the figure variations introduced may be found a shortened—possibly hollow and narrowed—chest length, increased upper back length and width, and prominent neck cords.

A *swayed back* will be evident by the forward tilt of the pelvis; a prominent abdomen and protruding buttocks result (see **Figure 3-8**). The abdominal curvature also will increase, as will the angle at the groin. Other probable figure variations include a shortened upper back length between waist and hip, and an increased length of buttocks to crotch.

A *slumped posture* is common; it results in a rounded upper back and shoulders, hollow chest, and forward head, in combination with a swayed back and prominent abdomen (see **Figure 3-9**). In addition to all the other figure variations that result from poor posture, it also may lead to the accumulation of excess weight at the base of the neck, commonly referred to as a dowager's hump. Slumped posture typically results in fatigue and backache, with discomfort increasing in the event of pregnancy. (A short-term counterbalance effect can be expected during pregnancy; as the bust and the abdominal area extends, the shoulders become overly erect and the arch in the back is increased.)

Rounded shoulders, a forward head and backward pelvic tilt is an uncommon postural variation. It is characterized by rounded back posture as previously discussed, in combination with an awkward tilt of the pelvis that pulls the waist area back and thrusts the hip joint and thigh forward. The buttocks are tucked under and knees may appear in a slightly bent position. The front abdominal curve will increase and buttocks curve will decrease. The individual appears to lead with the hips when walking. (See **Figure 3-10.**)

If no other means are available to evaluate your posture, you may resort to the use of a wall. Assume a normal stance with your back against the wall; your weight should be evenly distributed over both feet. Your body alignment is good if your shoulders, shoulder blades, and buttocks touch the wall. The space between the wall and the small of your back should be just large enough to insert a flat hand.

If only the shoulders touch the wall, your posture is overly erect. If only your shoulder blades touch the wall, you have rounded posture. If only your buttocks touch the wall, you have a swayed back. (An exception to this would be the individual with large buttocks.) If both shoulder blades and buttocks touch the wall and there is a large space between your waist and the wall, you probably have slumped posture.

If poor posture is prolonged, the stress and strain on muscles, bones, and joints will contribute to fatigue and health problems common in later years. However, poor posture *can* be corrected, if the individual is committed to the effort required. Try the following posture exercises:

- Assume corrected posture while aligned against a wall; maintain this posture and walk away from the wall
- Stop and hold correct posture for a short period of time
- Force a mental image of correct posture while walking; practice often
- Evaluate your posture often, in front of a mirror or as you pass a window
- Practice good posture while walking, sitting, or bending

The time used in improving poor posture is time well spent. It can improve your health and reduce or eliminate figure variations, fitting problems and pattern or garment alterations that result.

CHAPTER 4

To keep fitting adjustments and pattern alterations to a minimum, choose an appropriate pattern in a size that fits the major areas of the body frame. Alter for larger or smaller muscle and other soft-tissue areas. To ensure the best fit when selecting a pattern, consider three body characteristics: *circumference, height and build,* and *posture*. The circumference determines the number size of the pattern. The height and build determine the pattern figure type. The build and posture determine the pattern company whose pattern will fit best.

Pattern Size—Body Circumference

The following circumference measurements are used to determine pattern size for the garments listed; compare your measurements with the size charts in the back of the pattern book.

BUST

The bust measurement is taken at the scye level (base of arm hinge) and is used for blouses, coats, dresses, jackets, jumpers, and vests. Keep the tape level across the back from side to side, then curve upward across the upper perimeter of the bust. Most pattern companies design for a person who wears a B-cup bra. The high bust measurement is used because it reflects the size of the body frame. The pattern is altered to correctly fit the amount of bust tissue.

If the size of the bra cup is C or larger and small bone structure is also involved, you may want to use the next smaller pattern size. Although the pattern will need added circumference to accommodate the larger cup size, the size of the armscye and the fit through the shoulders and other areas of the bodice may be better for the small bone structure.

Conversely, if the bra cup is A and the bone structure is large in relation to the bust, you may want to buy the next larger pattern size. The excess circumference at the bust may be removed if the armscye and other areas fit properly.

Once the correct size is determined, purchase the same size for all the garments listed above. The varying amounts of livability and ease have been incorporated into the pattern.

HIP

The hip measurement is taken around the body at the level of the hip joint and is used for pants and skirts. The hip joint measurement is used because it reflects the size of the frame as well as the crotch and leg size. The pattern is then altered to correctly fit the amount of thigh and buttocks tissue. The waist size is more easily adjusted than the hip, especially when pleats or similar lines are involved.

Figure Type—Height & Build

The back bodice length is used as the indicator for body height. This measurement is taken from the prominent vertebra at the base of the neck to the waistline when the person being measured is looking straight ahead.

Sometimes the names of figure types are misleading since they seem to indicate the age of the person. In actuality, figure development begins and ends at various ages. Final mature height and build may place a shorter, older person in the junior figure type even though these pattern styles are designed for the adolescent. Conversely, a tall young person's height may place her in the misses figure type before her bust and hips have fully matured even though misses patterns are designed for adult tastes and figures. For these reasons, design adjustments and pattern alterations may have to be made to accommodate personal tastes and the body build of the person wearing the garment.

Following are descriptions of the major figure types. They are arranged in order of body development, height, and sex. All height measurements are taken without shoes.

CHILDREN

The children's basic bodice and pants pattern does not distinguish between the sexes. In developing the basic bodice sloper, a waist dart is sometimes included. This dart is released in shirts and blouses. In the dress bodice the dart may be used or transferred into the side seam.

Toddlers: Height 28 inches to 40 inches (71 cm to 102 cm) These patterns are designed for a figure between baby and child. The trunk (dress) length is shorter than the children's length. The pants have an allowance for a diaper that makes the crotch deeper and the hip area larger.

Children: Height 35 inches to 48 inches (88 cm to 122 cm) These patterns are designed for a figure that is 7 inches (17.5 cm) taller than the toddler and therefore slimmer in appearance but not in circumference measurement. The crotch depth of the pants is shorter since no allowance is needed for diapers.

Girls: Height 50 inches to 61 inches (127 cm to 155 cm) The shape of the basic bodice changes and the waistline dart is made slightly wider. These patterns are designed for the girl whose bust and hips have not begun to mature.

Boys: Height 48 inches to 58 inches (122 cm to 147 cm) The shape of the basic bodice changes; the dart increase for boys is transferred to the shoulders and released to give width. These patterns are designed for boys whose shoulders have broadened and legs have lengthened.

DEVELOPING & MATURE FEMALES

The size of the dart in the basic sloper increases as the difference between the scye measurement and the measurement at fullest bust increases. At the present time no pattern company fully meets the needs of the taller figure. Patterns for these women require alterations in length and width both above or below the waist.

Young Junior/Teen: Height 5 feet 1 inch to 5 feet 3 inches (1.55 m to 1.60 m) These patterns are designed for the developing preteen and teen figure.

Junior Petite: Height 5 feet to 5 feet 1 inch (1.52 m to 1.55 m) These patterns are designed for a well-proportioned, small-scale figure.

Junior: Height 5 feet 4 inches to 5 feet 5 inches (1.63 m to 1.65 m) These patterns are designed for a well-proportioned, shorter-waisted figure with a high small bust and small hips.

Miss Petite: Height 5 feet 2 inches to 5 feet 4 inches (1.57 m to 1.63 m) These patterns are designed for the shorter but well-proportioned and fully developed figure.

Misses: Height 5 feet 5 inches to 5 feet 6 inches (1.65 m to 1.68 m) These patterns are designed for the well-proportioned and fully developed figure of average height.

Half Size: Height 5 feet 2 inches to 5 feet 3 inches (1.57 m to 1.60 m) These patterns are designed for a fully developed figure with narrow shoulders and a short back waist length. The waist and hips are larger in proportion to the bust than the other figure types.

Women: Height 5 feet 5 inches to 5 feet 6 inches (1.65 m to 1.68 m) These patterns are designed for the mature figure that has increased in circumference beyond the misses figure.

DEVELOPING & MATURE MALES

Teen Boys: Height 5 feet 1 inch to 5 feet 8 inches (1.55 m to 1.73 m) These patterns are designed for young men who have not yet reached adult stature.

Men: Height 5 feet 10 inches (1.78 m) These patterns are sized and designed for men of average height and build. At the present time no pattern company fully meets the needs of the taller male figure. Patterns for these men may require alterations in length or width (or both) above and below the waist.

PATTERN COMPANY—BUILD & POSTURE

An individual's body build and posture determine the company whose pattern will fit best. Following is an analysis of the basic patterns for the companies listed (see **Figures 4-1** through **4-3**).

Burda

A Burda pattern is designed for the smaller, shorter European figure. The bodice back is shorter from underarm to waist than American patterns.

The shoulder slope and dart size indicate a figure with a slightly rounded upper back and a forward arm joint. The sleeve cap also is designed for a forward arm joint and a thin arm. The neck opening is designed for an erect head and a narrow neck from side to side but with a low base at the front. The width of the entire lower bodice front is narrower by one size than American patterns. When Burda is compared to other patterns, the shorter length of the side seam, the larger underarm dart, and equal center front length indicate an erect figure with a forward thrust of the rib cage.

The sleeve circumference is approximately 1 inch (2.5 cm) smaller at the capline than American patterns. The placement of the elbow dart above the midpoint of the underarm seam also reflects a shorter waist length.

The skirt back is slightly wider at the hip than Butterick or Vogue but not as wide as McCall's. The back and front width is the same as Simplicity. The single front waist dart of the skirt is placed near the side seam over the hip bone, approximately one-third the distance from side to center front. The side seam is more sloped from hem to waist than Butterick or Vogue, and the narrow width of the single waistline dart indicates that part of the basic dart has been transferred to the hem and released for flare. This transfer provides a wider sweep at the thighline and hemline, thus allowing more room for thigh fullness and for sitting and walking.

Simplicity

Simplicity patterns are designed for the individual who is of average height or slightly shorter, with a narrow rib cage and a rounded upper back.

The back bodice length is ⅛ inch (0.3 cm) shorter than Butterick and Vogue and ½ inch (1.2 cm) shorter than McCall's. It is ⅛ inch (0.3 cm) longer than Burda. The back shoulder slope and dart indicate a slightly forward arm joint. The sleeve cap is slightly flattened in the back, and the shoulder position is forward by ¼ inch (0.6 cm), also indicating a forward arm joint.

The chest width of the bodice front is slightly narrower than the other patterns. The curve on the lower armscye of the front is more rounded than Burda, Butterick, and Vogue but is the same as McCall's. The bust tip is higher than Burda, Butterick, and Vogue and is the same height as McCall's. The distance between the center and the bust tip is the same as Burda, Butterick, and Vogue but narrower than McCall's. This suggests a youthful mature bust. The sleeve cap is ¼ inch (0.6 cm) shorter than Butterick and Vogue but the same height as Burda and McCall's. The circumference at the elbow is the same as McCall's and wider than Butterick and Vogue by ⅜ inch (0.9 cm). The single elbow dart is midway down the underarm seam. The narrow width of the elbow dart indicates that a small amount of the basic dart has been transferred to the wristline, which increases the circumference of the lower arm and wrist.

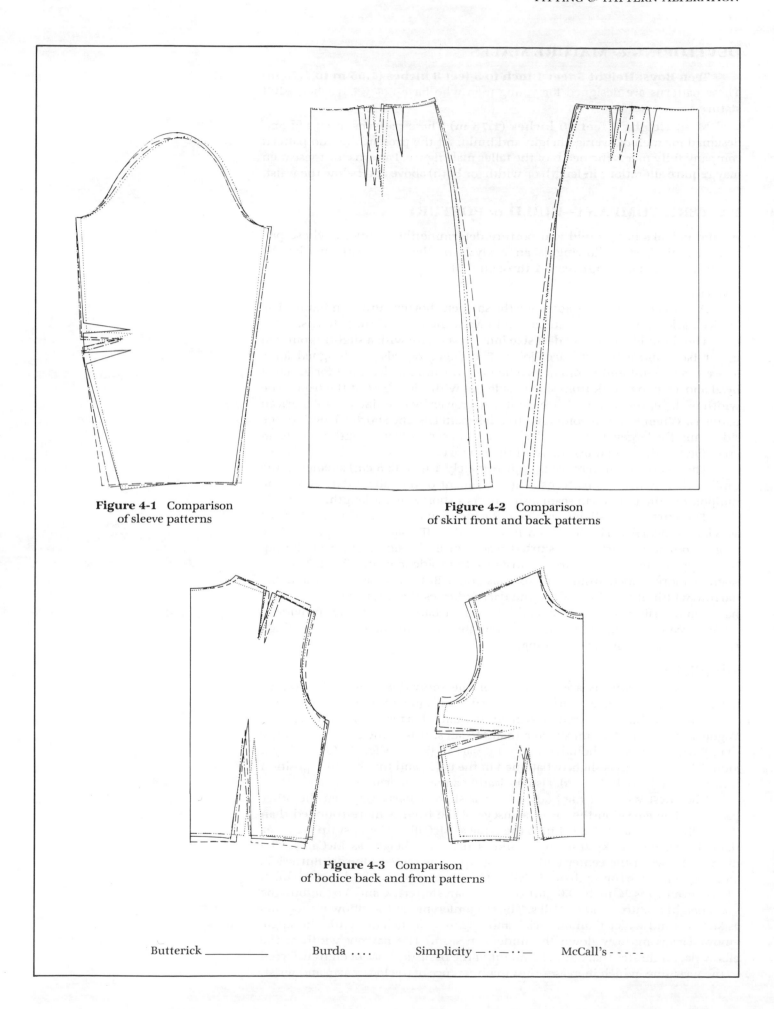

Figure 4-1 Comparison
of sleeve patterns

Figure 4-2 Comparison
of skirt front and back patterns

Figure 4-3 Comparison
of bodice back and front patterns

Butterick _____   Burda . . . .   Simplicity —··—··—   McCall's - - - - -

The skirt back at the hip is the same width as Burda; it is slightly wider than Butterick or Vogue but not as wide as McCall's. The single waist dart divides the waistline area approximately in half. The side seam from hem to waistline is sloped, indicating that part of the basic dart has been transferred to the hem. This provides a wider sweep at the hemline, thus allowing more room for thigh fullness and for sitting and walking.

Butterick & Vogue

Both Butterick and Vogue patterns are designed for the average-to-tall erect figure, and they vary very little.

In the back bodice, the shoulder dart is smaller and the width across the blade is narrower than Burda and McCall's. The back width is the same as Simplicity. The back length is ⅛ inch (0.3 cm) longer than Simplicity and ¼ inch (0.6 cm) longer than Burda; it is ¼ inch (0.6 cm) shorter than McCall's.

The front neck depth is shorter than Burda and McCall's but the same as Simplicity. The width of the front neck curve is less than McCall's and Simplicity but wider than Burda. The bust tip position is low when compared to the other patterns. The width from center front to bust tip is approximately the same as Burda and Simplicity but narrower than McCall's. The lower front armscye is less curved. The center front length at the waistline is ⅛ inch (0.3 cm) longer than McCall's and Burda and the same as Simplicity. The sleeve cap is higher and slightly wider at the top than the other pattern companies. The elbow position is approximately midway down the underarm seam. The sleeve fits tighter in the lower arm because the full amount of the basic dart has been used at the elbow position.

The skirt side seam from hip to waistline is almost straight. The shaping for the circumference difference is accomplished by two darts on the back and front pattern sections. The two darts provide better potential for a custom fit. The darts are spaced so they divide the waist and hip area approximately in thirds. The back dart nearest the side seam accommodates the flesh in the upper hip area; the one near center back contours the pattern for the buttocks. Butterick and Vogue are the only patterns that have two back and two front skirt darts.

McCall's

McCall's pattern's are designed for the average-to-tall figure with a slightly rounded upper back.

The bodice back length is ¼ inch (0.6 cm) longer than Butterick and Vogue, ½ inch (1.2 cm) longer than Simplicity, and ⅝ inch (1.5 cm) longer than Burda. The width across the back blade is ¼ inch (0.6 cm) wider than any of the other patterns. The dart placement on the front bodice indicates a bust tip position ¼ inch to ½ inch (0.6 cm to 1.2 cm) higher and ⅝ inch (1.5 cm) farther from center than other patterns.

The sleeve cap is ¼ inch (0.6 cm) shorter and slightly narrower than Butterick and Vogue. It is the same height as Burda and Simplicity, but the curve at the top of McCall's sleeve is symmetrical, like Butterick and Vogue. The elbow position is midway on the sleeve underarm. The circumference at the elbow is ⅜ inch (0.8 cm) larger than Butterick and Vogue. Part of the elbow dart has been transferred to the wrist, which increases the circumference of the lower arm and wrist.

The skirt has the largest hip circumference and sweep at the hem of any of the patterns. The hip measurement of the pattern is larger and therefore will accommodate a figure approximately one size larger than the body measurement given on the pattern envelope. The side seam from hem to waistline is more sloped. There is less darting from the waistline, indicating a dart transfer from waist to hemline. This gives more room for full thighs and for sitting and walking. The front waist dart is placed closer to the hip bone, approximately one-third the distance from side to center front.

CHAPTER 5

LEARNING FROM THE CONTENTS OF A PATTERN

There is more to a pattern than first meets the eye. Patterns are one of the best buys on the market when you consider the engineering that is involved, and the information and help they provide. Use them to continually update your knowledge and improve your skills as new fabrics, equipment, notions, and construction techniques are developed and discussed. The format used on the envelope, pattern tissue, and guide sheet is somewhat different for each pattern company. Better garment fit and construction should result if the pattern is read, understood, and properly used.

Pattern Companies

Major U.S. companies are Butterick, McCall's, Simplicity, and Vogue. These companies mass-market their patterns nationwide and in some foreign countries. Information printed on these patterns is written in Spanish and French as well as English. An illustrated guide sheet is supplied with each pattern but the directions are written only in English. The patterns contain very complete markings for layout, cutting, and construction. Seam and hem allowances may vary in width, but the amounts are stated on the hem areas. Vogue Designer Patterns have the most complete construction directions. These generally feature some couture sewing techniques.

Other U.S. pattern companies are Kwik-Sew, Sew Easy, Sunrise and Enchanted Forest. All information is written in English. Sunrise designs only for infants through preteen sizes. Sew Easy designs are mainly sportswear intended for knit fabric. Enchanted Forest designs for young children, some of these patterns are available through the McCall Pattern Company.

The Burda pattern is produced in Germany. Pattern information and guide sheets are written in English, Spanish, French, Swedish, Danish, and Dutch in addition to German. The English translation is not always fluent. The number and types of pattern markings are somewhat limited on these patterns. Each pattern piece is graded in three or more sizes on the same sheet of paper. The various sections for each size have to be traced onto a separate paper if the master pattern is to remain intact. Burda prints all sizes in the same color but uses different outlining for each size. Seam or hem allowances are not included, and information on the guide sheet is limited in comparison to U.S. patterns.

The price of a pattern may reflect the company's philosophy about the expected customer. Some pattern styles are directed to a wide variety of ages and lifestyles. Models in these illustrations usually suggest youthfulness because many young people are involved in learning-to-sew projects and sewing courses. Young people usually have less money to spend, and are often part of a total family for whom clothing money must be divided. Consequently, manufacturers allocate less time, labor, and production money to patternmaking for this market. These patterns are designed by a salaried company designer or patternmaker. They can sell for a low to moderate price because mass sales allow a lower profit margin per pattern.

Other patterns are styled for people who desire more exclusive designs. These patterns sell for moderate to high prices. The pattern pieces are more complex. More time, labor, equipment, and therefore, costs are involved in their production. Generally, an expensive garment prototype is purchased from an accomplished independent designer. This designer is often internationally known and can, therefore, demand high payment for a design. A large part of the resulting cost must be passed on to the consumer. The smaller market necessitates a higher profit margin for each pattern. Models in these pattern illustrations usually suggest sophistication and subtle, adult tastes. Adults are more financially independent and have more money to spend on clothing. Those who want exclusiveness in design are also more willing to pay a higher price per pattern.

The Pattern Catalogue

Today's pattern catalogue is an exciting preview into the world of fashion. The current fashion story is presented in color on glossy paper. Photographs of the latest designs appear with supporting background personality to suggest a lifestyle or activity suitable for the design. The catalogues contain a variety of fashions for all ages and both sexes. Ordinary styles as well as specialized designs directed to people with specific wants or needs are available. Costumes, home furnishings, and crafts are also featured.

The four major companies issue a large, complete catalogue either quarterly, bimonthly, or monthly. Each issue features the company's newest designs as the first entries. A four-digit stock number is listed with each design on these pages, but the remaining particulars are found later within the catalogue. These opening photographs give an instant overview of current fabrics, colors, textures, and styles. The silhouette and the fashion trends concerning shoulder shaping, sleeve style, waistline placement, hem length, accessories, and important garment combinations are revealed in the main body of the catalogue. The catalogue pages are numbered in continuous sequence from one issue to the next. Breaks occur in the page numbering sequence when designs are discarded.

Available patterns are classified into various categories. Each category is easily identified with dividers that have the category name or a trade name on the tab. Sometimes a design appears in more than one category. Style variations included in each pattern choice are accompanied with essential information. Line drawings are shown for each back view. A chart lists the size range available and the required yardage for each style variation. A fashion description, the finished garment lengths, and hem circumferences are sometimes listed and suitable fabric choices are suggested.

In the back portion of the catalogue, instructions are given for measuring a figure to determine the correct pattern size. This instruction is given for all age or figure-type groupings. A classified index lists each pattern number by category or purpose. The numerical index lists available pattern stock numbers in sequence within the classification category. A break in numbering occurs between categories. The higher numbers within the category indicate the most recent styles. When the numbering reaches a predetermined point, the sequence for the category begins again at the original low point. You can determine the approximate "age" of a pattern design number by its relative position in the listing for the specific category. With access to a collection of a

Fabric Width Conversion Chart

FABRIC WIDTH YARDS (METERS)	32" (81 cm)	35"–36" (90 cm)	39" (100 cm)	41" (104 cm)	44"–45" (115 cm)	50" (127 cm)	52"–54" (140 cm)	58"–60" (150 cm)
	1⅞ (1.75)	1¾ (1.60)	1½ (1.40)	1½ (1.40)	1⅜ (1.30)	1¼ (1.15)	1⅛ (1.05)	1 (0.95)
	2¼ (2.10)	2 (1.85)	1¾ (1.60)	1¾ (1.60)	1⅝ (1.50)	1½ (1.40)	1⅜ (1.30)	1¼ (1.15)
	2½ (2.30)	2¼ (2.10)	2 (1.85)	2 (1.85)	1¾ (1.60)	1⅝ (1.50)	1½ (1.40)	1⅜ (1.30)
	2¾ (2.55)	2½ (2.30)	2¼ (2.10)	2¼ (2.10)	2⅛ (1.95)	1¾ (1.60)	1¾ (1.60)	1⅝ (1.50)
	3⅛ (2.90)	2⅞ (2.65)	2½ (2.30)	2½ (2.30)	2¼ (2.10)	2 (1.85)	1⅞ (1.75)	1¾ (1.60)
	3⅜ (3.10)	3⅛ (2.90)	2¾ (2.55)	2¾ (2.55)	2½ (2.30)	2¼ (2.10)	2 (1.85)	1⅞ (1.75)
	3¾ (3.45)	3⅜ (3.10)	3 (2.75)	2⅞ (2.65)	2¾ (2.55)	2⅜ (2.20)	2¼ (2.10)	2 (1.85)
	4 (3.70)	3¾ (3.45)	3¼ (3.00)	3⅛ (2.90)	2⅞ (2.65)	2⅝ (2.40)	2⅜ (2.20)	2¼ (2.10)
	4⅜ (4.00)	4¼ (3.90)	3½ (3.20)	3⅜ (3.10)	2¾ (2.55)	2¾ (2.55)	2⅝ (2.40)	2⅜ (2.20)
	4⅝ (4.25)	4½ (4.15)	3¾ (3.45)	3⅝ (3.35)	3⅜ (3.10)	3 (2.75)	2¾ (2.55)	2⅝ (2.40)
	5 (4.60)	4¾ (4.35)	4 (3.70)	3⅞ (3.55)	3⅝ (3.35)	3¼ (3.00)	2⅞ (2.65)	2¾ (2.55)
	5¼ (4.80)	5 (4.60)	4¼ (3.90)	4⅛ (3.80)	3⅞ (3.55)	3⅛ (3.10)	3⅛ (2.90)	2⅞ (2.65)

Figure 5-2. Typical conversion chart showing yardage needed for various fabric widths. Reprinted courtesy of New Jersey Cooperative Extension Service, Rutgers, The State University

company's catalogues, any pattern stock number can be traced to its actual date of issue.

A source index listing distributors of fabrics used in the photographed styles is also included in the back of the catalogue. Write to the specific company to locate the nearest retail source of a fabric used in the photograph.

A fabric yardage conversion chart is included. Use this chart to determine the amount of fabric required when its width is not included on the yardage chart listed with the pattern. These converted yardages are estimates only, based on the comparable number of square feet of fabric needed. Due to the complexity of the shapes of pattern pieces, the converted amount may not be the correct amount required.

To determine the actual amount of fabric needed when a different width of fabric is to be used, indicate the folded or single fabric width (as indicated by the layout code) on a countertop or table. Lay the pattern pieces in place. Measure the total length used and purchase this amount plus an allowance for straightening and shrinkage if necessary. Make a drawing of the "trial layout" for later use with the fabric if the layout was changed from that furnished on the pattern guide.

The Pattern Envelope

The pattern envelope, as well as the guide sheet and pattern pieces, provides information for the sewing/learning process. The envelope heading includes the *name of the company* and the pattern *stock number.* The envelope heading also includes the *pattern size number, figure type,* and *purchase price.*

The *trade name of the style category* is noted on the front of the envelope. Each category is intended for a specific audience, need, or purpose. Each company features some patterns under exclusive trade name categories and others that are common to all companies.

The front of a pattern envelope features *illustrations of all style choices* for which pieces are provided. Art work is intended to make the style appear attractive, design lines more noticeable, and the pattern more saleable. Each model illustrates a different style choice. Each choice is coded with a letter or number. The drawings for the back views are coded with the same letter or number. Examination of these illustrations reveals styling details on the bodice, sleeve, and skirt, as well as accessory details. Illustrations give an idea of the difficulty of the construction and allow the customer to evaluate the style's ability to emphasize or minimize figure variations. These drawings suggest a type of fabric: plain, print, plaid, or stripe. The fabric in the illustration may not be the best choice for the style, or for the individual. (See **Chapter 1** for ways to create harmony between pattern, fabric, and wearer.) Fashion illustrations show a lengthened figure. Consumers will avoid disappointment by learning to interpret the illustrations in terms of the actual figure. (This is easier to do if the pattern envelope shows a photograph in addition to sketches of the model.)

The back of the envelope contains vital information. *Line drawings* for back views of each style choice are shown. Belts are not drawn in a fastened position, but are left off or drawn as though hanging untied, thus exposing the waistline. A belt drawn in place on the fashion illustration may not reveal whether the dress has a waistline seam. *A written fashion description* accompanies the sketch. It includes an analysis of design lines and details, and describes the style variations of necklines, skirts, sleeves, and so forth.

The total *number of pattern pieces* included for all style choices may be stated on the envelope back. Generally, the fewer the pieces, the simpler the construction. Sometimes small scale drawings of the pattern pieces are shown. These help to assess the difficulty of the pattern, and the time and skill required to do a professional job.

The back of the envelope always contains a *chart of standard body measurements,* cross-referenced in all sizes in which the pattern is available.

Bust, hip, and waist circumferences, along with the back waist length, are listed in inches and centimeters. McCall's shades the metric measurements in blue. The chart states the amount of fabric required for each style variation. Amounts are given for outer fashion fabric, interfacing, lining, and any trim fabric, based on fabric width, pattern size, style choice, and the nature of the fabric, i.e., with or without "nap." "Nap" in this instance refers to all fabrics that require the upper edges of all pattern pieces to lie in one direction; whether because of the nap, one-way color shading, a one-way design, or a one-way fabrication (such as knits and pile weaves). One-way layouts usually require more fabric. Although the charts list ample fabric amounts, there may not be adequate yardage if length losses occur before cutting the pattern pieces. Prior to purchase, analyze the fabric loss that will result from straightening the crosswise grain, anticipated shrinkage, lengthening of the pattern pieces, or for style adaptations, and large-scale fabric design. Add the amount of anticipated loss to the yardage suggested. *Notions* needed to complete the garment are listed, including type and length of zipper, number and size of buttons, hooks and eyes, and lace or other trimmings.

Charts may contain some *measurements for the finished garment.* Hem circumference may be given for dresses, skirts, and pants. This indicates the amount of basic ease or fullness added at the hemline but disregards fullness included in pleats and ruffles. The center-back length on dresses and jackets is stated, indicating the distance from the back neckline to hemline. This measurement reveals where the jacket edge will cross the hip area. The side length of pants sizes is also given. These measurements alert the reader to the need for style adaptation or pattern alteration.

The back of the pattern envelope lists *suggested fabrics* that are suitable for the garment design. These fabrics are compatible in texture, weight, and drapability to the one used by the designers. Every fabric will not make up well in every style. Note such words as "lightweight" and "heavyweight" in the fashion description. If the pattern is intended for knits with crosswise stretch, a fabric stretch-guide is illustrated. Such patterns have a smaller finished circumference due to less darting and ease needed with knitted fabrics; they cannot be used with woven or firmly knit cloth unless alterations are made. Be certain to use a crosswise fold of fabric when consulting the stretch guide; only fabric with inherent elasticity that matches the stretch-guide is suitable. The envelope back may list fabrics that are inappropriate for the pattern, such as plaids, border fabrics, prints, and diagonal stripes or weaves. It may indicate that extra fabric is required for matching plaids, stripes, and one-way designs.

The Guide Sheet

The guide sheet contains a wealth of information in addition to the "how-to" directions. It features *fashion drawings* for all front views. Each view is designated by the same code letter or number used on the front and back of the envelope. A set of labeled drawings or a list of *pattern pieces needed for each style* choice is shown. Use these lists when sorting the pattern pieces needed for a specific style choice. In this way the required pieces may be checked against the available fabric. Some pattern pieces are used for more than one style choice. Separate pattern pieces may be included for linings and interfacings; if not, areas on specific pattern pieces will be labeled "interfacing," "facing," or "lining," and these pattern pieces will be used a second time for cutting the additional garment area. Occasionally a pattern border will be labeled, "Cut here for facing." Each pattern piece is assigned a code number or letter according to the sequence of its use in the construction process as outlined in the guide sheet.

The guide sheet contains *suggestions for minor alterations* of pattern sections. Usually the examples show only even amounts of change in length and procedures are limited to slash method. Illustrations are accompanied with little explanation of how and why. Remember that altering only the length will not make most patterns fit well. A thorough knowledge of pattern alteration is invaluable for the individual who intends to sew and fit clothing . . . for anyone. This text explains and illustrates the total scope of fitting and pattern alteration. Changes for body width and contour are presented in addition to those for length.

Instructions for preparing and cutting the fabric are given. *Methods of transferring pattern markings* to the fabric are suggested. Read this information before using the pattern. It includes the initial steps for achieving correct fit and is not repeated in the step-by-step instructions.

Layout diagrams are given on the guide sheet. These diagrams show the exact placement of the pattern pieces when the grainlines are placed in the suggested relationship to the fabric fold or selvages. Be alert to fabric that is folded crosswise instead of lengthwise. Note also that the lengthwise fold is not always placed at the center of the fabric. All parts of the drawings are in the same scale.

Following the layout guide assures that all necessary pieces can be cut from a specific length of fabric. *Remember* to take into account, however, the possibility of fabric loss from preshrinking and grain straightening, and the extra fabric needed because of pattern alterations for enlarging pattern pieces or for style adaptations. Often individuals who are experienced in sewing can use less fabric by changing the position of the fabric fold or by dovetailing small and large pattern pieces to better advantage than is shown on the guide. The new fold need not be along the center of the fabric, but it must be parallel to the selvages or cut edges.

All pattern pieces can be laid with the printed side upward or downward, so long as the fabric is doubled. Those pattern pieces that are to be cut singly must be laid with the printed surface of the pattern and the face of the fabric in a consistent direction. Disregarding this rule can cause a pattern piece to be cut for the opposite side of the body or produce two pieces for the same body area.

A *layout code* is built into the diagrams to show the relationship between the printed side of the pattern piece and how it is to be laid against the fabric. The usual coding is a white sketch representing the pattern pieces placed with the printed surface upward and a shaded sketch representing the pattern pieces placed with the printed surface downward. Additional codings indicate that a pattern piece must be cut a second or third time or after the fabric is opened to a single layer. Each pattern guide sheet has a *legend to explain the coding*.

The largest portion of the guide is devoted to written descriptions and illustrations for the *sequence of construction*. Construction steps are numbered in the order of assembly and are placed in columns that are read vertically like a newspaper. Drawings illustrate the finished product.

Consider the construction guide as a help and a learning tool. Periodically they present new ideas and use of new equipment and techniques. Although all necessary information is given for the suggested techniques, it may be desirable to substitute methods that are less complicated, faster, or that produce superior quality. Many pattern guides present simplified speed techniques; however, some of these techniques yield a lower quality of construction and durability. Learn to substitute procedures appropriate to the needs and purposes of the sewn product.

The Pattern Pieces

Crucial information is provided by the marks and labeling on pattern pieces. These markings help keep the fabric under control and create the fit and style intended by the designer. The preciseness with which they are used affects the fit and final appearance of the garment. The number and the complexity of the markings indicate the difficulty of the construction.

Some pattern labeling is used only for *identification* purposes. These labels include the brand name, stock number, size, style choice, code number or letter, and the name of the pattern piece.

Other markings are used to indicate *natural positions for fitting* the pattern and the garment to the body. They include labeling the center front, center back, and natural waistline, hipline and crotchline so the pattern or garment sections can be correctly positioned on the body. They help you plan and evaluate the potential fit of the pattern before cutting the fabric. Allow additional length if blousing of the bodice is desired. The distance the fashion neckline lies below the natural neckline at the center back may be stated. No indication is given for neckline depth on the front pattern. Analysis of the position of the finished front neckline must be made before cutting the fabric if a specific neckline depth is desired.

The sleeve, bodice front and back are marked with *alteration lines* for body and arm length changes. These alteration lines are placed near the waistline and wrist, but the garment length may need to be changed above the bust or elbow. Additional figure variations will require pattern alterations not indicated on the pattern.

The *markings for pattern layout and cutting* are very important; they are marked on all printed patterns. Each pattern contains an arrow to indicate the relationship between the pattern grainline and the lengthwise direction of the fabric. Pattern pieces with a straight arrow will have cut edges all around the fabric piece; they may be placed against the selvages, next to the fabric fold, or on the interior of the fabric. The arrow must be placed parallel to the fabric selvages unless intentionally changed for purposes of design. The arrow placement controls the grain and drapes the fabric on the body in a manner that achieves the effect the designer intended. If the grain is parallel to center front or center back and a zipper or other closure is not involved, the seam can be eliminated by placing the center stitching line exactly on the fold of the fabric.

On other pattern pieces the tips of the grainline arrows are turned to point toward the line at the pattern edge. This pattern edge *does not* include a seam allowance; it must be placed exactly on a fabric fold. Inaccuracies that result from improper placement of these pattern pieces will double when the cut fabric is opened flat.

The number of pieces to cut for each pattern section is indicated with the instructions, "Cut 1," "Cut 2," and so forth. Sometimes these instructions are in the margins near small pattern pieces rather than on the pattern area. Transfer this information to the pattern piece to clarify the cutting of the pattern when used again or by another individual.

An arrow or scissor drawn at the pattern edge indicates the *direction to cut* along the pattern edge; however, a more consistent and accurate edge is produced by cutting so the fabric scrap falls to the right when using right-hand shears or to the left when using left-hand shears. An accurate edge is absolutely necessary to achieve a correct fit.

Several *construction markings* are printed on the pattern, such as the size and location of buttons and buttonholes, flaps, pockets, welts, trim, casings, and appliqués. Lines for gathering and foldlines for tucks, pleats, facings, and hemlines are also marked. Stitching lines for darts and the width of seam allowances are marked and labeled.

Notches along the pattern edges help identify adjoining garment sections. These notches are numbered in the order of use according to the sequence of construction stated in the guide sheet. Single notches usually indicate garment front pieces; double notches usually indicate back pieces. Cut the notch outward from the seam allowances or cut the edge smooth and make a *short* snip into the fabric edge exactly in the center of the notch. During layout, identically numbered notches should lie on identical horizontal and vertical color bars of a stripe, plaid, or similar motif. This ensures that the motif will match at the stitching line.

Precision marks are located along the stitching lines. These small, solid dots align corresponding sections and corners of adjoining seamlines so precisely that the fabric pieces balance correctly on the body. Using precision marks correctly will prevent rounded corners, curving seamlines, unequal extensions, and unintentionally eased or stretched areas. Poor fit and a cheapened appearance result when the fabric is forced to drape incorrectly or is under tension on the body.

Large solid dots indicate that stitching should begin or end at that spot; they may be used for a zipper or other opening or for matching the top of the sleeve to the basic shoulder seam position. Vogue patterns also use squares and triangles to help position adjacent fabric sections accurately.

Use a color-code system of tailor's tacks for transferring precision marks. Transfer all small circles with one color of thread, large circles with another color, and so on for other markings. During garment assembly the shape of the mark will no longer be a concern; pink thread will match pink thread, and so forth.

CHAPTER 6

RECOGNIZING CORRECT FIT

Beautiful and well-fitted clothes are not only attractive in themselves, but they also enhance the appearance of the wearer. Clothes too large can get in your way and create a comic appearance. Clothes too small restrict movement, appear immodest and offensive. In either case, poorly fitted clothes distract attention, emphasize a figure variation, and undermine the confidence of the wearer.

Well-fitted clothes camouflage a figure variation and direct attention away from areas considered less than ideal. They allow the wearer to be the center of interest and contribute to a sense of poise and self-confidence. Clothing that fits, looks, and feels comfortable and allows the body to move naturally is worn more frequently and yields a greater dollar value.

Basic Fitting Standards

The degree of harmony achieved through the application of the elements and principles of art to the design of a garment determines the attractiveness of a garment. When the structural divisions and decorative design of the garment are in harmony with the body, the garment is attractive on the figure. Correct fit is evaluated by attention to line (an art element), balance (an art principle), and fabric ease, (a fitting principle). (See **Figure 6-1**.)

USING GRAINLINE &
BALANCE TO EVALUATE FIT

The foremost fabric characteristic to consider when adjusting the fit of a garment is *grainline*. The designer or patternmaker has predetermined how the fabric is to hang on the body to give the garment a specific character. By placing the grainline arrows in a precise position on each pattern piece, the designer causes the fabric to be controlled in the desired manner. To reproduce this in a garment, however, both the lengthwise and crosswise fabric grains must be perfectly aligned at 90-degree intersections before the pattern pieces are cut. If the yarns are not aligned perfectly, they will not be in the correct position in the completed garment. The planned effect is altered. Even very small differences of poor grain alignment can produce noticeable changes in the hang of the fabric and the fit of the garment. Seamlines become crooked or tilted and the fabric behaves differently on the opposite sides of the body.

Fabric grainline is easily distinguished in cloth with woven or knitted stripes but is sometimes difficult to distinguish in cloth with plain textures or floral patterns. Easy recognition of the grainline makes fitting adjustments easier, less tiring and quicker to accomplish. To aid identification of grainline position in the completed garment, mark fitting grainlines on the fabric pieces with pencil, transfer paper, or thread, depending on the type of fabric and the use of the garment. Mark horizontal fitting lines at the hip, the chest and shoulder blade, the bust, the waist, and the sleeve capline. Mark vertical fitting lines at center front and center back, the midfront and back (center of leg, bust, and blade), the side seam positions, and the sleeve center. When a dart or seamline occurs at any of these fitting grainline locations, that stitched line becomes a fitting line.

Observing the position in which the fabric grain or marked grainlines lie on the body provides the first clue to the accuracy or deviation of the fit. Correcting the deviations creates balance in the garment; that is, on a symmetrical figure, both sides of the garment will lie equally smooth and relaxed because the pull of gravity will be equal. On a basic-fitting garment, the length grain should lie perpendicular to the floor at the sides, the center front and center back; the crossgrain should lie parallel to the floor across the center front and center back. With training, the eye will quickly perceive alignment of the grain with the body and distinguish even subtle needs for adjustment. Until this skill is developed, true vertical grain alignment can be checked with a plumb line (a weight suspended on a string). Gravity has the same effect on this line as it has on the grainline of the fabric.

On figures that vary from average, the fitting grainlines will lie slanted or bowed because each figure variation requires an increase or decrease in the existing length or width of the fabric. Insufficient or excess fabric length or width causes tension wrinkles or loose folds in the garment area and the grainline becomes distorted. The greater the variation from standard, the more the grainline will slope or bow as fabric ease is "borrowed" and pulled to another area or allowed to sag.

USING STRUCTURAL LINE & BALANCE TO EVALUATE FIT

The second clue to the accuracy or deviation of fit in a garment is the manner in which its structural lines align with the body and divide it into pleasing proportions. The eye is quickly drawn to any structural line of the garment. Darts, seams, pleats, tucks, and trim quickly attract attention and hold it for a short time period. Simultaneously, the eye compares the garment to the corresponding vertical or horizontal center of the body area and tries to align the two. The eye also makes a comparison between the corresponding structural lines on the left and right of the garment. These subconscious perceptions and comparisons quickly judge the degree of balance of the garment. To review, balance results from visually equal garment weight, size, or the distance from the body center line. A balanced garment gives a feeling of equilibrium; the observer does not tire from trying to visually move the fabric to improve the balance.

When the garment pulls or droops from its expected position on the body, the observer feels a sense of instability and discomfort. The greater the mislocation of the structural lines or degree of snugness and looseness in the

Figure 6-1 Correctly fitted basic garment

garment areas, the greater the lack of balance in the fit of the garment. When all the stitched lines divide the body into becoming proportions, the garment will be in harmony with the body. Both the wearer and the observer will sense its visual and physical comfort.

Poor posture and asymmetrical figure variations affect the balance of a garment by changing the position of its structural lines. Either of these conditions affects the amount of fabric needed and the alignment between the structural lines of the garment and the body centers. Strain pulls the garment fabric to the larger area and changes the position of structural lines. Smaller than average body areas permit excess relaxation in the garment fabric and create an illusion that the underlying body area is even smaller.

USING BASIC EASE TO EVALUATE FIT

Basic ease is an amount of garment fabric required in addition to the circumference of the body. The extra fabric permits the garment to accommodate such natural body movements as breathing, walking, raising and swinging the arms, climbing the stairs, sitting, bending, and stooping. All these movements cause expansion of the body area involved; extra fabric is required for mobility and comfort. Shoulders should raise and lower easily; arms should raise easily to a 90-degree angle to the body; each hand should touch the opposite shoulder easily. Following a body movement, the garment should resume its natural position without needing adjustment.

Lack of sufficient basic ease causes the garment to lose its flow of style lines. It appears tight and wrinkled. It becomes figure revealing instead of figure flattering, and variations in the figure are exaggerated. The garment is uncomfortable to wear. The strain also lessens the durability of the garment and causes it to wear out faster. *Do not* assume the amount of ease allowed by the designer is sufficient for your figure.

The amount of basic ease required is determined by the style of the garment and the acitivity the garment is intended for. Strapless bodices, halter necklines, sleeveless bodices, and swimsuits require little, if any, ease. Sportswear requires more ease than business-wear. Other factors affecting appropriate ease allowance include the size of the body frame, texture of the fabric, and personal preference.

Standards for Fitting a Basic Garment

The chart of fitting standards was developed to help you identify the positions for the grainlines, darts, and seamlines of a well-fitted basic garment on a standard figure. Use it as a checklist to evaluate fit and for making any needed adjustments to bring the garment fit into harmony with these standards.

Standards for Fitting Fashion Garments

Basic design becomes fashion design when added fullness or style ease has been introduced somewhere in the pattern and is intended to create a mood or characteristic. The amount added is subject only to the designer's discretion. It can be incorporated into the skirt, pants, bodice, and sleeve sections. This fullness is held in control by gathering, tucking, pleating, and flaring. It is further controlled by stitching, darts, or an appropriate adjacent garment section such as a band, yoke, collar, or cuff. Fitting standards may be used to evaluate each of these design techniques and control features regardless of their location or use in a design.

FLARE

Flared garment sections are created by adding fullness into the pattern edge that hangs free on the garment (see **Figure 6-2**). As flare is introduced to a

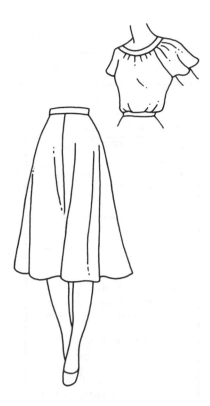

Figure 6-2 Flare

Figure 6-3 Pleats and tucks

Standards for Fitting a Basic Garment

LOWER TORSO & LEGS		UPPER TORSO & ARMS	
Center Back and Center Front Seam or Fitting Lines: • are perpendicular to the floor • are centered on the body • are straight lines **Side Seamlines:** • are perpendicular to the floor • divide the body into becoming proportions • appear as straight lines on the body • appear to intersect the waistline at 90-degree angles • create equal visual distances beyond the edges of the legs when the garment is viewed from front, back or side **Darts:** • point toward the crown of the curve being accommodated • appear as straight lines on the body • end approximately 1 inch (2.5 cm) short of the fullest part of the curve • are sewn to conform the fabric to the shape of the body surface • have no fabric strain, bubbles, or wrinkles at the dart tip area • are positioned to create pleasing proportions **Waistline:** • divides the body into pleasing vertical proportions • is parallel to the floor across the front • follows the body contour across the back • is loose enough to allow shoulders to rise and arms to move • is loose enough to allow the body to expand during sitting, breathing, and eating	**Hip Area:** • grainline is parallel to the floor at the center front and center back • circumference is adequate to permit fabric to relax • allows for movement without straining the fabric • does not gap at center front or center back when button closures are used • is free from diagonal, horizontal, or lengthwise distortion • is controlled with correctly fitted darts to accommodate the curves **Hemlines:** • are parallel to the floor • lie slightly above or below the largest part of the leg (hip) • divide the body into pleasing proportions	**Center Back and Center Front Seam or Fitting Lines:** • are perpendicular to the floor • are centered on the body • are straight lines **Side Seamlines:** • slope forward from underarm to waist • divides the body into pleasing proportions • are straight lines • create enough ease to permit the arms to swing without pulling the sleeve **Darts:** • point toward the crown of the curve being accommodated • appear as straight lines on the body • end approximately 1 inch (2.5 cm) short of the fullest part of the curve • are sewn to conform the fabric to the shape of the body surface • have no fabric strain, bubbles, or wrinkles at the dart tip area **Neckline:** • crosses the back of the neck through the center of the prominent vertebra • lies smooth against the base of the neck at front, sides, and back • crosses near the top of the ends of the collar bone or at the base of the throat depression • does not chafe the neck cords **Shoulder Seamline:** • divides the neck, shoulder, and arm into pleasing proportions • is inconspicuous from front and back • lies close to the body without strain at any point along its length • is a visually straight line from neck to armscye	**Blade and Chest Areas:** • have horizontal and vertical grainlines that lie parallel and perpendicular to the floor • lie smooth against the body between the creases of the arm • allow the arms to move comfortably without strain at the shoulders or armscye **Armscye:** • lies about ½ inch (1.2 cm) from the outer surface of the arm • is in line with the back arm crease when the hands are crossed at the front • is in line with the front arm crease when hands and arms are relaxed at the sides • neither constricts nor cuts the body, nor pulls away from it at any area **Bust:** • grainline is parallel and perpendicular to the floor at center front • has adequate ease to permit body movement and prevent gaps at closures • is free from diagonal or horizontal distortion **Sleeve:** • outer edge extends ½ inch (1.2 cm) from armscye, then drops vertically • has horizontal and vertical grainlines that lie parallel and perpendicular to the floor at the capline • underarm seam is in line with center of wrist • hemline maintains a pleasing relationship to the body and to other style lines

garment section, the opposite edge also changes in shape. Grainline position on the pattern can be used to determine the location of flare in the garment section; flare will occur only at a bias area of fabric. To create a more pleasing appearance, flare may be repositioned within a garment section by changing the angle of the grain on the pattern.

Flared areas should flow over the body and hang freely rather than protrude. Fabric at or above the flared area should fit in a relaxed manner. Sufficient basic ease should be present to prevent strain on the stitching. The amount of flare should be proportional to the body area. On a symmetrical design, the corresponding ripples on each side of the garment should be equal in size and begin at the same height.

A flared garment unit can be divided into panels or gores that vertically divide the body area into sections. The width of the center section should produce a pleasing space relationship across the body.

PLEATS, TUCKS, VENTS, & SLITS

Pleats or tucks can be controlled by stitching along part or all of their length (see **Figure 6-3**). The pleat or tuck should lie smoothly against the body without tension or excess fullness in the controlled area. The unstitched portion of a pleat should hang flat when the body is in a standing position. Sufficient ease should be allowed in the garment to permit the pleats, vents and slits to hang in a closed position except when the person is walking or seated.

Unstitched pleats should hang free and fold in place without gaping or opening when the person is standing. When placed over a bulge, such as the bust, an inner control panel or lining is required. The fit of pintucks is evaluated like gathers when stitched only part of their length; accordion and umbrella pleats are evaluated like flared garment sections.

GATHERS

Converting stitched darts to ease, gathers, open-end darts or unpressed pleats may improve both the appearance and fit of the garment on some figures. Gathers are tiny folds that fall vertically or radiate from a designated point. Their purpose is to give soft fullness to an area.

Gathers that lie against the body should fall softly over the body bulge with no large smooth areas or the appearance of tension (see **Figure 6-4**). When a gathered area is controlled at both the upper and lower edges, there should be sufficient lengthwise ease to allow for body movement. Again, there should be no tension on the fabric. When gathers are controlled from the top only, they should fall free in vertical folds.

Gathers that extend away from the body, such as in puffed sleeves, peasant or bishop sleeves, a blouson bodice, or a harem skirt or pants, require additional length for puffing or blousing (see **Figure 6-5**). This additional length may be added to the top or bottom of the garment, or both, and allows the garment to stand away from the body. The amount of added length, the contour of the edge, the ratio of gathered area to the flat control area, and the direction the gathered seam is turned determine the character of the additional fabric. The gathered area of a garment requires little pressing; the control area requires careful pressing. All these factors need to be taken into consideration when creating the illusions about the body underneath.

DRAPE

The success and fit of a draped area depends on the correct amount of tension introduced to pliable fabric that is gathered, folded or flared on the bias (see **Figure 6-6**). When an area of soft fabric is concentrated into gathers or folds at a given point, the lack of ease within the area creates the desirable amount of tension and causes the folds to radiate outward to the garment area diagonally opposite.

Figure 6-4 Straight-hanging gathers

Figure 6-5 Full-rounded gathers

Only actual fitting of draped designs on the body during construction can ensure a custom fit. The closeness of fit may vary slightly depending on the figure type, fabric characteristics, and garment use. The shape of the pattern edge for draped designs is unique. This edge must be strictly maintained during construction: garments must be cut accurately and matched with precision.

DARTS

Fashion garments may feature curved, straight, or angular darts such as the French or English darts. A dart or a dart-equivalent seam will be a smooth flowing line whether it appears on the body as a straight or curved line. A single dart will point to the crown of the body bulge. Two or more darts may be placed equidistant from the bulge or one may point to the crown while the second (usually smaller and shorter) lies nearer the outer area (see **Figure 6-7**). Two or more narrow darts are more attractive on a large body curve than is one large dart. The darts should give a feeling of buoyancy, moving the eye upward. They should not repeat or otherwise emphasize body variations. All other standards that apply to basic darts also apply to fashion darts and their equivalents.

COLLARS

For fitting purposes, collars may be classified according to the way they stand or roll around the neckline: standing band, full roll, partial roll, or flat (see **Figures 6-8** and **6-9**).

The collar stand should fit smoothly against the back of the neck. The crease or roll line should be a smooth, continuous line. The stand of the collar should be in proportion to the length of the individual's neck. The outer edge of a collar should lie smoothly against the garment and should cover the seamline at the back of the garment neckline. The collar ends should lie symmetrically against the chest. The roll of a lapel should taper to the level of the top button or designated termination point. The collar and lapel should balance both horizontally and vertically on the body. Style edges and lapels

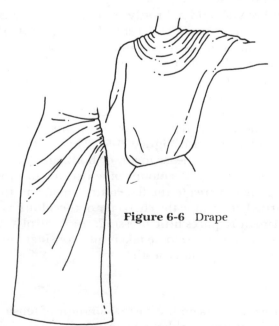

Figure 6-6 Drape

Figure 6-7 Darts

should be in proportion to the body and to the garment areas on which they lie. Close-fitting collars should provide sufficient ease to lie comfortably around the neck.

When constructing a rolled collar, the outer layer of collars and lapels should be slightly larger than the underlayers and should be eased into place to prevent distortion of fabric and fit.

Variations in the slope of the shoulder will affect the fit of the collar. Changes in the curvature of the collar neckline seam may be required. If changes are made on the garment neckline or the slope of the shoulderline during fitting, the collar also must be changed. Otherwise it will not hug the neckline nor roll or ripple as designed. For example, on someone with uneven shoulders the point of the collar will lie lower on the low shoulder unless the collar pattern is altered. Allowing this to occur will accent the lack of balance caused by the asymmetrical figure variation.

POCKETS

Pockets may be applied to the garment surface, inserted into a slash, hidden in a seam, or designed as part of a yoke (see **Figure 6-10**). They may be functional, decorative, or both. They are a design detail that can be used to create a point of emphasis or to divert attention from a figure variation.

The fitting of the garment precedes pocket application. The marks for the position of the pocket are checked at the first fitting. Check placement and size of the pockets as they relate to body size, and garment balance, proportion and scale.

Pockets should lie smoothly against the body unless designed to extend away from the body. If designed to extend away from the body, the line of the pocket should relate to the contour of the body. When placed over a body curve, the pocket should have sufficient ease to lie flat and smooth. The outer layer of lined patch pockets and pocket flaps should be made slightly larger than the under layers, then eased into place to prevent distortion of fabric and fit. There should be sufficient ease in the circumference of the garment to allow a vertical pocket opening to lie closed, or to prevent the outline of an interior pocket from being visible.

Figure 6-10 Pockets

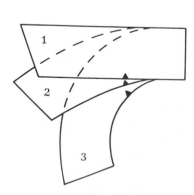

Figure 6-8 Comparison of collar neckline curves

    1. Full roll
    2. Partial roll
    3. Flat

Standing band

Full roll

Partial roll

Flat

Figure 6-9 Completed collars

A positive attitude and a desire to accomplish the task are keys to a successful fitting experience. When coupled with a sound, dependable method of fitting clothing, a seemingly impossible fit becomes possible. All too often fitting becomes a negative experience because of poor surroundings, an untidy personal appearance, or a lack of knowledge or low opinion of the value of fit. This unpleasant experience is often assumed to be the fault of the garment, and negative feelings develop about fitting or sewing in general. The positive control of attitudes, surroundings and personal appearance can lead to a more productive fitting experience on oneself or someone else, whether constructing the first basic fitting garment or a later fashion style. Attention to detail makes the difference.

Fitting Area

A *full-length mirror* is essential. While being fitted in front of a mirror, you can easily watch the fit of your garment develop, make suggestions to the fitter and give immediate response to questions. The effect can be evaluated on the total figure rather than on isolated areas only. A three-way mirror is ideal because it reflects the back, front and side images simultaneously.

Adequate space to permit walking several steps toward or away from the mirror gives you better perspective. It also allows you to check the fit from the back, front, and side views while the body is in motion.

Good lighting helps the fitting progress more efficiently and effectively. It can reveal fabric distortion and reduce visual strain. A source of light above or to the side of the mirror prevents glare and shadows.

A *chair* allows you to observe both the figure and the garment when seated. View the garment while sitting in the usual positions appropriate for the garment. A chair also permits the fitter to sit while adjusting your skirt or pants and the fabric is seen at eye level. Needed change in fabric position is more easily recognized when the fitter is looking straight ahead at the garment rather than having to look down at it. Work progresses more quickly and with less strain on both persons.

A *counter, table, or tray* at a convenient standing height is useful for holding pins, tape, and other fitting equipment.

Proper ventilation is very important, especially when working with several individuals in the room. A supply of fresh circulating air helps prevent the person being fitted from feeling faint or nauseous when standing for long periods of time.

A nearby *closet or rack* is very useful for hanging cut fabric sections, garment units, or completed garments during the fitting and construction process. Wooden or padded hangers help retain the shape of the garment. Cloth or plastic garment bags help keep the clothing clean.

Ideally, room decor should be plain and in soft, neutral colors. Extreme colors or patterns in wall, window and floor coverings detract from and conflict with the garment color and style lines. They may also irritate some individuals.

Personal Appearance

Personal cleanliness should be maintained at all times. When people must work closely together, breath, body, or foot odor can be not only offensive but nauseating.

An *attractive hair style* adds to a positive self-image. Hair length, however, should not interfere with fitting. If your hair is shoulder length or longer, wear it in a style that holds it off your neck and shoulders. Apply your usual *makeup*. If you make your appearance as pleasing as possible, it contributes to a more positive fitting experience for all concerned.

Choose well-fitted *underwear*. Each piece should provide proper support for normal, excess, or sagging tissue and serve as a foundation for outerwear.

Underwear should minimize, not emphasize figure variations or create additional unnatural contours. Consider the effect of underwear seams and elastic. They should not be visible through outer clothing. A waist-height panty and one-piece slip are recommended. If bikini or hipline briefs are worn, the elastic should be soft, smooth and wide enough to prevent a depression and bulge across the hips. Wear the same underclothing styles during fitting that will be worn with the finished garment. The same underwear styles should be worn during each fitting session to avoid unnecessary changes in darts, waistline position, and the amount of ease needed.

Shoes should be comfortable and allow you to stand for fairly long periods of time during fitting. They should be of the proper heel height and style to be worn with the garment. This will help to establish pleasing garment proportions and contribute to the overall harmony between the garment and figure. Negative surprises and disappointments are prevented if the preceding hints are followed.

Efficiency & Accuracy

Effective fitting begins long before making adjustments on the pattern or garment. Some people are reluctant to put forth the time and effort required to achieve a good fit. Others attempt to overlook errors by convincing themselves that their sewing results are "just fine." Rather than learn from reliable instruction, some individuals learn only from sad experience and repeated disappointment. Others give up sewing entirely or continue with consistently substandard results and never achieve an attractive fit. Make the necessary preparation that contributes to a successful fitting experience.

- Evaluate the figure and posture realistically (see **Chapter 3**).
- Assemble needed tools and equipment. Understand their role in producing good fit (see **Chapter 2**).
- Select a pattern in the most appropriate size, figure type, and brand (see **Chapter 4**). A basic dress pattern should have a close-fitting neck, standard armscye, waistline, and straight skirt. These features are necessary so that the fabric requirements for the lengths and widths of all body areas can be adequately determined. These areas include the size of the neck, the slope and length of the shoulder, the width of the back and chest, the fullness of the bust and thighs, the circumference of the hip, and the lengths of the back and front of both the upper and lower torso. The crux of creating well-fitted clothing is to begin with a pattern that has the most potential to fit the given individual. The standard ⅝ inch (1.5 cm) seam allowance and the given hem allowance permit little room for adjustment. On the other hand, cutting an extra-wide seam allowance on all edges creates problems at curved areas, such as the armscye and neck openings.
- Learn to use your patterns skillfully (see **Chapter 5**).
- Select and prepare fabric properly. Straighten the grain and preshrink if necessary (see **Chapter 8**).
- Each aspect of garment production is interrelated and affects the final fit. Unskilled fabric selection, handling, construction, and pressing (or lack of pressing) at any stage not only causes varying degrees of poor fit, but starts a chain reaction that compounds the chance of poor fit in all succeeding steps. Fitting the units separately saves time and effort.

During the fitting process the *assistance* of another individual is quite necessary for the novice. Choose an assistant who can be available when needed, and is observant, objective, reliable in judgment, and interested in fitting. If at all possible, your assistant should also be knowledgeable in clothing construction processes.

Schedule *short fitting sessions* at close intervals to ensure continuity in the fitting procedure. This also helps avoid undue mental, emotional, or physical fatigue and prevents loss of interest in the project.

Work quickly. Standing still too long often causes faintness because the blood circulation is inhibited. Locking your knees will increase the possibility of fainting. To help prevent feeling faint, wiggle your toes and relax your knees occasionally. When the garment is on the body, pin-baste the adjustment only enough to indicate the problem areas and the amounts of change required. The complete adjustment can be made more quickly and accurately when the garment unit is on the work table.

Make math work for you. If the length of one stitching line changes, the length of corresponding lines on adjoining parts must change an equal amount. For example, if a garment neck opening is made smaller, make the same reduction in the neckline of the facing and the collar. A change in the length of an armscye requires the same amount of change in the height of the sleeve cap or an adjustment in the position of the top-of-cap mark. When the adjustment of one stitching line involves only a change in position or in shape but not in length, the adjoining stitching line requires no length change. For example, an adjustment for sloping or squared shoulders only changes the pitch of the shoulderline and height of the underarm. It does not change the size of the armscye, therefore no sleeve adjustment is needed.

Fitting Guidelines

Attempt to solve each fitting problem on the basis of a few underlying principles. Apply similar adjustment procedures to similar problems. *Choose the simplest,* neatest procedure that corrects a problem without causing additional ones. Multiple figure variations may require only a single alteration procedure to correct several fitting problems.

Work from the simple to the complex. Begin fitting with the garment section for the area of the body which has the least complicated contours. This is usually a skirt, since the lower torso has fewer pronounced curves and contours and the corresponding pattern has fewer pieces. Pants are next in a logical fitting sequence. Principles and procedures for fitting a skirt apply directly and proceed naturally to the pant. Pants require the same adjustments as the skirt and for the same reasons. Additional fitting areas include the inseam and crotch seam. Learning to fit pants at the crotch area has a direct relationship to fitting the bodice armscyes. Fitting principles that apply to adjusting the length and shape of the crotch curve and the depth from front to back also apply to adjusting the fit of the sleeves. Proceeding from the simple to the complex makes the fitting of the armscyes a review instead of a new challenge.

Begin to fit each garment unit at the largest area of the body where the fabric touches the figure. Garment circumference must be adequate to encircle the body and close without strain. To check the fabric adequacy for the lower and upper torso, use the following formula.

- Measure the circumference of the waist, hip, and bust.
- Subtract the personal body measurements from the corresponding standard measurements on the pattern envelope chart.
- Divide the difference between each set of measurements by four. (Four seam edges are involved.)
- Add or subtract the divided difference parallel to the side seam of the pattern or garment.
- Measure the arm circumference of the biceps and add 1 inch to 2 inches (2.5 to 5 cm) for ease. Subtract this from the sleeve pattern about 2 inches (5 cm) below the capline. Divide the difference by two and add or subtract this amount parallel to the underarm seam of the pattern or garment.

Fit the garment right side out since this is how the finished garment will be worn. (If the garment is fitted wrong side out and then worn right side out asymmetrical alterations will be on the incorrect half of the body.) Place the garment on the body carefully to avoid stretching the unfinished edges. Pin the closure together accurately. Match garment center lines or other closure markings. All seam allowances and dart folds should lie smoothly against the body and the fabric surface should be free from any distracting construction. (An exception occurs when the dart-folds on a fashion garment lie on the outside for design interest.)

Once the garment is on and closed, fitting problems involving length should be adjusted first, before those involving circumference so that garment shaping is level with the appropriate body contour.

While being fitted, stand away from but look straight ahead into the mirror. Stand erect with body weight balanced in a natural stance. Assume this posture during each fitting. A change in posture always produces a change in fit. If the person being fitted turns to watch the fitting process, the body automatically becomes asymmetrical and the garment twists out of its natural alignment. (If the torso is asymmetrical, however, adjust the garment for asymmetry [see **Chapters 3** and **10**]. If one leg is shorter, level the body by placing a flat object under the foot of the shorter leg.)

In general, *work from the top to the bottom* of the individual garment unit as you work on the most obvious problems first. Progress toward the lower edge. The myriad of minor problems seen at first may become insignificant or disappear altogether as your work progresses logically.

Always keep the garment centers in line with body centers and work from side to side within the same area to achieve balance. It also prevents incorporating too much ease on one side of the garment.

To achieve the illusion of pleasing figure proportions, *work from the front to the back* of the garment. The *position* of the side or shoulder seamline can be changed without increasing the total size of the garment. To make the front appear smaller, move the seamline forward by letting out the back and taking up the front an equal amount. Reverse the procedure to make the back appear smaller. Portions that are more nearly equal create a feeling of balance.

Look for related variations, side to side, front to back, and top to bottom. The body usually counterbalances itself. If an individual has rounded shoulders, the chest is usually hollow. A high hip on one side may be accompanied with a high shoulder on the opposite side of the body. If the figure is asymmetrical, determine which side of the body is causing the most distortion in the fabric; adjust only that side of the garment when the figure differences of the two sides are slight. If the figure difference is more extreme, adjust each side of the garment as needed.

Adjust the position of the garment hemline last. Body contour, frame and build help determine the appropriate positions that will enhance appearance. The adjustment in hemline position is made an even amount at the hem edge of the various garment pieces. Unevenness of a hemline is a signal that adequate fit has not been accomplished, unless bias fabric areas are involved.

Fitting Procedure

Learn to evaluate the fit of the garment unit in relation to the body structure. To determine whether a need for improvement of fit exists, be observant and think analytically in terms of cause, effect and solution (review **Chapter 6**).

Figure Analysis
Analyze the body structure to determine the cause of an incorrectly fitted pattern or garment area (see **Chapter 3**).

Fitting Analysis
Locate the wrinkles and identify their direction and character. If a garment

area is too large, either loose horizontal or vertical folds form, the garment stands away from the body, or sags against it depending on the fabric texture. If a garment is too small, tension wrinkles form horizontally, vertically, or diagonally over the tight area. Learning to evaluate wrinkles is a beginning step in learning to fit. Removing wrinkles by preventing their formation is the fitter's goal.

- When horizontal tension wrinkles form, the garment circumference is smaller than the body circumference at or below the wrinkled area (see **Figures 7-1, 7-2**).
- When loose horizontal folds or soft wrinkles form, the garment is longer than the body at the area of the fold or wrinkle (see **Figure 7-3**).
- When vertical tension wrinkles form, the garment is shorter than the body area underneath the wrinkled area (see **Figure 7-4**).
- When loose vertical folds, diagonal folds or puffs form, the garment length or width is excessive over a body bulge. The accommodating dart is too wide (see **Figures 7-5, 7-6**).
- When tight diagonal wrinkles form, the garment length and width is too small over the body bulge at the top of the wrinkles. The accommodating dart is too narrow (see **Figures 7-7 to 7-9**).
- Not infrequently, combined directional wrinkles form (see **Figures 7-10 to 7-13**).

Fabric Requirement

Analyze the need for change in garment measurements. If a garment has the same measurement and shape as the body plus enough ease for natural body movement, the garment will fit smoothly. No change is needed. If a garment has a different measurement or shape than the body plus ease, some part of the garment must change in length or width.

When a flat piece of paper or fabric is formed into a tube and placed on the body, the excess fabric lying at the edge of each body bulge or hollow forms a dart. A dart-equivalent seam forms along each body slope, such as the shoulders, sides of the rib cage, and hips. Dart-equivalent seams also join fabric sections at natural body divisions. Darts and dart-equivalent seams add the dimension of depth to the length and width of the garment. A darted garment area that requires a change in length and/or width nearly always requires a change in the size of the dart. The larger the body bulge or the greater the body slope, the wider the fitting dart must be. The smaller the bulge or the less the body slope, the narrower the fitting dart must be.

When the two halves of the body are asymmetrical, the lengths and widths of the garment sections and the corresponding width of the dart must differ accordingly. The tips of corresponding dart end on a line parallel to the floor and the same distance from the garment center line.

When expressing needed changes in a garment area, use terms that describe the size or shape of the body area. For example, "To fit larger-than-average shoulder blades, increase the length and width of the fabric over the shoulder blade area." Using descriptive words in logical sequence makes pattern alteration and future fitting a simpler task.

Garment Alteration

Choose an appropriate method to adjust the tissue pattern or fabric garment. Two methods commonly used include *the slash and spread or lap methods* and *the pivot-slide method*. See garment alterations for specific figure variations in **Part Two.** Comparing body measurements plus ease to a garment or pattern is a third method of determining where and how much adjustment is needed (see **Chapter 8,** measurement method).

The slash method is limited to trial-fitting garments because the interior of the garment is cut and increased with an inserted strip of fabric, or made smaller by stitching a tuck to remove the excess. The pivot method involves moving the stitching line and can be used on fitting of fashion garments.

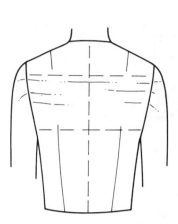

Figure 7-1   Broad upper back

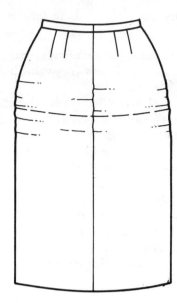

Figure 7-2   Broad lower hip

Figure 7-3   Short midriff

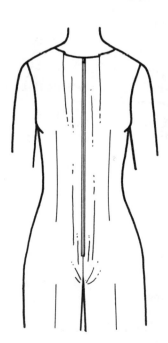

Figure 7-4   Long torso

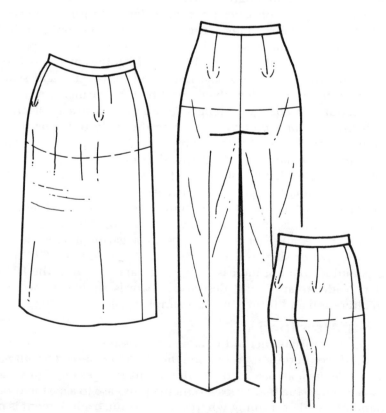

Figure 7-5   Flat buttocks

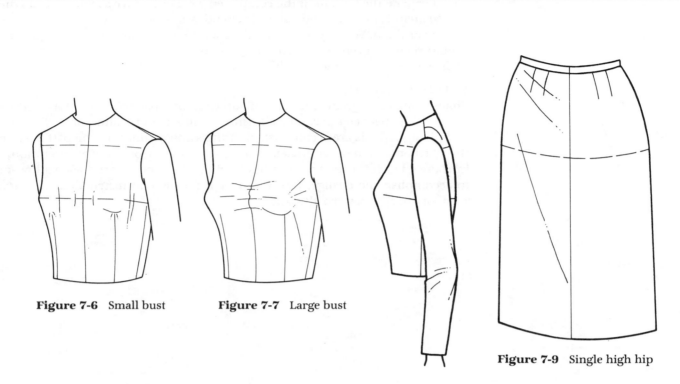

Figure 7-6 Small bust   **Figure 7-7** Large bust

Figure 7-9 Single high hip

Figure 7-8 Large elbow

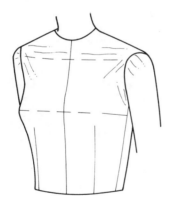

Figure 7-10 Broad, square shoulders

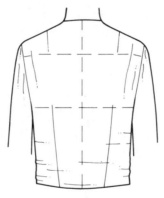

Figure 7-11 Narrow shoulders, broad lower back and large waist

Figure 7-13 Protruding abdomen, full front thigh and hyperextended calf

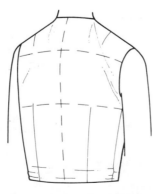

Figure 7-12 Rounded upper back, sloped shoulders and large waist

Evaluate the total fit of the completed garment. Move as you would when the garment is in use. Stand, sit, walk, bend, and stoop. Swing your arms; raise and lower them. When you are standing with your usual posture, the garment should relax and return to a correctly fitted position without help. Refine the fit as needed on any questionable area.

Pattern Alteration

Choose an appropriate method of altering the pattern. There is a direct relationship between garment adjustment and pattern alteration. The slash and pivot methods are accomplished in the same manner on the pattern as on the garment. A new approach, the seam method of pattern alteration, is introduced in this text. The seam method involves moving the seam allowance to accomplish the change. (See **Chapter 9** for general instructions and **Part Two** for specific pattern alterations.)

CHAPTER 8

This chapter discusses three fitting methods.

- Pinned Pattern Method
- Trial Garment Method
- Measurement Method

They have been tested in a variety of classroom situations. The procedures in each method will produce accurate results if understood and applied correctly. Each method may be used separately, or parts of the three may be combined on the same pattern piece. The result is an artistic composition of fabric, garment, and figure.

Pinned Pattern Method

In this method, the paper pattern pieces are pinned together as though they were the corresponding pieces of fabric. Units are then adjusted directly on the body.

When assembling the pattern pieces, do not pin seam allowances facing each other in the usual manner. Pinned so they extend away from the body, the resulting "wings" are unattractive and make the body appear larger. Pinned with seam allowances turned toward the body, these nonpliable, thickened areas of paper use up ease and make the pattern appear tighter than it actually is. In either case, curved seams with edges that do not curve identically are strained and buckle, become lumpy, or tear. Instead, *overlap the seam allowances* and pin them together *with stitching lines coinciding,* or turn the one seam allowance under (preferably the nondarted and the outwardly curved edges) and pin in place on the corresponding pattern edge. In either procedure the stitching lines must match. The pattern can then lie smoothly on the body and units are easily reversed to try on either half of the body. Fit each garment unit separately to avoid excess damage to the pattern.

Once mastered, this method has the following *advantages:*

- Pinning the pattern together can be done quickly and easily.
- Reliable results can be obtained for the *primary* fitting.
- Both unaltered and altered patterns can be pin-fitted successfully.
- People with limited time but determination can achieve an attractively fitted garment.
- People who wish to work quickly with a minimum of detail can obtain success.
- The garment can be worn sooner. Less time is spent fitting the garment itself.
- The fashion fabric is not overhandled.
- Seeing the pattern pinned together provides motivation to complete the garment.
- The sequence of construction is learned indirectly as the paper sections are pinned together. (If the pattern guide sheet is to be used during construction, the pinning sequence follows the guide. Notches on adjoining seam allowance edges are numbered according to the sequence shown on the guide sheet.)
- A preliminary check of fitting ease and the effect of the fashion ease can be made quickly.
- This method is particularly efficient for easy-to-fit figures and simple or loose garment styles.

The following *limitations* should be taken into consideration when learning the pinned pattern method:

- An assistant is very helpful.
- The person being fitted must stand very still to prevent damage to the pattern.

- The upper arm must be held away from the body; nonreinforced tissue tears easily and may become wet at the underarm area.
- Gathered areas, pleats, and tucks must be pinned in place. This can be very involved on some patterns.
- The amount of available ease may be difficult to determine, especially by a beginner.
- Pattern tissue is semi-rigid. The corresponding fabric pieces are pliable and fit somewhat differently according to the texture and other inherent characteristics of the fabric. However, minor differences are easily adjusted during the refined fitting procedures if the pattern has been appropriately fitted prior to cutting.
- Due to the rigidity of the paper, larger-than-average figure variations will not cause grainlines to bow as in fabric but rather cause the pattern area to appear tight and the edge to ripple.
- The asymmetric figure causes the fitting lines to tilt toward the higher or fuller side. Duplicates must be made of the main pattern pieces so that the left and right pattern pieces can be adjusted separately.

PREPARING THE PATTERN FOR FITTING

1. Cut pattern pieces apart, leaving generous margins along the side and shoulder seam allowances.
2. Select the necessary pattern pieces.
3. Using a dry iron to prevent shrinkage, press the pattern pieces flat and wrinkle free.
4. Reinforce the unprinted surface of the pattern, if desired. Use a light press-on pattern backing or thin, fusible interfacing. These will reinforce paper patterns. Plastic-coated freezer wrap pressed onto paper patterns gives additional firmness and durability. Keep the backing material and the patterns totally wrinkle-free while reinforcing. If possible, use a thick table cover that is firm but porous enough to

Figure 8-1 The pinned pattern illustrating the fitting units

allow pins to be inserted. Such materials as a large piece of cardboard, a sewing cutting board, or a cork-top table are convenient. Lay the reinforcement material, fusing side up, over the table covering. Anchor to the cover. Lay the untrimmed pattern, labeled side up, over the reinforcement material. Anchor to the reinforcement and the table covering to prevent slippage. Keep both layers smooth and produce a wrinkle-free pattern. Press the pattern area lightly with a dry iron to fuse the layers. Begin at the center and work outward to edges and corners. Press along the cut edge of the seam allowance but not past the pattern margin. Use a disposable press cloth, if necessary, to prevent fuse-agent residue from collecting on the iron; fusing agents and plastic are difficult to remove. The fusing agent on interfacing and pattern backing will adhere better if a strip of aluminum foil is placed under the covering of the pressing board. This reflects the heat back into the pattern materials.

5. Trim the excess pattern tissue from the armscye, neckline, waistline, and crotch seam allowances.

6. Fold hems and pin in place.

7. Lap darts closed. Pin through all thicknesses of paper near the base of the darts.

8. Lap the seam allowances with stitching lines coinciding. Pin along the seamline each 3 inches to 6 inches (7.5 cm to 15 cm). For safety and efficiency, place pins either horizontally across the seam allowance or parallel to the stitching line with the tips pointing downward.

FITTING PROCEDURE FOR EACH UNIT

1. Pin pattern pieces together to form the major garment units such as the skirt or bodice.

2. Place a narrow fitting band snugly around the body at the scyeline, waistline, and fullest hipline, as needed for the unit you are fitting.

   • Fold one end of each fitting band under and lap this over the other end; pin closed.
   • Mark along the endfold and again at the exact point where the fold lies; unpin and remove the bands. Label the marks *center front*.
   • Match the two marks on each band and fold the band in half; mark the new foldline. Label the mark *center back*.
   • Replace the bands on the appropriate body areas. Align the marks on the bands exactly at center back and center front of the figure. Fasten the bands to underclothing if necessary to keep them from slipping while the pattern is fitted.

3. Place the pinned-together pattern unit on the body (see **Figure 8-1**). For garments comprised of two or more units, fit the skirt first, then the vest, bodice, or jacket, and the sleeve last. In this way you proceed from units that are less difficult to those that require more complex fitting.

For skirts and pants
   • Pin the center back and center front of the pattern at corresponding marks on the fitting bands for waist and hip. The waist stitching line should lie even with the *bottom* of the band.

For the bodice
   • Slide the arm through the pattern armscye. The person being fitted should rest the back of her hand on her hip or raise her hands and cup them around her jawline.
   • Pin the center back and center front of the pattern at corresponding marks on the fitting bands at the scyeline and waistline. The stitching line at the pattern waistline should lie even with the bottom edge of the band.

For sleeves
- Leave the bodice pinned to both fitting bands at center back and center front.
- Slide the sleeve onto the relaxed arm.
- Overlap the sleeve cap onto the bodice. Match the stitching lines and pin at each set of notches. Pin the top of the sleeve to the bodice shoulderline.

4. Determine the fitting adjustments required. Anchor the center front and center back of the pinned units to the appropriate fitting band. Using one or more of the following procedures, mark or make temporary adjustments while the unit is on the figure.
   - Indicate the amount of adjustment necessary with a pin or pencil mark.
   - Remove excess length and width by pinning tucks through the interior of the pattern area.
   - Increase pattern size by unpinning seam allowances and adjusting at the edges, or cut through a too-small area and insert extra length or width.

   When cutting is necessary, slash as near the closest affected seamline as possible to prevent large distortions in the pattern. Use marking or cellophane tape to hold the opened adjustments in place or pin the cut edges directly to underclothing. If necessary, make a note to indicate the location and amount of adjustment.
   - Evaluate hemline position, ensuring that it falls at an attractive place on the figure.
   - Coordinate hemlines on all pinned units. Adjust as necessary to create pleasing, interrelated proportions for the entire garment.

5. When properly fitted, the garment will incorporate appropriate fitting standards (see **Chapter 6**).
   - Vertical centers of pattern pieces coincide with body centers.
   - Dartlines point toward but stop approximately 1 inch (2.5 cm) from the fullest part of the body bulge.
   - All other fitting lines and pattern edges are in proper position and location.
   - Pattern tissues lie smoothly against the body and are free from distortion.

6. Remove the adjusted garment unit from the body and separate the pattern pieces.
7. Alter each pattern piece as necessary.
   - Use slash, seam, or pivot method for pin-marked or tucked adjustments.
   - Use slash method to alter slashed-and-spread areas of the pattern. Pin strips of tissue under opened areas or *lightly* fuse strips of pattern backing underneath the pattern.

8. If necessary, pin the garment unit together again on the figure to evaluate the alterations. Adjust as needed.
9. Perfect all edges and stitching lines. Permanently fuse pattern backing to the tissue if desired.

Trial Garment Method

A trial garment teaches how to determine body areas that vary from standard and how to adjust fabric to improve fit. This garment is often referred to as a *muslin*. A fashion garment, or any unit of it, may be constructed on a trial basis to assess the accuracy of fit and determine the effect of fabric texture.

If learning to fit is the objective in making a trial garment, good quality muslin or another solid-color fabric should be used. Select plain weave, medium-weight fabric with warp and filling yarns of the same size and a close, balanced thread count. The texture should be pliable enough so that figure variations can affect the fabric, yet firm enough to prevent distortion with handling. Extra fashion fabric, or a less expensive fabric that duplicates its texture as closely as possible, may be used for trial units.

If the purpose of a basic garment is to recognize figure variations or to use fitting principles and procedures, it is cut without any adjustments. Differences in the amount of fabric needed and the effect of figure variations on the fabric can then be determined. Differences in size and shape can then be built into the basic pattern and will become a part of the garment area for every commercial or self-designed pattern thereafter. A pattern for a trial fashion garment should be adjusted as much as possible prior to cutting the fabric, thus eliminating unnecessary handling of the fabric.

Markings are vital in the trial garment method. Mark all stitching lines on the fabric. Always mark the center front and center back of a garment unit on both pattern and fabric. It is helpful to mark crosswise lines at hip, chest, blade, and sleeve cap. This procedure helps distinguish the amounts of adjustment needed while the garment is on the figure. Adjustments will be equal on both sides for the symmetrical figure. By keeping the center back and center front of the trial garment at the body center and perpendicular to the floor, asymmetrical figure variations are more easily recognized. Amounts of difference in the left and right sides of the garment are more effectively determined.

Fabric sections may be pin-, hand-, or machine-basted, depending on the purpose of the garment, the complexity of the style, and the desired construction procedure (mass production, custom, or couture). When basting by any method, sewing lines must match exactly. Fitting time is saved if the units are pin-basted for the first fitting. Pin basting is quick and advisable for simple styles with only a few large sections or in the preliminary fitting of any style, including the basic muslin.

Hand-basting is very easily removed while the garment is on the figure; use fastening stitches instead of knots to prevent snagging the fabric when removing the basting. Long thread ends also facilitate removal. Hand-basting is advisable for complex styles, for styles with several small pattern pieces, and for garments with seamlines that require easing to produce the desired shape.

Care must be used with machine-basting especially on trial fashion garments. Needle size and condition, thread, fabric, and machine feed must be controlled correctly to prevent fabric slippage or damage. The machine needle must be sharp and its size appropriate for the weight of the fabric. Thread should be a pastel color or white to prevent dye from rubbing (crocking) onto the fabric. If long lengths of thread are pulled through a synthetic fabric, stitch marks are often heat-set into the fabric. *Do not* allow the machine foot to push the top layer of fabric or the feed dogs to ease in the underneath layer. Each of these actions distort the grain, and the ends of the seams will curve away from the eased side of the fabric. Final fitting stitches should be done on the machine or by hand rather than with pins.

Pressing is a vital part of fitting, regardless of the method of attaching garment sections. Pressing produces a smooth garment and enhances its overall appearance. Leave the basic garment basted together so it may be stored for future fittings as they become necessary.

The trial garment method is recommended for anyone with a desire to produce well-fitted clothing, to determine figure variations for asymmetrical and other difficult-to-fit figures, and to personalize basic patterns that will be used repeatedly.

This method has the following *advantages:*

- The fabric of the finished garment lies as smoothly on the various contours of the body as during the fitting process.

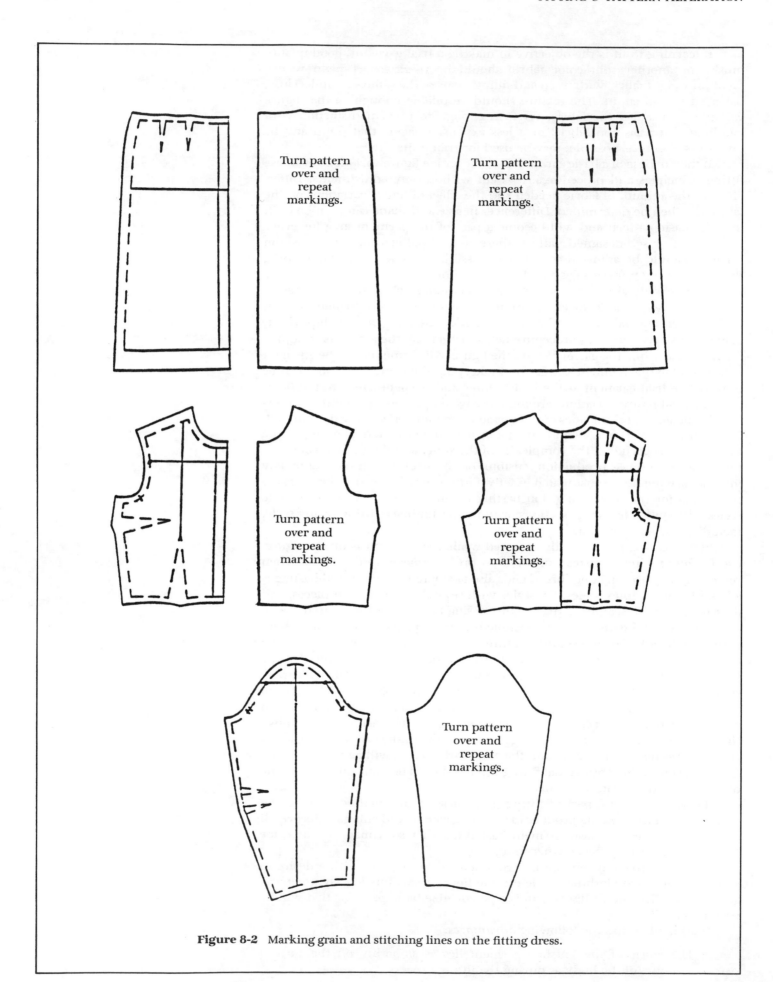

Figure 8-2 Marking grain and stitching lines on the fitting dress.

- The interlaced yarns allow the fabric to move with the body so that adequate ease is determined during fitting.
- Figure variations cause the fabric line and grain to tilt, bow, sag, or strain, thus revealing garment areas that need adjustment.
- Inexpensive fabric similar to the fashion fabric can be used to determine drape and grain direction before cutting fashion fabric.
- Amounts of ease and added fullness are easily recognized.
- Stitching lines are easily changed to increase or decrease length or width.

The following *limitations* are associated with the trial garment method and should be taken into consideration:

- Extra time and effort are required.
- Extra financial expense is often involved.
- If the adjusted basic garment is cut apart along the stitching lines and used as a pattern, a new trial garment must be constructed if the body changes size and shape.
- If the trial garment is cut apart on the stitching lines then copied onto a pattern material, the grain on each fabric section must be aligned exactly as when cut or the copied pattern will be distorted and will not fit. Identical fit is assured only if the fabric is grain perfect before the initial cutting and after the separated garment pieces are placed onto tracing paper.

PREPARING THE PATTERN

1. Cut apart the pattern pieces you will use for the garment. Leave generous margins along *all* edges. These margins will be useful for adjustments when the pivot method of alteration is used.
2. Using a dry iron to prevent shrinkage, press the pattern pieces flat and wrinkle free.
3. Mark the lengthwise fitting lines at the center of each pattern piece (see **Figure 8-2**).

   - On a sleeve, fold the portion *above the elbow* in half lengthwise. Extend the crease straight for the full length of the pattern. Mark the crease.
   - On pants, fold the leg portion in half *at the knee*. Extend the crease on the grain the full length of the pant leg. Mark the crease.
   - On bodices, vests, skirts, and jackets, mark the center front and center back when the marked lines or seamlines are not at these positions.

4. Mark the crosswise fitting lines along the hip, chest and blade lines, and sleeve capline. Mark the hipline parallel to the hemline (see **Figure 8-2**).

PREPARING THE FABRIC

1. Block the fabric grain with the yarns crossing at 90-degree angles. Remember that tearing or cutting along one crosswise thread or one row of knit does not straighten the grain; it only makes the ends follow a single row of weave or knit.

   - Fold the fabric in half lengthwise. Place the right sides of the fabric inward if a fashion fabric is being used.
   - Match the cut edges at one end so the fabric edges form 90-degree angles at the corners and lie parallel to the table edges.
   - Match the selvages in a straight line perpendicular to the pinned end and parallel to the table edge.

- Match the fabric edges at the other end. Pull taut so the fabric corners form 90-degree angles. If the table has a porous surface, pin the fabric to the table.
- Using a steam iron, press the fabric smooth while following the *lengthwise* grain. Work from the selvages toward the fold. Do not press a crease at the fold.

2. Pin the trimmed pattern exactly on grain. Point pins diagonally toward the pattern edges. This prevents bubbling of the pattern, which could result in cut fabric pieces that are smaller than the original pattern pieces. If the table has a porous covering, insert pins vertically through the pattern and fabric into the covering. Place pins about 2 inches (5 cm) away from the pattern cutting line to keep them out of the way of the shears.

3. Cut around pattern pieces smoothly and accurately.

4. Use contrasting pen or pencil on trial fitting fabric or thread on fashion fabric to clearly transfer all grainline and fitting lines, center front and center back markings to the face of the fabric. On trial fitting garments, mark all stitching lines. On fashion garments, transfer all additional marks and lines for trimmings, casings, and other design details.

JOINING THE FABRIC PIECES

1. Use either the *unit method* or the *assembly-line method* of construction. In the *unit method* each garment section such as the skirt is constructed independently. The completed units are then joined to one another. In the *assembly-line method,* a specific construction technique such as darting is completed on all garment pieces before progressing to the next technique.

2. If possible, plan a center-front opening for fitting purposes.

3. To prevent fabric damage, use only sharp pins. Use a contrasting pastel thread, somewhat lighter than the fabric. (On white fabric use a pale blue thread.)

4. Join the pieces exactly on the stitching lines.
   - Plan the marked surface as the *outside* of the garment to facilitate fitting on the figure.
   - To *pin-baste,* fold the fabric along one dartline and lay the fold even with the other line. Pin through folded fabric. Fold one seam allowance under along the stitching line (preferably the nondarted or outwardly curved edge) and align it with the seamline on the adjoining fabric section. Pin through folded fabric.
   - To *hand-baste,* first pin as above. Then slip-baste along the folded edge of fabric.
   - To *machine-baste,* stitch the darts and seam allowances so they lie *inside* the garment. Pin dartlines and fabric sections together with dart areas or seam allowances facing each other, as for regular machine sewing. Machine baste using the longest stitch and balanced tension. Begin sewing seams and darts at the intersecting *seamline.* Do not backstitch. Leave 2-inch to 3-inch (5-cm to 7-cm) thread ends to facilitate removal later.

5. To maintain accuracy and a pleasing appearance, press all darts and seams before crossing them with an additional line of stitching.

FITTING TRIAL GARMENTS

1. Beginning with the simplest unit, fit each unit separately. Refine the fit of each as necessary before joining to another unit (see **Figure 8-3**).

2. Mark or make temporary adjustments while the unit is in place on the figure. Depending on the use of the garment, choose an appropriate method from the following procedures:

   - Remove stitching from a too-tight area. Let out or take up darts and seam allowances.
   - Pin tucks through the interior of the garment to remove excess length or width.
   - On a fitting garment, cut along the grain through a too-small area. Cut near the garment edge to allow the garment to increase in size. Insert a wide strip of scrap fabric under the slash. Allow the area to spread as necessary and pin the slashed edges to the inserted fabric.

3. When it is properly fitted, the garment will incorporate the appropriate fitting standards:

   - Vertical centers of the patterns coincide with the body centers and are perpendicular to the floor.
   - Dartlines point toward the fullest part of the body bulge.
   - All horizontal fitting lines are level.
   - All garment edges are in attractive and proper positions.
   - There is appropriate ease for the figures. Fabric lies smoothly against the body and is free from distortion and tightness.

4. Stitch the separately fitted units together, then refine the fit of the total garment. Coordinate hem with horizontal seam positions to create pleasing, interrelated proportions.
5. Perfect all stitching lines.
6. Using the slash, seam, or pivot method, transfer all adjustments to the paper pattern if it is to be used again.

Figure 8-3 The trial fitting garment illustrating the fitting units

Measurement Method

Fitting by measurement is accomplished by comparing body measurements to those of the pattern. After specific body measurements are taken, an ease allowance is added to the measurements for the areas of the body that move or expand. The total measurement or body-plus-ease is then compared to the corresponding pattern measurement. Measurements may also be obtained by measuring a basic garment or personalized basic pattern.

The measurement method for checking fit potential offers the following *advantages:*

- Measurements can be taken quickly.
- Vital information is obtained by beginners or professionals with minimal cost in time or money.
- Basic information is easily recorded for further reference and refinement.
- Experienced seamstresses and tailors can cut to fit so little refined fitting is needed.

The measurement method has several *limitations* that should be taken into consideration:

- When only a minimum number of body measurements are taken, more refined fitting is often required after the garment is cut.
- Practice in taking body measurements is needed to become an accurate fitter.
- A body is slightly smaller in the morning than in the afternoon. This sometimes results in inaccurate measurement.
- Soft body tissue may indent or expand with slight shifts in body stance. If the individual being measured turns or bends as the measurements are taken, mistakes result.

MARKING THE FIGURE FOR MEASUREMENTS

To facilitate taking body measurements, use marks, tapes, elastic, or other similar means to locate and define the points from which measurements originate and at which they terminate. Assemble the following: measuring tape, chart for recording measurements, pen or pencil, a necklace, elastic, straight pins, a flexible ruler, and a right angle or tailor's square.

TAKING & RECORDING BODY MEASUREMENTS

The individual being measured should stand erect in a natural, relaxed position and look straight ahead while measurements are being taken.

Measure the lower torso first, particularly if you are a beginner at taking measurements. There are fewer complicated bulges and curves. Work quickly and accurately so the person being measured does not become tired. A rest may be taken after the lower torso has been measured. (Check the position of waistline tape and other tapes before measuring is resumed.) Another rest may be taken before the arm is measured.

The measurements that follow are listed in the same sequence as on the **Measurement Chart (Part Three).** Remember to record the body measurement *plus* any indicated ease.

Lower Torso (for skirt or pants)

1. *Centers:* Measure from the waistline to the floor, beginning at the bottom of the waistline tape. (See **Figures 8-4a** and **8-4b.**)
2. *Inseam:* Take the measurement from the front of the figure, measuring from the crotch straight down to the floor. The person being measured may hold the end of the measuring tape at the crotch if a tailor's tape is not available. (See **Figure 8-4c.**)

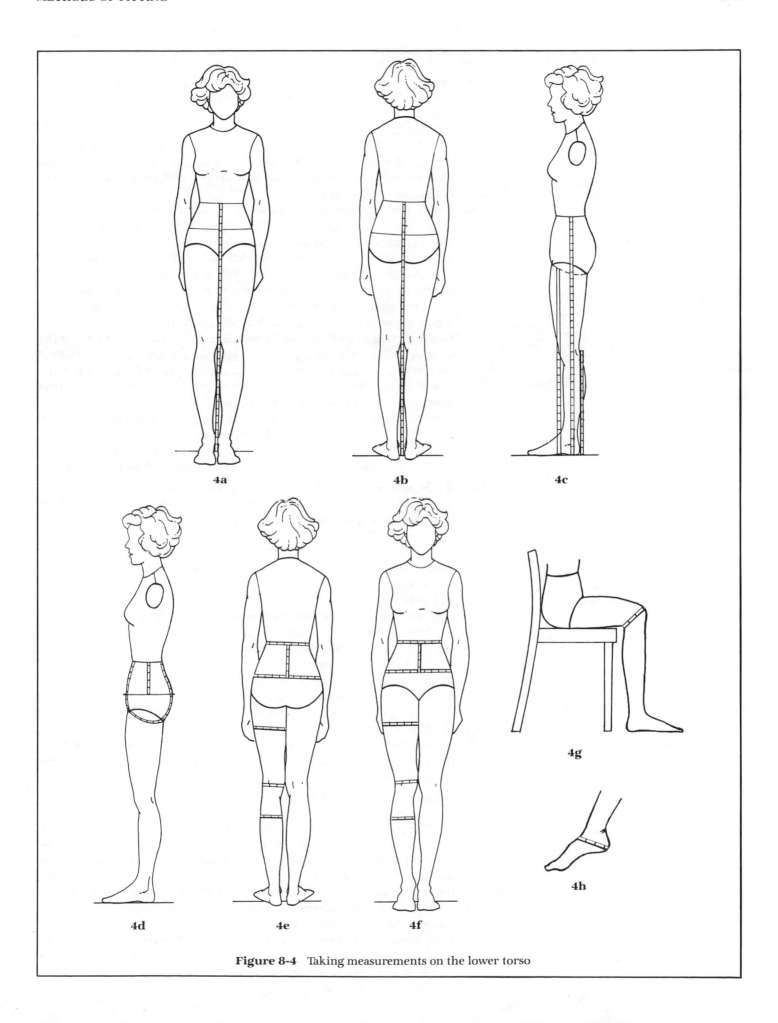

Figure 8-4 Taking measurements on the lower torso

3. *Knee position:* Measure from the floor to the middle of the kneecap. (See **Figure 8-4c.**)

4. *Side seam:* Measure over the hip from the waistline to the floor. Note the variation in lengths if both sides are not the same. (See **Figure 8-4c.**)

5. *Hip depth:* Measure from the waistline down to the tape at the hip joint level. Measure at center front, center back, and both sides. If side hip depths are not the same, record variations on the chart. Also note protruding hip bones or a rounded abdomen. (See **Figures 8-4d, 8-4e,** and **8-4f.**)

6. *Crotch length:* Measure from the waistline at center front, through the crotch, to the waistline at center back. (See **Figure 8-4d.**)

7. *Waist circumference:* Measure from center back to the tape at each side and from center front to each side. Record back and front measurements separately. (See **Figures 8-4e** and **8-4f.**)

8. *Hip circumference:* Measure from center back to the tape at each side and from center front to each side. Record back and front measurements separately. Note the conformation of the buttocks. Does the area protrude more than standard or is it flat? Is the fullest part of the buttocks curvature placed high or low in relation to the hip joint? Record this information on the chart. (See **Figures 8-4e** and **8-4f.**)

9. *Thigh circumference:* Measure around each leg at the fullest part above the knee. Record the distance between the waist and the thigh. Observe the conformation or shape of the thigh. Does the silhouette extend beyond the abdomen? Do inner thigh muscles touch or rub when walking, or is there a space between them? Record your observations on the chart. (See **Figures 8-4e** and **8-4f.**)

Optional Measurements (for close-fitting pants)

10. *Knee circumference:* Measure around the bent knee while the person is seated (see **Figure 8-4g**). Observe the conformation or shape of the knee area. When the person is walking or standing with the feet slightly apart, do the knees touch? Is the area between the knees greater or smaller than the area between the ankles when the person is standing? Record the conformation on the chart. (See **Figures 8-4e** and **8-4f.**)

11. *Calf circumference:* Measure around each leg at the fullest part below the knee. Observe the conformation of the calf. When viewed from the side, do the legs bow to the back? If so, is the plumb line at the side of the body in line with or near the front of the knee? When viewed from front or back, is the calf width more than 1½ times that of the knee? When standing, is the area between the calves greater than the area between the ankles? Record your observations on the chart. (See **Figures 8-4e** and **8-4f.**)

12. *Heel-instep circumference:* Measure around the foot diagonally from the heel over the instep when toes are pointed downward. (See **Figure 8-4h.**)

Upper Torso (for the bodice)

13. *Body centers:* Measure the back length from the center of the prominent neck vertebra down to the lower edge of waistline tape. Measure the front length from the necklace or line at the top of the collarbone down over the bustline tape to the lower edge of the waistline elastic. Also record the distance from the waistline to the maximum fashion neckline depth. (See **Figures 8-5a** and **8-5b.**)

14. *Full bodice length:* Measure the back from the shoulder/neck point straight down over the shoulder blade to the lower edge of the waist tape. Repeat on the front over the bust. (See **Figures 8-5b** and **8-5c.**)

15. *Blade and bust height:* Measure from the waist up to the tape at blade and bust tip level. (See **Figures 8-5a** and **8-5b.**)

16. *Side seam length:* Measure from the underarm level or scyeline ¾ inch to 1 inch (2 cm to 2.5 cm) below the level of the arm hinge to the waistline. (See **Figure 8-5c.**)

17. *Width of shoulders:* Measure across the upper back from shoulder tip to shoulder tip (between armscye elastics or marks). Repeat for the front. (See **Figures 8-5d** and **8-5e.**)

18. *Shoulder slope:* Measure each shoulder diagonally from the waistline at center back over the shoulder blade to the shoulder tip. Repeat on the front over the bust contour. (See **Figures 8-5d** and **8-5e.**)

19. *Length of chest and bust contour:* This measurement is required for empire waistlines and similar styles. Measure from the midshoulder down over the contour of the bust to the rib cage at the under edge of the bust. (See **Figure 8-5f.**)

20. *Shoulder length:* Measure from the side neck out to shoulder tip. (See **Figures 8-5g** and **8-5h.**)

21. *Width across shoulder blade area or chest:* At a level 1 inch to 1¼ inches (2.5 cm to 3 cm) above the arm hinges, measure across the shoulder blades from arm crease to arm crease. Repeat for the front across the chest from arm crease to arm crease. (See **Figures 8-5g** and **8-5h.**)

22. *Distance between blade and bust tips:* Measure from blade to blade and from bust tip to bust tip. (See **Figures 8-5g** and **8-5h.**)

23. *Full bodice width:* At scye level measure across the back from body center to each side. At fullest bust level, measure across the front from the body center to each side. Note that these measurements are not taken at the same level on the body. Back measurement indicates rib cage size while front measurement includes rib cage and bra cup size. (See **Figures 8-5g** and **8-5h.**)

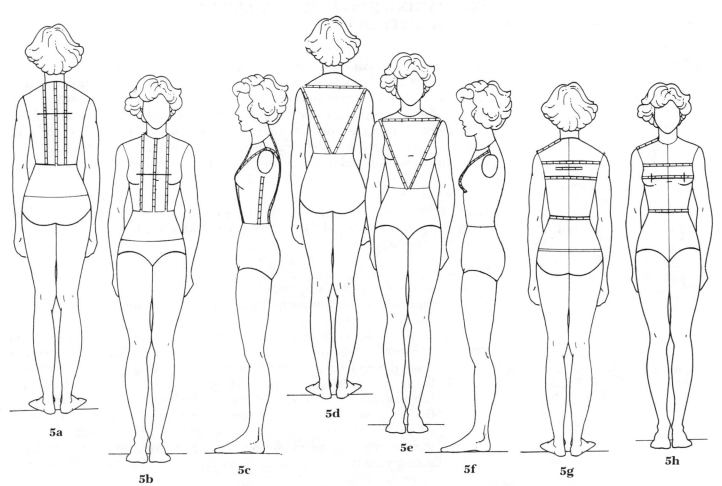

5a

5b

5c

5d

5e

5f

5g

5h

Figure 8-5 Taking measurements on the upper torso

Arm (for the sleeve)

24. *Underarm length:* Take this and following measurements with the arm hanging in a relaxed position. Measure at the side at a level ¾ inch to 1 inch (2 cm to 2.5 cm) below the arm hinges. Measure down the inside arm, following the contour of the arm to the wristline above the little finger. (See **Figure 8-6c.**)
25. *Elbow tip position:* Above the little finger, measure from the wristline to the elbow tip. (See **Figure 8-6a.**) (The elbow divides the underarm length approximately in half.)
26. *Overarm length:* Measure down the outer arm following the contour from the shoulder tip across the elbow tip to the wristline above the little finger. (See **Figure 8-6a.**)
27. *Biceps circumference:* Measure around the fullest part of the biceps. (See **Figure 8-6b.**)
28. *Elbow circumference:* Bend the arm to form a right angle. Measure around the arm diagonally from the elbow tip over the crease. Keep tape measure out of the crease. Check for the possibility of inward rotation of the elbow: relax the arms in a downward position with the palms of the hand forward. Do the elbow joints curve toward the waist and the wrists extend away from the hips 3 inches (12 cm) or more? Record your observations on the chart. (See **Figure 8-6b.**)
29. *Wrist circumference:* With two fingers under the measuring tape, measure around the arm at the wristbone. (See **Figure 8-6b.**)
30. *Hand circumference:* Place your thumb in line with your index finger. Measure around the hand at the base of the thumb. (See **Figure 8-6d.**)

COMPARING BODY MEASUREMENTS TO THE PATTERN

Work with a smoothly pressed, untrimmed pattern, the body measurement chart, and a ruler, tailor's square, or an accurate tape measure.

Use the body measurements-plus-ease in the sequence indicated in the instructions below. Compare body measurements to the corresponding location on the pattern piece. *Do not* include in the measurements the seam or hem allowances, button closures, or other extensions beyond the center; the area enclosed in the darts, stitched pleats, and tucks; or other similar details. Width must be allowed in addition to the body measurement for gathering, for unstitched pleats, released darts or tucks, and flare.

Begin measuring the pattern from the location designated in the instructions. With a pencil, mark the pattern where body measurements end or where they extend beyond the pattern edge. Add tissue to extend the pattern edge if necessary.

Lower Torso (skirt) (Figure 8-7)

1. Compare center body lengths to the pattern centers from hemline to waistline (see *measurement 1* on chart).
2. Compare side body length to the pattern along side seam contour from hemline to waistline (see *measurement 4* on chart). Side length minus desired hem level from the floor equals skirt length.
3. Compare the hip depth of the body to the pattern as follows. Mark side hip level on the pattern, 7 inches to 9 inches (18 cm to 23 cm) below the waistline or 1 inch to 1½ inches (2.5 cm to 4 cm) below the point where the side seam becomes a straight line. Draw the hipline across the pattern parallel to the hemline. Now use the body hip depth measurement to measure up from hipline to waistline (see *measurement 5* on chart).

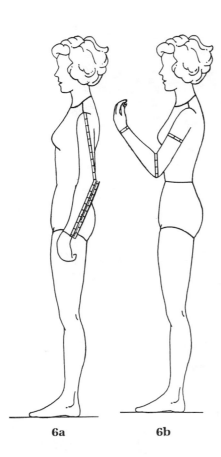

6a   6b

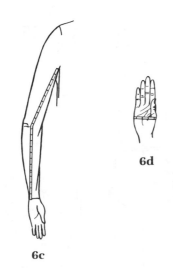

6d

6c

Figure 8-6 Taking measurements on the arm

To alter the pattern:

If chart measurements 4 and 5 differ from the pattern the *same* amount, change the pattern length above the hipline **(Figure 8-8)**. If chart measurements 1 and 4 agree with the pattern but measurement 5 differs, change the pattern length above the hipline then restore the pattern to its original length at cut edge of hemline **(Figure 8-9)**. If chart measurement 5 agrees with the pattern but measurements 1 and 4 differ, change the pattern length at the cut edge of hem **(Figure 8-10)**. If chart measurements 4 and 5 differ from the pattern an *uneven* amount, make the pattern length changes for measurement 5 above the hipline and the changes for measurements 1 and 4 at the cut edge of hem.

4. Compare the waistline circumference of the body to the pattern from center-line to side seamline (see *measurement 7* on chart; see **Figure 8-11**).
5. Compare the hipline circumference of the body to the pattern at hip level from center line to side seamline (see *measurement 8* on chart; see **Figure 8-11**).

To alter the pattern:

If chart measurements 7 and 8 differ from the pattern an *even* amount make pattern width change along the side seamline or at the marks indicating the side seam position **(Figure 8-12)**. When a side pocket is involved, make the change between the pocket and the dart or tuck. If chart measurements 7 and 8 differ an *uneven* amount, make the change at the side seam, dart, or a style seam near the side **(Figure 8-13)**. If prominent thighs were noted at the side, add width at the side of the pattern. If thighs are prominent at the front, increase the waistline curve by transferring part of the waist dart to the hemline.

Lower Torso (pants) (Figure 8-14)

1. Compare the inseam length of the body to the pattern front from crotch seamline to hemline (see *measurement 2* on chart). Where the body measurement ends, mark a new hemline parallel to the original one **(Figure 8-15)**.
2. Compare the knee position of the body to the pattern front by measuring up from the new hemline (see *measurement 3* on chart; see **Figure 8-16**).
3. Compare side body length to the pattern along the contour of the side seam from the new hemline to waistline (see *measurement 4* on chart; see **Figure 8-16**).

To alter the pattern:

If chart measurement 3 differs from the pattern, change the kneeline on the pattern if the pants leg is a fitted style. Retain the new hem length. If chart measurement 4 differs from the pattern, change the pattern length above the hipline **(Figure 8-16)**.

4. Compare the hip depth of the body to the pattern as follows: Mark the side hip level on the pattern 7 inches to 9 inches (18 cm to 23 cm) below the waistline or 1 inch to 1½ inches (2.5 cm to 4 cm) below the point where the side seam becomes straight. Draw the hipline across the pattern parallel to the hemline. Now use the body hip-depth measurements to measure up from hipline to waistline. If the pants leg is close fitting, there should be additional length 1 inch to 1⅜ inches (2.5 cm to 3.5 cm) above the depth measurement of the body at the back waistline (see *measurement 5* on chart; see **Figure 8-16**).

To alter the pattern:

If chart measurements 4 and 5 differ from the pattern the *same* amount, change the pattern length at the hipline **(Figure 8-16)**. If chart measurements

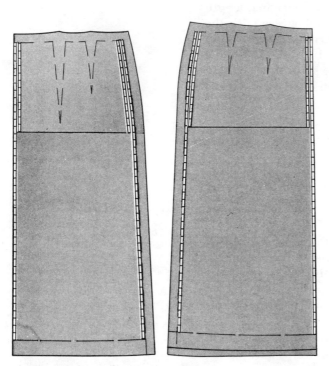

Figure 8-7 Body measurements indicate that skirt lengths are correct and require no change.

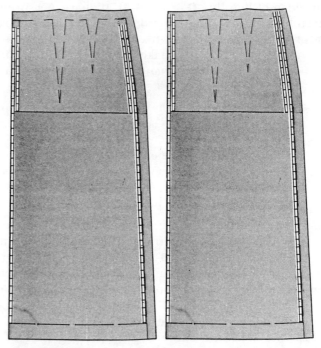

Figure 8-8 Body measurements indicate that skirt length requires alteration above the hipline to change total length and hip depth.

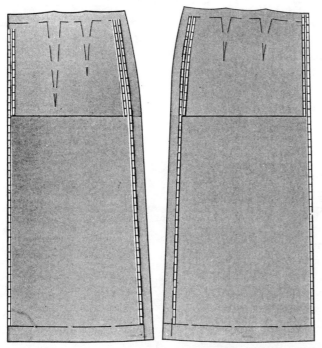

Figure 8-9 Body measurements indicate that skirt length requires alteration above the hipline to change hip depth at the center only.

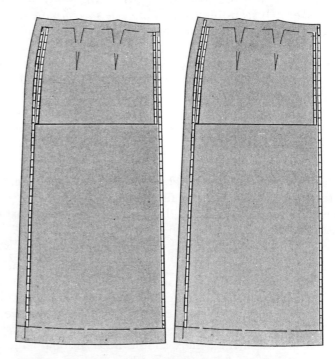

Figure 8-10 Body measurements indicate that skirt length requires alteration below the hipline to change the position of the skirt on the leg.

Figure 8-11 Body measurements indicate that skirt widths are correct and require no change.

Figure 8-12 Body measurements indicate that the skirt requires alteration at waist and hip side seams to change the width of both.

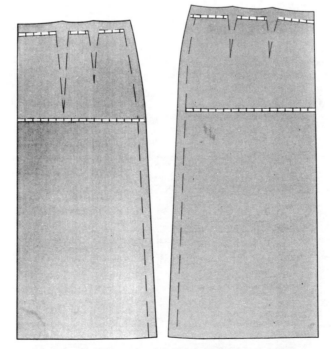

Figure 8-13 Body measurements indicate that skirt width requires alteration at the side to change the width at hip and waistline.

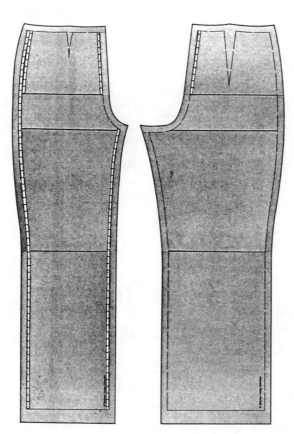

Figure 8-14 Body measurements indicate that pant lengths are correct and require no change.

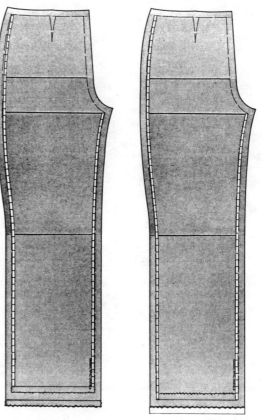

Figure 8-15 Body measurements indicate that pant length requires alteration below the crotch line to change the leg length.

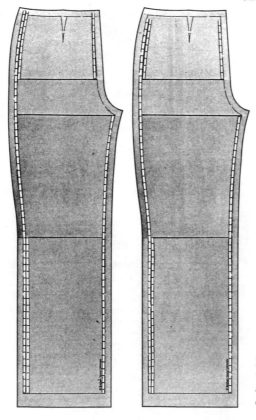

Figure 8-16 Body measurements indicate that pant length requires alteration at or above the hipline to change the hip and/or crotch depth.

4 and 5 differ from the pattern an *uneven* amount, change the pattern length at the waistline.

5. Compare the crotch length of the body to the pattern. Measure center front and center back from the waistline seam down to inseam. Combine front and back pattern measurements. To facilitate measuring, stand a flexible ruler or tape measure on edge along the seamline (see *measurement 6* on chart; see **Figure 8-17**).

    If chart measurement 6 still differs after making length adjustments above the crotchline, make the adjustments for the remaining crotch length difference at the crotch extensions. Divide the measurement difference into thirds. Alter the front extension equal to one-third. Alter the back extension equal to the remaining two-thirds **(Figure 8-18)**.

6. Compare the waistline circumference of the body to the pattern waistline from center line to side seamline (see *measurement 7* on chart; see **Figure 8-19**).

7. Compare the hipline circumference of the body to the pattern at hip level from center line to side seamline (see *measurement 8* on chart; see **Figure 8-19**).

8. Compare the thigh circumference of the body to the pattern from inseam to side seam approximately 1⅜ inches to 2 inches (3.5 cm to 5 cm) below the crotchline (see *measurement 9* on chart). Check the conformation noted when taking measurements.

To alter the pattern:
If chart measurements 7 and 8 differ from the pattern an *even* amount, make the pattern width change along the side seam or at the marks indicating the side seamline position. When a pocket is involved at the side, make the change between the pocket and dart or tuck (see **Figure 8-19**). Change the width of the front extension one-fourth of the side change. Change the back extension one-half of the side change.

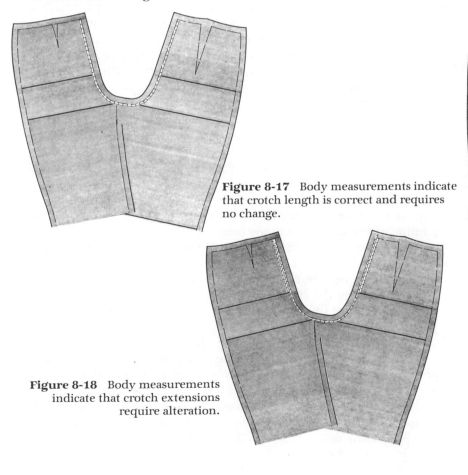

Figure 8-17 Body measurements indicate that crotch length is correct and requires no change.

Figure 8-18 Body measurements indicate that crotch extensions require alteration.

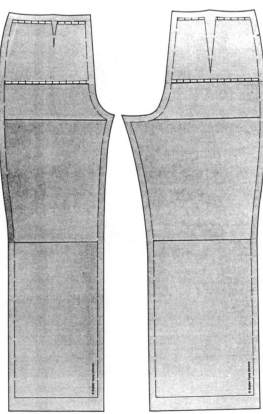

Figure 8-19 Body measurements indicate that pant widths are correct and require no change.

If chart measurements 7 and 8 differ from the pattern an *uneven* amount, make the change at the side seam, dart, or style seam nearest the side. Change the front extension one-fourth of the width change at side hip level. Change the back extension one-half of the width change at the side hip level.

If chart measurement 9 differs from the pattern, make the pattern change at the side seam and inseam. Only the degree of curve of the inseam may require change instead of the width of the extension. If prominent thighs were noted at the side, add width at the side of the pattern. If thighs are prominent at the front, increase the waistline curve by transferring part of the waist dart to the front extension.

Close-fitting Pants

9. Compare the knee circumference of the body to the pattern approximately halfway between the hipline and ankle or at the marked knee position (see *measurement 10* on chart). Measure from inseam to side seam of back and front and combine the measurement. Check the conformation noted when measurements were taken.

10. Compare the calf circumference of the body to the pattern from the inseam to side seam approximately 4 inches to 5 inches (10 cm to 12 cm) below the knee position (see *measurement 11* on chart). Check conformation of calf as noted on measurement chart.

11. Compare the instep circumference of the body to the pattern at the hemline of full-length pants (see *measurement 12* on chart).

To alter the pattern:
If chart measurements 10 and 11 differ from the pattern, change the pattern by even amounts along the inseam and side seam. Some pants have slits or plackets at the hem to allow the foot to slide through. Check for this styling before adding width.

Bodice Lengths (Figure 8-20)

12. Compare center lengths of the body to those of the pattern from waistline to neckline. If a low neckline is featured, use the maximum neckline depth measurement and measure from the waistline up to the neckline (see *measurement 13* on chart; see **Figure 8-21**).

13. Compare the full bodice length of the body to the pattern parallel to the center line (see *measurement 14* on chart; see **Figure 8-21**). Measure from the waistline up to the shoulder/neckline point. If the neckline is a widened style, extend the shoulderline toward the center line then compare the body measurement to the pattern from the waistline to the extended shoulderline. Measure about 2⅜ inches to 2¾ inches (6 cm to 7 cm) away from the pattern center and parallel to it.

14. Compare the shoulder blade height and bust height to the pattern (see *measurement 15* on chart; see **Figure 8-21**). Measure along the foldline of the waist dart if one originates at the waistline. If there is no waist dart, measure along the pattern center from the waistline and square a line out at the height of blade or bust. A princess line usually passes near but not over the bust point. Often the middle of an eased area on the center panel of the pattern may be used as the indicator for bust height, or the fullest point of the curve on the side panel may be used.

15. Compare the side seam length of the body to the pattern from the waistline along the side seam (or the marks indicating the side seam position) to the armscye (see *measurement 16* on chart; see **Figure 8-21**). Side seams of sleeveless tops may rise higher at the underarm than side seams of tops with sleeves. The side seams of jackets, coats, jumpers, and vests have been lowered at the armscye to accommodate blouses or other garments that are worn under such apparel. A

garment also may be designed with a lowered armscye for fashion purposes.

To alter the pattern:
If chart measurements 13, 14, 15 and 16 differ from the pattern the *same* amount make the change below the bustline (see **Figure 8-21**).

16. Compare the shoulder-tip width of the body to the bodice pattern (see *measurement 17* on chart; see **Figure 8-22**). Extend the pattern center line, then square and measure across to shoulder-tip. Mark the pattern level with the shoulder-tip. Measure and mark again above or below the tip, then draw a line through the two points. This line is parallel to the center. The shoulder width of a jacket or coat is wider than the basic bodice. For clothing styles with lowered, widened necklines, remove the ease in width and length to allow the neckline to lie smoothly against the body.

17. Compare the shoulder slope of the body plus shoulder pad height and shoulder extension (see *measurement 18* on chart; see **Figure 8-22**). Measure from the waistline at center, diagonally upward to the shoulder tip. The body measurement plus pad height and shoulder extension will touch the vertical line previously drawn through the shoulder tip.

To alter the pattern:
If chart measurement 16 agrees with the pattern but measurements 13, 14 and 18 differ the same amount, make the change between the scye and shoulder to alter the armscye depth (see **Figure 8-22**). If chart measurements 13 and 14 agree with the pattern but measurements 16 and 18 differ, make the change at the shoulder and underarm to raise or lower the armhole position (see **Figure 8-23**). If chart measurements 15, 16 and 18 agree with the pattern but measurements 13 and 14 differ, make the change at the neck and shoulder to alter center lengths and the shoulder slope (see **Figure 8-24**). If chart measurement 16 agrees with the pattern but measurements 13 and 14 differ the *same* amount and 18 differs less, make the change at the fullest part of the bulge. This will alter the size of the dart(s) in the area (see **Figure 8-25**).

18. On styles with empire waistlines and other similar styles, compare the length of the chest and bust contour to the pattern from the center of the shoulder down to the empire seamline below the bust area (see *measurement 19* on chart; see **Figure 8-26**).

To alter the pattern:
If chart measurements 13 and 19 differ from the pattern but measurement 16 agrees, make the change on the upper bodice at the empire line (see **Figure 8-26**). If a princess line is involved, make the change at the bust level of both pattern pieces.

Bodice Widths (Figure 8-27)

19. Compare the shoulder length of the body to the pattern from the shoulder tip to the neckline (see *measurement 20* on chart). Jackets and coats extend ½ inch to ⅝ inch (1 cm to 1.5 cm) at the shoulder, but their wider neckline may shorten the shoulder by ⅛ inch (0.3 m) or more. Check shoulder-tip width (chart *measurement 17*) as an indicator of shoulder length for designs with extended shoulders or for designs that do not extend to the body neckline.

20. Compare the width across the shoulder blades or chest to the pattern at the narrowest point of the armscye if the armscye is standard (see *measurement 21* on chart). If the sleeve is raglan style, measure across the bodice at the armscye notch nearest the side seam.

21. Compare the blade and bust-tip widths to the pattern at the line marking the height of the blade or bust (see *measurement 22* on chart). Begin measuring from the center line.

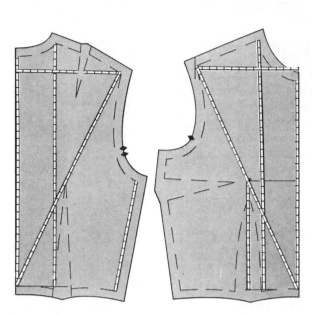

Figure 8-20 Body measurements indicate that bodice lengths, and shoulder tip width and slope are correct and require no change.

Figure 8-21 Body measurements indicate that bodice length requires alteration below the bustline to change the midriff length and correctly position bust darts.

Figure 8-22 Body measurements indicate that the bodice length requires alteration between the armscye and the shoulder to change the armscye depth.

Figure 8-23 Body measurements indicate that bodice length requires alteration at the shoulder tip and underarm to raise or lower the armhole position.

Figure 8-24 Body measurements indicate that bodice length requires alteration at the neck and shoulder to change the center lengths.

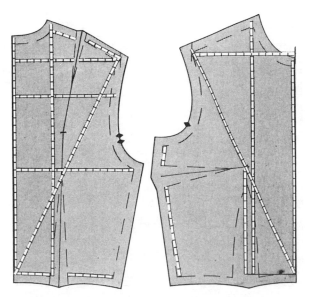

Figure 8-25 Body measurements indicate that bodice length requires alteration through the bust dart to increase size.

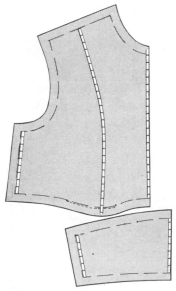

Figure 8-26 Body measurements indicate that bodice length and dart size require alteration at the bust on fashion patterns.

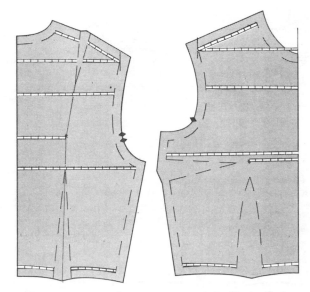

Figure 8-27 Body measurements indicate that bodice widths are correct and require no change.

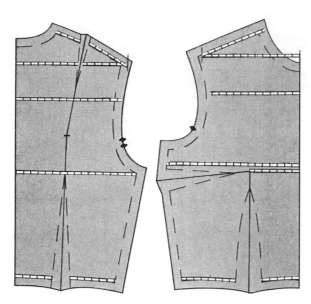

Figure 8-28 Body measurements indicate that bodice width requires alteration at the armscye to change the shoulder length.

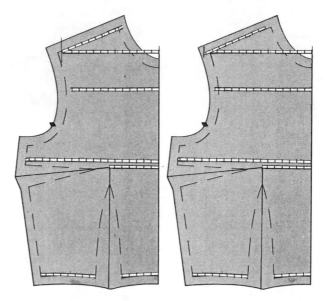

Figure 8-29 Body measurements indicate that the bodice width requires alteration at the neck and armscye to change the neck and chest width.

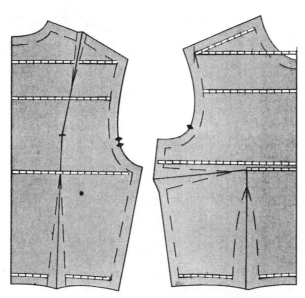

Figure 8-30 Body measurements indicate that bodice width requires alteration at the side seam and lower armscye to change width through the bust and rib cage.

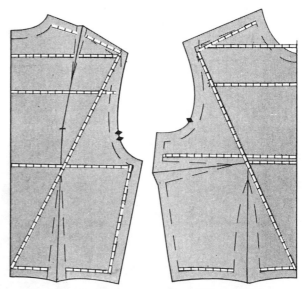

Figure 8-31 Body measurements indicate that the bodice width and shoulder slope require alteration at the shoulder tip and armscye to change the position of the shoulder and armscye seams.

22. Compare the full bodice width of the body to the pattern at scye level in the back (see *measurement 23* on chart). On the front compare the body measurement from the center line toward the side seam at bust level. There will be more ease in a jacket or coat to allow for the blouses, etc., worn under them.

23. Compare the waist circumference of the body to the pattern along the waistline seam or waistline mark at the narrowest part of the pattern waistline area (see *measurement 7* on chart). Jacket waistlines are loose to allow for a skirt, etc., to be worn under them.

To alter the pattern:

If body measurements 17, 21, 22, 23 and 7 differ from the pattern an *even* amount, make the change between the center line and the dart, and extending through the shoulderline (broad or narrow body center).

If chart measurements 17 and 20 differ the *same* amount and 21 is less, make the pattern change at the armscye unless that will make unpleasing proportions for a yoke or princess line at the shoulder (see **Figure 8-28**).

If 20 agrees, but 17 and 21 disagree, make the change for 20 at the neckline. Make the change for 17 and 21 at the armscye (see **Figure 8-29**).

If only chart measurement 22 differs from the pattern, change the position of the dart or princess line.

If only chart measurement 23 differs from the pattern, make the change at the side seam (see **Figure 8-30**). If the design features a yoke or princess line, make the change on the side panel at the princess seam. If no length change occurred on the center panel, the width adjustment must not change the length of the side panel.

If chart measurements 22 and 23 differ from the pattern, make the changes at the same time.

If only measurement 7 differs from the pattern, make the change at the side and/or at the dart.

Sleeve Lengths (Figure 8-32)

24. Compare the underarm length to the pattern from the capline to the wristline along the front underarm seam or from the marks indicating the seam position (see *measurement 24* on chart).

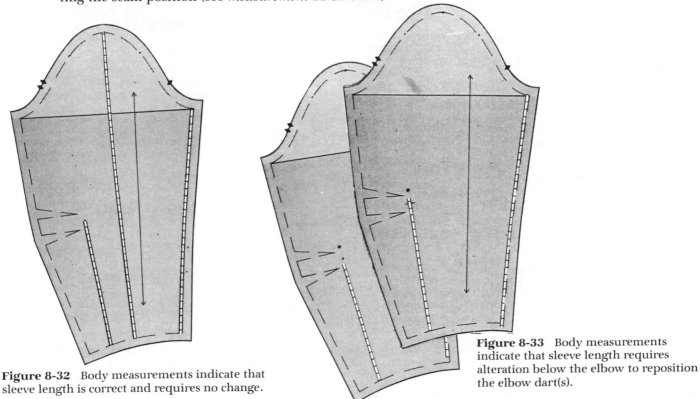

Figure 8-32 Body measurements indicate that sleeve length is correct and requires no change.

Figure 8-33 Body measurements indicate that sleeve length requires alteration below the elbow to reposition the elbow dart(s).

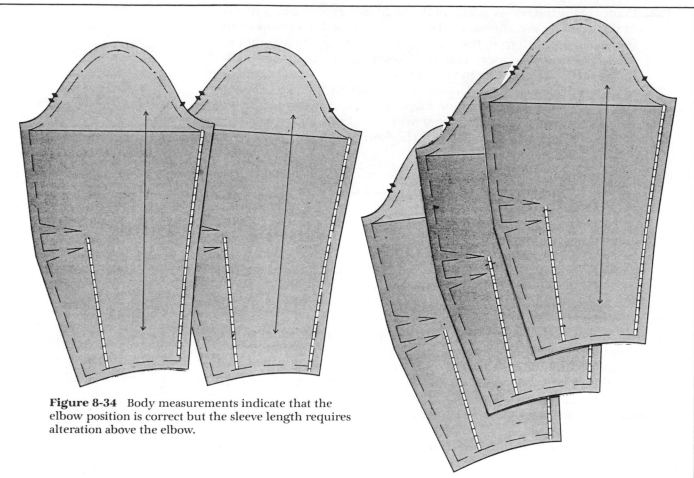

Figure 8-34 Body measurements indicate that the elbow position is correct but the sleeve length requires alteration above the elbow.

Figure 8-35 Body measurements indicate that alteration is required above and below the elbow to reposition the elbow dart(s) and to retain or alter length.

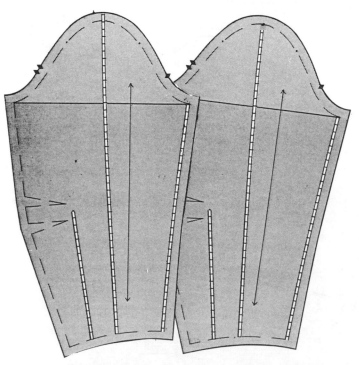

Figure 8-36 Body measurements indicate that the sleeve length requires alteration above the capline.

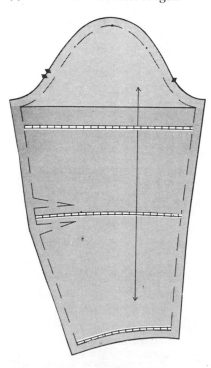

Figure 8-37 Body measurements indicate that the sleeve width is correct and requires no change.

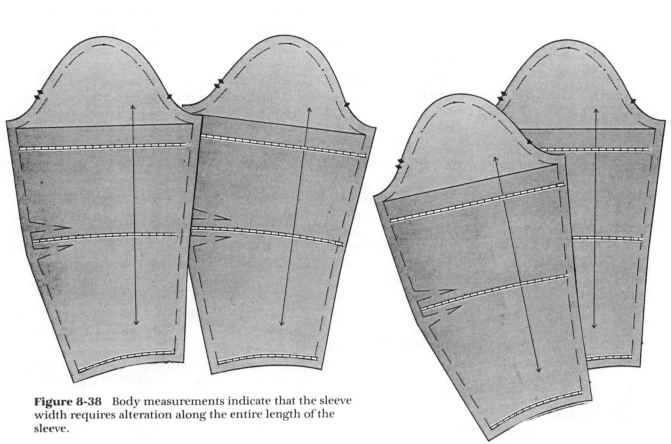

Figure 8-38 Body measurements indicate that the sleeve width requires alteration along the entire length of the sleeve.

Figure 8-39 Body measurements indicate that the sleeve width requires alteration above the elbow.

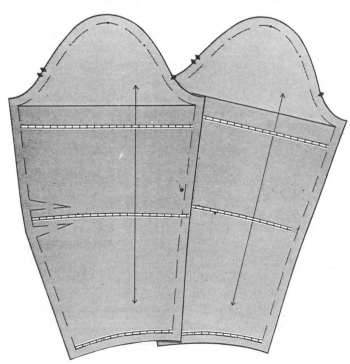

Figure 8-40 Body measurements indicate that the sleeve width requires alteration at the back dart level.

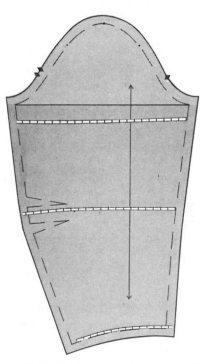

Figure 8-41 Body measurements indicate that the underarm seam requires repositioning and the dart size increased to accommodate the elbow.

25. Compare the height of the elbow to the pattern from the back quarter of the wristline to the elbow mark or dart tip (see *measurement 25* on chart). If there is no dart in a full-length sleeve compare at approximately half the pattern underarm length.

To alter the pattern:

If chart measurements 24 and 25 differ from the pattern by the *same* amount, make the change below the elbow position (see **Figure 8-33**).

If only measurement 24 differs from the pattern, make the change above the elbow position (see **Figure 8-34**).

If only measurement 25 differs from the pattern, make the change below the elbow position and then restore the underarm length above the elbow (see **Figure 8-35**).

26. Compare the overarm length of body to the pattern from the center of the wristline to the shoulder mark (see *measurement 26* on chart). The height of the shoulder pad (if a shoulder pad is used) must be added to the body measurement before making the comparison. On a kimono or raglan sleeve a notch often designates the end of the shoulder.

To alter the pattern:

Adjust the height of the sleeve cap as necessary (see **Figure 8-36**).

Sleeve Widths (Figure 8-37)

27. Compare the biceps circumference to the pattern across the pattern 1 inch to 1½ inches (2.5 cm to 4 cm) below the capline from underarm seam to underarm seam (see *measurement 27* on chart). Jacket sleeves are wider than dress sleeves by 1 inch (2.5 cm), coat sleeves by 2 inches (5 cm). Some dress designs are loose and therefore have more than minimum sleeve ease.

28. Compare the elbow circumference to the pattern at the elbow dart level from underarm seam to underarm seam (see *measurement 28* on chart). Jackets and coats will be larger here also. On full-length sleeves without a dart, measure across the sleeve halfway between the capline and the wrist. Was elbow rotation noted when taking measurements?

29. Compare the wrist circumference to the pattern from underarm seam to underarm seam along the wristline (see *measurement 29* on chart). Jacket and coat sleeves are wider than fitted dress sleeves. If a wrist placket is not featured, compare the hand circumference (chart *measurement 30*) with the pattern wristline or the sleeve-band circumference.

To alter the pattern:

If chart measurements 27, 28, and 29 differ from the pattern by the same amount, change the pattern at the center of the sleeve and at the underarm (see **Figure 8-38**).

If only measurement 27 differs, make the change at the underarm seams above the elbow (see **Figure 8-39**).

If only measurement 28 differs, change the width and dart size at the back underarm seam (see **Figure 8-40**).

If elbow rotation was noted, swing the front underarm seam forward until the wristline moves ½ inch to ¾ inches (1.2 cm to 1.8 cm). Pivot at the elbow level. Adjust the wrist and back seams so the dart increases no more than the amount of the forward change (see **Figure 8-41**).

CHAPTER 9

METHODS OF PATTERN ALTERATION

The alteration of a pattern is a fundamental step in achieving attractive and correctly fitted clothing. Information learned from a personal figure evaluation and in a measurement or fitting experience can be easily incorporated into the paper pattern to ensure a better fit in a fashion garment. The variety of methods presented in this chapter permit selection of a procedure most nearly suited to your needs, purposes, and ability. We will discuss the following methods:

- Slash Method
- Seam Method
- Pivot Method

The advantages and disadvantages of these methods are identified to aid you in selecting a suitable method. Each alteration procedure is either entirely new or is an improvement over past methods; each is intended to be logical, reliable, and complete. Consistent procedures have been used to define cause, effect, and alteration solutions for the specific figure variations in **Part Two**. The methods are equally effective for altering patterns for men, women, and children.

Alteration Procedures

1. Assemble equipment needed in the alteration process.
2. Review the amounts of necessary change determined during fitting or measurement.
3. Analyze each garment adjustment independently and as it relates to other adjustments. Consider the alterations to be made on a single pattern piece in order to plan for a series of alterations resulting from multiple figure variations.
4. Choose the most appropriate pattern alteration method for a particular adjustment or combination of adjustments.
5. Pattern preparation for all methods:

   - Work with a pressed pattern. (Press with dry heat to prevent shrinkage.)
   - Work with a reinforced pattern (see **Chapter 7**).
   - Work with the printed side of the pattern up and on top of the alteration paper.
   - Work over a flat, porous surface such as corkboard, a pattern cutting board, or a large piece of corrugated cardboard so that pins may be inserted to hold patterns firmly in place.
   - Draw alteration lines in red to draw attention to them.

6. Incorporate the correct amount of fitting adjustment at each area requiring a change on the pattern piece. Use a systematic procedure.

   - Make those changes that *evenly* increase or decrease the *length* of the pattern piece. (The width may be accurate when the pattern is positioned correctly on the body.)
   - Make those changes that involve *uneven* adjustments in the *length* of the pattern piece.
   - Make those changes that involve *even* adjustments in the *width* of the pattern piece.
   - Make those changes that involve *uneven* adjustments in the *width* of the pattern piece.

7. Check all pattern pieces adjoining an edge that has been altered in length or width. Changes must be in equal amounts at the stitching line on all adjoining edges or the pattern pieces will not match during construction.
8. Evaluate the accuracy of all alterations.

- The original style of the garment must be retained unless a change was intentional.
- A pattern lies flat before an alteration; there should be no puckers, puffiness, or wrinkles after the alteration is completed.
- Center front and center back seamlines on a basic pattern must be kept straight.
- When the length change of a pattern involves the center front or center back, the amount of change occurring at center front or center back must be even for a distance of about 3 inches or 4 inches (7.5 cm to 10 cm) from the centers. Seamlines that intersect the center front or center back must lie at right angles on the basic pattern.
- The hem corners of all basic skirt pattern pieces must form right angles or the hemline will be uneven.
- Double check the accuracy of each change.

9. True the pattern edges and make necessary restorations.

- Use rulers and french curves to restore the accuracy of lines and edges and to make them conform to the curves and planes of the body.
- When a dart is altered in length, position, or size, its base shape and the pattern edge will change too. Fold the dart into the closed position and cut along the pattern edge. This will automatically shape the dart base correctly.
- Restore any original pattern markings disturbed during the alteration process.

The Slash Method

The slash method is based on the traditional theory that pattern alterations should lie in the same area of the body requiring change. Alterations by this method are made by cutting through the interior of the pattern in approximately the same area that the body requires an adjustment for proper fit. The slashed pattern piece is then spread to increase a pattern area or overlapped to decrease an area.

The slash method offers the following *advantages:*

- The method is similar to slash adjustments in the fitting garment.
- Even amounts of change are readily accomplished for the specific body area.
- Changes will neither be forgotten nor cut off when the fabric is cut because alterations have been made in the interior of the pattern area.
- The original seam allowances remain intact on the pattern edge.

The slash method offers the following *disadvantages:*

- Distortion of dart size and pattern edge usually occurs when uneven changes are made and when the slashed edge is slanted or curved.
- Distortion increases in proportion to the distance the alteration is made from the pattern edge. (Resulting dart size is not in proportion to the amount of change when the alteration is too far from the edge.)
- Exact duplication of all adjustments in the fitting garment cannot be accomplished in paper patterns because fabric and paper do not respond identically. To keep the patterns flat and the edges smooth, additional procedures must be done.
- Multiple figure variations do not lend themselves to combined alterations; the slashed areas often overlap or cross each other and can lead to confusion and increased pattern distortion.
- Because of the flimsy texture of tissue patterns, the shape of the pattern pieces may be difficult to maintain.

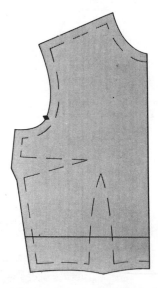

Figure 9-1 Establish slash lines for even amounts of change that affect the entire width or length (long or short waist).

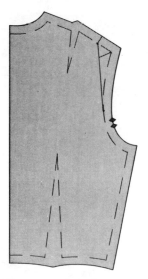

Figure 9-2 Establish slash lines for uneven amounts of change that affect the length of only one edge (broad or narrow shoulders).

- The cut pieces may become a "jigsaw puzzle" and be lost or confused during reassembly.
- Producing altered patterns that accurately fit most figure variations may be too difficult for the novice.
- Many illustrations in available references are either inaccurate, incomplete, or cannot be reproduced as illustrated because the drawing is not factual.
- The individual whose pattern has been altered may not feel good about the self or the pattern, since the altered pattern looks appreciably different from the original.

Approach the slash method of pattern alteration in the following sequence:

1. To keep distortions to a minimum, plan alterations near the edge that requires change.
2. Establish guidelines for slashing the area where the figure variations occur.

   - When an even amount of change is to be made in the length or width, a line will extend through the entire area to be altered, crossing both pattern edges (see **Figure 9-1**).
   - When the length of only one seamline is adjusted, one alteration line crosses the seam to be changed and extends to another stitching line at the point where the figure variation tapers to nothing; an additional line is made to the corner in the area between the two affected points (see **Figure 9-2**).
   - When only the interior is adjusted without changing the length of any seamline, a line will extend from one stitching line to another within the affected area; additional lines are made as necessary to a corner, where the figure variation is the greatest, and through the center of the darts in the area (see **Figure 9-3**).
   - When the adjustment involves both an even and uneven amount of change, one line will extend through the pattern edge needing a length change and will end at another stitching line or corner where the figure variation tapers to nothing. Lines are made to the corner where the variation changes from an even to an uneven amount in addition to the one through the center of darts in the area (see **Figure 9-4**).

3. Establish clip lines across the appropriate seam allowance area to form "hinges" on the stitching line (see **Figure 9-5**). These lines should extend diagonally across seam allowances at corners or straight across other seam allowances to meet the end of interior slash lines. The hinges permit movement of the pattern sections and allow the seam allowance to lie flat.
4. Place alteration paper under the affected area.
5. Cut the pattern along the established slash lines. Clip to, but not through, the stitching line to form hinges.
6. Secure the edge of the unchanged pattern area to the alteration tissue.
7. Manipulate the loosened pattern areas to make the adjustment (see **Figures 9-6** and **9-7**).

   - To *increase an even amount* of length or width, separate the pattern pieces a parallel amount.
   - To *decrease an even amount* of length or width, overlap the pattern pieces a parallel amount.
   - To *increase an uneven amount* of length or width, pivot the pattern edge away from the interior of the pattern.
   - To *decrease an uneven amount* of length or width, pivot the pattern edge onto the interior of the pattern.

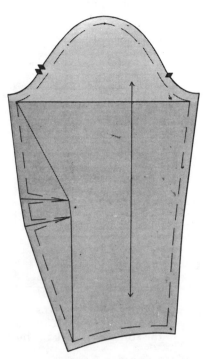

Figure 9-3 Establish slash lines for uneven amounts of change that affect only the interior (large or small elbow).

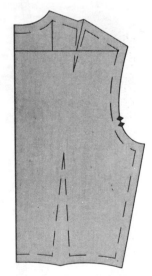

Figure 9-4 Establish slash lines for even and uneven amounts of change that retain the shape of the separated edge of the pattern (rounded or overly erect back).

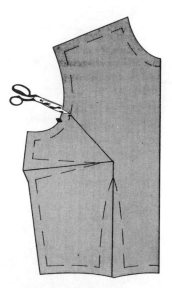

Figure 9-5 Clip across seam allowance to form a "hinge" on the stitching line (large bust).

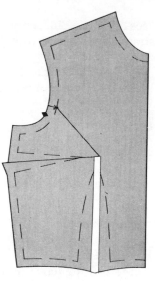

Figure 9-6 Manipulate the pattern area for an even amount of change (large bust).

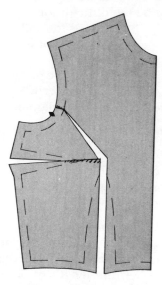

Figure 9-7 Manipulate the pattern area for amount of change (large bust).

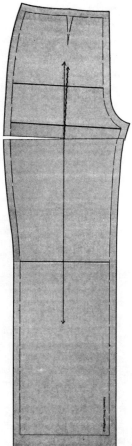

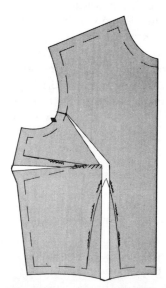

Figure 9-9 True the pattern edges and dartlines (large bust).

Figure 9-8 True the pattern grain to restore proper drape (bowed legs).

- To accomplish *an even and uneven amount* of change, make the even change first by separating or overlapping the affected area, then pivot the remaining section(s) until the pattern edges align.

8. Secure the changed pattern area to the alteration paper.
9. True the original grain if affected by the pattern alteration (see **Figure 9-8**).
10. True the pattern edges and make the necessary restorations (see **Figure 9-9**).

The Seam Method

The seam method illustrates the theory that the closer the alteration is made to the edge of the pattern, the less the pattern will be distorted. The process involves cutting the affected seam allowance free from the point where a figure variation begins to the point where it ends. The seam allowance is then moved away from, or overlapped onto the pattern to alter the affected area. Although the change is apparent only at the pattern edge, the adjustment is incorporated at the area where the fitting adjustment is necessary. This is due to the strategic placement of length changes and pivot points.

The seam method offers the following *advantages:*

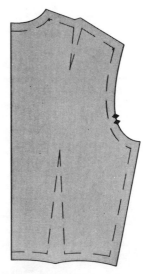

Figure 9-10 Establish pivot points for an uneven amount of change (square or sloping shoulders).

- The method can be easily carried out by the beginner.
- Alterations for multiple figure variations can be accomplished in an efficient and logical manner.
- Alterations can be accomplished in a short time.
- The interior of the pattern remains uncut and the original seam allowance is retained.
- Distortion is minimal; tiny amounts occur only at altered corners and at curved edges of seam allowances.
- The grainline does not become distorted.
- Tucks, pleats, and other construction details in the affected area remain undisturbed.
- The appearance of the altered pattern is more pleasing.
- The individual whose pattern has been altered is more likely to feel good about the self and the pattern, since the altered pattern does not look appreciably different from the original.

The seam method presents the following *disadvantages:*

- Because of the flimsy texture of typical commercial patterns, the shape of seam allowances may be difficult to maintain.
- Small pieces of seam allowance may be lost or misplaced during the alteration process.
- No known references other than this text contain directions for these newly developed procedures.

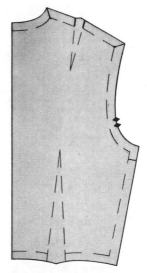

Figure 9-11 Establish clip lines to create "hinges" at stitching lines (square or sloping shoulders).

Approach the seam method of pattern alteration in the following sequence:

1. Locate the appropriate stitching line affected by the figure variation.
2. Establish pivot points on the pattern stitching line as necessary (see **Figure 9-10**):

   - at the point where the figure variation is greatest
   - at the point where a figure variation diminishes to nothing
   - where an adjustment changes from an even to an uneven amount
   - at the base of affected darts
   - at affected corners

3. Establish clip lines diagonally across the seam allowance at corners or straight across other seam allowances to meet the pivot points (see **Figure 9-11**).

4. Place alteration paper under the affected area.
5. Free the affected seam allowance by cutting near the stitching line in the garment area (see **Figure 9-12**).
6. Cut the designated clip lines across the seam allowances to create a "hinge" on the stitching line at each pivot point (see **Figure 9-13**). (*Do not* cut through the stitching line.) Hinges permit movement of the seam allowance, and these clips permit the seam allowance to lie flat.
7. Secure the pattern area to the alteration paper.
8. Move the seam allowance the appropriate amount and in the appropriate direction (see **Figure 9-14**):

   • To *increase an even amount* of length or width, slide the seam allowance away from the pattern area.
   • To *decrease an even amount* of length or width, slide the seam allowance onto the pattern area.
   • To *increase an uneven amount* of length or width, pivot the seam allowance away from the pattern.
   • To *decrease an uneven amount* of length or width, pivot the seam allowance onto the pattern.
   • To accomplish alterations of *both even and uneven amounts*, slide the section of freed seam allowance that is to be moved evenly, then pivot the remaining section.

9. Secure the changed seam allowance to the alteration paper.
10. True the pattern edges and make necessary restorations (see **Figure 9-15**).

The Pivot Method

The pivot method is based on the theory that regardless of where or how a pattern or garment is altered, it is the contour of the outer edge that ultimately changes. The method, however, does incorporate the change into the area of the pattern where the fitting adjustment occurs because of the strategic

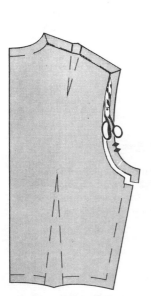

Figure 9-12 Free the seam allowances to reposition the stitching lines (square or sloping shoulders).

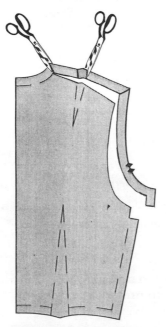

Figure 9-13 Clip across seam allowances to form "hinges" on the stitching lines (square or sloping shoulders).

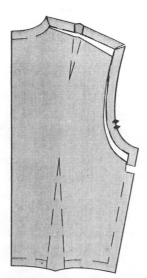

Figure 9-14 Manipulate the loosened seam allowance for the uneven amount of change (square shoulders).

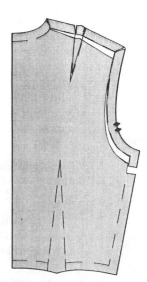

Figure 9-15 True the pattern edges and restore dart length (square shoulders).

placement of the length changes and pivot points. The process involves obtaining a duplicate of the affected pattern area. The pattern, a tracing of the pattern, or a ruler which matches the pattern edge may be used. This duplicate is then slid or pivoted over the pattern or tracing and retraced to incorporate the amount of adjustment. The fabric will be cut according to the corrected alteration line. Avoid confusing the two lines by consistently tracing the corrected line—which is always the fabric cutting line—in red.

The pivot method offers the following *advantages:*

- Multiple alterations for figure variations that occur in combinations are efficiently accomplished.
- Since the tracing is the new working edge of the pattern, the pattern may be retraced when the body weight or size changes or when the pattern is used by more than one person. Only decreased areas require cutting the original pattern.
- Distortion of the pattern edges is slight.
- The grainline does not become distorted.
- Tucks, pleats, and other construction details in the affected area remain undisturbed.
- The process can be used to alter the pattern before the fabric is cut, during the cutting process, during the construction process on the garment or on ready-to-wear garments that have adequate seam allowances.

The pivot method presents the following *disadvantages:*

- The shape of the cut edge may be difficult to trace accurately because of the flimsy texture of commercial patterns.
- Unless a contrasting color is used for the new cutting line, alterations may be unnoticed and habit may cause you to cut on the original cutting edge of the pattern.
- Alterations which involve darts are rather advanced for beginners.
- Few sources are available that explain pivot procedures for more than a few common figure variations or pattern shapes.

Approach the pivot method of pattern alteration in the following sequence:

1. Establish pivot points on the pattern stitching line as necessary (see **Figure 9-16**):

   - where the figure variation is greatest
   - where the figure variation diminishes to nothing
   - where a change is no longer an even amount
   - where an affected dart stitching line meets the cutting line being traced

2. Duplicate the pattern area to be altered by making a tracing or using a ruler with the appropriate shape. For relocation purposes, make matching marks on both the pattern and the duplicate. Use a black pencil for the tracing (see heavier outline in **Figure 9-17**).
3. Duplicate the pattern edge by making a tracing or by using a ruler which matches the original pattern edge.
4. Slide or pivot the duplicate of the pattern area the needed amount and in the appropriate direction. Trace the new cutting line *in red:*

   - To *increase* an even amount of length or width, slide the duplicate beyond the pattern or traced area.
   - To *decrease* an even amount of length or width, slide the duplicate onto the pattern or traced area (see **Figure 9-18**).
   - To *increase* an uneven amount of length or width, use the pivot point(s) along the stitching line and pivot the duplicate away from the pattern or traced area.

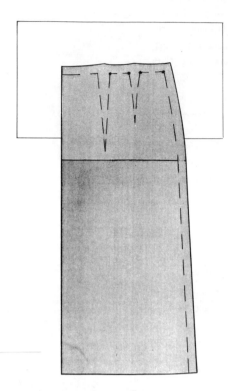

Figure 9-16   Establish pivot points for an uneven amount of change (sway back).

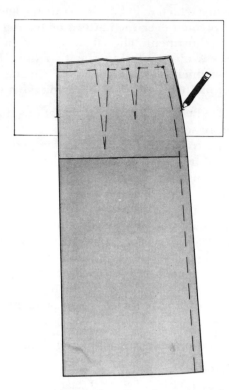

Figure 9-17   Trace the affected area (sway back).

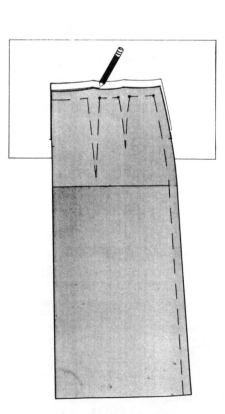

Figure 9-18   Slide and trace affected area for an even amount of change (sway back).

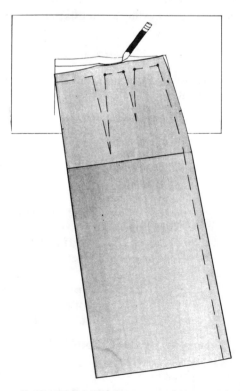

Figure 9-19   Pivot and trace uneven amount of change (sway back).

- To *decrease* an uneven amount of length or width, use the pivot point(s) on the stitching line and pivot the duplicate onto the pattern or traced area (see **Figure 9-19**).
- To accomplish alterations of even and uneven amounts, slide and trace the duplicate in the area to be altered the even amount. Pivot and trace the duplicate.
- To accomplish an even and uneven amount of change, make the even change first by sliding the duplicate away from or onto the pattern or tracing (see **Figure 9-20**). Then pivot and trace the duplicate until the seams and darts are aligned (see **Figure 9-21**). Mark the position of notches and the ends of the dartlines when tracing the altered area (see **Figure 9-22**).

5. If a tracing was used, secure the tracing to the original pattern. Match the first traced line (black) with the cutting line on the original pattern (see **Figure 9-23**).
6. True the pattern edges to make the necessary restoration (see **Figure 9-24**).
7. Cut along the corrected (red) line when cutting the fabric.

Alterations for Asymmetrical Variations

When the left side of the body differs significantly from the right side, the fitting pattern must be duplicated to have a pattern for each side of the body. Each is then altered as necessary. On some figures, the original pattern may fit one side of the body correctly, while the other side requires a change. It is also possible that the original pattern will fit neither side correctly. For this figure each half of the pattern must be altered according to need. This results in different pattern outlines for each side of the body for the bodice, skirt, or sleeve units. The two halves of the patterns must be identical in length at center front and center back. The center pattern lines remain as straight lines. The changes are tapered into each other at or near the center back and center front (see **Figure 9-25**).

When altering only one side of a pattern, taper the increase or decrease in size back to the original at the center back or center front so it may be joined properly with the unaltered side.

When you alter both sides of a pattern, the increase or decrease on each side must be tapered to create the same measurement at the center front or center back to join the pattern at the appropriate angle.

Specific alteration procedures are not presented for all possible asymmetrical figure variations. Essentially the procedures are accomplished in the same manner as alterations for the symmetrical figure but are confined to the appropriate half of the pattern.

To create a feeling of levelness and balance, the dart tips on both sides of a front or back pattern are kept the same height from the floor (see **Figure 9-26**).

Maintain the same distance from the center front or center back to corresponding dart tips and dart base seamlines (see **Figure 9-27**). (A significant difference in the size of one breast or shoulder blade would be an exception to this advice.)

Be aware of related alterations. For example, waistline height added to the skirt side seam to accommodate a high hip may require a reduction in the length of the bodice side seam.

Even though more time and effort is involved in altering for the asymmetrical figure, the results are worthwhile. When alterations are accomplished correctly, differences between the right and left sides of the figure are less easily detected, or at least minimized, depending on the degree of variation. The wearer's comfort is certain to improve. Major variations require increased care in the selection of flattering styles so that, in combination with the pattern alteration, the camouflaging effects may be utilized to the greatest degree. An illusion of symmetry is generally the goal.

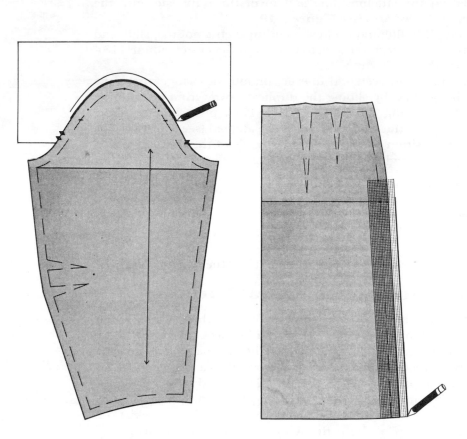

Figure 9-20 Slide and trace for an even amount of change (short arm joint and wide hips).

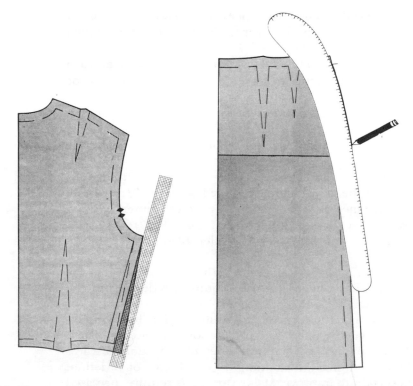

Figure 9-21 Pivot and trace for uneven amount of change (narrow waist and wide hips).

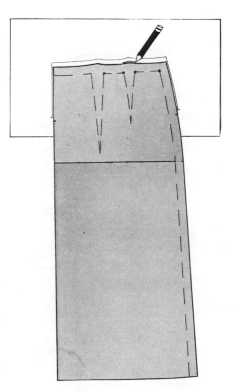

Figure 9-22 Level the pattern across the dart base to maintain equal dartline length (sway back).

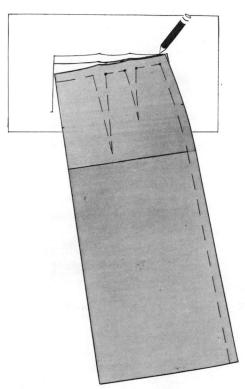

Figure 9-23 Pivot and trace to complete the uneven amount of change (sway back).

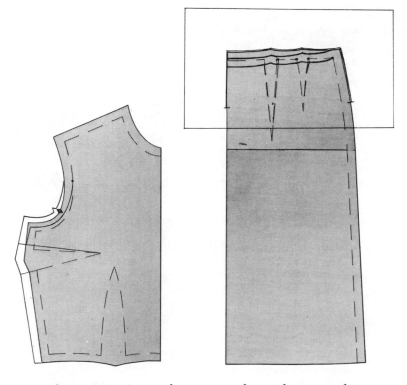

Figure 9-24 Secure changes, true dart and pattern edges.

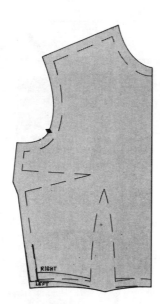

Figure 9-25 Blend asymmetric alterations to nothing at pattern center.

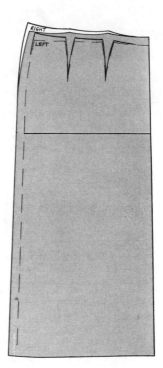

Figure 9-26 Waist dart tips remain the same height from the floor on asymmetric alterations.

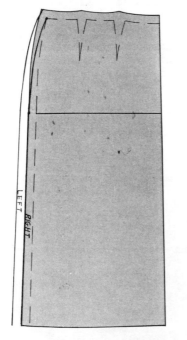

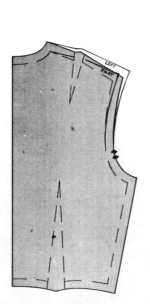

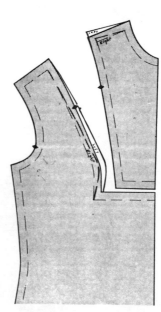

Figure 9-27 Dart tips and base seamlines are equal distances from center on asymmetric alterations.

CHAPTER 10

PERSONALIZED PATTERNS & SLOPERS

Once the fitting adjustments have been completed in the trial garment and general alteration procedures are understood, it is relatively easy to convert the fitting adjustments into pattern alterations. This procedure *personalizes* the basic pattern.

Figure 10-1 illustrates the before and after appearance of a straight skirt style modeled by a person whose figure has three symmetrical variations. The lower torso area differs from the standard in hip circumference, center back length from waist to hip, and length of the leg. Evaluate the appearance of the unadjusted skirt. The fitting grainlines are level and plumb. The skirt balance is correct. The skirt, however, lacks adequate ease at the hipline and horizontal wrinkles have formed around the body. The swayed posture is causing a loose horizontal fold in the fabric across the "small" of the back below the waist. The skirt length is too long in proportion to the leg length and creates an appearance that may be seen as dowdy.

In the adjusted skirt, increased width has been added at the hip to restore ease. The center back length was decreased above the hipline to smooth the fabric against the body. The skirt was shortened to create better proportions between the figure and the garment.

Using the skirt adjustments illustrated in **Figure 10-1** as an example, practice converting the adjustments to pattern alterations. (Use half-scale patterns if they are available.) The alteration procedures that follow are intended to be a review and an application of the alteration methods presented in **Chapter 9**. Separate procedures are explained and illustrated for each pattern alteration method.

As a beginning step, analyze each one of the fitting adjustments both independently and in relation to adjacent changes, then answer the following questions.

- Is the adjustment an increase or a decrease in size?
- Is the amount of adjustment even, uneven, or a combination of the two?
- What are the total amounts of change for each adjustment?
- Are the adjustments identical or different for each side of the body?
- Does the adjustment affect one or more garment sections?
- Which of the adjustments will be the simplest to accomplish first?
- Which alteration method will be the simplest and easiest to use to accomplish the adjustment?

Simplicity, efficiency and neatness usually result if the alterations in each pattern piece are made in the following order.

Length adjustments
- Even amounts of change.
- Uneven amounts of change.
- Combined even and uneven amount of change.

Width adjustments
- Even amounts of change.
- Uneven amounts of change.
- Combined even and uneven amount of change.

Use the following guides for completing the pattern alterations. Refer to figure variations 23, 8, and 12, respectively, located in **Part Two** of this text.

1. EVEN LENGTH CHANGES:
Hemline Adjustment (back and front patterns)

Note whether the pattern has a marked hemline. Measure and mark the finished length desired for the skirt. Determine the appropriate hem width for the garment style and the fashion fabric. This amount is an addition to the finished length.

Slash Method (see Figure 10-2): Determine the necessary length change to establish the alteration lines, draw a crosswise slash line below the hipline.

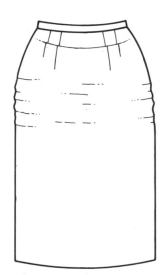
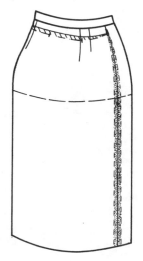

Figure 10-1 Skirt illustrating poor fit and the adjustments for proper fit.

Draw a second line parallel to the slash line. The distance between the two lines will be equal to the amount of change needed. Cut along the slash line then slide the cut edge of the pattern to meet the second line. Keep center back and center front line straight. Secure the lapped edges. True the side seam on the lower portion of the pattern by extending the pattern edge of the upper portion in a straight line to the hem edge. Repeat for the other pattern piece.

Seam Method (see Figure 10-3): If a hem allowance has not been drawn on the pattern, mark the hemline parallel to the cut edge. Determine the necessary length change. In the skirt area above the marked hemline, draw an alteration line parallel to the hemline leaving a space equal to the amount of change needed. Free the hem allowance by cutting in the skirt area just above the marked hemline. Lap the hem area over the skirt area until the hemline and alteration line meet. Keep the center back or center front straight. Secure the lapped edges. True the side seam across the hem by extending the pattern edge in a straight line to the hem edge. Repeat for the other pattern piece.

Pivot Method (see Figure 10-4): Mark the finished skirt length on the pattern. Mark the new hem allowance width below this mark. Draw the new hem cutting line parallel to the original edge of the hem. Cut along the new hem edge. Cross out any original hem markings. Repeat for the other pattern piece.

2. COMBINED EVEN & UNEVEN LENGTH CHANGES: Waistline Contour (back pattern only)

Slash Method (see Figure 10-2): Establish the pivot points. Mark the points on the waist stitching line where the adjustment changes from even to uneven amounts. Mark another at the termination point of the uneven change.

Establish the alteration lines. Below the waistline, draw a crosswise slash line from the center back toward the side seam until in line with the first pivot point. Angle the line from this point up to the termination point. Draw a slash line through the center of the dart near the side seam. Draw a lengthwise slash line from the horizontal line up to the waist seamline at each pivot point.

Place the waistline area over alteration paper. Slash along the alteration lines; cut along the crosswise line from the center back to the termination point. Cut through the center of the dart near the side seam. Cut along each

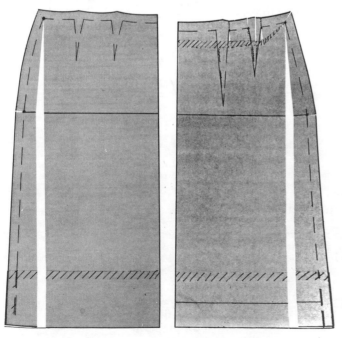

Figure 10-2 Completed patterns altered by slash method.

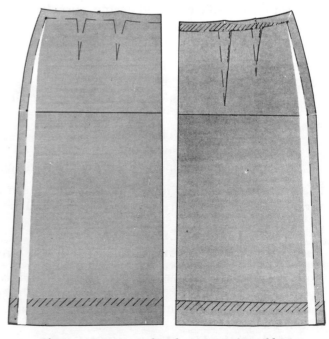

Figure 10-3 Completed patterns altered by seam method.

vertical line up to the pivot points. At each pivot point, clip across the seam allowance from the cutting line to the stitching line. Leave a tiny, uncut area at the stitching line so that hinges form on the seamline.

Secure the unaffected portion of the pattern to the alteration paper. Adjust the position of the slashed pattern; across the center back area, lap the slashed edges to decrease the length evenly as needed. Keep the center back line straight. At the pivot point nearest the center back, begin tapering and decrease as needed to the second dart. Level the area across the dart base. Taper to nothing at the termination point. The adjusted dart width maintains the waistline circumference. Keep all corresponding dartlines equal in length. Secure the cut edges to the alteration paper.

Seam Method (see Figure 10-3): Establish the pivot points. Mark the point on the waist stitching line where the adjustment changes from even to uneven amounts. Mark another at the termination point of the uneven change. Place alteration paper under the waistline area.

Free the affected seam allowance; cut near the stitching line just inside the garment area. At each pivot point, clip across the seam allowance from the cutting edge to the stitching line. Leave a tiny, uncut area at the stitching line so that hinges form on the seamline. Cut through the center of the dart near the side seam.

Secure the pattern area to the alteration paper. Adjust the position of the freed seam allowance: across the center back area, lap the seam allowance over the skirt area to decrease the length evenly as needed. Keep the center back line straight. At the pivot point nearest the center back, begin tapering and decrease the change as needed to the second dart. Level the area across the dart base. Taper to nothing at the termination point. The adjusted dart widths maintain the waist circumference. Keep all corresponding dartlines equal in length. Attach the cut edges to the alteration paper.

Pivot Method (see Figure 10-4): Establish the pivot points. Mark the points on the waistline where the adjustment changes from even to uneven amounts. Mark another at the termination point of the uneven change.

Establish the new cutting edge of the pattern. Use a duplicate of the original contour of the waistline. Match the duplicate to the original pattern edge. Mark the pivot points on the duplicate. Across the center back area, slide the duplicate into the pattern area to decrease the length evenly as needed.

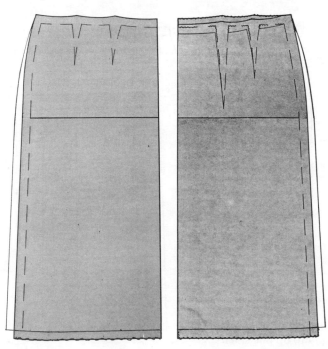

Figure 10-4 Completed patterns altered by pivot method.

Trace along the duplicate edge for a distance equal to the even adjustment. Mark any dart ends in the traced area. At the pivot point nearest the center back, pivot the duplicate up until the duplicate touches the original waistline at the side seam. Trace the waistline between the two darts and mark the end of the first dartline. Match the duplicate to the remaining original seam. From the termination point, pivot the pattern down until the unmarked dart end is level with the marked dart end. Trace the waistline and the dart end. The dart width adjustment maintains the original waist circumference. True the dart base. All corresponding dartlines should be equal in length. If a tracing was used for the adjustment match the cutting lines of the original and the tracing. Secure the tracing to the pattern.

3. COMBINED EVEN & UNEVEN WIDTH CHANGES: Hipline Circumference (back and front patterns)

Slash Method (see Figure 10-2): Establish the pivot points. Mark the point on the side seamline where the adjustment changes from an even to an uneven amount. Mark another at the termination point of the uneven change.

Establish the alteration lines. Draw a lengthwise slash line from the termination point to the hem edge. Draw a crosswise slash line between the lengthwise line and the pivot point at the hip area. Place the side area of the pattern over alteration paper.

Slash along the alteration lines. Cut along the vertical slash line from the hem edge to the termination point. Cut along the crosswise line over to the pivot point. At each pivot point, clip across the seam allowance from the cutting line to the stitching line. Leave a tiny, uncut area at the stitching line so that hinges form on the seamline.

Secure the unaffected portion of the pattern to the alteration paper. Adjust the position of the cut areas of the pattern; below the hipline, spread the slashed edges to increase the width evenly as needed. At the hipline pivot point, begin tapering and decrease to nothing at the termination point. Attach the cut edges to the alteration paper. The side section will rise slightly at the hem. True the distorted corner at the hem by continuing the hem edge and the side seam cutting lines until they intersect. Repeat for the other pattern piece.

Seam Method (see Figure 10-3): Establish the pivot points. Mark the point on the side seamline where the adjustment changes from an even to an

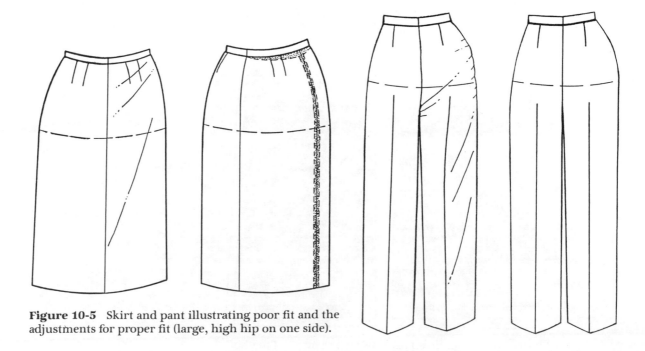

Figure 10-5 Skirt and pant illustrating poor fit and the adjustments for proper fit (large, high hip on one side).

uneven amount. Mark another at the termination point of the uneven change. Place the side area of the pattern area over alteration paper.

Free the affected seam allowance. Cut near the stitching line just inside the garment area. At each pivot point, clip across the seam allowance from the cutting edge to the stitching line. Leave a tiny, uncut area at the stitching line so that hinges form on the seamline.

Secure the pattern area to the alteration paper. Adjust the position of the seam allowance. Below the hipline, move the seam allowance beyond the pattern area to increase the width evenly as needed. At the hipline pivot point, begin tapering and decrease to nothing at the termination point. Attach the cut edges to the alteration paper. The seam allowance will rise slightly at the hem. True the distorted corner at the hem by continuing the hem edge and the side seam cutting lines until they intersect. Repeat for the other pattern piece.

Pivot Method (see Figure 10-4): Establish the pivot points. Mark the point on the side seamline where the adjustment changes from an even to an uneven amount. Mark another at the termination point of the uneven change.

If the pattern edge has been trimmed, attach alteration paper to the side of the pattern.

Establish the new cutting edge of the pattern. Use a duplicate of the original contour of the side seam. Match the duplicate to the original pattern edge. Mark the pivot points on the duplicate. Adjust the new cutting edge of the pattern. Below the hipline, slide the duplicate beyond the pattern area to increase the width evenly as needed. Trace along the duplicate edge from the hem edge until even with the pivot point. At the hipline pivot point, pivot the duplicate until it meets the original and is even with the termination point. Complete the tracing. True the distorted corner at the hem by continuing the hem and side seam cutting lines until they intersect. Repeat for the other pattern piece.

Figures 10-2, 10-3 and **10-4** illustrate the appearance of the altered patterns. Regardless of the methods used, the owner of the skirt pattern is assured that fashion skirts will fit properly if made from this pattern or from one compared and correlated to it. Sewing time is reduced. The fabric will remain new and fresh during construction because of less handling. Poise and self-confidence increase and a feeling of well-being is the end result.

Figure 10-5 illustrates the before and after appearance of a straight skirt and pants modeled by a person whose lower torso area is asymmetric. It differs from standard in the height of the left and right hip and in the amount of fullness in the upper hip area.

Evaluate the appearance of the unadjusted skirt. The fitting grainlines are neither level nor plumb. The skirt is out of balance and the hem is not level. On this first evaluation, the ease at the hipline may appear to be adequate but the skirt is binding against the full, high hip.

When the skirt is adjusted for the fuller hip, the front and back waistline and the entire side seam on the left-hand side is released to permit the crosswise fitting grain and hem to become level. In turn, this permits the center lines to become plumb. The ease is restored across the fuller hip area. This adjustment causes excess ease to appear in the fabric over the flatter hip; the excess is then removed by taking in the side seam.

Figure 10-6 illustrates the patterns altered by a combination of methods. Since commercial patterns are printed to represent the right-hand side of the body, the original pattern area is altered to correspond to the right-hand fitting adjustments. The pivot method is used for the alterations necessary for the left-hand side.

When a pattern for an asymmetrical figure is cut from fabric, time is saved and frustration is prevented by cutting duplicate garment pieces to correspond to the *larger* side of the body. After cutting, mark and trim the garment pieces for the smaller side according to the corresponding pattern.

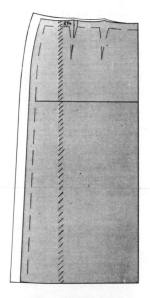

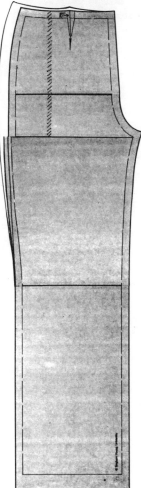

Figure 10-6 Completed patterns altered by slash and pivot method.

Checking the Finished Patterns for Accuracy

Basic patterns or slopers are only as effective as their internal accuracy permits. Inaccuracy in either one will be duplicated in each altered or self-designed fashion pattern. To prevent mistakes, check the following:

- Center back, center front and side seamlines should meet hemlines at right angles (see **Figure 10-7**).
- Necklines and waistlines should meet center lines at right angles (see **Figure 10-7**).
- The entire center back and center front edges should be straight (see **Figures 10-7, 10-8** and **10-9**).
- The skirt side edges below the fullest body bulge should be straight (see **Figures 10-7** and **10-9**).
- Corresponding dartlines and seamlines should be the same length (see **Figures 10-7** and **10-8**).
- Corresponding waistline areas of bodices and skirts or pants should be identical (see **Figure 10-8**).
- All curved edges should be smooth and free from bumps or indentations (see **Figures 10-9** through **10-12**).
- The degree of flare on the skirt side seams below the fullest body bulge should be identical on back and front (see **Figure 10-9**).
- The curved portions of the front and back crotch seamlines should form a continuously smooth line where they intersect at the inseam (see **Figure 10-10**).
- Waistlines should form a continuously smooth line where they meet at the side seam line (see **Figure 10-11**).
- Necklines should form a continuously smooth line where they meet at the shoulder (see **Figure 10-12**).
- Armscye seamlines should form a continuously smooth line where they meet at the underarm and at the shoulder (see **Figure 10-13**).
- Waistlines of front and back skirt or pant pieces should be approximately ¼ inch (6 mm) larger than the corresponding waistband areas (see **Figure 10-14**).
- The spaces between the sleeve underarm seamlines and the notches should be ⅛ inch to ⅜ inch (3 mm to 9 mm) larger than corresponding areas on the bodice armscye (see **Figure 10-15**).
- Back and front sleeve cap seamlines should each be ¾ inch to 1 inch (1.2 cm to 2.5 cm) larger than the corresponding areas on the bodice (see **Figure 10-15**).

Personalized basic patterns and slopers provide a record of an individual's measurements, size, and shape with a minimum of ease included (see **Figures 10-16** and **10-17**). Use them to compare the fit of fashion patterns, make alterations and design new patterns. They are invaluable tools for individuals:

- who have a creative interest in clothing design.
- who desire or require simple design changes in commercial patterns.
- who design and alter simultaneously during the process of patternmaking or cutting from fabric.
- who sew for anyone with significant figure variations, including themselves.
- who live alone and have little or no access to help for fitting.

Preserving a Personalized Pattern

Press basic pattern pieces flat. Use a warm, dry iron. Excess heat shrinks backing material containing polyester, and steam shrinks paper. Avoid using tape in the alteration process, it shrinks if touched with the iron.

Checking the finished pattern for accuracy.

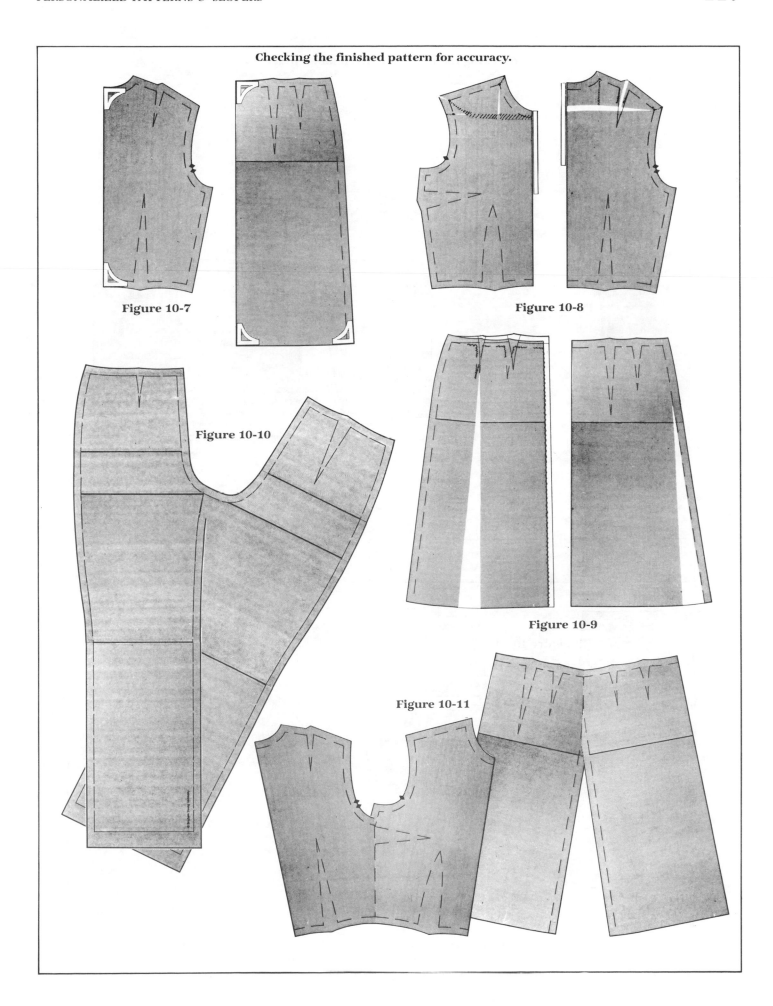

Figure 10-7

Figure 10-8

Figure 10-10

Figure 10-9

Figure 10-11

Checking the finished pattern for accuracy.

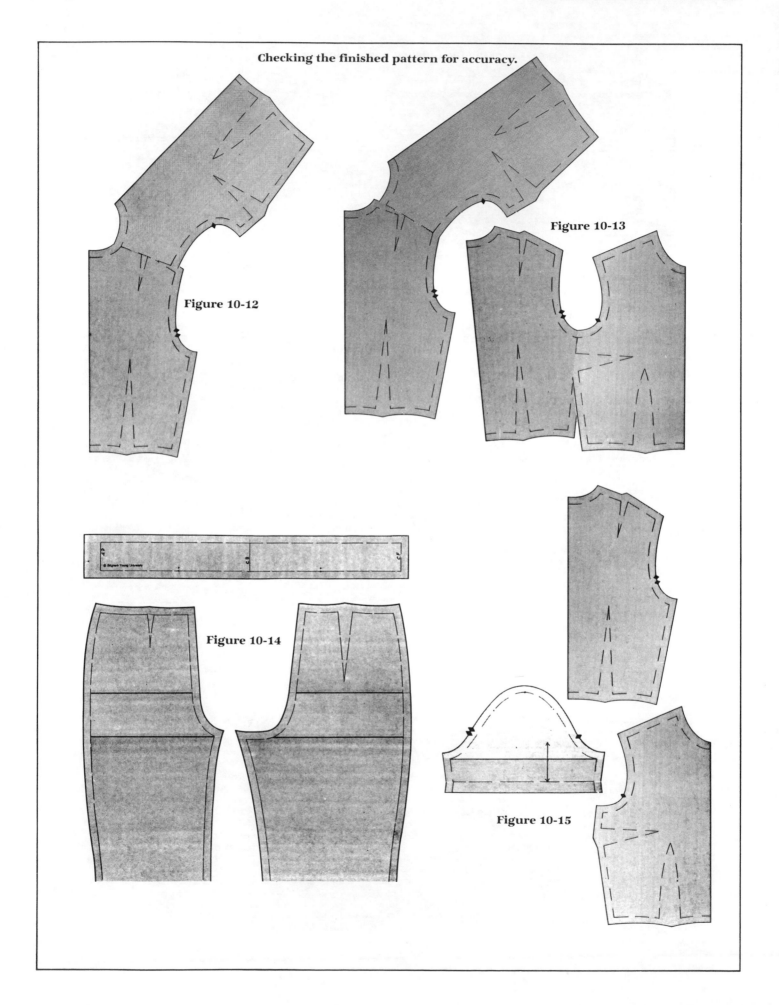

Figure 10-12

Figure 10-13

Figure 10-14

Figure 10-15

If the pattern has not previously been reinforced, do so now. You may wish to consider a fusible material or plastic lamination, depending on storage space. At this point, your personalized basic pattern is ready to use in checking the potential fit of fashion patterns and for simple design projects.

For more extensive design work, a *sloper* is needed. A sloper (master or block) is a basic pattern with seam allowances, hem allowances, and dart interiors removed. The cut edges of the sloper are equivalent to stitching, fold, or hem lines. A personalized sloper can be purchased only through a personalized fitting service. It can be made from a *personalized basic pattern* very easily.

If the *basic pattern is to be an integral part of the sloper*, it can be double-laminated or adhered to a suitable material. Consider the following materials: tagboard or lightweight cardboard, heavyweight nonwoven fabric, wallpaper lining, window shade backing, heavyweight wrapping paper, craft paper, smooth grocery bags, and plastic-coated freezer paper with two layers fused together.

The material chosen should not damage working surfaces or fabric. It should remain wrinkle-free and be able to retain the shape of the edges. Use sheets large enough to cut bodices in one piece; skirts, sleeves, and pants in no more than two or three pieces. When large pattern pieces are divided, leave a $1/16$ inch (2 mm) space between the separated sections. Adhere a pliable, strong tape along the joint on *both* sides of the material. This permits folding without tearing or loosening the tape. A material that can be rolled is useful only if the sloper will also unroll and lie flat for use.

Once the pattern is laminated or adhered to a material, trim away seam and hem allowances, and cut out dart interiors with straight, not curved lines. (Curved lines cannot be folded during the design process.) Darts may be stitched as curved lines later, during construction.

If the *basic pattern is to be kept as a pattern separate from the sloper*, anchor it temporarily to the sloper material. *Trace* stitching, fold, hem, and dart lines. Use curved and straight rulers to aid accuracy.

To mark each notch on the sloper, draw a line through the center at right angles to the pattern edge and extend it across the stitching line. Repeat for the top-of-sleeve mark and any other marks used for matching garment sections. Draw all darts using straight lines. Check sloper tracings for accuracy and true any crooked lines. Make short, very narrow slits at each notch location on the stitching lines, if desired.

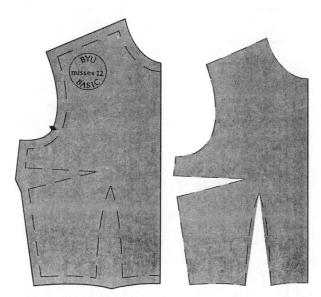

Figure 10-16 A standard basic pattern and a standard basic sloper represent an average figure.

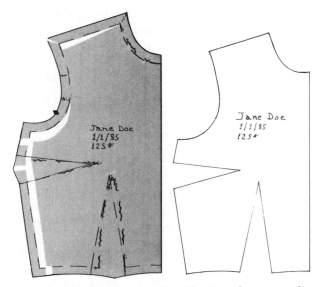

Figure 10-17 A personalized basic and a personalized sloper have been altered to fit the figure of a specific individual.

If *separated sections of the adjusted fitting garment are to be used as the shaping basis for the slopers,* use a pencil to mark seam and dart stitching lines, ·center front, center back, and hemlines of each garment section. (The hemline may be left stitched in place if desired. The folded edge is the finished hemline.)

Cut the sections apart exactly on all marked lines, or carefully remove the basting stitches. Do not pull or stretch the fabric. Press the separated sections on the lengthwise grain. Again, do not pull or stretch the fabric off grain. Anchor the pressed fabric section, right side up, to the material used to create the sloper. Complete the slopers as instructed above.

Using separated sections of a fitting garment to produce slopers is relatively fast since you progress directly from the fitting of the basic trial garment to making the sloper. Little knowledge of pattern alteration is necessary. However, accuracy in size and shape is difficult to maintain. Fabric is pliable and cut garment sections are easily distorted. In addition, the altered fitting garment is no longer available to put on and adjust if and when figure changes occur.

Label each completed sloper section. Record the location and amount of each alteration on the appropriate sloper. (See pattern adjustment record at the end of **Part Two.**) (This information is particularly helpful when altering a fashion pattern that is identical in brand, size, and figure type.)

Store slopers appropriately, according to the sloper material used.

As wear and tear appear on the edges of a sloper, make a new working copy. (Keep the original basic pattern for reference.) As figure changes occur, adjust the fitting garment, basic pattern, and sloper to reflect the changes.

Using a Basic Pattern or Sloper to Compare Fit & Determine Alterations

If the *fashion pattern is the same brand,* size, and figure type as your basic pattern, make the same adjustments in size and location. This retains the fashion fullness and design lines the designer intended. Analyze design lines and edges, such as the armscye and neckline. If they are different from the basic pattern for reasons other than style, alteration may be needed in these areas. For example a lowered neckline eliminates the need to alter for a low neck base at center or for full collarbones. A widened neckline may eliminate alteration for a high or low neck base. The fashion neckline depth may require raising or lowering for personal preference.

If the armscye depth has been lowered, check the sleeve capline and bodice bustline width for enough design ease for a loose fit. If the shoulder tip width appears too narrow or too wide, check the fashion description for puffed sleeves or an extended shoulderline. The shoulder tip will be higher to accommodate the thickness of shoulder pads—check the notion list on the pattern envelope.

If the *fashion pattern differs* from your basic pattern in brand, size, or figure type, compare the two and alter the fashion pattern to conform to the measurements of the basic pattern or sloper at specific body locations. Analyze the design to determine how much fashion fullness the designer used and where it was placed. Analyze design lines and edges, such as the neckline or armscye. If they vary from the basic, alterations may be necessary in those areas as described above.

To compare the fit of the two patterns, lay the fashion pattern over the basic or sloper. Match the bodices at center front, center back, and at the natural waistline. Match the skirts at the center front, center back, and at the natural waistline. Match the sleeve cutting lines at the underarm extension and at the vertical centers of the sleeve.

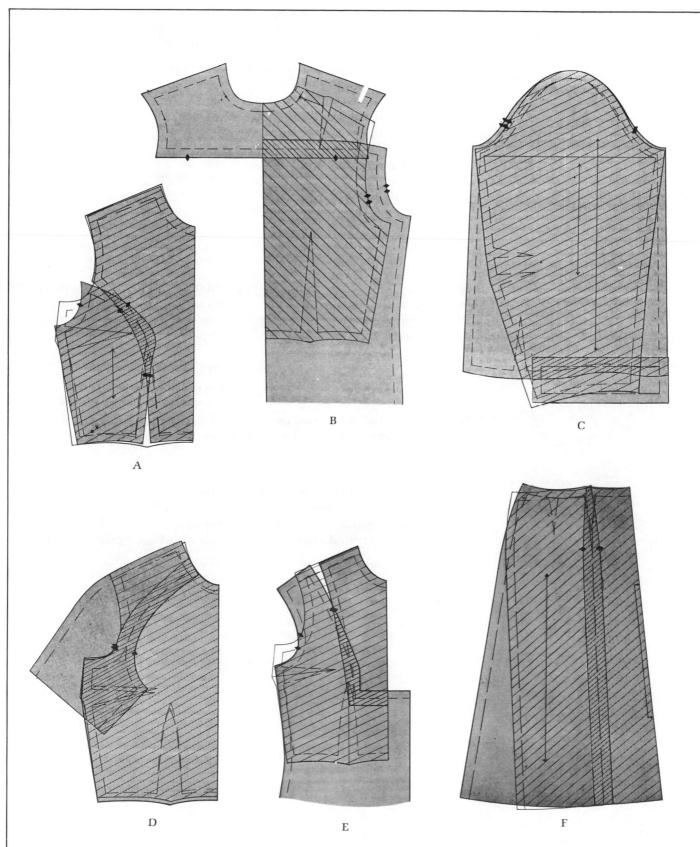

Figure 10-18 Fashion patterns compared to the personalized basic or sloper.

Basic pattern only (clear).   Fashion pattern only (gray).   Fashion and basic pattern overlap (wide lines).

Fashion pattern overlap (narrow lines).

The outside edges of the two patterns may not coincide. However, the following specific areas of the fashion pattern must be at least as large as the basic or the fashion garment will not be large enough:

- Width from center back or center front to shoulder tip
- Shoulder slope
- Chest and blade width
- Length and width at bust level
- Armhole depth and width
- Back and front waist lengths
- Waist circumferer.ce
- Hip circumference
- Crotch depth and length
- Thigh circumference
- Skirt and pant length
- Elbow dart position
- Long sleeves length

When a single basic pattern piece is compared to a fashion pattern with two or more pieces in the same area, match the corresponding stitching lines at the bustline, hipline, and sleeve capline and check circumference. Manipulate pattern pieces to match other for further comparison. See **Figure 10-18.**

Using a Basic Pattern or Sloper to Design New Patterns

A basic pattern or sloper can be used as a tracing template to create new patterns according to personal taste and need. Design features that can be incorporated include:

Dart changes:
- Move darts from one seamline to another.
- Release dart for a loose fit.
- Change darted area into gathers, unpressed tucks, or pleats.
- Convert darts to design seamlines, such as yokes or princess seamline.

Added Fullness
- Add flare at lower edges.
- Add extra fullness for gathers, unpressed or pressed pleats or for tucks.

Finishing Details
- Design facings, collars, yokes, pockets, and belts.

To pretest a design, make a small-scale pattern and construct a small-scale garment. If available, critique the finished garment on a small-scale mannequin. A disappointing design in small scale is more easily corrected or forgotten than a full-scale version. A successful design viewed in small scale may provide the motivation to produce a full-scale version.

part two

illustrated alteration guide

hip area

1 Long Lower Torso

2 Short Lower Torso

3 Large Waist

4 Small Waist

5 Prominent Hip Bones

6 Prominent Abdomen

7 Flat Abdomen

8 Sway Back

9 Pelvis Tilts toward Back

10 Prominent Upper Hip Curve

11 Sloping Upper Hip Curve

12 Broad Hips

13 Narrow Hips

14 Cylindrical-shaped Torso (hip area)

15 Flattened Oval-shaped Torso (hip area)

16 High Buttocks Contour

17 Drooped Buttocks

18 Large Buttocks

19 Flat Buttocks

20 Prominent Pubic Area

21 Recessed Pubic Area

BASIC FITTING THEORY

Figure Analysis
The pelvic cradle is longer than average. The distance increases between the waist and the fullest part of the buttocks. The bone structure has no effect on the position of the abdomen curvature.

Fitting Analysis
The fabric is loose above the hipline along the side seams and below the back dart tips because the fabric shaping is above the corresponding body contour. On a skirt, the hip fitting line remains level. On pants, it bows downward across the body centers because the fabric binds against the crotch. The pant fabric either pulls into the crotch crevice or forms into diagonal wrinkles from the crotch to the hip bones and the buttocks. The hem position may be too high.

Fabric Requirements for Proper Fit
The longer torso area requires more fabric length from the waist to the buttocks and longer *back* darts. The shaping of the longer garment area aligns with the body curvature. On pants, this relieves the strain at the crotch and the hip fitting line becomes level.

GARMENT & PATTERN ALTERATIONS FOR SYMMETRICAL FIGURES

Change Required
Increase the length above the hipline *or* lower the curvature on the side seamlines.

Slash Method—fitting garment only
Slash around the entire garment below the front dart tips. Cut parallel to the waistline. Insert a strip of fabric. To increase length, spread the cut edges evenly until the shape of the garment aligns with the curvature of the body. Adjust the hemline position as needed to create good proportion between the garment and the wearer.

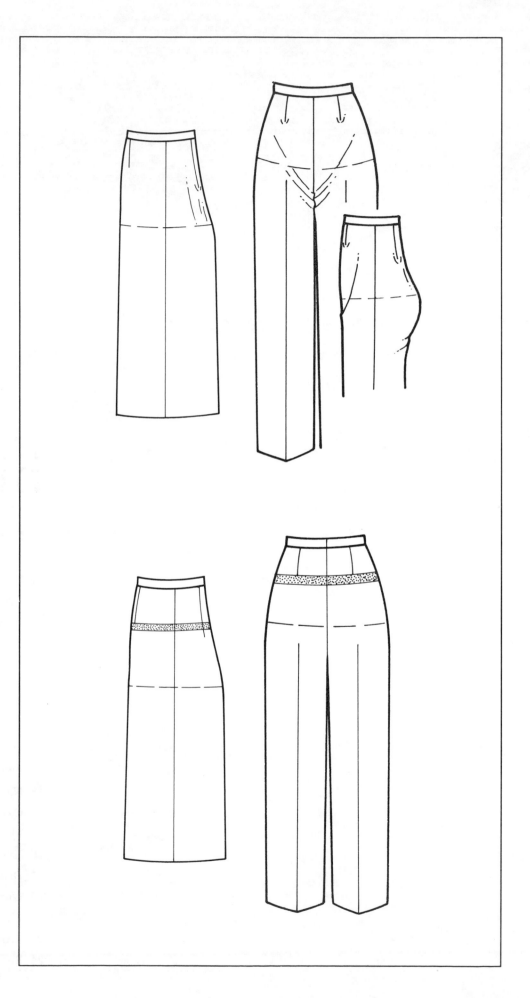

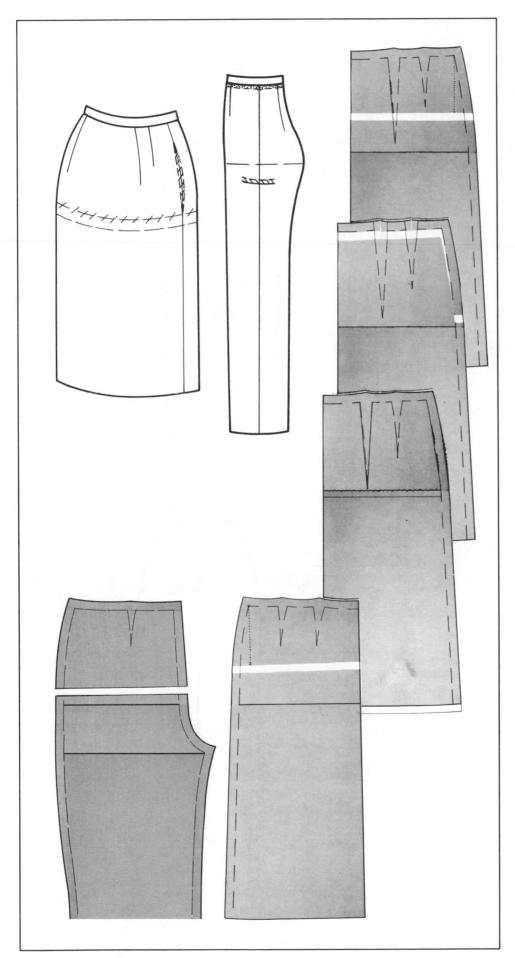

Pivot Method

To reposition the side seam curve, release the side seams from the waistline to the hipline. Take in the garment areas equally on the back and front to remove the excess fabric above the hipline. Blend into the original seamline toward the waist and the hipline. Mark the dart tip positions for longer back darts. For a fitting garment, mark the new hipline.

On pants, increase the crotch depth by lowering the crotch seamline: Form a new stitching line *below* the original. Across the inseams, mark parallel to the existing seamline. Blend into the original stitching near the hipline on the back and the front. Trim the excess from the widened seam allowance area.

Adjust the hemline position on both skirts and pants as needed to create good proportion between the garment and the wearer.

BASIC FITTING THEORY

Figure Analysis

The pelvic cradle is shorter than average. The distance decreases between the waist and the fullest part of the buttocks. The bone structure has no effect on the position of the abdomen curvature.

Fitting Analysis

The fabric is snug at the hipline along the side seams and across the back darts because the body contour is above the corresponding fabric shaping. The buttocks may lift the fabric into a horizontal fold across the back darts. This causes the hip fitting line to rise across the center back and the side seams to slant toward the back at the hem. On pants the crotch seam is below the body level. This inhibits walking comfortably and causes strain on the stitching of the crotch seam.

Fabric Requirements for Proper Fit

The shorter torso area requires less fabric length from the waist to the buttocks and shorter *back* darts. The shaping of the shorter garment area aligns with the body curvature and the hip fitting line becomes level. On pants, the crotch seam is nearer the body surface. The wearer can move their legs more freely.

GARMENT & PATTERN ALTERATONS FOR SYMMETRICAL FIGURES

Change Required

Shorten evenly *above* the hipline or raise the curvature on the side seamlines.

Slash Method—fitting garment only

To reduce length, form a parallel tuck around the entire garment below the front dart tips. Adjust the tuck width evenly until the shape of the garment aligns with the curvature of the body. Adjust the hemline position as needed to create a good proportion between the garment and the wearer.

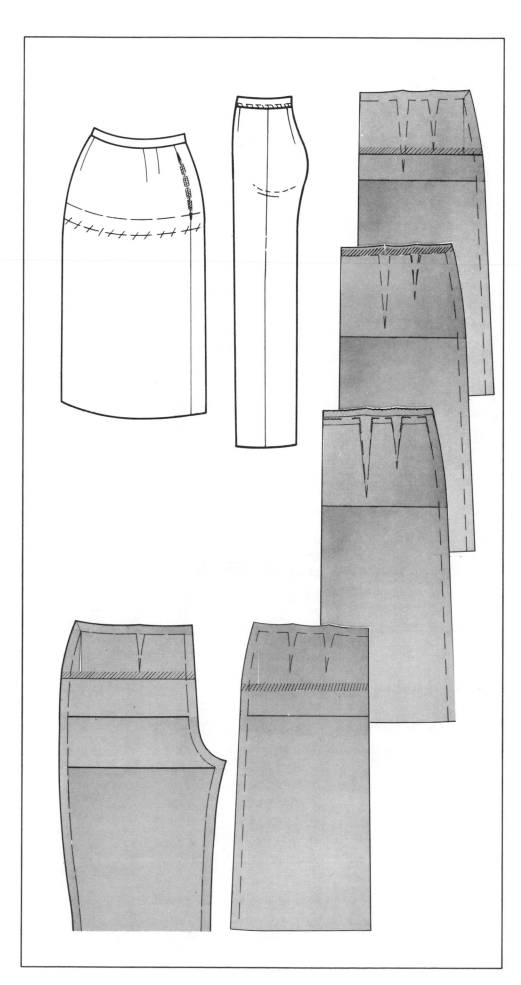

Pivot Method

On pants, release the entire waistline seam. To decrease the crotch depth, lift the garment evenly until the shape of the garment aligns with the curvature of the body. Clip the widened waistline seam allowance at 2 inch (5 cm) intervals to release the strain and mark the new waistline. To restore the waist circumference, widen the darts and take in the side seams as needed on the front and back. Trim the widened seam allowances. Adjust the hemline position to create good proportion between the garment and wearer.

On a skirt, realign the hipline curve by releasing both side seams from the hipline to the waistline. Let out the seam allowances equally on the back and front to release the tightness and restore the proper ease. Blend into the original stitching near the waist- and the hiplines. Shorten the darts as needed. On a fitting garment, mark the new hip fitting line.

BASIC FITTING THEORY

Figure Analysis
The waist indents less than average because of greater amounts of body tissue, flaccid muscles or slumped posture.

Fitting Analysis
Forcing the garment to close constricts the body at the waist and compresses the soft tissues. This compression causes body tissues to expand below and above the waist. The force lifts the fabric into a horizontal fold around the waistline. The hip fitting line remains level. The hem position rises.

On pants, the fold is smaller or may not form because the fabric binds against the crotch. This strain causes the fabric to pull into diagonal wrinkles from the crotch toward the hip bones. The hip fitting line pulls downward at the body centers. The taut fabric at the crotch causes discomfort.

Fabric Requirements for Proper Fit
The larger waist circumference requires more fabric width at the waistline. The wider garment area relaxes and lowers to the correct position over the body contour. This figure variation also affects the bodice waistline (see **Upper Torso, 70 Large Waist**).

GARMENT & PATTERN ALTERATIONS FOR SYMMETRICAL FIGURES

Change Required
Widen the waistline area at the side seams.

Slash Method—fitting garment only
Mark each side seam at the place above the hipline where the tightness begins. Release the waist seam across each side seam area. On both the back and front, cut through the waistline seam allowance near each side seam. Continue cutting diagonally to the corresponding adjustment mark on each side seam. Do not cut through the side seam allowances. Insert fabric strips. To gain the needed width, spread each set of cut edges equally at the waistline until the garment fastens comfortably and smoothly and the ease is incorporated. Taper to nothing at the side seams. Let out the waistband or bodice side seam

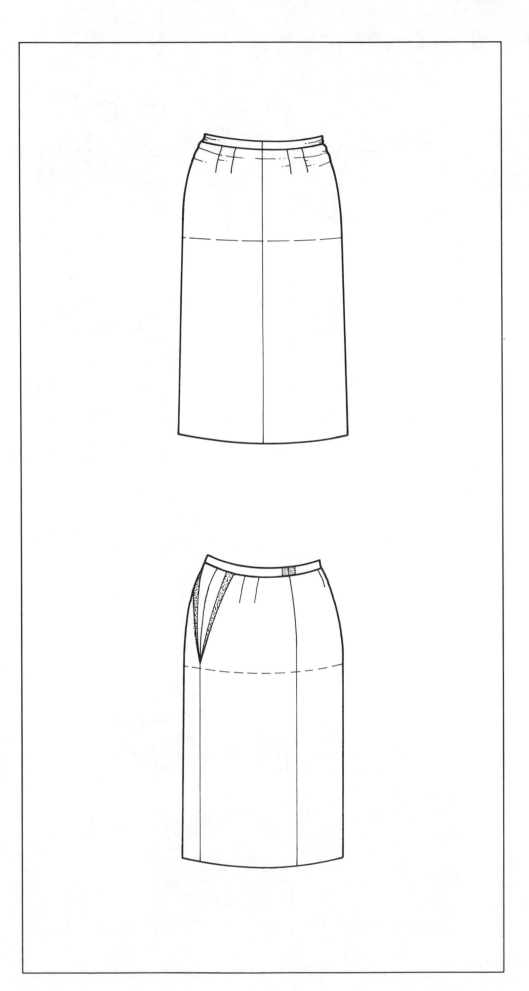

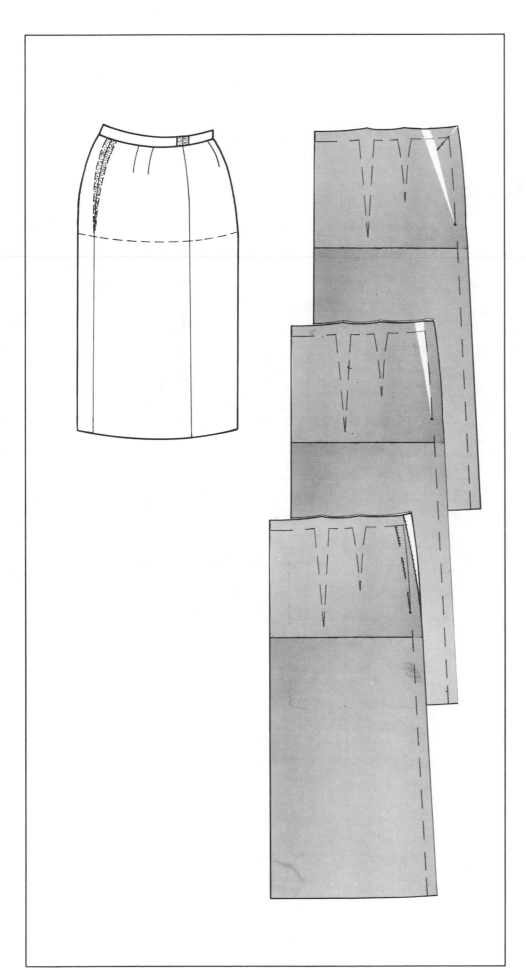

allowance equal to the change in
the skirt or pants. See **70 Large
Waist**.

Pivot Method
Release the waistline seam across
each side seam area. Release the
side seams from the waistline to the
place near the hipline where the
tightness begins. To increase width,
let out each seam allowance equally
at the waist so that the garment
fastens comfortably and sufficient
ease is incorporated. Blend into the
original stitching near the hipline.
Let out the waistband or bodice
side seam allowances equal to the
change in the garment. See
70 Large Waist.

BASIC FITTING THEORY

Figure Analysis
The waist indents more than average because of smaller deposits of body tissue, taut muscles or overly erect posture.

Fitting Analysis
The edges of the garment opening lap beyond the closure line. When fastened on the closure line, the waist, hip and hem lines of the garment drop below the corresponding positions of the body. As a result, the fabric near the side seams is loose. The hip fitting line remains level.

On pants, the crotch seam is below the body surface. This inhibits walking comfortably and causes strain on the crotch seam. The hemline position lowers.

Fabric Requirement for Proper Fit
The smaller waist circumference requires less fabric width at the waistline. The narrower garment area aligns with the waist and lifts the fabric shaping to the correct position over the body contour. This variation also affects the bodice waistline (see **71 Small Waist**).

GARMENT & PATTERN ALTERATIONS FOR SYMMETRICAL FIGURES

Change Required
Narrow the waistline area at the side seams.

Slash Method—fitting garment only
Release the waistline seam across each side seam area. Near each side seam, on the back and front, form a tuck through the waistline to remove the excess fabric equally. Retain enough ease for the fabric to relax. Taper each tuck to nothing along the side seam where the looseness ends. Take in the waistband or bodice at the side seams equal to the change in the skirt or pants. See **71 Small Waist**.

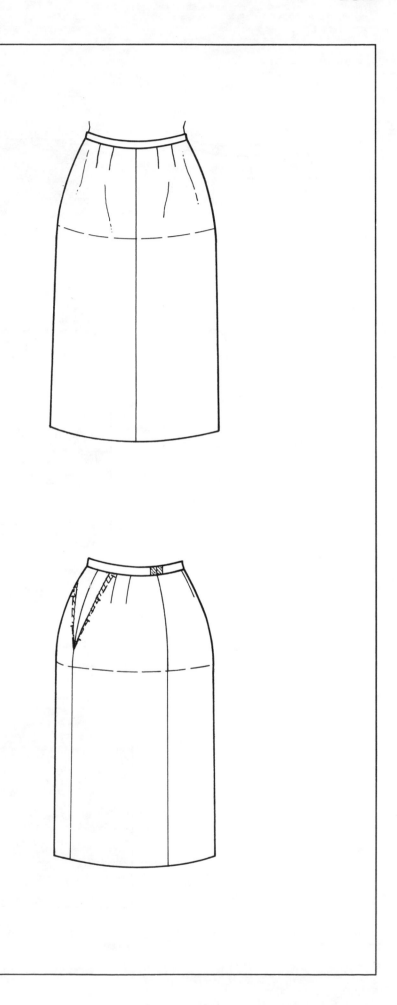

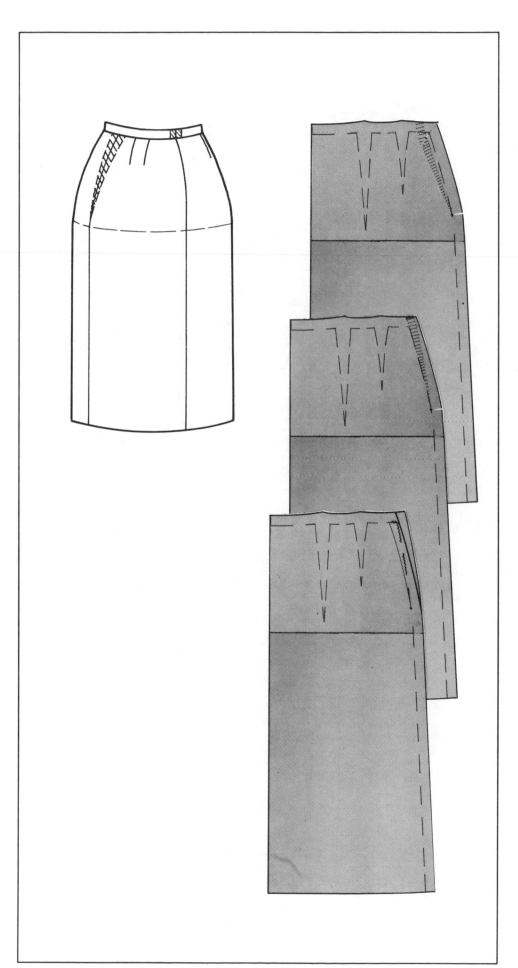

Pivot Method
Release the waist seam. Release the side seams between the waistline and the place above the hipline where the figure variation begins. To decrease width, take in the side seam areas equally at the waistline to remove the excess fabric. Blend into the original stitching near the hipline. Trim the widened seam allowance. Take in the waistband or bodice at the side seam equal to the change in the skirt or pants. See **71 Small Waist**.

BASIC FITTING THEORY

Figure Analysis

The upper tips of the pelvic cradle protrude more than average because either the bone structure is larger, more angular, or the muscles over the areas are light and taut. The abdominal area may appear indented.

Fitting Analysis

The fabric is taut over the hip bones. The strain causes diagonal wrinkles to radiate toward the side seams and the center front. The hip fitting line may rise toward each hip bone. A slight horizontal wrinkle may form near the waistline above each bone.

Fabric Requirements for Proper Fit

The fullness of the bone structure requires more fabric width and length over the hip bone areas. This results in wider front darts which may require repositioning and straighter stitching lines. Darts nearest the center front may be unnecessary but may be retained and made very narrow or converted to ease or gathers for a more aesthetic appearance. The larger garment areas relax and lower to the correct position over the body contour. The hip fitting becomes level.

GARMENT & PATTERN ALTERATIONS FOR SYMMETRICAL FIGURES

Change Required

Lengthen and widen the area over the hip bones.

Slash Method—fitting garment only

Clip the garment near the waistline halfway between the center front and each side seam. Continue cutting diagonally to the corresponding side seam just above the hipline. Insert fabric strips. To gain width and length, spread each set of cut edges equally at the dart tips until the fabric relaxes. Taper to nothing at the side seams and the waistline. Reposition the darts if needed.

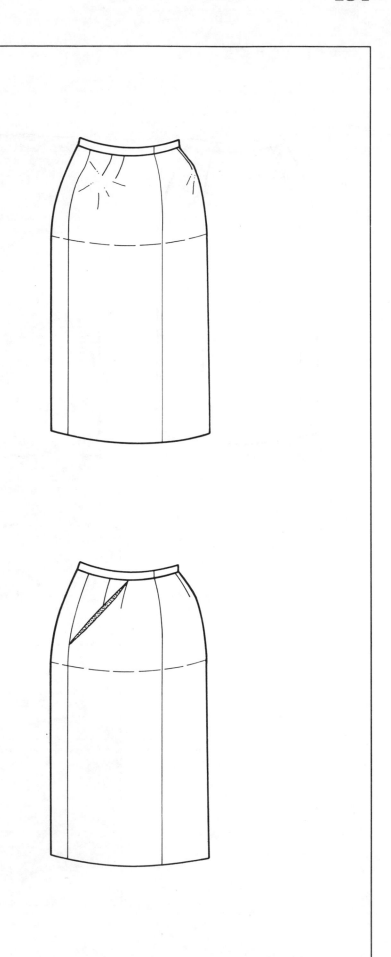

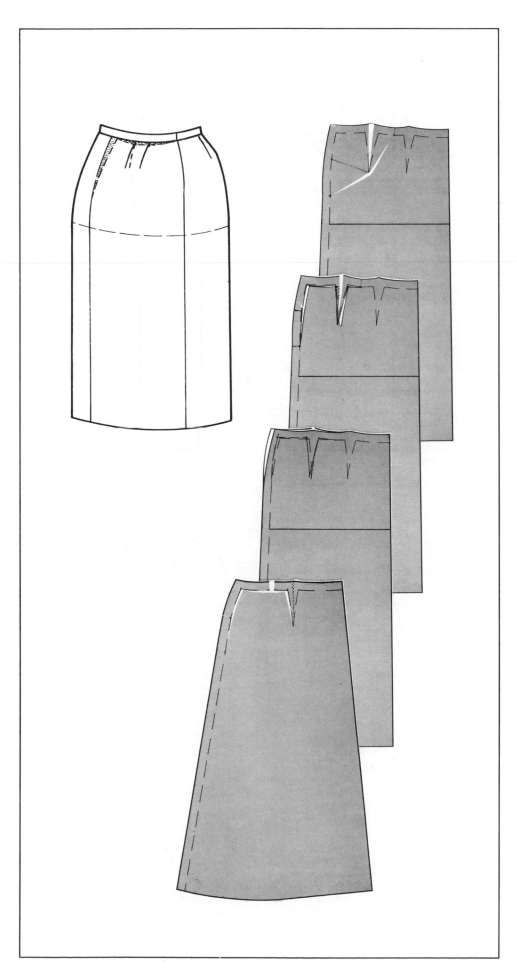

Pivot Method
Release the side seams above the hipline. Release the waist seam above the hip bones. Reposition the side darts, if necessary, and increase their widths to relax the fabric over the hip bones. To gain width and length, let out the side seam allowances of the *front* at the waistline to restore the waistline circumference. Blend into the original stitching above the hip. Lower the loosened waistline areas until the fabric relaxes over the hip bones and the hip fitting line is level. Blend into the original stitching near the center front and at the side seams.

BASIC FITTING THEORY

Figure Analysis
The abdominal muscles lack tone and permit the abdomen to protrude more than average. Excess fatty tissue and slumped posture may intensify the roundness.

Fitting Analysis
The fabric is taut across the abdomen. The side seam above the hip curve bows forward. The strain may cause a horizontal fold of fabric to form at the front waistline. At the center front the skirt cups under the abdomen, the hip fitting line rises and the hemline protrudes. Diagonal wrinkles pull from the abdomen to the side seams and cause the seams to slant toward the front at the hem. Elasticized waistbands on pants may curve downward at the center front. Pants with fitted waistbands bind uncomfortably tight against the crotch and cause diagonal wrinkles to form from the crotch to the hip bones.

Fabric Requirements for Proper Fit
The roundness of the abdomen requires more fabric width and length along the entire center front. This results in wider darts. The dart stitching lines bow toward each other. The larger garment area relaxes over the abdomen and relieves the tightness at the pant crotch. The skirt fabric hangs straight from the abdominal curve. Elasticized waistbands on pants align with the waist above the abdominal curve. The side seams hang plumb and the hip fitting line becomes level.

GARMENT & PATTERN ALTERATIONS FOR SYMMETRICAL FIGURES

Change Required
Widen the midfront area; lengthen the upper center front area.

Slash Method—fitting garment only
Release the center front seam or slash along the center front fold and insert a strip of fabric. To increase width, spread the center front edges evenly until the fabric relaxes across the abdomen. Mark the darts in their new position and shaping.

To increase the center front length, cut across the garment front just below the dart tips. Insert a strip of

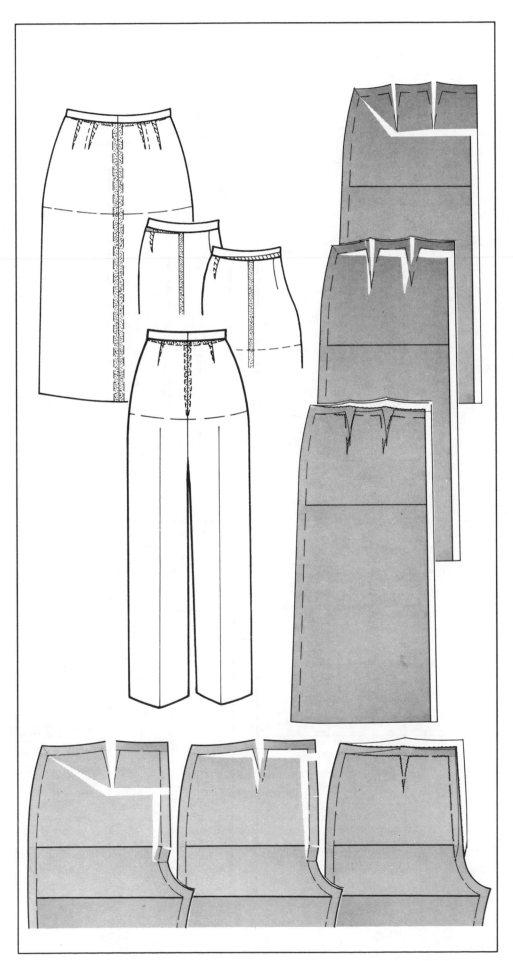

fabric. Spread the cut edges equally across the center until the fitting line is level. Taper to nothing at each side seam.

Pivot Method

On a skirt, release the front waist seam. To gain width, release either the center front seam or both side seams their entire lengths. Let out the *front* seam allowances equally until the fabric relaxes across the abdomen. Stitch the new seamlines parallel to the original ones. Widen the darts to restore the waistline circumference. Mark the correct dart shaping. Restitch the darts.

For pants follow the same procedure, but increase the width only at the center front. Let out both edges evenly as needed from the waist to the hipline. Blend the seamline back to the original stitching at the crotch curve.

To increase the center front length, let out the waistline seam allowance evenly across the center front area until the hip fitting line is level. Blend into the original stitching at the side seam.

The back waistline may be lifted instead. On pants, the back crotch curve may then need more depth. See **17 Drooped Buttocks**.

BASIC FITTING THEORY

Figure Analysis
The abdominal area is flat because of taut abdominal muscles, overly erect posture or lack of fatty tissue.

Fitting Analysis
The fabric over the abdomen is loose. Vertical folds hang below the darts nearest the center front because the darts create excess shaping in the fabric. The hip fitting line may drop across the center front.

Fabric Requirements for Proper Fit
The flatness of the figure requires less fabric shaping over the abdomen. The darts nearest the center front may be eliminated for some figures. Occasionally less length is needed at the center front. The very narrow darts prevent excess shaping in the fabric but maintain an aesthetic appearance. The smaller garment area lies smoothly against the body.

GARMENT & PATTERN ALTERATIONS FOR SYMMETRICAL FIGURES

Change Required
Narrow the midfront area; shorten the upper center front area.

Slash Method—fitting garment only
To decrease the dart width and center front length, form a parallel tuck across the center front below the dart tips. Adjust the width until the hip fitting line is level. Taper to nothing at the side seams. Follow the crosswise grain.

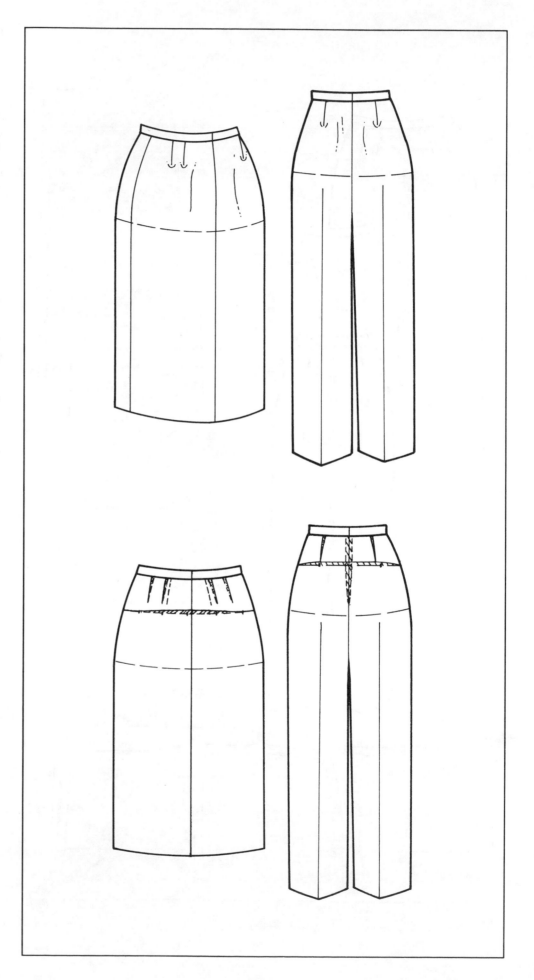

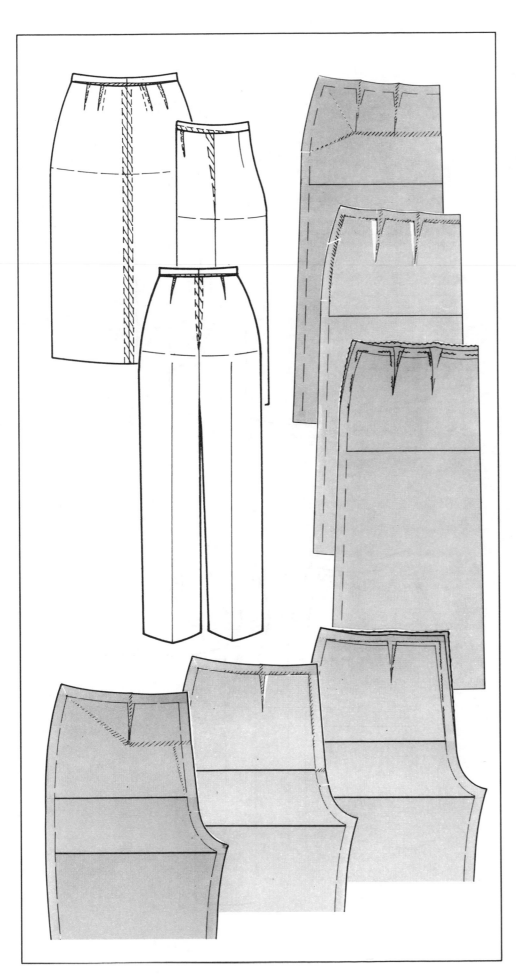

Pivot Method

Release the front waistline seam and the front darts. Release the side seams above the hipline. To decrease width, narrow the darts to smooth the fabric across the abdomen. Take in the *front* areas equally at both side seams to restore the waist circumference. If necessary, lift the fabric across the center front to remove excess length. Trim the widened seam allowances.

On pants, release the front waist seam, the center front seam, and the darts. Narrow the darts to smooth the fabric across the abdomen. Take in the excess width equally at the center front. Taper to nothing at the hipline. If necessary, lift the fabric evenly across the center front to remove excess length. Blend into the original stitching at the side seams. If a zipper is already at the center front, the excess waist width may be removed at the side seam as for the skirt.

BASIC FITTING THEORY

Figure Analysis

The pelvic cradle does not lie plumb. As the top tilts forward, the coccyx tilts outward and upward. This causes the buttocks to protrude and the groin to indent more than average. The distance increases from the fullest part of the buttocks to the central axis of the body. The distance decreases from the hipline to the waist across the center back area.

Fitting Analysis

On a skirt, a tapering, horizontal wrinkle forms at the back waistline because the garment area is too long. The hip fitting line remains level. On pants, the wrinkle may not form because the fabric binds against the crotch. The fabric under the buttocks is taut and pulls into wrinkles which slant toward the inseams. When the variation is extreme, the strain may pull the waistband and hip fitting line down across the center back area.

Fabric Requirements for Proper Fit

On a skirt, the shorter body measurement at the center back requires less fabric length. For pants, the increased profile depth of the buttocks requires a wider crotch extension. When the variation is extreme, length may be needed below the hipline. This increases the dart created by the slanted center back seam. The adjustments in length and width relax and smooth the fabric. The hip fitting line becomes level.

GARMENT & PATTERN ALTERATIONS FOR SYMMETRICAL FIGURES

Change Required

Shorten the upper center back area; widen the back crotch extension.

Slash Method—fitting garment only

On a skirt, form a parallel tuck near the waistline to remove the excess fabric length. Taper to nothing at or near the side seams.

If a pant waistband pulls down at the center back, reposition the back crotch length by widening the back crotch extension.

Place one pant leg inside the other so the garment is wrong side out. Match and pin the inseams together from the crotch to the kneeline.

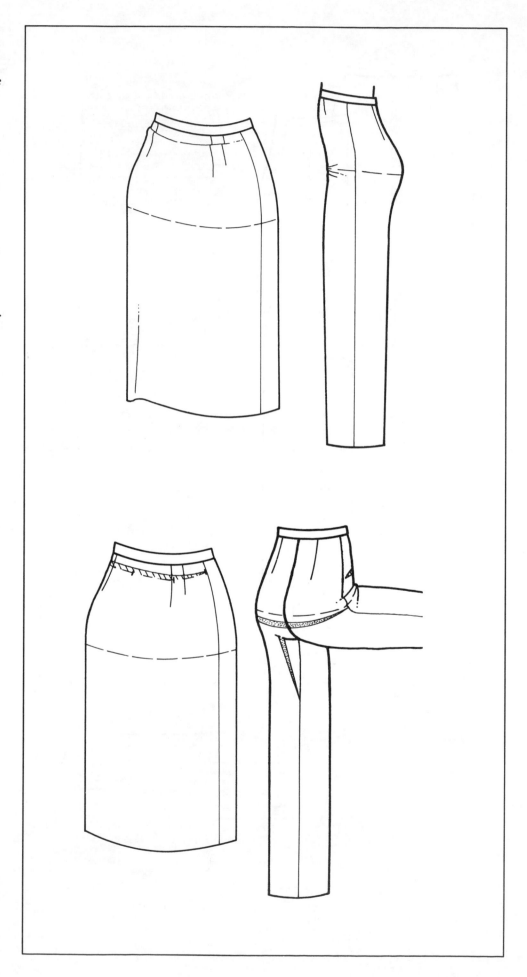

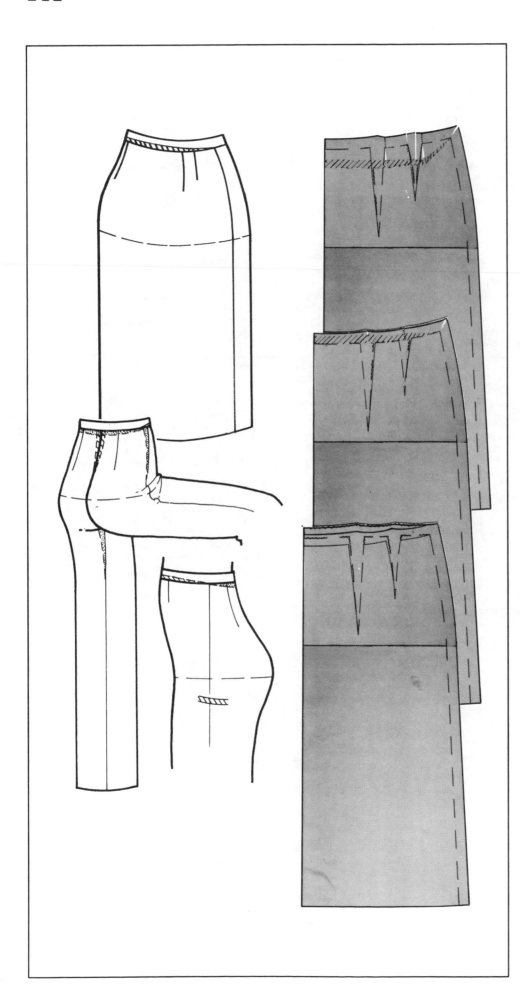

About 2 inches (5 cm) away from the inseam, cut vertically through the *back* crotch extension and follow the grain to the inseams. Turn the pants right side out and separate the legs. Lay each set of cut edges over a fabric insert and spread them equally at the crotch to relax the fabric. Taper to nothing at the inseams.

If the variation is extreme, increase the center back length also. Cut across the entire back just below the hip fitting line. Insert a strip of fabric. Spread the cut edges evenly across the center back area until the hip fitting line becomes level. Taper to nothing at the side seams.

Pivot Method
On a skirt, release the back waist seam. To reduce the center back length, lift the waistline evenly across the center back area until the fabric is smooth. Mark the new waistline at the center back area. Blend into the original stitching near the side seams. Trim the widened seam allowance. Restore the dart widths. Check for correct dart length.

On pants, if the waistband pulls down at the center back, reposition the back crotch length by widening the back crotch extension: release the crotch seam across the inseams. Release the inseams from the crotch to the kneeline. At the crotch, let out the *back* inseam allowances enough to relieve the strain. Blend into the original stitching near the kneeline.

If a wrinkle now forms across the center back, release the back waist seam and the side seams to the hipline. Take up the center back seam at the waistline until the fabric lies smooth. Blend into the original stitching at the hipline. To restore the waistline circumference, let out the side seam allowances equally at the back. Blend into the original stitching near the hipline. When seam allowance width is minimal, release the waist seam except at the center back area. Lift the waistline evenly across the *center front* area until the garment is smooth. Blend into the original stitching near the *back* darts. Restore the dart widths and lengths. The crotch seam may require lowering equal to the change at the waistline. (See **1 Long Lower Torso.**) Trim the widened seam allowances.

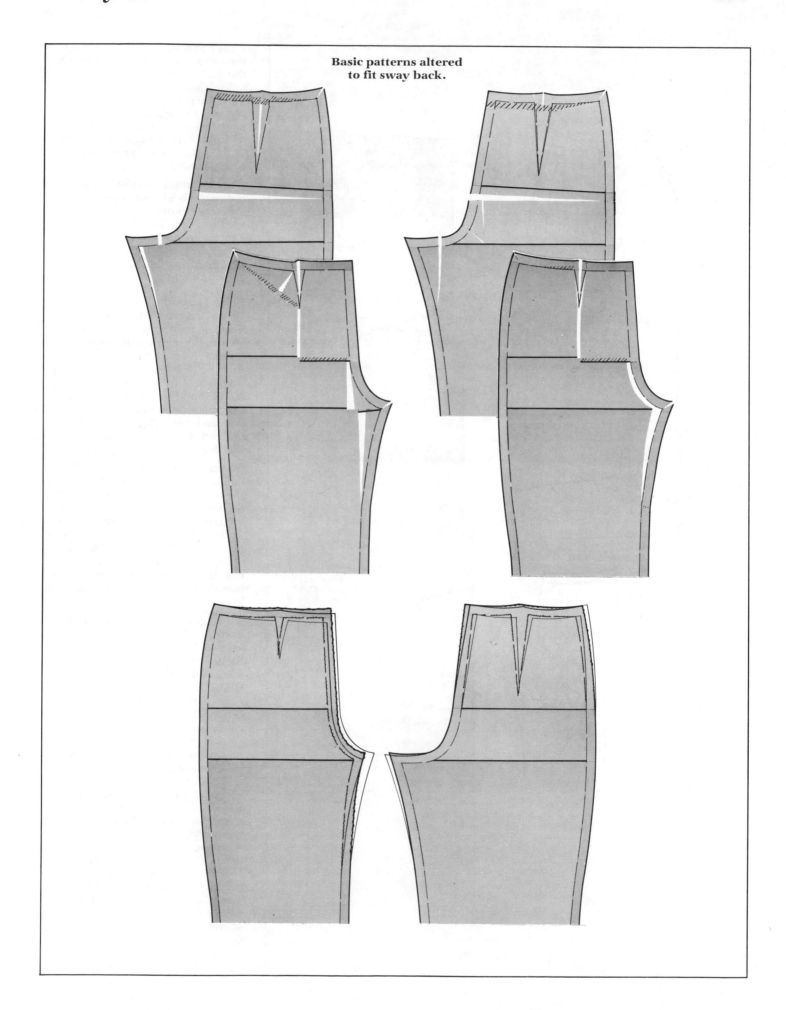

**Basic patterns altered
to fit sway back.**

Fashion patterns altered to fit sway back.

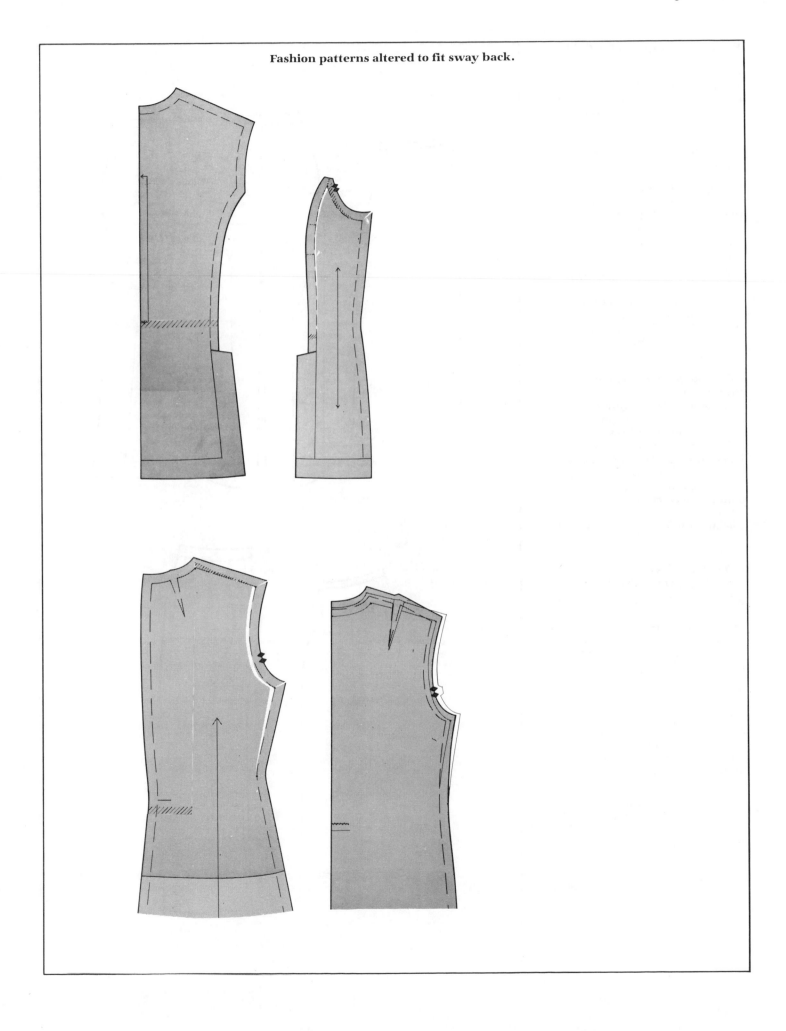

BASIC FITTING THEORY

Figure Analysis
The pelvic cradle does not lie plumb. As the top tilts backward, the coccyx rotates closer to the central axis of the body and the pubic bone moves farther away. The buttocks protrude less than average.

Fitting Analysis
The hem of a skirt hangs against the back of the legs. The side seams slant forward at the hem. Diagonal wrinkles sag from the side seams toward the center back.

On pants, the fabric sags diagonally under the curve of the buttocks and at the back creaselines. The front of the pants may bind against the crotch. The hip fitting line and hemline drop in the back and rise in the front.

Fabric Requirements for Proper Fit
The flatness of the buttocks requires less fabric length and width at the center back area. When the variation is extreme, the longer front surface of the body may require more garment length across the center front. The adjustments relax and smooth the fabric. The side seams hang plumb. The hip fitting line becomes level.

GARMENT & PATTERN ALTERATIONS FOR SYMMETRICAL FIGURES

Change Required
Shorten the upper center back area; lengthen the upper center front area, if necessary.

Slash Method—fitting garment only
Across the upper center back, form a parallel tuck to remove the excess fabric length. Adjust the tuck width until the hip fitting line is level. Taper to nothing at the side seams or near the front darts.

On pants, if horizontal wrinkles now form under the buttocks, deepen the back crotch curve also. See **17 Drooped Buttocks.**

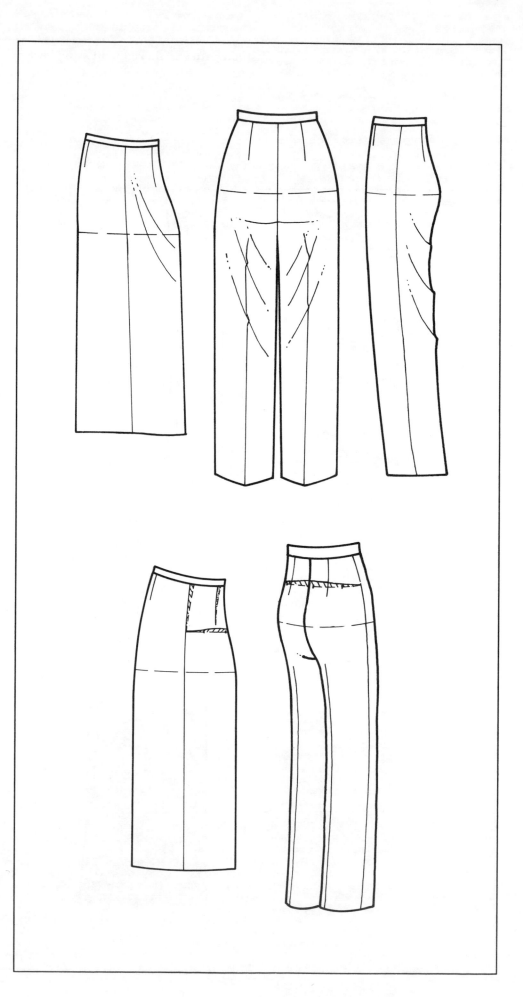

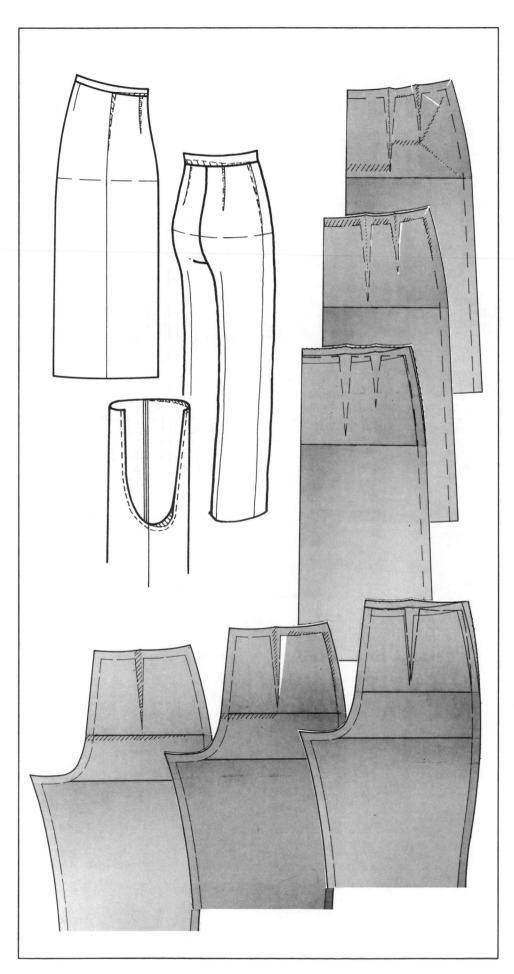

Pivot Method

Release the back waist seam and the side seams to the hipline. To decrease center back length, raise the waistline evenly across the center back until the hip fitting line is level. Blend into the original stitching near the side seams. Narrow the dart widths, if necessary. Check the dart lengths. To restore the waist circumference, take up the back side seams equally at the waistline. Trim the widened seam allowances.

On pants, if horizontal wrinkles form under the buttocks, deepen the back crotch curve. See **17 Drooped Buttocks**.

BASIC FITTING THEORY

Figure Analysis

The upper tips of the pelvic cradle flare wider than average. This causes the sides of the torso to curve out abruptly below the waist. The upper hip area may be wider than that at the level of the hip joints.

Fitting Analysis

The fabric along the side seams is taut over the upper hip area. On a skirt, horizontal wrinkles form across the side seams just below the waistline. The hip fitting line bows upward at the sides as the garment rises to accommodate the prominent bulges. On pants, diagonal wrinkles form from the upper hip areas to the crotch. The hemline rises at the sides.

Fabric Requirements for Proper Fit

The prominent hip contours require more fabric in width and length at the upper side seams because the most prominent curvature of the side contour occurs near the waistline. The larger garment area relaxes the fabric over the hips. The hip fitting line becomes level.

GARMENT & PATTERN ALTERATIONS FOR SYMMETRICAL FIGURES

Change Required

Widen the upper hip area at the side seams; lengthen the side seams at the waistline, if necessary.

Slash Method—fitting garment only

Only the curvature and length of the side seamlines require change. Cutting the interior causes unnecessary trueing of curved edges. Follow **Pivot Method**.

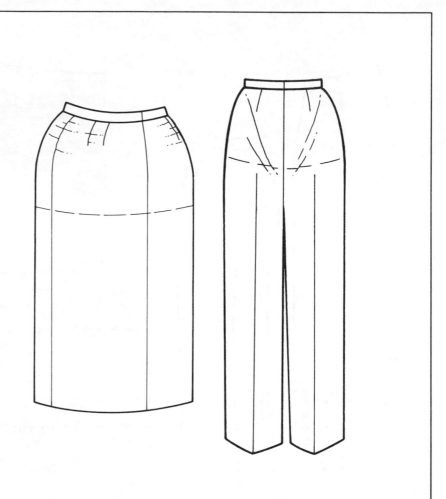

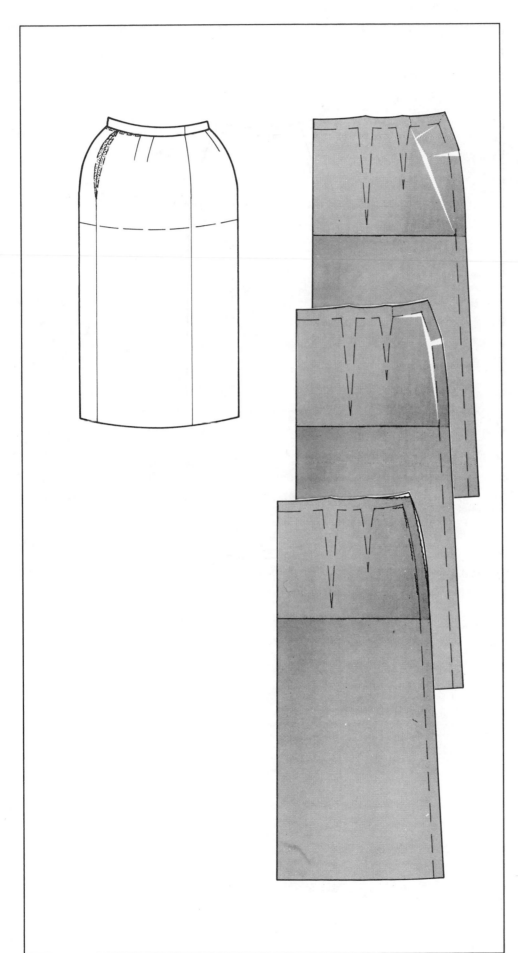

Pivot Method

Release the waistline seam across each side seam area. Release the side seams above the hipline. To increase width, let out side seam allowances equally on both the back and front until the fabric relaxes across the hip curve.

To increase length, let out the waistline seam allowance above the side seams until the hip fitting line becomes level. Blend into the original stitching near the darts.

This figure variation may be more easily accommodated by purchasing a pattern and ready-to-wear garment in the next larger size. Reduce the waistline at the side seams instead.

BASIC FITTING THEORY

Figure Analysis
The upper tips of the pelvic cradle flare less than average and cause this part of the hip structure to be narrower than that at the level of the hip joints. The sides of the torso slope toward the waist instead of curving.

Fitting Analysis
The fabric is loose along the side seams near the upper hip areas. The hip fitting line is not affected.

Fabric Requirements for Proper Fit
The flatter body contours require less fabric in width and length at the upper side seams. The only curvature along the side contour occurs at the hipline.

GARMENT & PATTERN ALTERATIONS FOR SYMMETRICAL FIGURES

Change Required
Narrow the upper hip area at the side seams; shorten the side seams at the waistline, if necessary.

Slash Method—fitting garment only
To flatten the side seam curvature, pin a tuck along each side seam where the looseness is greatest. Taper the tuck to nothing toward the waist- and hiplines.

If a decrease in length is necessary, form a horizontal tuck near the waistline across each side seam to lift the fabric until it lies smooth. Taper the tuck to nothing near the darts at both back and front.

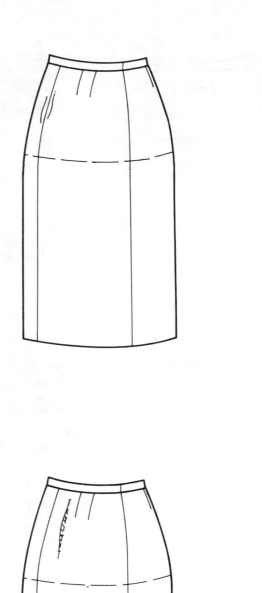

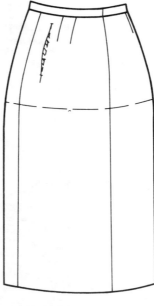

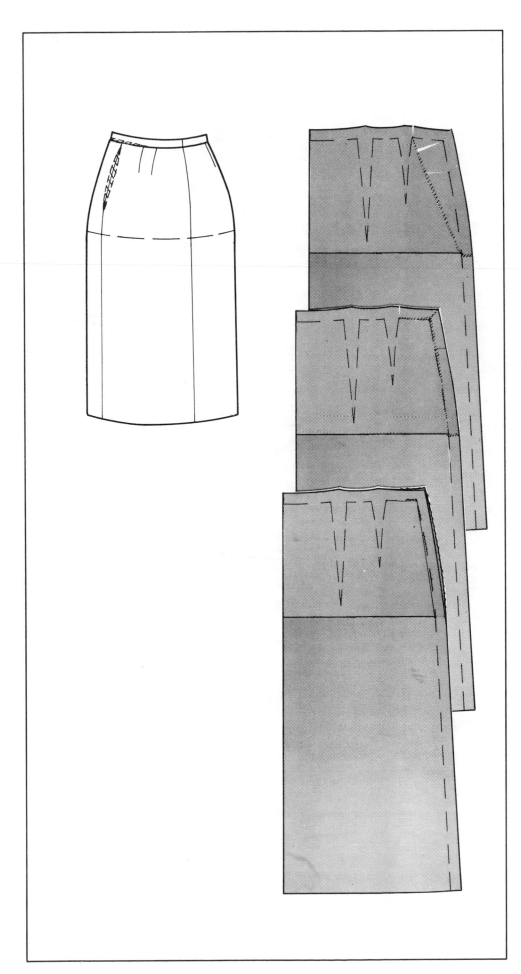

Pivot Method
Release the side seams above the hipline. To flatten the side seam curve, take in the curved area of the side seam equally on both the back and front until the fabric becomes smooth.

If a decrease in length is necessary, release the waistline seam across the side seams and lift the garment until the fabric is smooth. Blend into the original stitching near the darts at back and front. Trim the widened seam allowances.

BASIC FITTING THEORY

Figure Analysis
The bone structures forming the pelvic cradle and the hip joints are larger and wider than average. Deposits of soft body tissues may lack tone and may be softer or more developed. The hip circumference is larger than average.

Fitting Analysis
The fabric pulls taut around the fullest part of the hips. The strain causes a skirt to rise gradually when the body is in motion. A horizontal fold forms around the waist. The hip fitting line and hemline position both remain level. On pants, the fabric cannot rise at the center front and center back because it binds against the crotch. Skirts and pants purchased by hip size will be too large at the waistline (see **4 Small Waist** for fitting procedures).

Fabric Requirements for Proper Fit
The wider, fuller hip area requires more fabric width and length at the fullest hip level. This results in longer side seams that are noticeably curved near the hipline. The larger garment area allows the fabric to relax and to lower into the correct position on the body.

GARMENT & PATTERN ALTERATIONS FOR SYMMETRICAL FIGURES

Change Required
Widen the side seam areas at the hipline.

Slash Method—fitting garment only
To determine the amount of fabric needed, subtract the total body hip measurement plus ease from the corresponding garment measurement. Divide the difference by four (four side seam areas). Release the waist seam across the side seam areas.

On both the back and front near each side seam, cut through the waist seam allowance downward to the hem, following the lengthwise grain. Cut through the hem edge on skirts and to the kneeline on pants. Insert fabric strips.

To increase width, spread the cut edges evenly along the entire slash on skirts and from the waist to the crotchline on pants. For the latter,

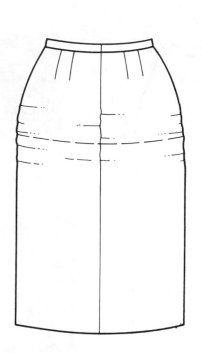

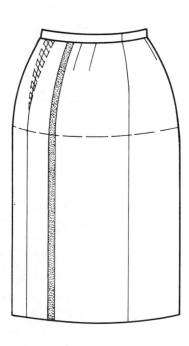

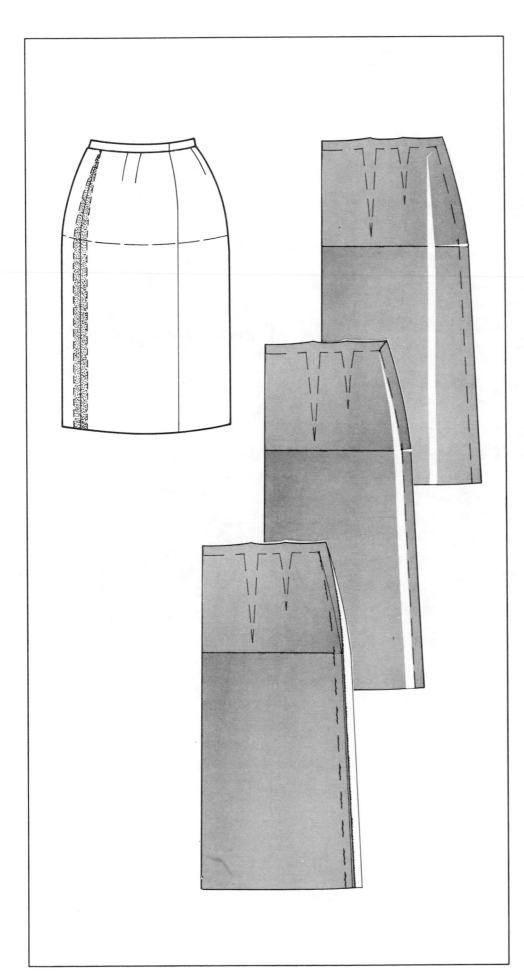

taper to nothing at the kneeline. At the waistline, take in the side seam areas equally to restore the waist circumference. Taper to nothing at the hip.

Pivot Method

To determine the amount of fabric needed, subtract the total body hip measurement plus ease from the corresponding garment measurement. Divide the difference by four (four side seam allowances).

On a skirt, restitch a new side seam to release the calculated amount evenly from the hem edge to hipline. Gradually blend the stitching back to the original seamline at the waistline.

On pants, mark a new side seam across the hipline area to release the needed width. Gradually curve back to the original seamline near the waistline and below the thighline. If a wider pant leg is desired, continue the new line parallel to the original from the hipline to the hem edge.

When adjusting a six-gore skirt, maintain pleasing proportions in the garment. Let out the edges of the *center panel* an even amount equal to one-fourth of the calculated adjustment. Let out the side seams equal to three-fourths of the needed amount.

**Basic patterns altered
to fit broad hips.**

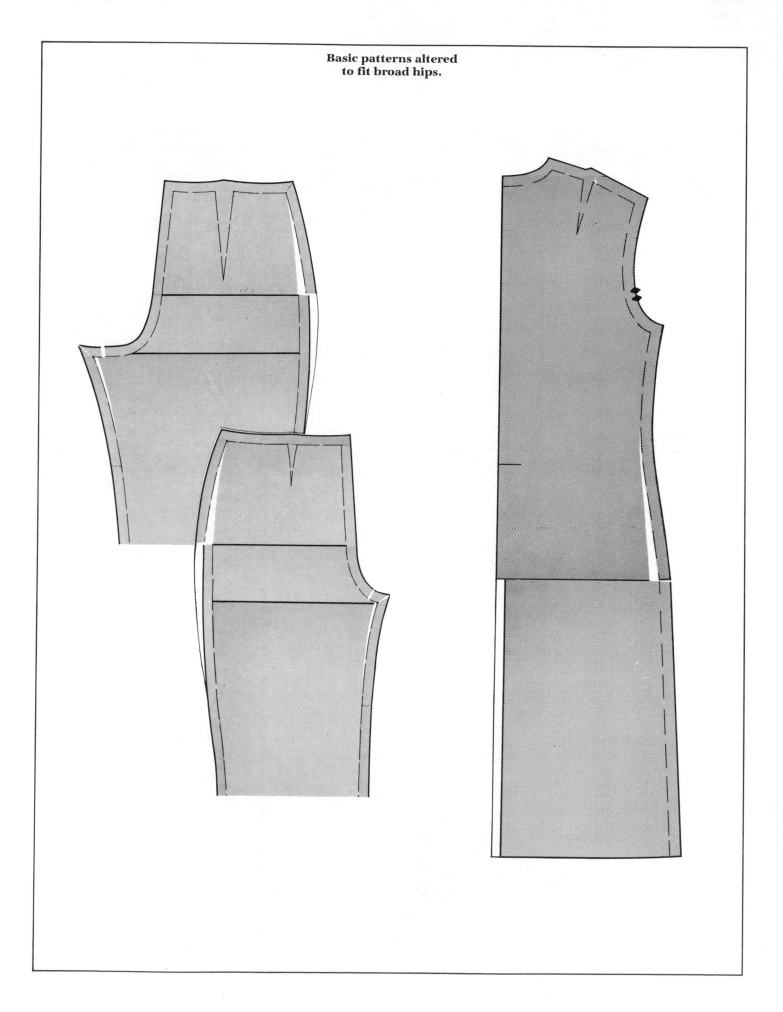

Fashion patterns altered to fit broad hips.

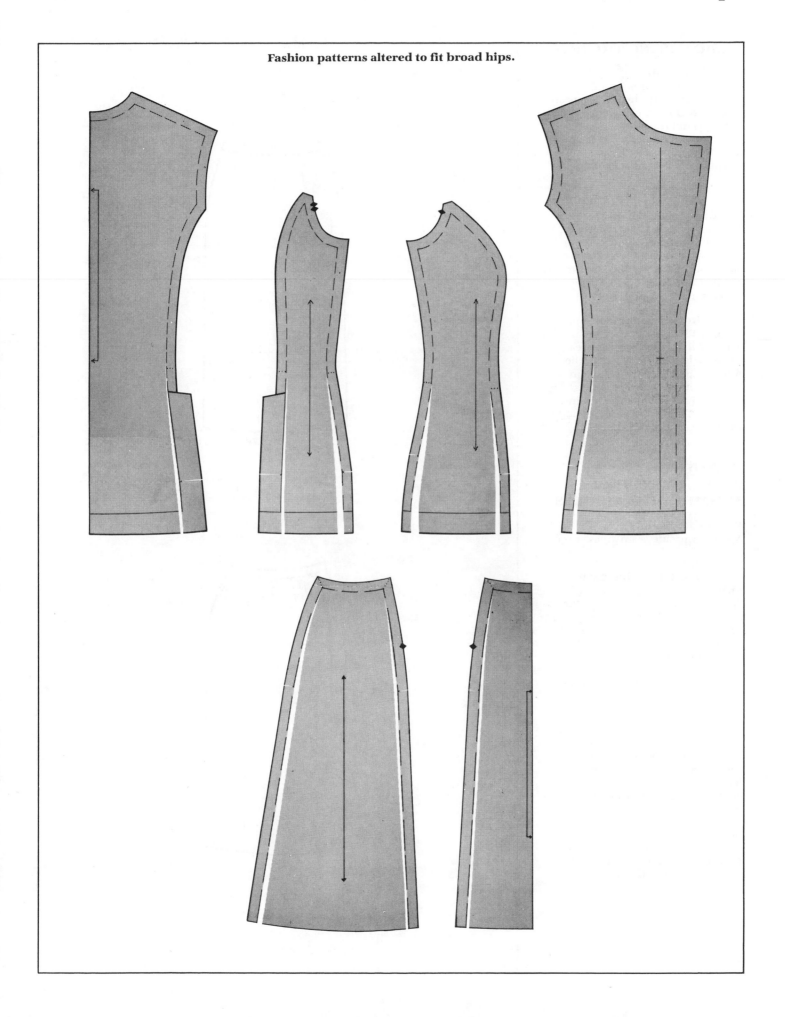

BASIC FITTING THEORY

Figure Analysis

The bone structures forming the pelvic cradle and the hip joints are smaller and narrower than average. Smaller amounts of soft body tissues or more taut muscles may also be present. The hip circumference is smaller than average.

Fitting Analysis

The fabric along the side seams is loose at the fullest part of the hips. The hip fitting line and hemline position are not affected. Pants and skirts purchased by hip size are too small at the waist (see **3 Large Waist** for fitting procedures).

Fabric Requirements for Proper Fit

The smaller, narrower hip area requires less fabric width at the fullest hip level. This results in shorter side seams that are less curved than usual at the hipline. The smaller garment area smooths the fabric against the body.

GARMENT & PATTERN ALTERATIONS FOR SYMMETRICAL FIGURES

Change Required

Narrow the side seam areas at the hipline.

Slash Method—fitting garment only

To determine the amount of excess fabric, subtract the total body hip measurement plus ease from the corresponding garment measurement. Divide the difference by four (four side seam areas). Release the waistline seam across the side seam areas.

On both the back and front near each side seam, form a parallel tuck from the waist seam allowance downward to the hem to remove the excess fabric. Follow the lengthwise grain. On skirts continue the tuck through the hem edge. On pants continue it evenly to the crotchline then taper to nothing at the kneeline. Let out the side seams equally at the waistline to restore the waist circumference. Blend into the original near the hipline.

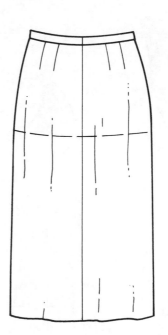

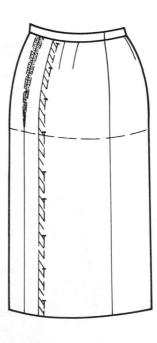

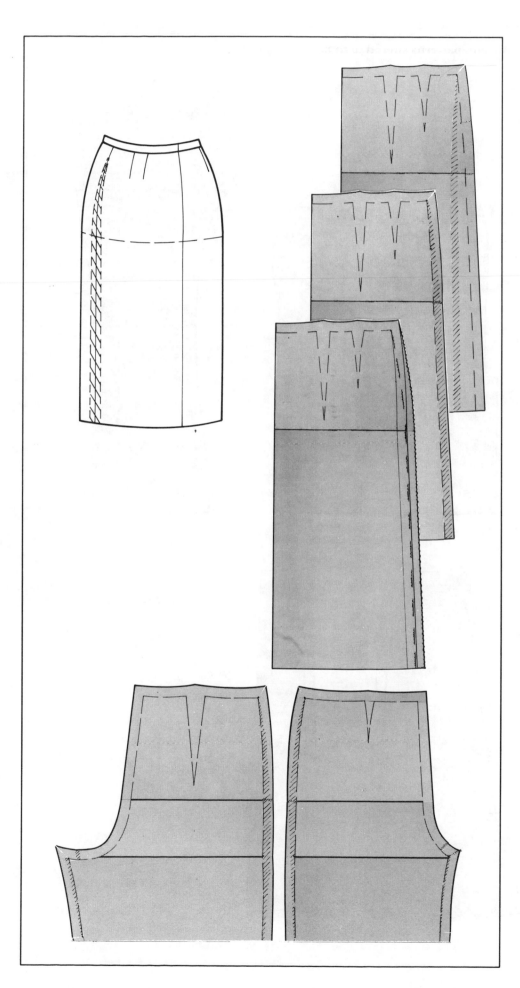

Pivot Method

To determine the amount of excess fabric, subtract the total hip measurement plus ease from the corresponding garment measurement. Divide the difference by four (four side seam allowances).

On a skirt restitch a new side seam to take in the calculated amount evenly from the hem edge to the hipline. Gradually blend the stitching back into the original seamline near the waistline. Trim the widened seam allowances.

On pants, mark a new side seam across the hipline area to take in the excess fabric. Gradually blend the stitching line back into the original near the waistline and at the thighline. If a narrower pant leg is desired, continue the new line parallel to the original from hipline to the hem edge. Trim the widened seam allowances.

When adjusting a six-gore skirt, maintain pleasing proportions in the garment. Take in the edges of the *center panel* an even amount equal to one-fourth of the calculated adjustment. Take up the side seams equal to three-fourths of the needed amount.

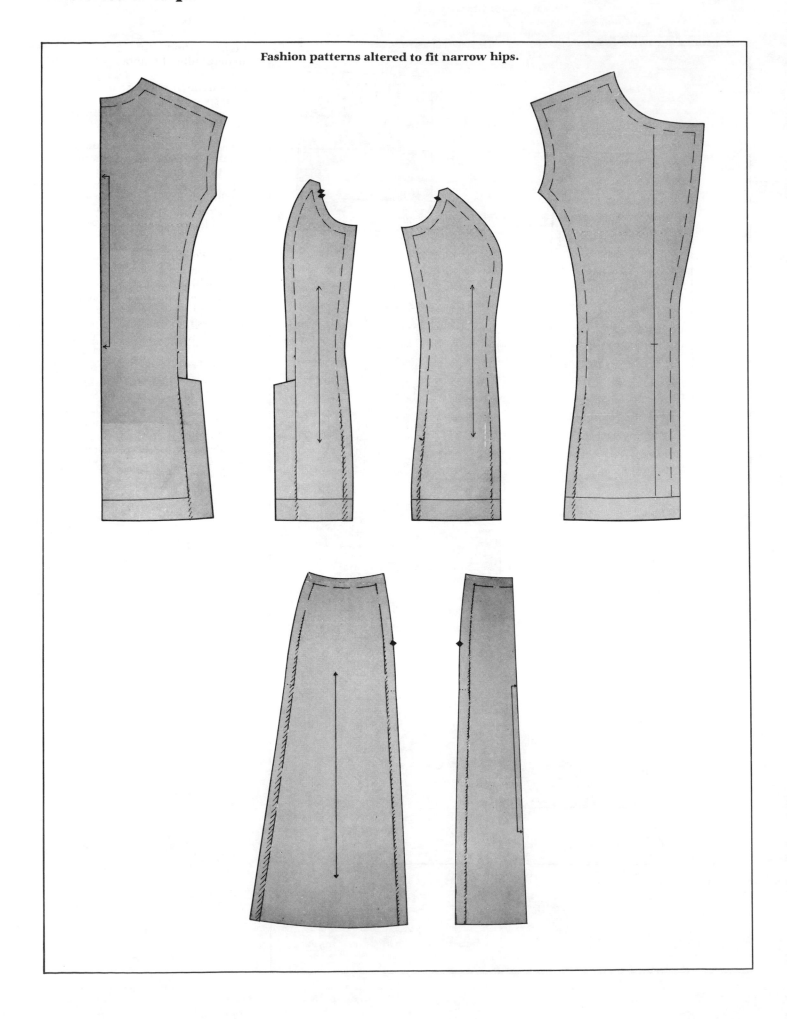

Fashion patterns altered to fit narrow hips.

BASIC FITTING THEORY

Figure Analysis
The bone structure forming the pelvic cradle is less oval than average. The torso is narrower from side to side and deeper from the center front through to the center back. The torso circumference does not change.

Fitting Analysis
This figure variation usually affects the fit only on *pants.* Tight diagonal wrinkles pull through the crotch area; they usually are more apparent from the back. The fabric may pull into the crotch crevice when the wearer walks, sits, or stoops. The strain pulls the waistline and hip fitting line downward across the center back.

Fabric Requirements for Proper Fit
The greater body profile depth requires wider crotch extensions. The larger garment area allows the fabric to relax and hang smoothly between the legs.

GARMENT & PATTERN ALTERATIONS FOR SYMMETRICAL FIGURES

Change Required
Widen the back and front crotch extensions.

Slash Method—fitting garment only
Place one pant leg inside the other so the garment is wrong side out. Match and pin the inseams together from the crotch to the knee line. About 2 inches (5 cm) away from the inseam, cut vertically through the *back* crotch extension and follow the grain to the inseams. Turn the pants right side out and separate the legs. To increase width, lay each set of cut edges over a fabric insert and spread equally at the crotch to relax the fabric. Taper to nothing at the inseams. On the pant *pattern* follow this process but add one-third of the adjustment at the front inseam and two-thirds at the back inseam.

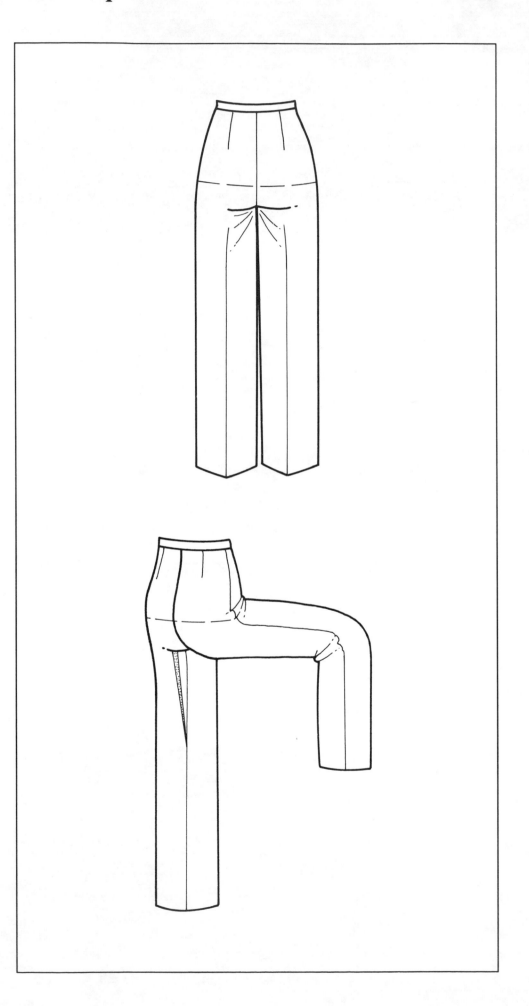

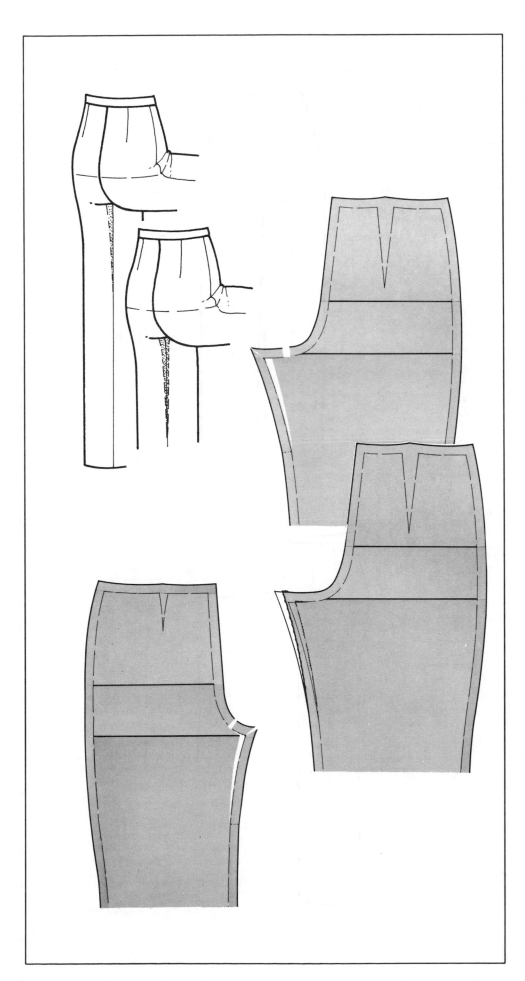

Pivot Method
Release the crotch seam across the inseam allowances. Release both inseams from the crotch to the kneeline. To increase width at the crotchline let out the *back* inseam equal to two-thirds of the needed amount. For the new front inseam let out an amount equal to one-half of the back adjustment. Blend the adjustments into the original seamline near the kneeline. Restitch the crotch seam.

BASIC FITTING THEORY

Figure Analysis

The bone structure forming the pelvic cradle is more oval than average. The torso is wider from side to side and more shallow from the center front through to the center back.

Fitting Analysis

This figure variation usually affects the fit only on *pants.* The fabric between the legs hangs in loose, vertical folds. The excess fabric is an annoyance and restricts walking and stooping.

Fabric Requirements for Proper Fit

The more shallow body profile depths require narrower crotch extensions. The smaller garment area prevents fabric bagginess, between the legs.

GARMENT & PATTERN ALTERATIONS FOR SYMMETRICAL FIGURES

Change Required

Narrow the back and front crotch extensions.

Slash Method—fitting garment only

Release the seam along the *back* crotch curve. On each pant leg form a vertical tuck at the back crotch curve to remove the excess fabric width. Following the lengthwise grain, taper the tucks to nothing at the inseam. On the pant *pattern*, follow this process but subtract one-third of the adjustment at the front inseam and two-thirds at the back inseam.

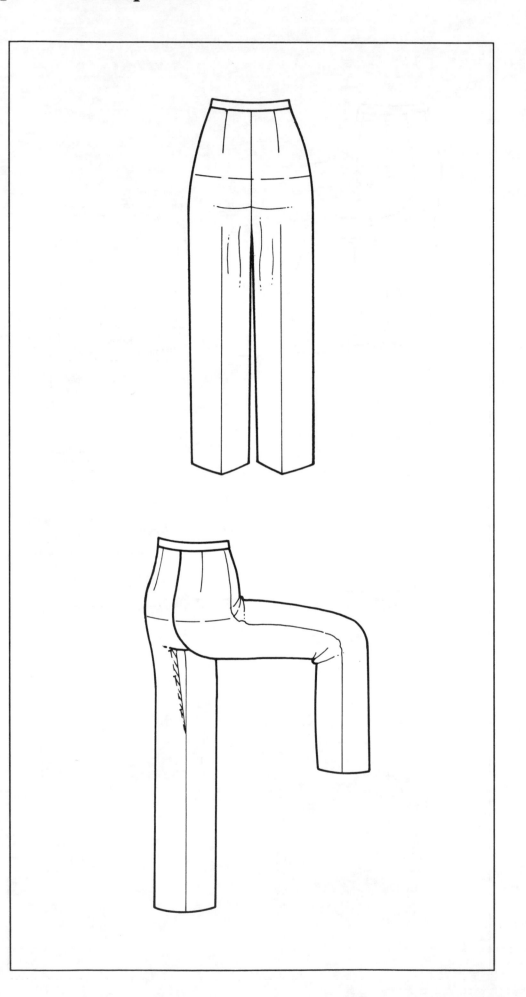

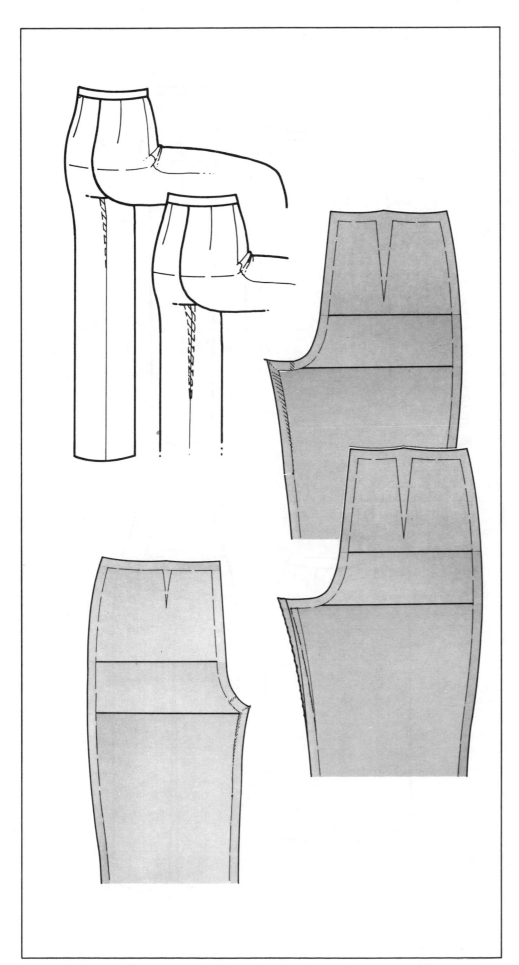

Pivot Method
Release the crotch seam across the inseam allowances. Release both inseams from the crotch to the kneeline. At the crotch, take in the back inseam area to remove two-thirds of the excess fabric. Take in the front inseam equal to one-half of the back adjustment. Blend the adjustments into the original seamline near the kneeline. Trim the widened seam allowances. True the front crotch curve. Restitch the crotch seam.

BASIC FITTING THEORY

Figure Analysis

The muscle development across the center back waist area is slight. The muscles forming the buttocks curve are taut and develop at a higher position than average. The buttocks contour is prominent because the shallow and full areas meet abruptly. The distance decreases from the waist straight to the fullest part of the buttocks.

When the variation is extreme, the depth increases from the fullest part of the buttocks to the central axis of the body. This causes the hip fitting line to drop at center back.

Fitting Analysis

On both skirts and pants, the fabric near the tip of the darts or below the yoke forms a loose horizontal fold across the center back. The hip fitting line remains level.

When the variation is extreme, pants bind against the crotch and the fabric forms into wrinkles that slant from the buttocks toward the inseams.

Fabric Requirements for Proper Fit

The shorter, upper center back area requires less fabric length above the hipline. This results in a need for shorter *back* darts. When the variation is extreme, the greater back profile depth requires a wider *back* crotch extension. Wearing a well-fitted girdle will minimize the need for adjustment in most clothing.

GARMENT & PATTERN ALTERATIONS FOR SYMMETRICAL FIGURES

Change Required

Shorten the upper center back area; widen the back crotch extension, if necessary.

Slash Method—fitting garment only

On both skirts and pants, form a parallel tuck across the center back just above the dart tips to remove the excess fabric length. Taper to nothing at the side seams.

When the variation is extreme, widen the back crotch extension. Place one pant leg inside the other so the garment is wrong side out. Match and pin the inseams together from the crotch to the kneeline. About 2 inches (5 cm) away from

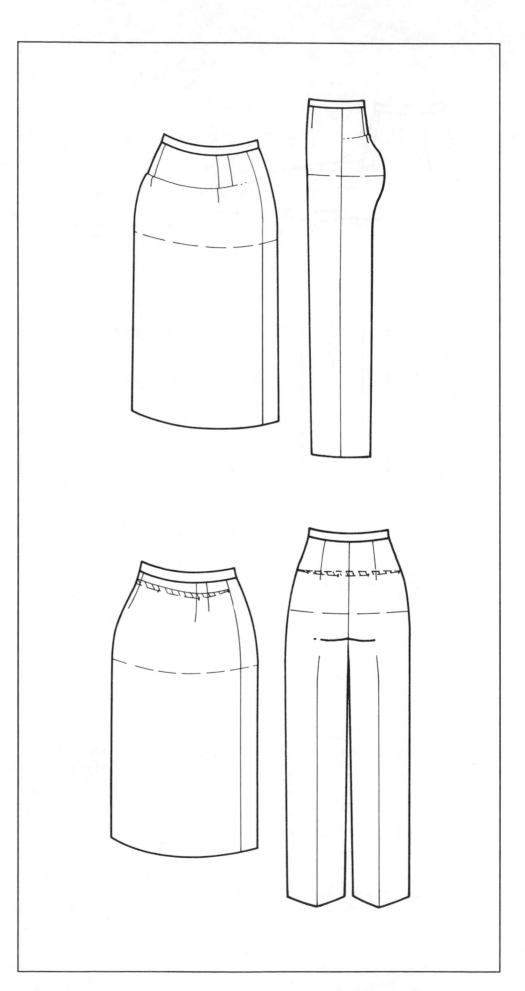

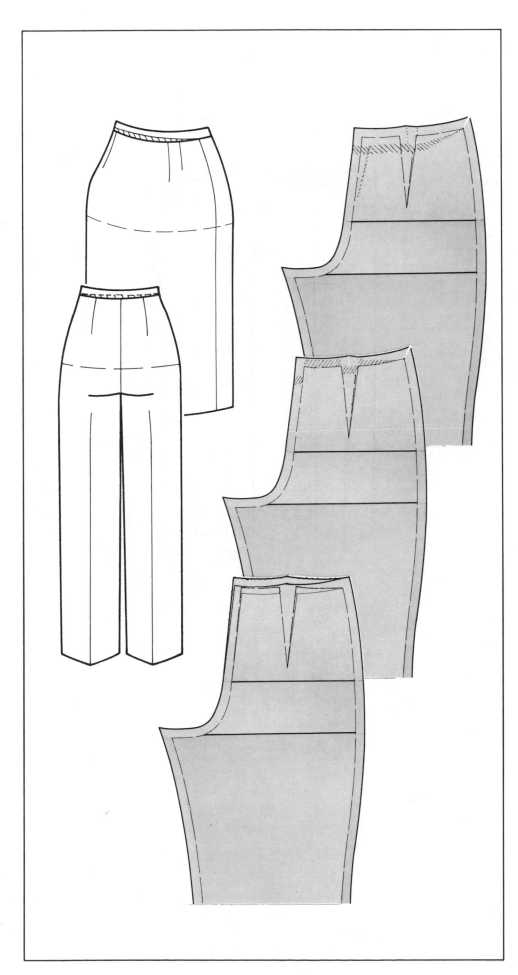

the inseam, cut vertically through the back crotch extension and continue along the lengthwise grain to the inseams. Turn the pants right side out and separate the legs. Lay each set of cut edges over a fabric insert, and spread equally at the crotch to relax the fabric and raise the hip fitting line to a level position.

Pivot Method
Release the back waistline seam. Lift the waistline evenly across the center back area to remove the excess fabric length. Blend into the original seamline at the side seams. Increase the back dart width to restore the waist circumference. Trim the widened waist seam allowance.

When the variation is extreme, let out the back crotch extensions. Release the stitching across the inseams. Release both inseams from the crotch to the kneeline. Increase width of the back extensions as necessary at the crotch. Blend into the original seamline at the knee.

BASIC FITTING THEORY

Figure Analysis
The buttocks contour is less prominent than average because the muscles and connective tissue forming the buttocks lose their tone and the flaccid tissue droops. This increases the crotch length below the hipline.

Fitting Analysis
This figure variation affects the fit only on *pants.* The fabric forms into horizontal wrinkles below the buttocks. The fabric may pull into the crotch crevice. The waistline and the hip fitting line drop across the center back.

Fabric Requirements for Proper Fit
The lowered contour of the buttocks requires a deeper curve along the back crotch seamline. In turn, a less curved seamline is required at the front crotch curve. This prevents a "peak" from forming at the inseam area in the new crotch seamline. The deeper curve in the back crotch seam permits the fabric to rise and lie smoothly under the buttocks.

GARMENT & PATTERN ALTERATIONS FOR SYMMETRICAL FIGURES

Change Required
Deepen the curve on the back crotch seamline; flatten the curve on the front crotch seamline.

Slash Method—fitting garment only
Pin a horizontal tuck at the wrinkled area to indicate the amount of adjustment.

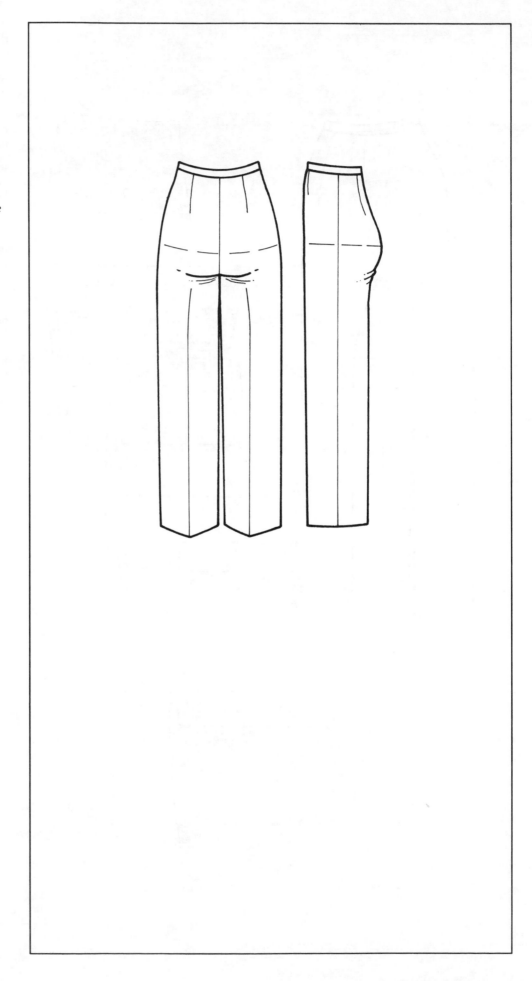

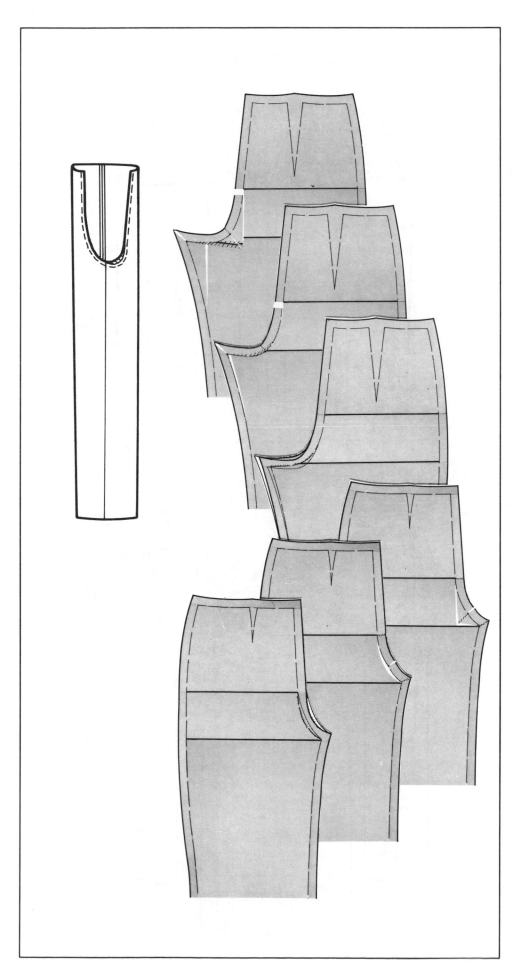

Pivot Method
Place one pant leg inside the other with the pants wrong side out. Match and pin the inseams together from the crotch to the kneeline. Along the back crotch seam, mark the midpoint between the hipline and the inseam. Repeat for the front. Below this point on the *back* curve, mark ½ inch (1.2 cm) *into the pants area.* At the midpoint on the front, mark *into the seam allowance* enough to form a smooth curve. Begin the new seam near the hipline at the back. Stitch a smooth curve through the back adjustment mark, then through the original intersection of the crotch and inseam. Continue stitching through the front adjustment mark and slope back to the original seamline at the hipline. Clip the widened seam allowance area.

Try on the pants and repeat the above procedure until the fabric lies smooth under the buttocks. Trim the widened seam allowances.

If the back pant legs tighten across the inside thigh, see **14 Cylindrical shaped Torso**. Let out only the back inseam allowance.

BASIC FITTING THEORY

Figure Analysis

The muscles and soft tissues which form the buttocks are more developed than average and may lack tone. This increases the hip circumference. The distance increases from the fullest part of the buttocks to the central axis of the body and to the waist.

Fitting Analysis

A basic garment pulls taut over the buttocks. The strain causes the fabric to cup under the abdomen. The side seams curve toward the back at the hipline and diagonal wrinkles radiate from the buttocks toward each side seam. On a skirt, the hip fitting line and hemline rise and the hem protrudes at the center back. On pants, the waistband and hip fitting line drop across the center back area because the fabric binds against the crotch.

Fabric Requirements for Proper Fit

The larger tissue structure requires more fabric length at the upper center back area and more width across the buttocks. The back darts become wider and longer. For pants, the greater back profile depth requires a wider back crotch extension. The adjustments in length and width relax the fabric. The hip fitting line and hemline become level. On pants, the waistband aligns with the body waist.

GARMENT & PATTERN ALTERATIONS FOR SYMMETRICAL FIGURES

Change Required

Widen the back at the hipline; lengthen the upper center back area; widen the back crotch extensions.

Slash Method—fitting garment only

Release the back waistline seam near the side seams. On skirts, cut the *back* from the edge of the waistline seam allowance downward through the hem edge. Follow the lengthwise grain. On pants, cut from the waistline to the kneeline. Insert fabric strips. To increase width, spread the cut edges evenly along the entire slash on skirts. On pants spread the cut edges evenly from the waistline to the crotchline, tapering to nothing at the kneeline. Increase the back

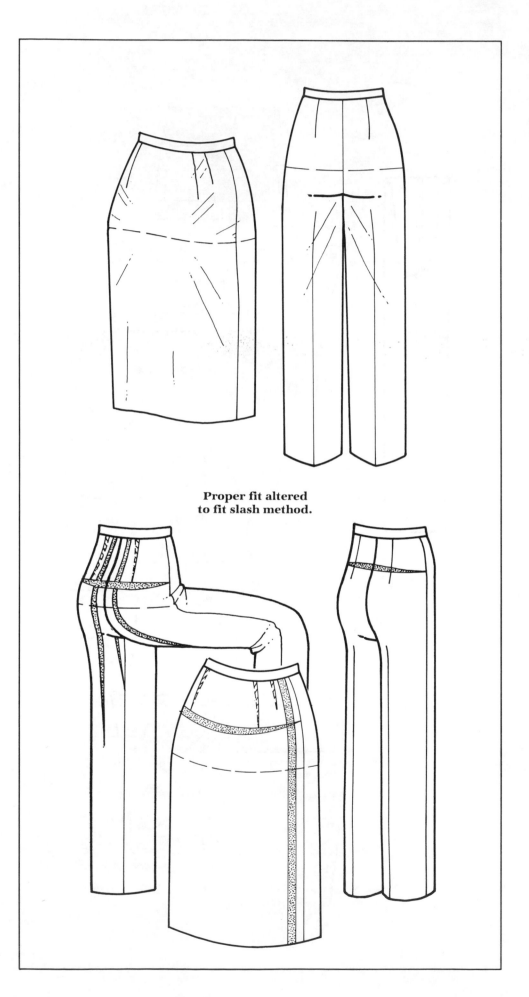

Proper fit altered to fit slash method.

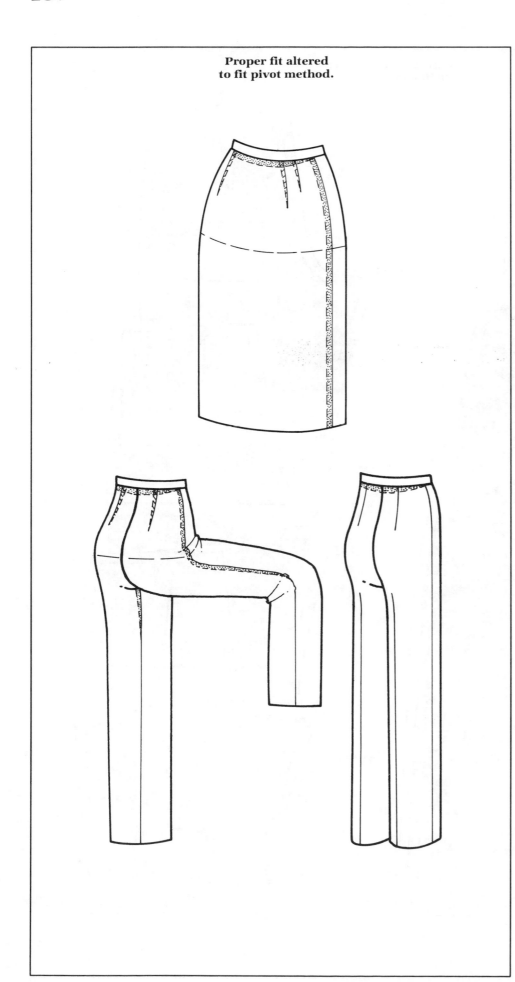

**Proper fit altered
to fit pivot method.**

dart widths on both garments to restore the waistline circumference.

To widen the pant back crotch extension, place one pant leg inside the other so the garment is wrong side out. Match and pin the inseams together from the crotch to the kneeline. About 2 inches (5 cm) away from the inseam, cut vertically through the *back* extension and follow the grain to the inseams. Turn the pants right side out and separate the legs. Lay each set of cut edges over a fabric insert and spread equally at the crotch to relax the fabric. Taper to nothing at the inseams.

To lengthen the center back cut across the entire back of the garment just below the back dart tips. Insert a fabric strip. Spread the edges evenly between the dart tips until the hip fitting line becomes level. Taper to nothing near each side seam. Reposition and lengthen the back darts, as needed.

Pivot Method
For skirts, release the back waistline seam and the side seams. For pants, release the side seams and inseams only to the kneeline. On either garment, increase width by letting out both *back* allowances of the side seams evenly at the hipline. Let out an even amount from the waist to the hem on a skirt, and from the waist to the crotchline on pants. On pants, blend into the original seamline at the kneeline. Increase the back dart widths to restore the waistline circumference. Lengthen the darts if necessary.

To increase the back crotch ease on pants, release the crotch seam across the inseam allowances. Release the inseam from the crotch to the kneeline. Let out the *back* inseam allowances equally at the crotch to relieve the strain on the fabric. Blend into the original seamline above the knee.

To lengthen the center back area, let out the waist seam allowance evenly across the center back until the hip fitting line is level. Blend into the original seamline at each side seam.

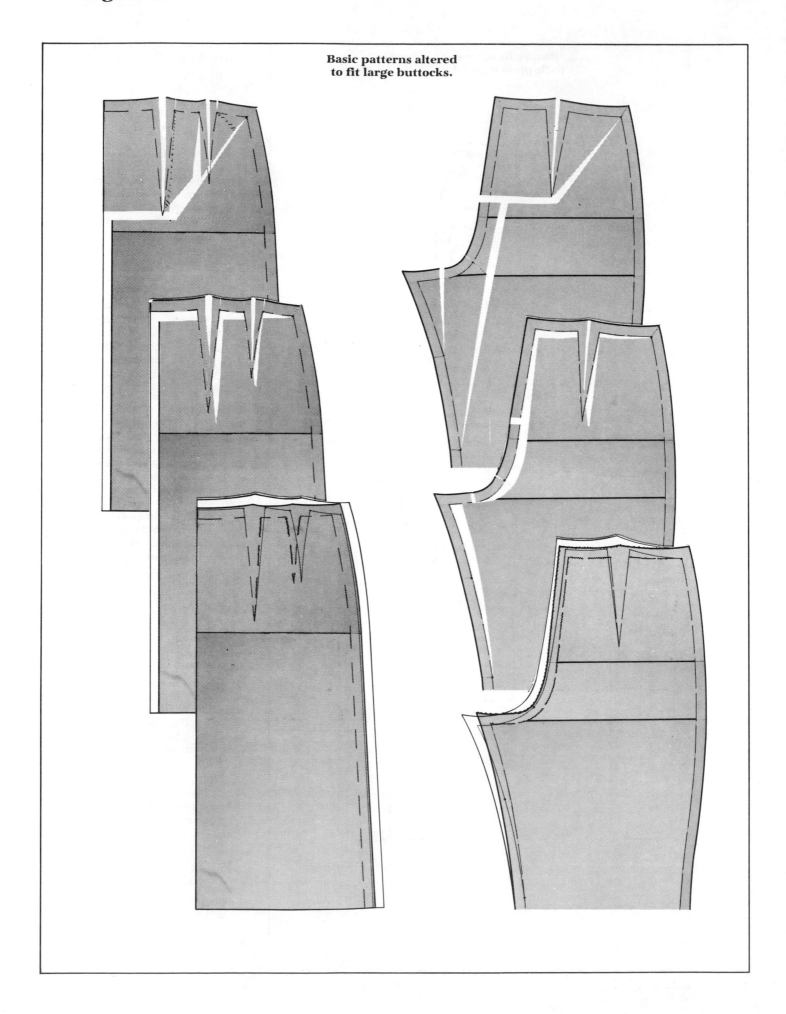

**Basic patterns altered
to fit large buttocks.**

Fashion patterns altered to fit large buttocks.

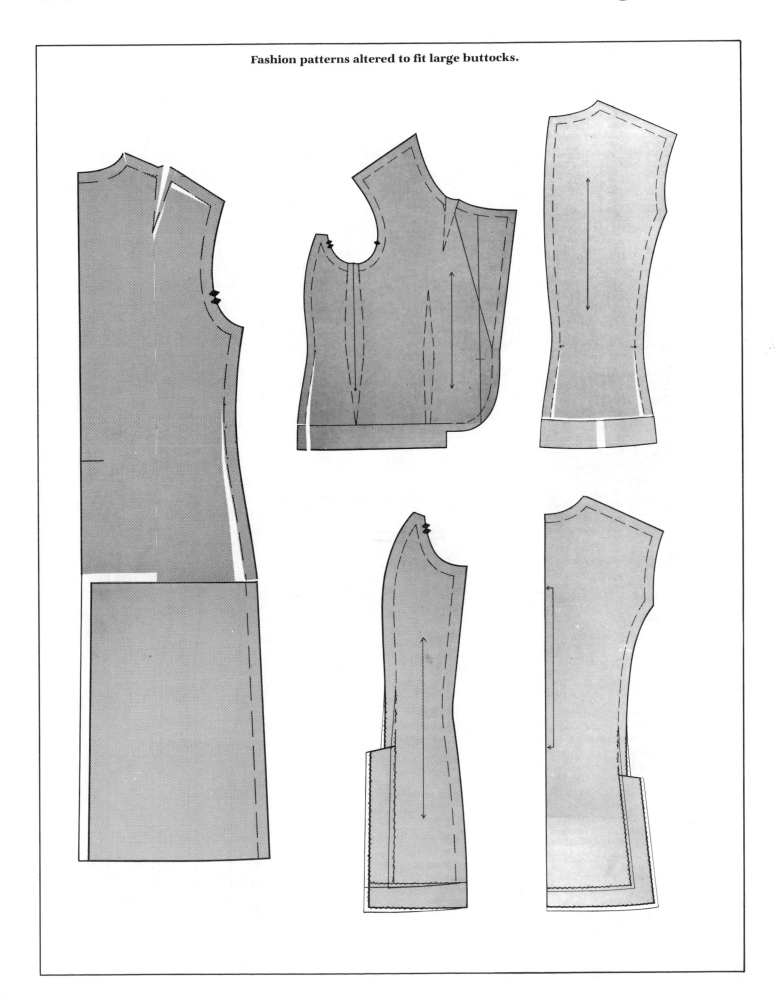

BASIC FITTING THEORY

Figure Analysis
The muscles and soft tissues which form the buttocks are less developed than average. This decreases the hip circumference. The distance decreases from the fullest part of the buttocks to the central axis of the body and to the waist.

Fitting Analysis
The garment is loose across the buttocks. Loose diagonal wrinkles droop from the upper side seam areas toward the buttocks. The hip fitting line drops across the center back area. On pants, loose diagonal wrinkles droop downward from the side seams and inseams toward the creaselines on each pant leg.

Fabric Requirements for Proper Fit
The smaller tissue structure requires less fabric length at the upper center back area and less width across the buttocks. The back darts become narrower and shorter. For pants, the more shallow back profile depth requires a narrower back crotch extension. The adjustments in length and width smooth the fabric against the body. The hip fitting line becomes level.

GARMENT & PATTERN ALTERATIONS FOR SYMMETRICAL FIGURES

Change Required
Narrow the back at the hipline; shorten the upper center back area; narrow the back crotch extensions.

Slash Method—fitting garment only
Release the back waistline seam near the side seams. To remove the excess fabric on the garment back, form a parallel, vertical tuck from the waistline toward the hem following the lengthwise grain. End at the hem edge on skirts. On pants begin tapering at the crotchline; taper to nothing at the kneeline. Decrease the dart widths to restore the waistline circumference. Shorten the darts as needed for the smaller curvature.

To narrow the back crotch extension on pants, release the stitching along the *back* crotch curve. To remove the excess fabric width on each pant leg, form a vertical tuck at the crotch. Following the lengthwise grain,

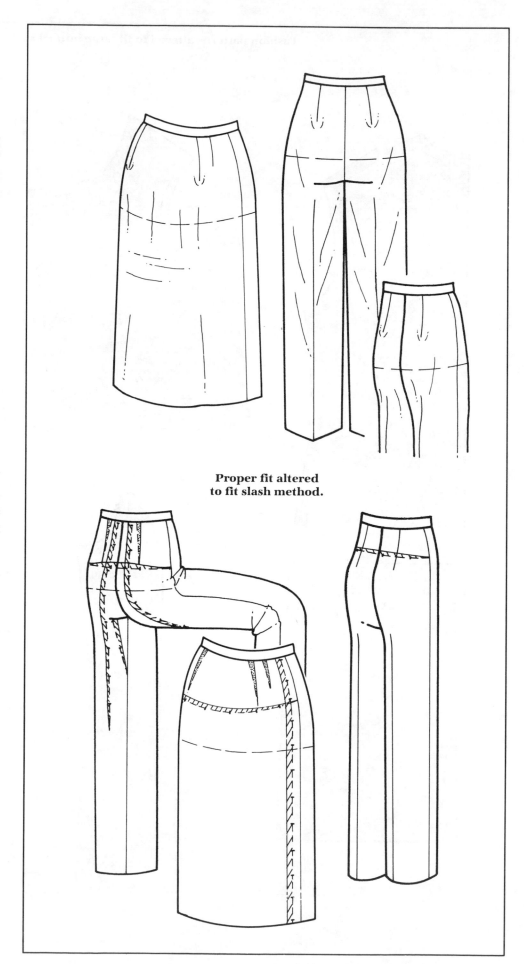

**Proper fit altered
to fit slash method.**

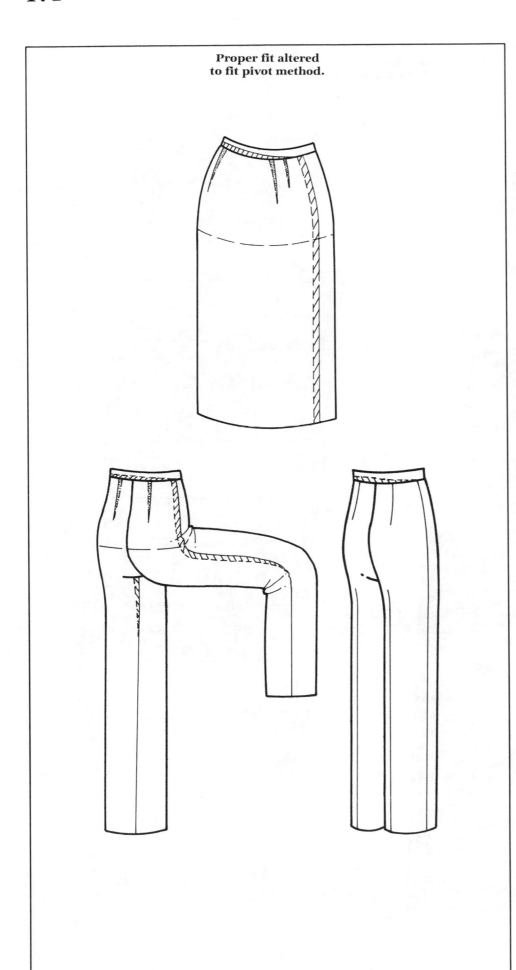

**Proper fit altered
to fit pivot method.**

taper the tuck to nothing at the inseam.

To shorten the center back, form a horizontal, parallel tuck across the garment between the back dart tips to lift the hip fitting line to a level position. Taper to nothing at the side seams.

Pivot Method

Release the back waist seam and the back waist darts. On skirts release the side seams. For pants release the side seams only to the kneeline. To narrow the garment, take in the back side seam an even amount from the waist through the hem on a skirt and from the waist to the crotchline on pants. Taper the pant side seam into the original seamline at the kneeline. Decrease the dart length and width as needed for the smaller curvature.

To reduce the back crotch looseness on pants, release the crotch seam across the inseam allowances. Release the inseam from the crotch to the kneeline.

Take in the *back* inseam area equally at the crotch to remove the excess fabric. Taper into the original seamline above the kneeline.

To shorten the center back area, lift the waistline evenly across the center back until the hip fitting line is level. Blend into the original seamline at each side seam.

**Basic patterns altered
to fit flat buttocks.**

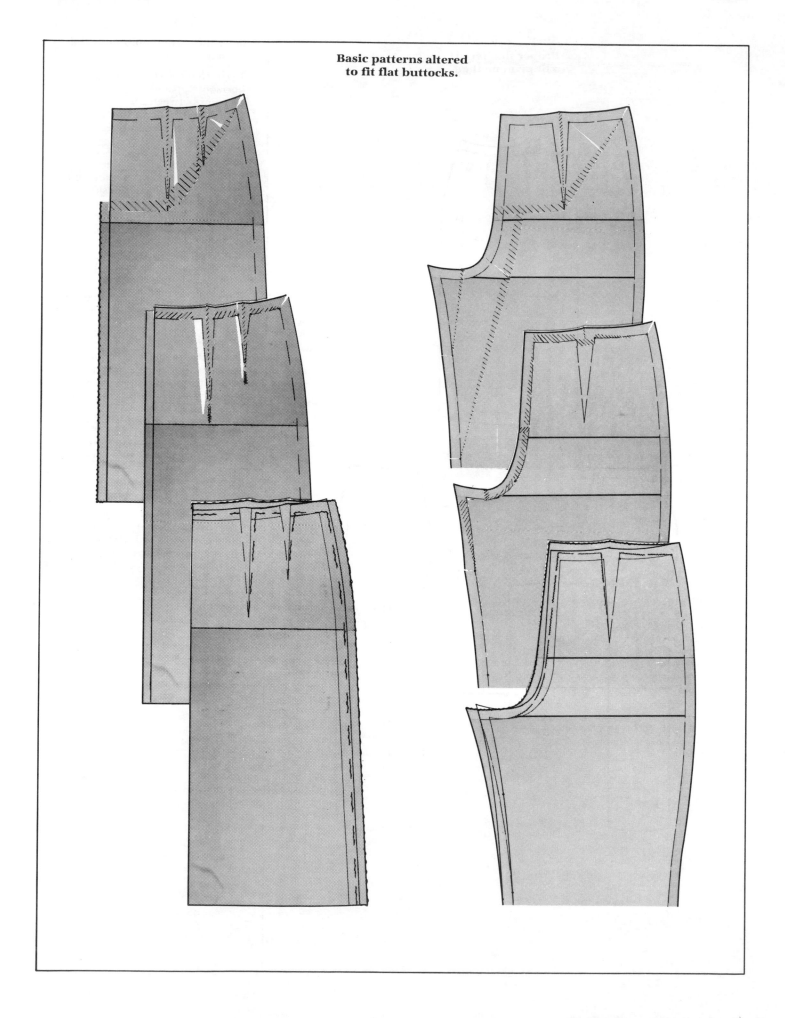

Fashion patterns altered to fit flat buttocks.

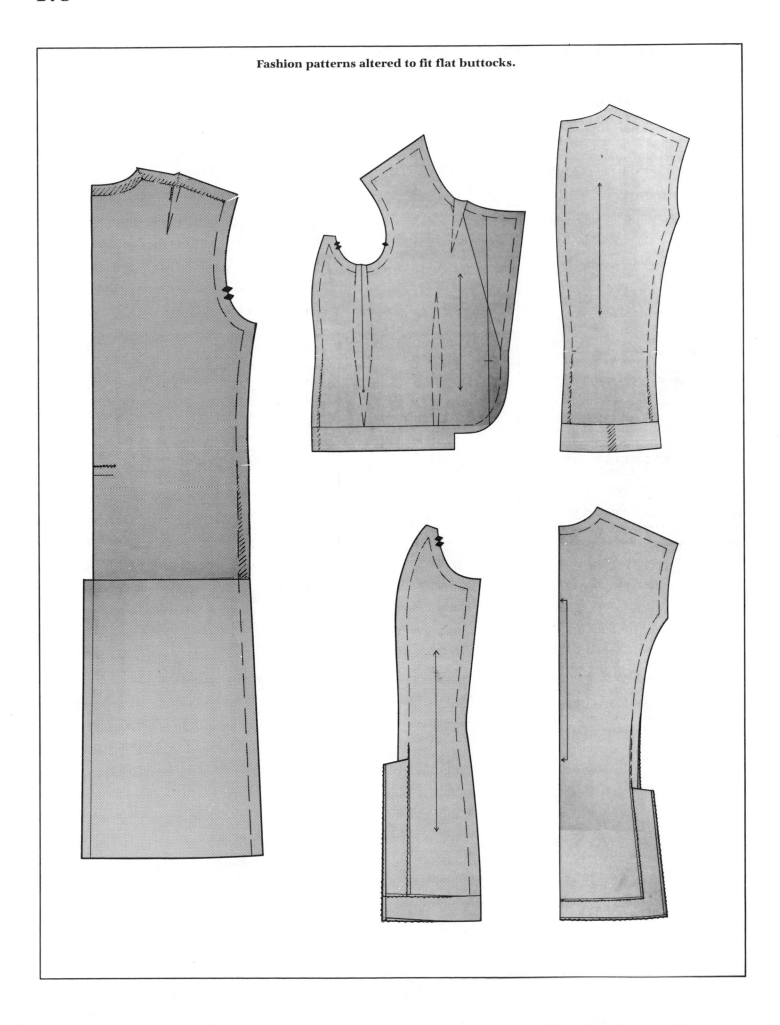

BASIC FITTING THEORY

Figure Analysis

The pubic bone or flesh may be more forward, lower, or larger than average. This creates a more abruptly curved contour at the front crotch. The front surface of the torso is vertical rather than being slightly sloped.

Fitting Analysis

This figure variation affects the fit only on pants. Wrinkles follow the contour of the front crotch curve or the fabric pulls into the crotch crevice because the curve on the front pants crotch is too shallow. The vertical fitting lines may pull toward each other at the front crotchline when the variation is extreme.

Fabric Requirements for Proper Fit

The more prominent bone structure requires a more abrupt curve at the front crotch seamline. When the variation is extreme the front crotch extension on the pants may need to be widened. The latter increases the crotch length from the hipline to the inseam.

GARMENT & PATTERN ALTERATIONS FOR SYMMETRICAL FIGURES

Change Required

Deepen the curve on the front crotch.

Slash Method— fitting garment only

Only the angle and curvature of the center front and the crotch seamline require change. Cutting the interior causes unnecessary trueing of sloped and curved edges. Follow the **Pivot Method**.

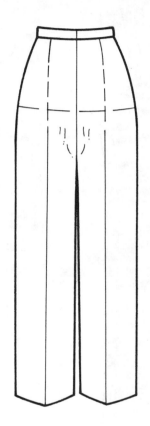

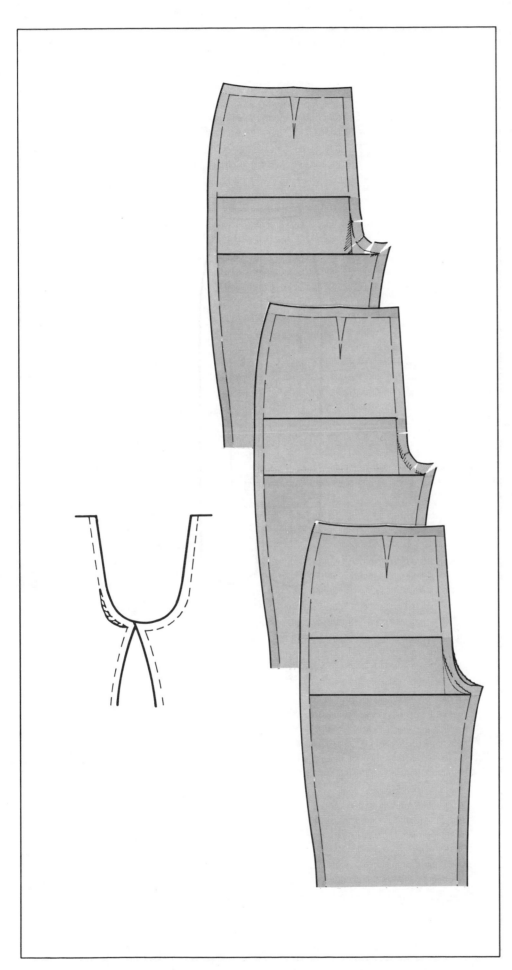

Pivot Method
Place one pant leg inside the other so the garment is wrong side out. Flatten the center front area of the pants and align the fabric grain. To relieve the strain at the crotch contour, draw a new, more rounded front crotch seamline beginning at the original center front/hipline intersection. Blend into the original crotch seamline at the inseam. The seamline on the back crotch curve may need to be flattened slightly to prevent a peak from forming at the inseam. Trim the widened seam allowance after stitching.

BASIC FITTING THEORY

Figure Analysis
The pubic bone or flesh may be smaller or the area may set back more deeply than average. This creates a crotch with a more sloping contour rather than curved. The front surface of the torso slopes noticeably.

Fitting Analysis
This figure variation affects the fit only on pants. Taut horizontal wrinkles pull across the seam at the front crotch area. The vertical grainlines pull toward each other at the groin.

Fabric Requirements for Proper Fit
The less prominent bone structure requires a flatter curve in the seamline at the front crotch.

GARMENT & PATTERN ALTERATIONS FOR SYMMETRICAL FIGURES

Change Required
Flatten the curve on the front crotch seamline.

Slash Method—fitting garment only
Only the angle and curvature of the center front and the crotch seamline require change. Cutting the interior causes unnecessary trueing of sloped and curved edges. Follow the **Pivot Method**.

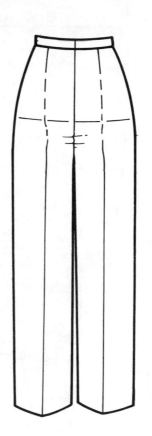

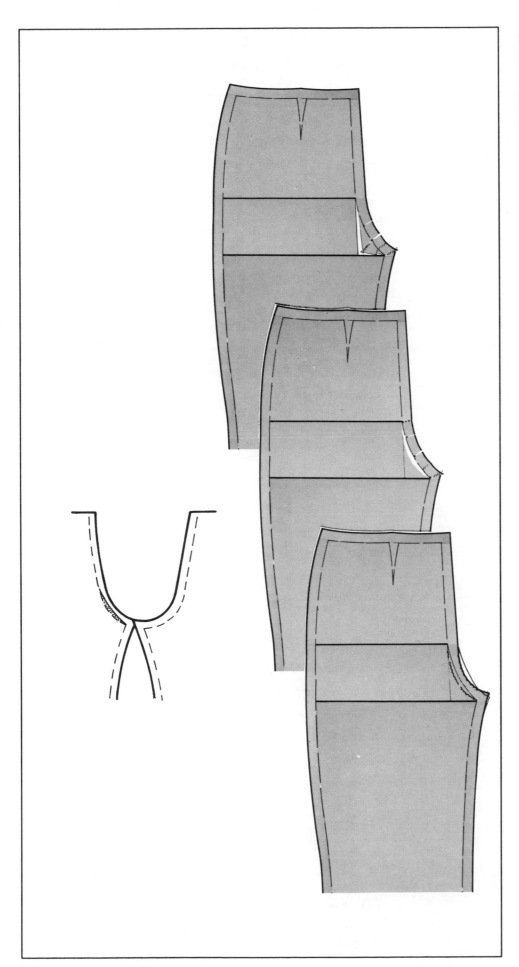

Pivot Method
Release the lower half of the front crotch seam. Put the pants on. Along the crotch curve, mark the place where the greatest amount of increase is needed. Remove the pants, and place one pant leg inside the other so the garment is wrong side out. Flatten the front area of the pants and align the fabric grain. To bring the stitching line closer to the body surface, draw a new, less curved front crotch seamline beginning at the center front/ hipline intersection. Continue through the adjustment mark and blend into the original crotch seamline at the inseam. The seamline on the back crotch curve may need to be deepened slightly to prevent a peak from forming at the inseam.

legs

22 Long Legs

23 Short Legs

24 Large Thighs at Inside

25 Shallow Thighs at Inside

26 Large Thighs at Front

27 Large Thighs at Sides

28 Outward Knee Rotation

29 Inward Knee Rotation

30 Hyperextended Calves

31 Large Legs

32 Thin Legs

BASIC FITTING THEORY

Figure Analysis
The leg bones are longer than average. The additional length may occur above or below the knee or may be distributed equally.

Fitting Analysis
The hem position is too high on the leg to create pleasing proportions. On closely fitted garments that flare near the knee, the flare origin may be too far above the knee to create pleasing proportions for an aesthetic appearance. On long tapered pants, the hem circumference may appear to be too small because it pulls taut against the leg. The hip fitting line remains level.

Fabric Requirements for Proper Fit
The additional leg length requires longer fabric areas below the thighline. On closely fitted garments that flare or taper near the knee, the extra length may be required either above or below the kneeline or distributed equally. Garments with ruffles, kick pleats, and other such details may need more length only in the garment area, or both in the garment and the detail. Proper adjustments in length will enhance the harmony between the garment and the wearer.

GARMENT & PATTERN ALTERATIONS FOR SYMMETRICAL FIGURES

Change Required
Lengthen the skirt and pants evenly below the thighline.

Slash Method—fitting garment only
Cut around the entire skirt or both pant legs below the thighline or above the design detail. Insert fabric strips. To increase the length, separate the cut edges evenly. Observe the proportions of the body, garment, and the detail on a fashion garment. Adjust each garment area to enhance the garment and wearer.

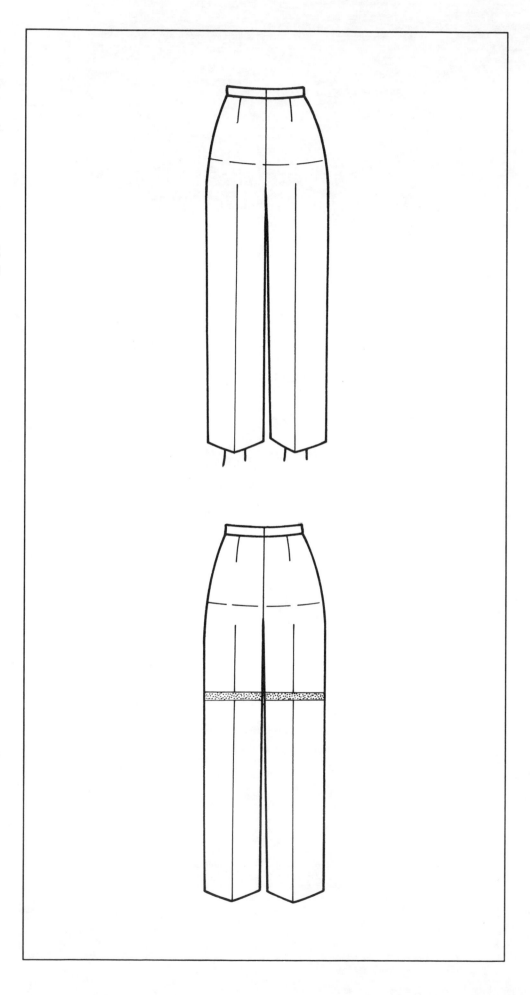

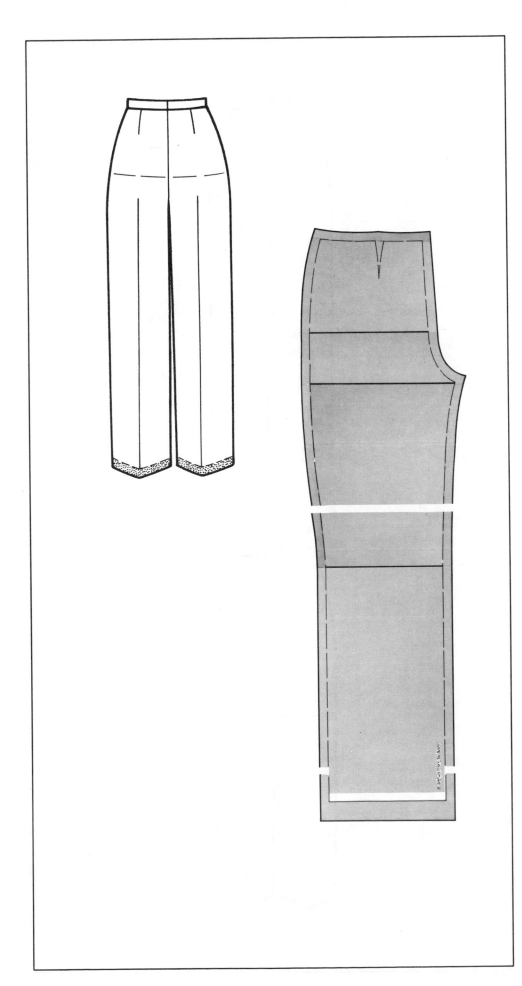

Pivot Method

Release the hem and press it flat. Mark the new hemline. If the resulting hem width is not wide enough for the style, fabric, or the wearer, face the hem edge. Hems that are too narrow appear skimpy and "remodeled" and detract from the total appearance.

Pants hems may taper ½ inch (1.2 cm) higher at the front crease to prevent excess "break" above the instep. Trim the hem allowance to an even width after tapering.

On closely fitted garments that begin to flare above the knee mark the appropriate place along the side and inseams for the flare to begin. Stitch new seams from the original seamlines at the hem edge to the adjustment marks near the knee-line. Blend into the original seamline in a slight curve.

Length also may be added to a skirt by restyling it with a yoke: lower the waistline and add a yoke wide enough to correct the total garment length. To adjust the garment width at the yokeline, narrow and shorten the darts, convert them to ease, or eliminate them. Adjust the side seam allowances as necessary.

BASIC FITTING THEORY

Figure Analysis

The leg bones are shorter than average. The shorter length may occur above or below the knee or may be distributed equally.

Fitting Analysis

The hem position is too low on the leg to create pleasing proportions. Pants hems that touch the floor fray quickly, hide the feet, and are dangerous. On closely fitted garments that flare near the knee, the flare origin may be too far below the knee for walking comfort or to create pleasing proportions for an aesthetic appearance. The hip fitting line remains level.

Fabric Requirements for Proper Fit

The decreased leg length requires shorter fabric areas below the thighline. On closely fitted garments that flare near the knee, the length may need reducing either above or below the kneeline or distributed equally. Garments with ruffles, kick pleats, and other such details may need less length only in the garment area or both in the garment and the detail. Proper adjustments in length will enhance the harmony between the garment and the wearer.

GARMENT & PATTERN ALTERATIONS FOR SYMMETRICAL FIGURES

Change Required

Shorten the skirt or the pants evenly below the thighline.

Slash Method—fitting garment only

To adjust for the *total* appropriate length, form a parallel tuck around the garment below the thighline or above the design detail. Observe the proportions of the body, garment, and detail for a fashion garment. Adjust each garment area to enhance the garment and the wearer.

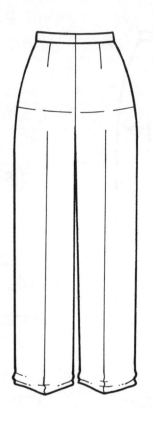

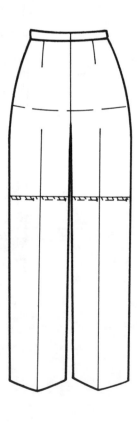

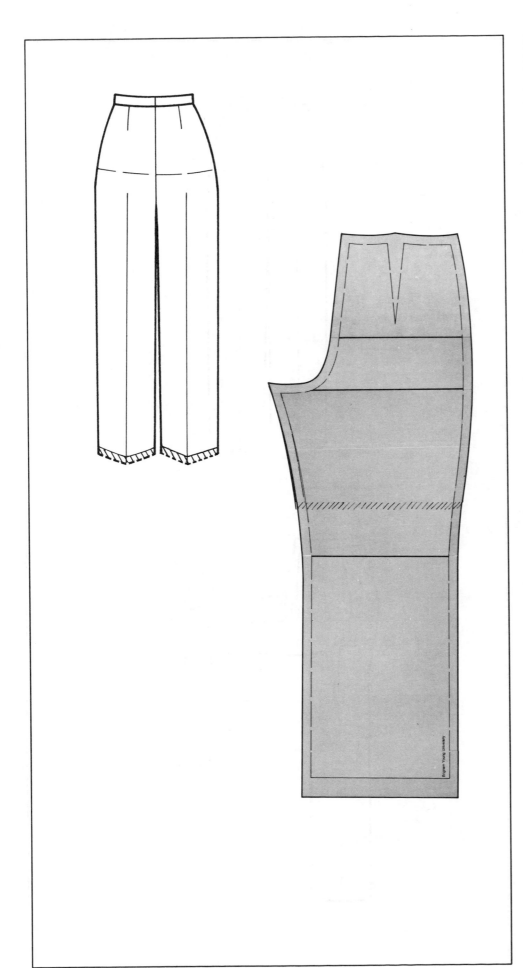

Pivot Method

Release the hem and press it flat. Mark the new hemline. Check the resulting hem width and remove the excess. Hems that are too wide for the fabric, style or the wearer are bulky and heavy and detract from the total appearance.

Pants hems may taper upward ½ inch (1.2 cm) at the front crease to prevent excess "break" above the instep. Trim the hem allowance to an even width after tapering.

On closely fitted garments that begin to flare or taper above the knee, mark the appropriate place on the side and inseams for the flare to begin both for fit and walking comfort. Stitch new seams from the original seamlines at the new hemline to the adjustment marks near the kneeline. Blend into the original seamline in a slight curve.

If a style detail is at the skirt hem, length may be reduced at the waistline instead: Release the waist seam and lift the garment an even amount until the hem position is correct. To restore the waistline circumference, form new darts, widen and lengthen the original darts or convert the increased width to gathers or tucks. Adjust the side seam allowances, as necessary, to remove excess fullness.

BASIC FITTING THEORY

Figure Analysis
The muscles and soft tissues forming the contour of the inner thigh areas are more developed than average. The inner surface of the legs may touch when the wearer stands and rub together as the person walks.

Fitting Analysis
This figure variation affects the fit only on pants. The fabric is taut across upper inseam and may rise to form tight horizontal wrinkles below the crotch. When the person walks, the fabric on the back pant leg pulls forward between the legs.

Fabric Requirements for Proper Fit
The fuller thigh area requires a wider *front* crotch extension and a straighter *front* inseam from the crotch to the knee. Excessive wear occurs on the fabric at the inseam area. Stable, closely-woven fabrics with relatively smooth textures are more durable and comfortable. Use a shorter stitch or double stitching on the crotch and upper inseams to strengthen the seams.

GARMENT & PATTERN ALTERATIONS FOR SYMMETRICAL FIGURES

Change Required
Widen the front crotch extensions.

Slash Method—fitting garment only
Place one pants leg inside the other so the garment is wrong side out. Match and pin the inseams together from the crotch to the kneeline. About 1 inch (2.5 cm) away from the inseam, cut vertically through the *front* extension and follow the lengthwise grain to the inseams. Turn the pants right side out and separate the legs. Lay each slashed area over a fabric insert. To increase width, spread the cut edges equally at the crotch as needed to relax the fabric. Taper to nothing at the knee.

If the seamline along the upper inseam area forms a curve, draw a new, straighter inseam seamline. Begin at the crotch/inseam intersection and taper to nothing at the knee.

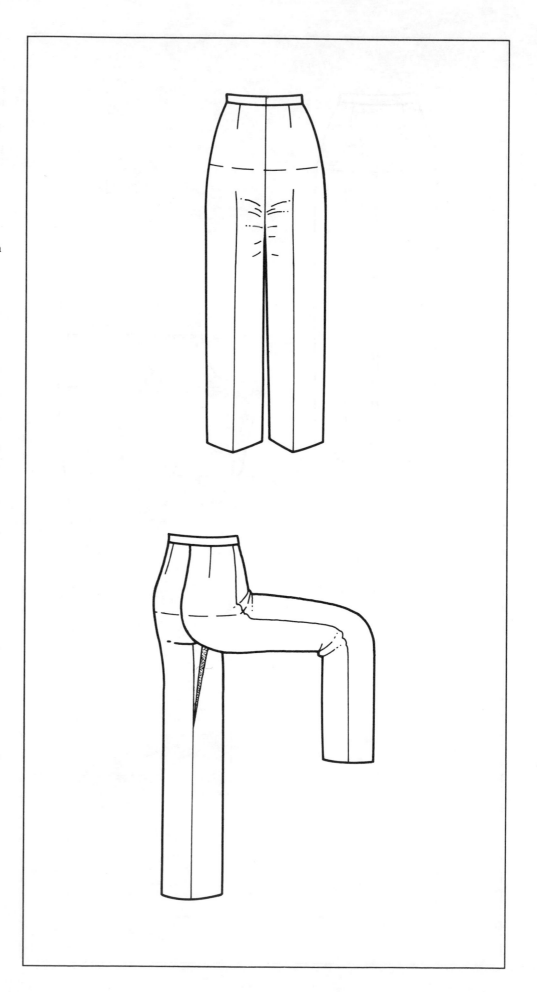

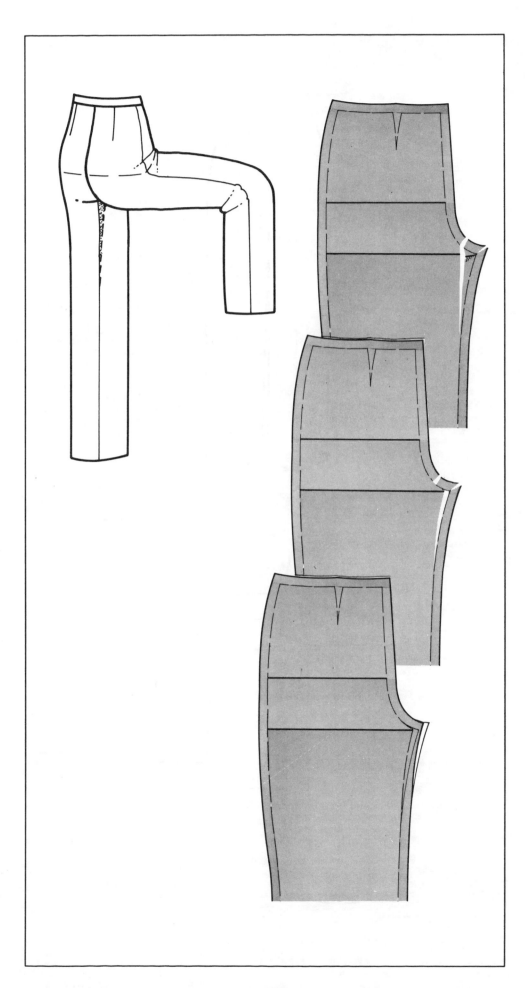

Pivot Method
Release the crotch seamline across the inseam allowances. Release the inseams from the crotch to the kneeline. To increase width at the crotch, let out the front inseam allowances equally at the crotch to relieve the strain. Form the new inseam seamline as a rather straight line. Blend into the original seamline above the kneeline. Check for fit and comfort. Repeat for the back crotch extension, if necessary.

BASIC FITTING THEORY

Figure Analysis
The muscles and the soft tissues forming the contour of the inner thigh areas are less developed than average. When the person stands, there is a definite, visible space between the legs from the crotch nearly to the knee.

Fitting Analysis
This figure variation affects the fit only on pants. The fabric is loose along the upper inseam and hangs in loose vertical folds.

Fabric Requirements for Proper Fit
The flatter inner thigh area requires a narrower *front* crotch extension. This results in a more vertical inseam.

GARMENT & PATTERN ALTERATIONS FOR SYMMETRICAL FIGURES

Change Required
Narrow the front crotch extensions.

Slash Method—fitting garment only
Release the seam along the *front* crotch curve. To remove the excess fabric width, form a vertical tuck on each crotch extension about 1 inch (2.5 cm) away from the inseam. Follow the lengthwise grain, tapering the tuck to nothing at the inseams just above the knee.

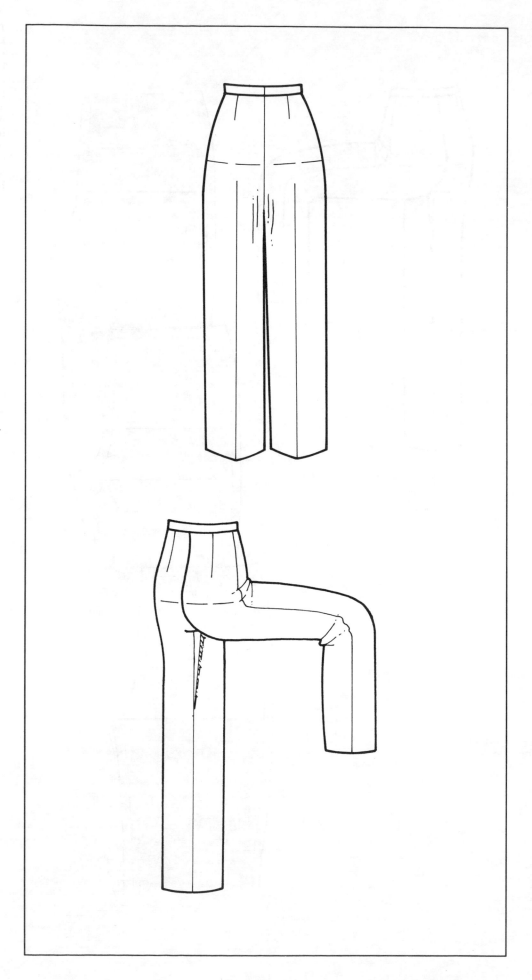

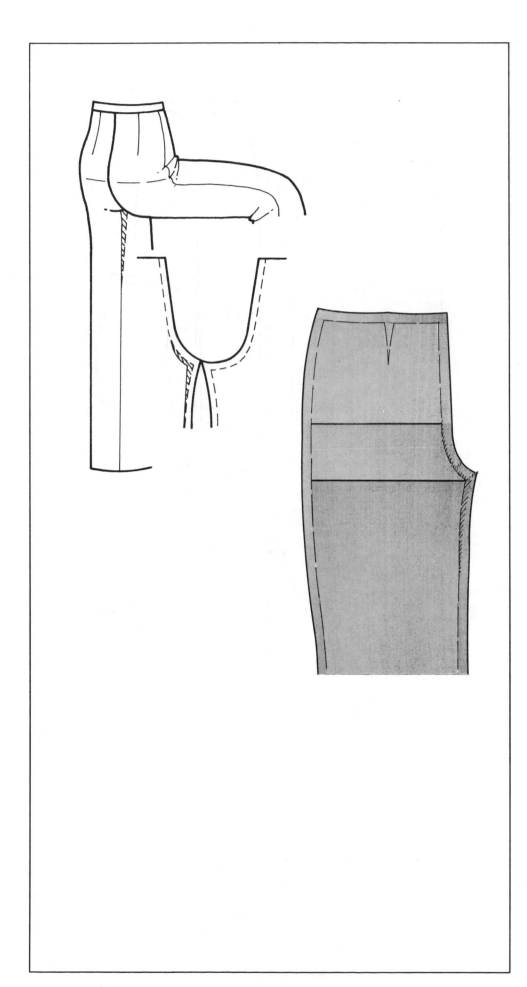

Pivot Method
Release the crotch seamline across the inseam allowances. Release the inseams from the crotch to the kneeline. To remove the excess fabric at the crotch, take up the front inseam areas equally as needed. Blend into the original center front at the hipline. Form a new inseam seamline as a rather straight line. Blend into the original seamline near the kneeline.

BASIC FITTING THEORY

Figure Analysis
The thigh muscles across the front of the legs are fuller than average. This creates the illusion that the recess at the groin is deeper than average.

Fitting Analysis
The fabric pulls taut across the front surface of the upper thigh areas and cups under the buttocks. The side seams curve toward the front. When the wearer walks, the front fabric of a skirt rises to form a horizontal fold at the groin. The hemline rises across the center front area. On pants, horizontal folds form across each inseam near the crotch and may cause the front creaselines to curve toward each other at the thigh and hang toward each other at the hem.

Fabric Requirements for Proper Fit
The thigh fullness requires more fabric width at the midfront areas. On a skirt, transfer the front dart to the hem edge to place the flare over the thigh. The wider garment area relaxes and hangs smoothly below the hipline. A-line, circular and gathered skirts include more fullness at the thigh level, therefore, may require no alteration and are more appropriate style choices.

On pants the dart transfer also increases the amount of fabric for the thigh by widening the area from the front creaseline to the crotch extension.

GARMENT & PATTERN ALTERATIONS FOR SYMMETRICAL FIGURES

Change Required
Widen the midfront areas.

Slash Method—fitting garment only
On skirts, slash halfway between each side seam and the center front from the hem to waistline. Follow the lengthwise grain. Insert fabric strips. To increase the width, spread the cut edges evenly from the hem to the thighline. Taper to nothing at the dart tip area or at the waistline as the body requires.

On pants, place one pant leg inside the other so the garment is wrong side out. Match and pin the inseams together from the crotch to the kneeline. About 1 inch (2.5 cm)

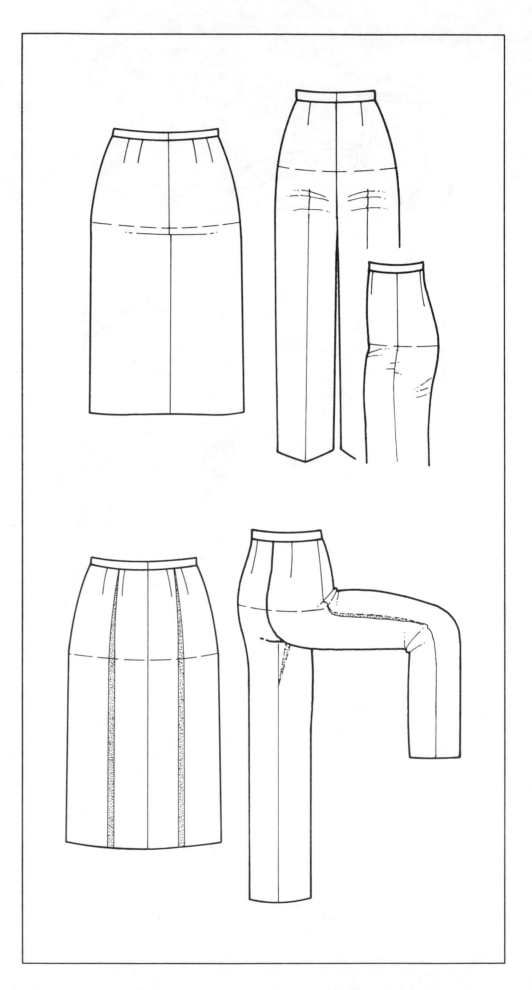

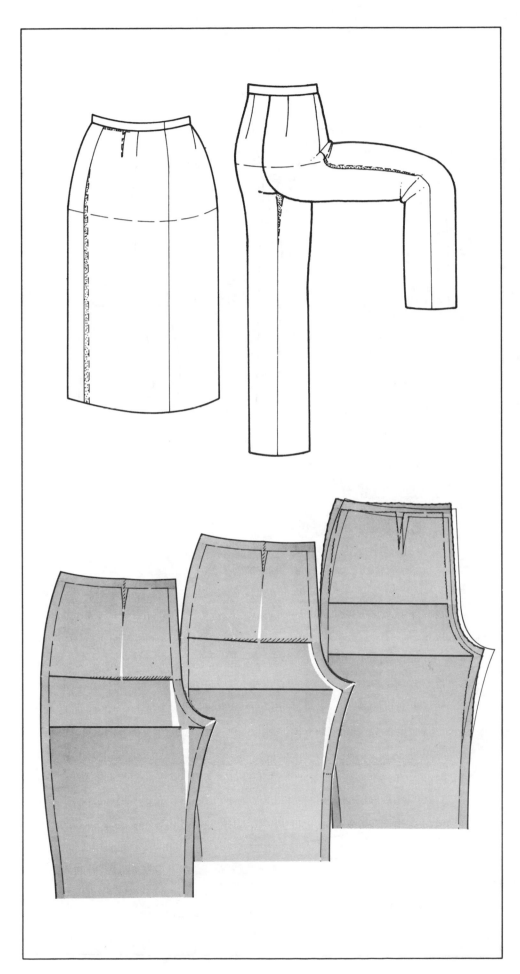

away from the inseam, cut vertically through the *front* extension and follow the lengthwise grain to the inseams. Turn the pants right side out and separate the legs. Lay each slashed area over a fabric insert. To increase width, spread the cut edges equally at the crotch as needed to relax the fabric. Taper to nothing at the inseams.

Release the side seam from the hip to the kneeline. Let out the seam allowance of the pants *front* until the front creaselines relax and hang plumb.

Pivot Method
On skirts, release the side seams from the hip to the hem. Determine the amount of width increase needed at the thigh level. Mark the new side seams parallel to the original seams from hem to thigh.

To transfer the waist dart to the hem edge, release the remaining side seam and the waistline to the dart. Decrease the side waist dart one-half of its width. When only one dart is present, decrease the width by one-third. To complete the dart transfer, lengthen the side seam at the waistline (approximately one-half the width change at the thigh). Taper back to the original seam at the dart.

To restore the side length, shorten the new side seam at the hem the same amount it was raised at the waist. Pin the side seams together up to the thigh level. Put on the skirt and taper the side seam to the waist. Mark the new front hemline.

On pants release the side seam from the hip to the kneeline, the waistline, the center front and the front crotch seam across the inseam allowances. Release the inseam from the crotch to the kneeline. Let out the front seam allowances of both the side and inseam as needed to relax the fabric and to allow the creases and side seams to hang plumb. The longer crotch extension may cause the fabric to sag against the groin. Raise the waist across the center front to remove the excess fabric. Mark a new waistline parallel to the original across the center front. Taper to the original at the side seam. The front crotch curve may need to be flattened slightly.

On the pattern, the increased width of midfront is obtained by transferring the dart to the center and inseam of the pattern.

BASIC FITTING THEORY

Figure Analysis

The muscles and soft tissues across the sides of the legs extend more than average and may lack tone. The greatest width and side curvature are below the hipline.

Fitting Analysis

The fabric pulls taut across the side seams at the thighline and cups under the buttocks. When the person walks, the garment rises and forms a horizontal wrinkle above each thigh. The hip fitting line rises at the sides.

On pants the fabric also pulls taut across the upper inseam area. The front creaselines curve outward at thigh level and slant away from each other at the hems.

Fabric Requirements for Proper Fit

The fullness at the side of the legs requires more fabric width below the hipline. The greatest curvature along the side seam occurs at the thigh level because the "dart" concealed in the side seamlines increases in width. The wider garment area relaxes over the thigh and the hip fitting line becomes level. A-line, circular and gathered skirts include more fullness at the thigh level, therefore, these styles may require no alteration and are appropriate choices.

GARMENT & PATTERN ALTERATIONS FOR SYMMETRICAL FIGURES

Change Required

Widen the side seam areas at the thighline.

Slash Method—fitting garment only

Adjust *both the front and back* of a skirt to keep the widths of the two areas balanced. Release the waist seam across the side seam areas. On both the back and the front near each side seam, cut from the edges of the waist seam allowance through the hem edge. Follow the lengthwise grain. Insert fabric strips. To gain the needed width, spread each set of cut edges evenly along the entire slash. Take in the side seams equally at the waist to restore the waist circumference. Taper to nothing just below the hipline.

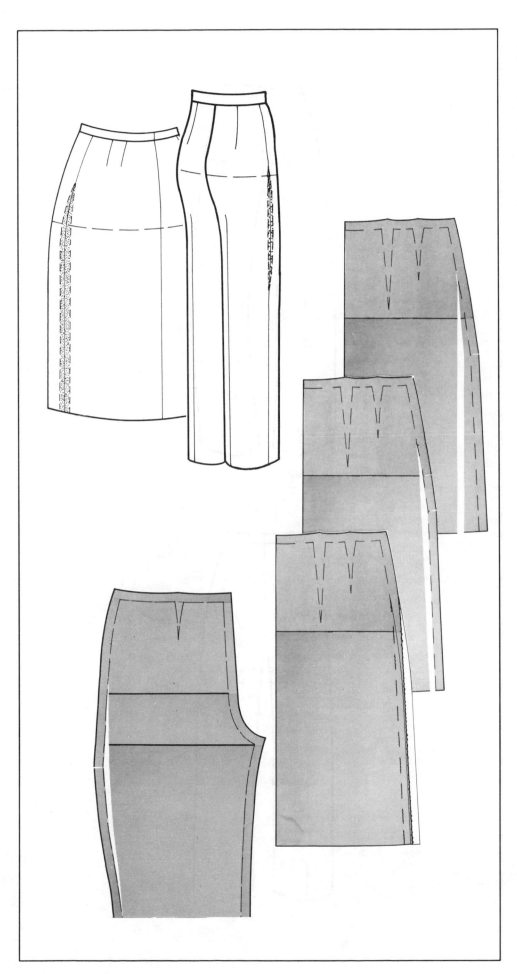

Pivot Method

On skirts, release the side seams from the hem past the hipline where the tightness begins. At the thighline, let out the back and front seam allowances equally until the fabric relaxes. Continue the adjustment an even amount through the hem edge. Blend into the original seamline as required above the hipline.

On pants, release the side seams from hip to kneeline. Let out the back and front seam allowances equally at the thighline. Blend into the original seamline near the ends of the opened areas.

BASIC FITTING THEORY

Figure Analysis
The legs bow outward with the greatest curvature occurring at the knee. Often the toes point inward to counterbalance the body.

Fitting Analysis
On pants the front creaselines bow outward at the knees and slant inward at the hems. At the kneeline, the fabric is taut along the side seams and loose at the inseams. Diagonal wrinkles form across the inseam at the kneeline. The hemline rises at the sides.

Fabric Requirements for Proper Fit
The outward curvature of the legs requires more length at the side seams and less at the inseams. The adjusted seam lengths reposition the fabric to relax and lie smooth. The hemline becomes level. Flared skirts and pants help to camouflage the figure variation and may require no adjustment.

GARMENT & PATTERN ALTERATIONS FOR SYMMETRICAL FIGURES

Change Required
Lengthen the side seams; shorten the inseams.

Slash Method—fitting garment only
Near the thighline, cut across both *side seams.* Continue cutting along the crosswise grain to the front and back creases. Insert fabric strips. To increase the side seam length, spread each set of edges equally at the side seams until the fabric relaxes and the front creaselines straighten below the *knee.* To shorten the inseams, continue following the crosswise grain with a tuck across each inseam to remove an amount equal to the side adjustment. Taper each adjustment to nothing at the creases. For a slight figure variation, decrease the inseam length by forming a tuck across each inseam at the thighline. Adjust the tuck widths equally until the front creaselines hang plumb. Taper each tuck to nothing at the side seams. On the pattern, establish a new grainline parallel to the original creaselines *below the knee.*

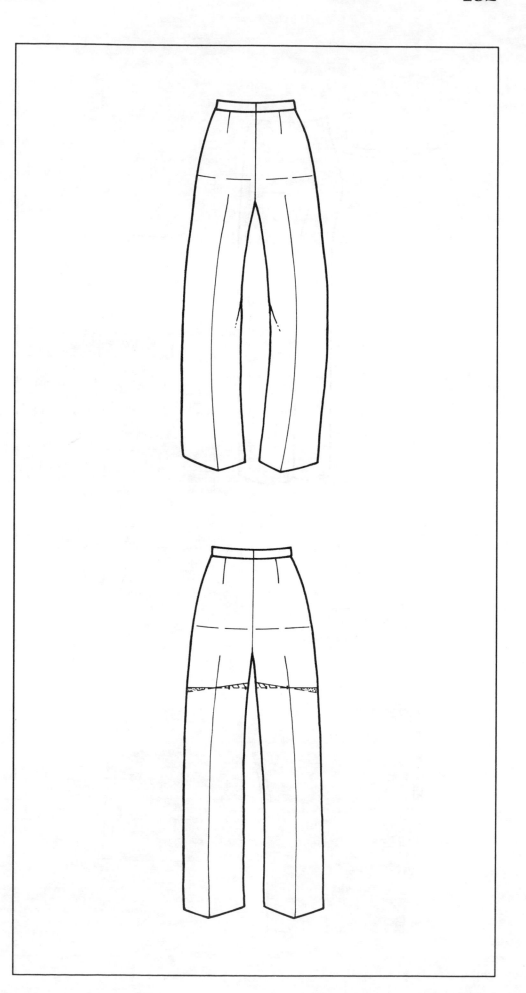

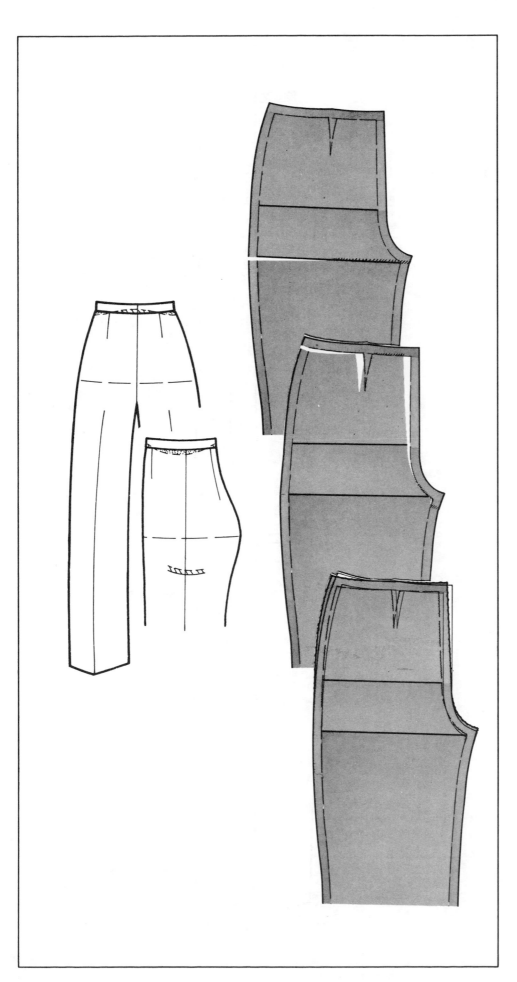

Pivot Method
Release the entire waistline. The center front and back areas require lifting; clip the crotch seam allowance at ½ inch (1.2 cm) intervals across the inseam area.

Put on the pants. Lift the waistline across the center front and back and lower it at the sides until the pant legs hang smoothly and the front creaselines straighten below the knee. Blend into the original waistline near the sides. Clip at the crotch to relieve any tightness. Stitch the new crotch seamline ¼ inch (0.6 mm) below the ends of the clips. Taper into the original seamline near the hipline. Trim the widened crotch seam allowance.

For a slight figure variation, release the back and front waistline across the side seam areas nearly to the centers. Lower the waist at the side seams to relieve the strain at the knee. Taper into the original waist seamline near the center front and back.

BASIC FITTING THEORY

Figure Analysis

The legs bow inward with the greatest curvature occurring at the knee. Often the toes point outward to counterbalance the body.

Fitting Analysis

The figure variation affects the fit only on pants. The front creaselines bow inward at the knees and slant outward at the hems. At the kneeline, the fabric is taut along the inseams and loose at the sides. Diagonal wrinkles form from the inner edge of each knee upward toward each creaseline. The hemline rises at the inseams. On tight-legged pants, a loose horizontal fold forms across each side seam at the kneeline.

Fabric Requirements for Proper Fit

The inward curvature of the legs requires more length at the inseams and less at the side seams. The adjusted seam lengths reposition the fabric to relax and lie smooth. The hemline becomes level. Pants that flare gently from the thighline to the hem help to camouflage the figure variation.

GARMENT & PATTERN ALTERATIONS FOR SYMMETRICAL FIGURES

Change Required

Shorten the side seams; lengthen the inseams.

Slash Method—fitting garment only

To decrease the side seam length, form a tuck across each side seam at thigh level. Adjust the tuck widths equally until front creaselines hang plumb. Taper each tuck to nothing at the inseams.

If tightness is present along the inseams at the knee area, release the stitching from the thighline to below the kneeline. Let out the seam allowances equally at the knee until the fabric relaxes. Taper into the original seamline near the crotch and hemline.

Check the hemline position and adjust evenly to create a pleasing proportion between the garment and the wearer.

On the pattern establish a new grainline parallel to the original creaselines below the knee.

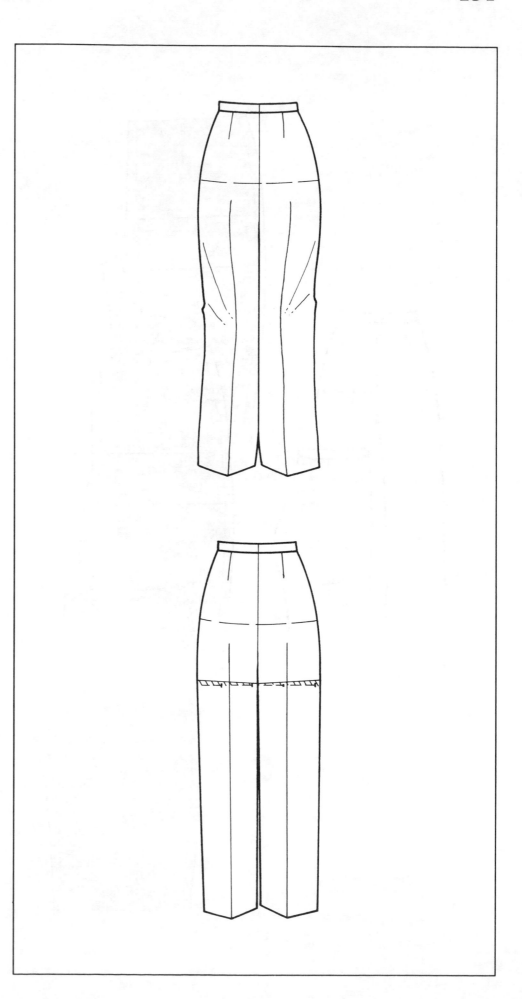

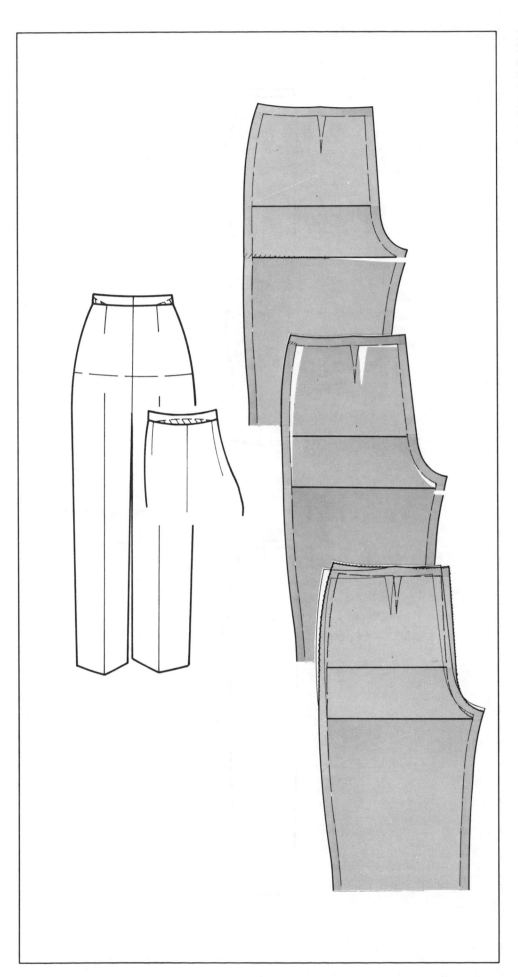

Pivot Method
Release the entire waistline except a short distance across the center front and center back. Lift the waist at the side seams until the pant legs hang smoothly and the front creaselines are plumb below the knee. Blend into the original seamline near the center front and the center back.

BASIC FITTING THEORY

Figure Analysis
The lower leg bones appear to bow toward the back. The back curvature may be the result of tense, "locked" knees. Back muscle development may be involved.

Fitting Analysis
On pants, the fabric forms a loose horizontal fold above the calves. The side seams may curve toward the back at the calf level. The hip fitting line remains level. The hemline rises slightly across the back.

Fabric Requirements for Proper Fit
Decreasing the length of the fabric across the upper center back area lifts the fabric so it can hang vertically from the buttocks curvature. This variation may require a deeper back crotch curve. Pants styles with fuller legs will camouflage this variation and may need no adjustment.

GARMENT & PATTERN ALTERATIONS FOR SYMMETRICAL FIGURES

Change Required
Shorten the upper center back area; restore the back crotch length by lowering the crotch curve.

Slash Method—fitting garment only
Below the crotchline, form a tuck across the creaseline to lift the fabric until it hangs smoothly and away from the surface of the calves. Taper to nothing at the side seams and inseams.

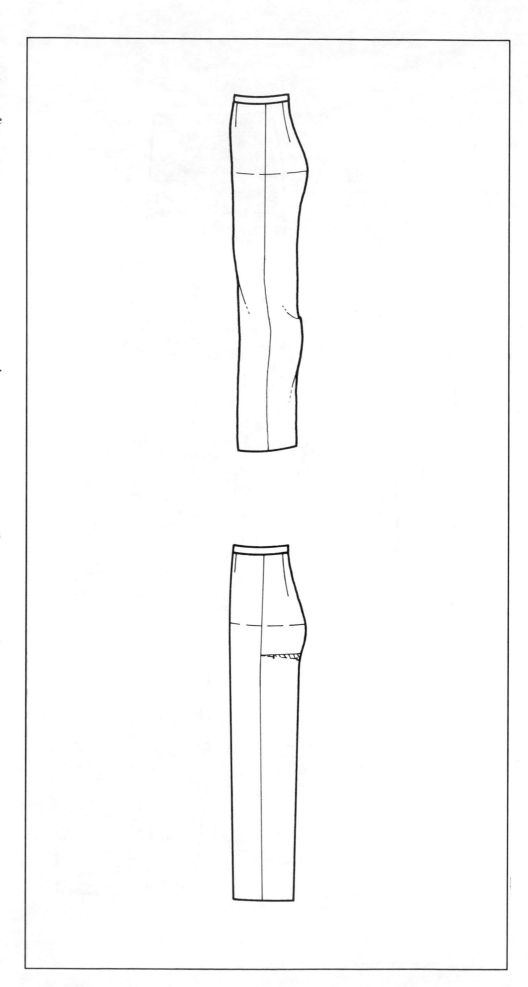

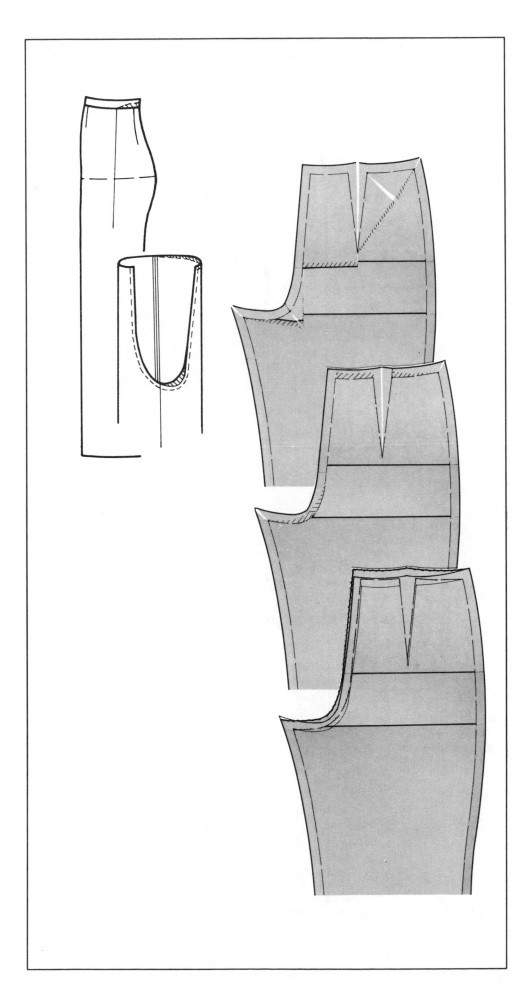

Pivot Method
Release the back waist seam. Before
the center back can be lifted, clip
the crotch seam allowance each
½ inch (1.2 cm) along the back
crotch curve. Put on the pants and
lift the waistline a parallel amount
across the center back until the
fabric hangs smoothly and away
from the surface of the calves.
Blend into the original seamline at
the side seams. Continue the clips
deep enough to relieve the strain at
the crotch. Stitch a new crotch
seam ¼ inch (0.6 mm) below the
ends of the clips. Blend into the
original seamline at back and front
near the hipline.

BASIC FITTING THEORY

Figure Analysis

The leg bones may be larger than average. The muscles and other soft tissues are more developed and may lack tone. The larger development may occur along the entire length of the leg or only over that of the upper or lower portion. Occasionally, excess soft tissues create fullness at the ankle and conceal the angularity of the bone structure at the ankle.

Fitting Analysis

This figure variation affects the fit of pants primarily. The fabric pulls taut around each leg and forms horizontal wrinkles at the crotchline. The hemlines rise and the upper part of the pants appears loose and bloused. For skirts refer to **12 Broad Hips** and **27 Large Thighs at Sides**. A slightly flared skirt with the hemline just above the fullest area of the calves helps to camouflage the fullness of the legs and creates a more pleasing proportion.

Fabric Requirements for Proper Fit

The larger circumference of the legs requires more fabric width below the hipline on both the back and front of the pants. The larger pant legs permit the upper pants area to lower to the correct position. The bloused appearance disappears. The larger leg areas relax over the figure and hang free. If a pants pattern is purchased in a larger size to fit the legs, the adjustment is simpler, the waistline circumference is reduced instead (see **4 Small Waist**).

GARMENT & PATTERN ALTERATIONS FOR SYMMETRICAL FIGURES

Change Required

Widen the back and front pant legs.

Slash Method—fitting garment only

Near the midfront and midback of each pant leg, cut along the lengthwise grain from the hem through the hipline. Insert fabric strips. From the hemline to the kneeline, spread the cut edges evenly to relax the fabric and restore the ease. Taper to nothing at the hipline.

On the pattern, one fourth of the increase should be added at each

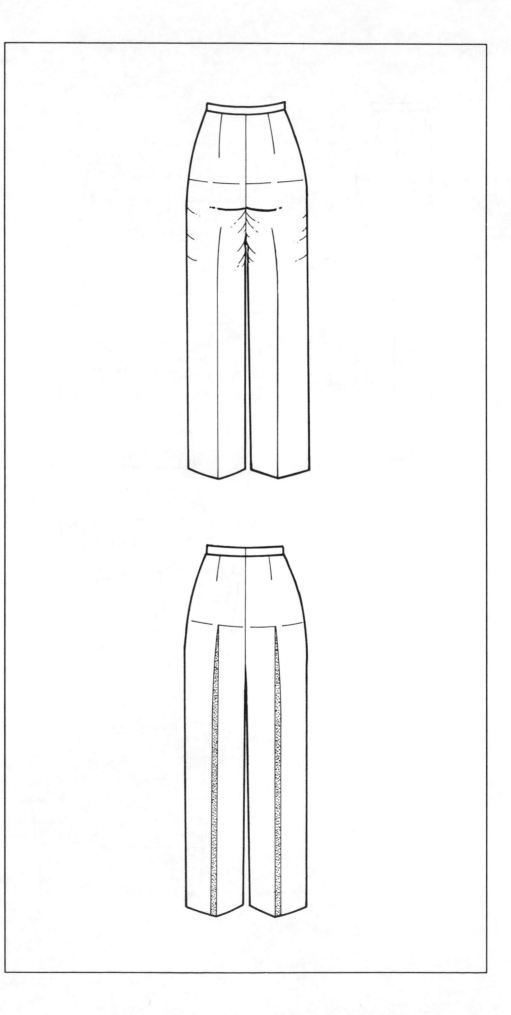

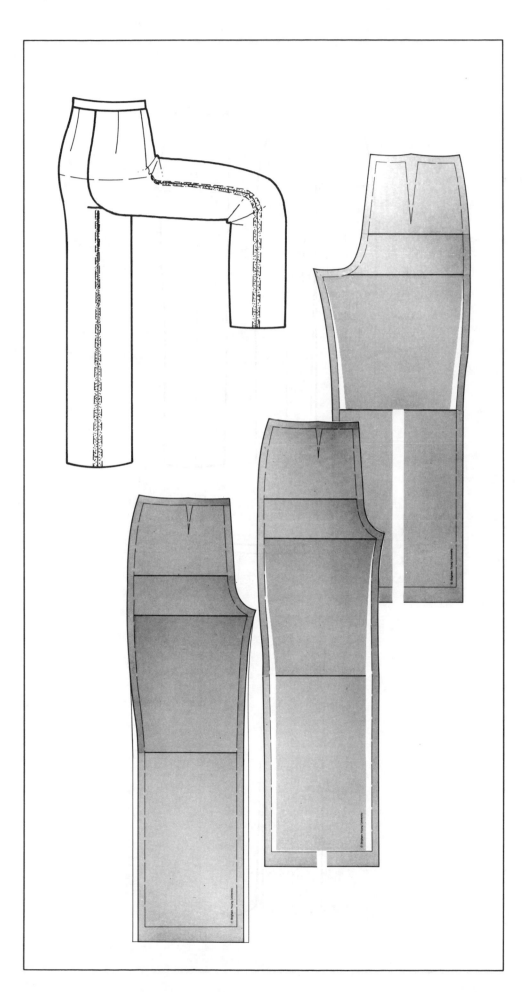

side seam and inseams to keep the pant leg balanced.

Pivot Method
Release the crotch seam across the inseam allowances. Release the inseams from the crotch to the kneeline. Release the side seams from the hem to the hipline. From the hemline to the kneeline, let out *front* and *back* side seam allowances evenly until the fabric relaxes and the ease is restored. Blend the side seam adjustments into the original seamline at the hipline. Let out the inseam even to the knee. Taper the inseam to the crotch. Decrease to one-half the amount at the crotchline.

BASIC FITTING THEORY

Figure Analysis

The leg bones may be smaller than average. The muscles and other soft tissues are firmer or less developed than average. The smaller development may occur over the entire length of the legs or only over the upper or lower portion. The angularity of the ankle bone structure is usually quite apparent.

Fitting Analysis

This figure variation affects the fit on pants primarily. The entire pants leg areas are loose and appear too large. The fabric hangs in slight vertical folds. The looseness begins at the hipline but is most apparent from the crotch to the kneeline. Closely fitted pants and straight or extremely full skirt styles will emphasize the thinness of the lower leg areas.

Fabric Requirements for Proper Fit

The smaller circumference of the legs requires less fabric width below the hipline on both the back and front of the pants. The narrower pant leg areas lie closer to the leg surfaces and enhance the proportions between the garment and the wearer.

GARMENT & PATTERN ALTERATIONS FOR SYMMETRICAL FIGURES

Change Required

Narrow the back and front pant leg areas.

Slash Method—fitting garment only

Along each creaseline of both pant legs form a parallel tuck from the hem to the crotchline. Adjust the tuck widths as needed to remove the excess fabric. Taper to nothing at the hipline. On the pattern, one-fourth of the total decrease should be removed at each side seam and inseam to keep the pant legs balanced.

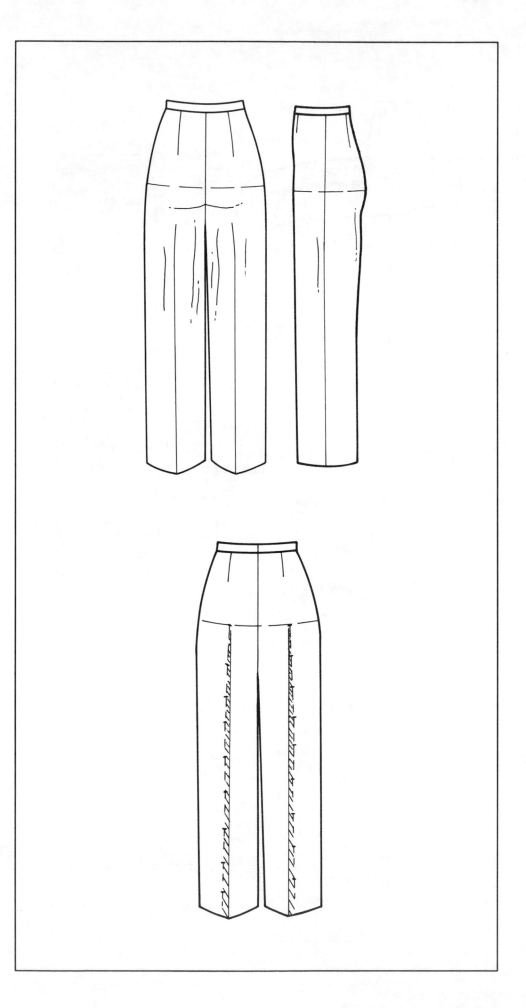

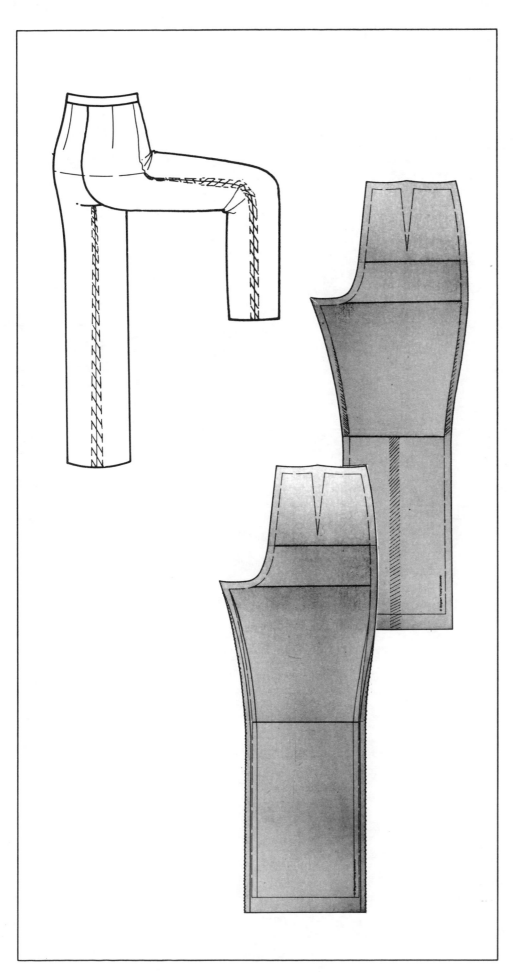

Pivot Method
Release the crotch seam across the inseam allowances. Release the inseams from the crotch to the kneeline. Along both the side seams and the inseams take in the back and front pant area evenly from the hem to the kneeline to remove the excess fabric. Blend the side seam adjustments into the original seamline at the hipline. Keep the inseam adjustment even to the knee, then taper to the crotchline. Remove the original stitching on the adjusted areas of the side seams and the remainder of the inseam.

neck

33 High Neck Base at Sides

34 Shallow Neck Base at Sides

35 Large Neck

36 Thin Neck

37 Forward Neck

38 Dowager Hump

BASIC FITTING THEORY

Figure Analysis

There is less than average angularity where the neck edges meet the shoulders. The heavier muscles and body tissues that fill this area create an illusion of sloping shoulders.

Fitting Analysis

The front neckline is uncomfortably tight. Diagonal wrinkles pull from the neckline toward the armscyes. A loose horizontal fold of fabric may form across the base of the neck. The back neckline may rise at the center back. The strain causes the armscye edges to ripple, making them appear too large. The chest and blade fitting lines rise at the body centers. A center front opening will not close properly at the neckline.

Fabric Requirements for Proper Fit

The neck fullness requires longer front neckline extensions and more length at the upper center back area. The back and front necklines should be widened. The larger garment areas relieve the tightness at the front neckline and permit the back neckline and the armscyes to relax and align with the body contours. The chest and blade fitting lines become level.

GARMENT & PATTERN ALTERATIONS FOR SYMMETRICAL FIGURES

Change Required

Lengthen the front neckline extensions and the upper center back area; increase the neckline width.

Slash Method—fitting garment only

On the garment front, slash through the neck seam allowance near each shoulder seam. Continue cutting across to each armscye seamline. Insert fabric strips. Spread each set of cut edges equally at the neckline until the fabric relaxes.

On the garment back, slash across the upper blade area from shoulder tip to shoulder tip. Insert a fabric strip. Spread the cut edges evenly below the neckline. Adjust until the tightness is relieved and both fitting lines become level. Taper the adjustments to nothing at the armscyes. Widen the neckline opening at the shoulder area, as needed.

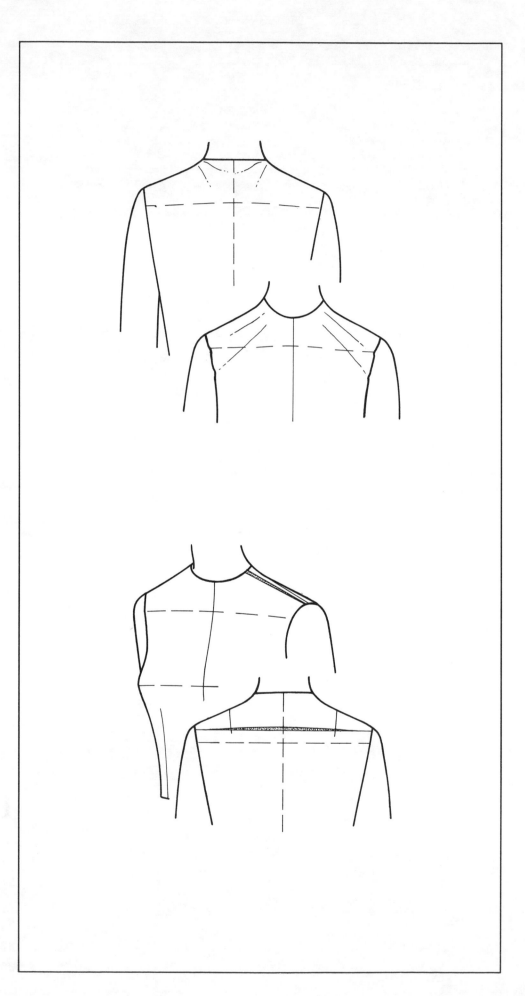

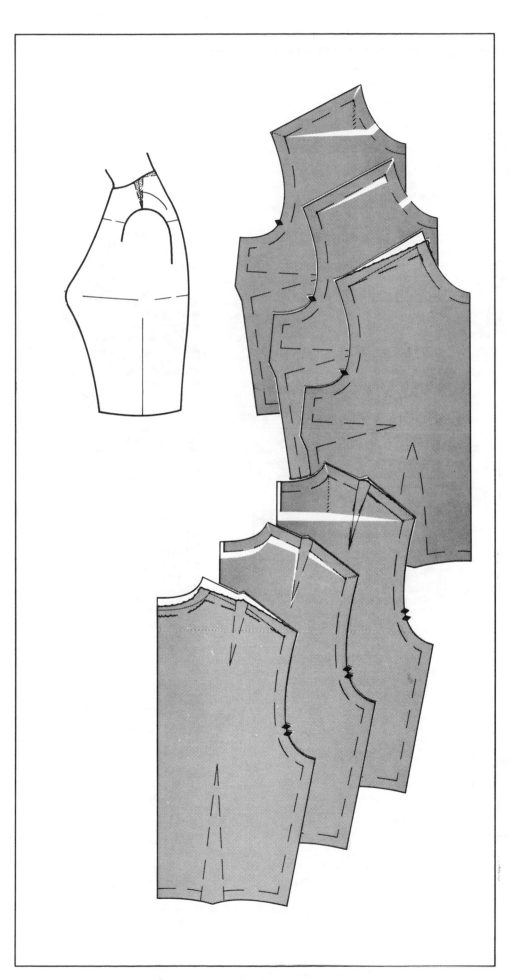

Pivot Method
Release the shoulder seams. At the neckline, let out the front and back seam allowances equally to relieve the tightness and to straighten the chest and blade fitting lines. Taper to nothing at the armscyes.

Across the center back raise the neckline seam equal to the change at the shoulders. Blend into the original at the new shoulder seamline. Widen the neckline opening at the shoulder area, as needed.

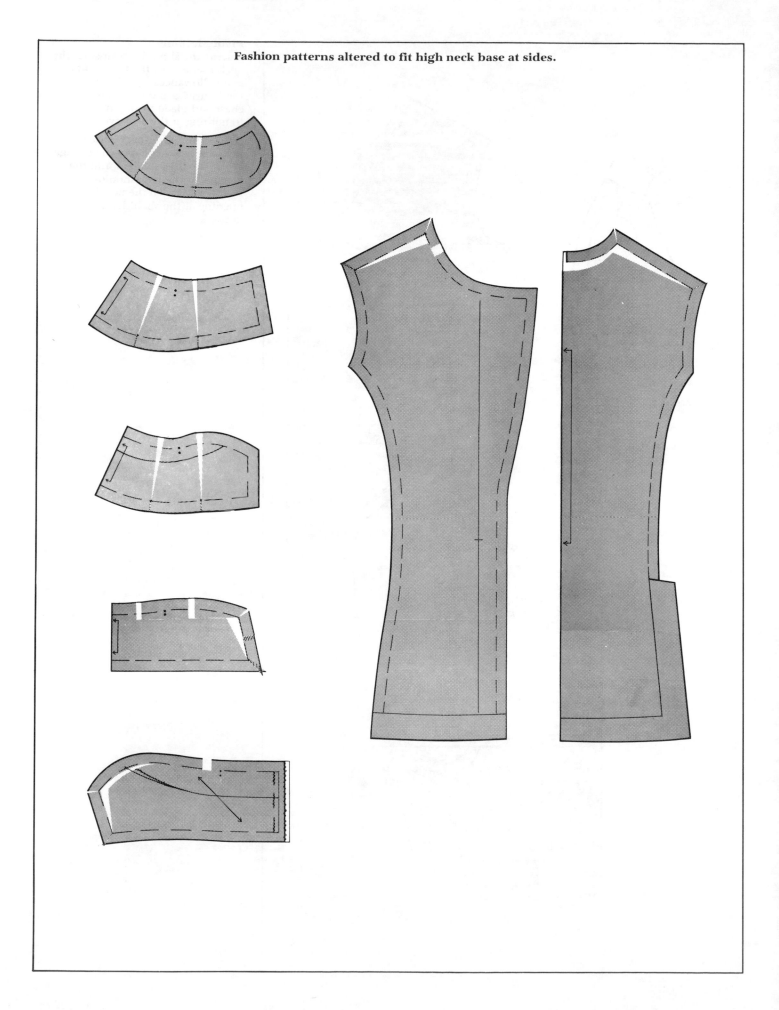

Fashion patterns altered to fit high neck base at sides.

Fashion patterns altered to fit high neck base at sides.

BASIC FITTING THEORY

Figure Analysis

A definite angle is defined where the neck edges meet the shoulders. The shallowness caused by lighter than average muscle development and smaller deposits of soft body tissues create an illusion of square shoulders.

Fitting Analysis

The neckline is loose at the shoulder area and may appear to be too low at the center front. A loose horizontal fold of fabric may sag across the center front and center back near the neckline. The chest and blade fitting lines remain level.

Fabric Requirements for Proper Fit

The shallow neck areas require shorter front neckline extensions and less length at the upper center back. The back and front neckline width may require adjustment. The smaller garment areas lie smoothly against the neck base at the back and front.

GARMENT & PATTERN ALTERATIONS FOR SYMMETRICAL FIGURES

Change Required

Shorten the front neckline extensions and the upper center back area; decrease the neckline width.

Slash Method—fitting garment only

On the garment front form a tuck through the neck seam allowance near each shoulder seam. Keep the shoulderline in the correct position. Adjust the width of the tucks until the excess fabric is removed at the neckline. Taper to nothing at each armscye.

Below the back neckline, form a parallel tuck across the center back area. Adjust the width of the tuck until the fabric lies smoothly against the body. Taper to nothing at each armscye.

Narrow the neckline opening at the shoulderline, as needed.

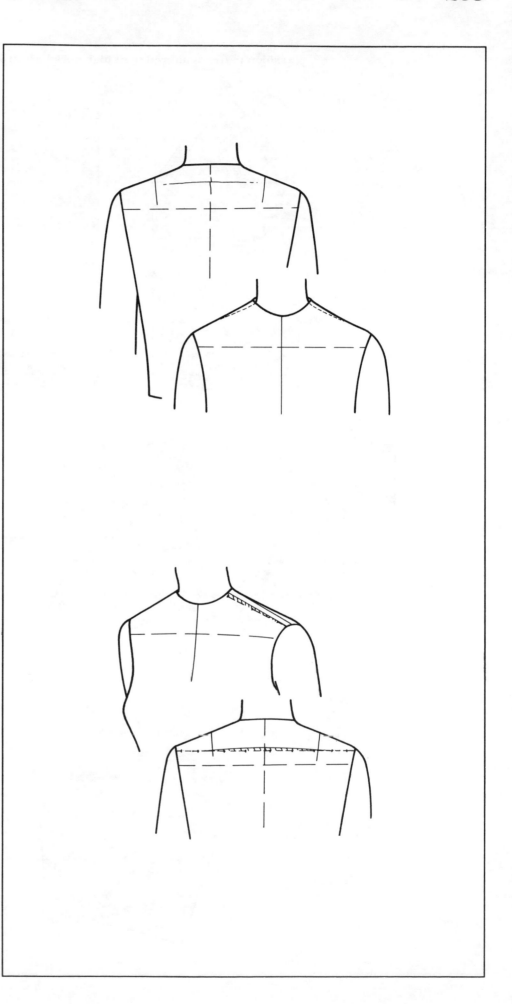

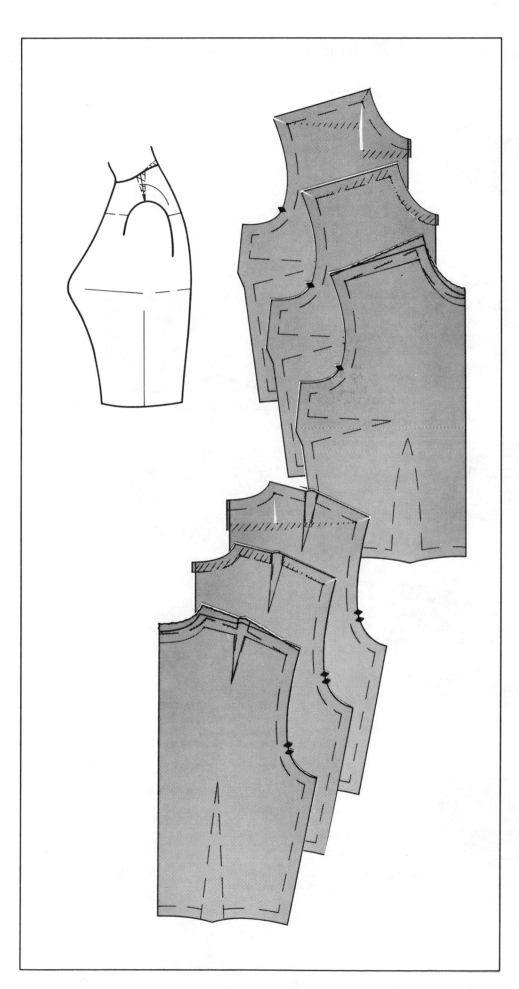

Pivot Method

Release the shoulder seams. At the neckline, take up the back and front seam allowances equally to remove the excess fabric. Taper to nothing at the armscyes.

Across the center back, lower the neckline seam equal to the change at the shoulders. Blend into the original at the new shoulder seamline.

Narrow the neckline opening at the shoulderline, as needed.

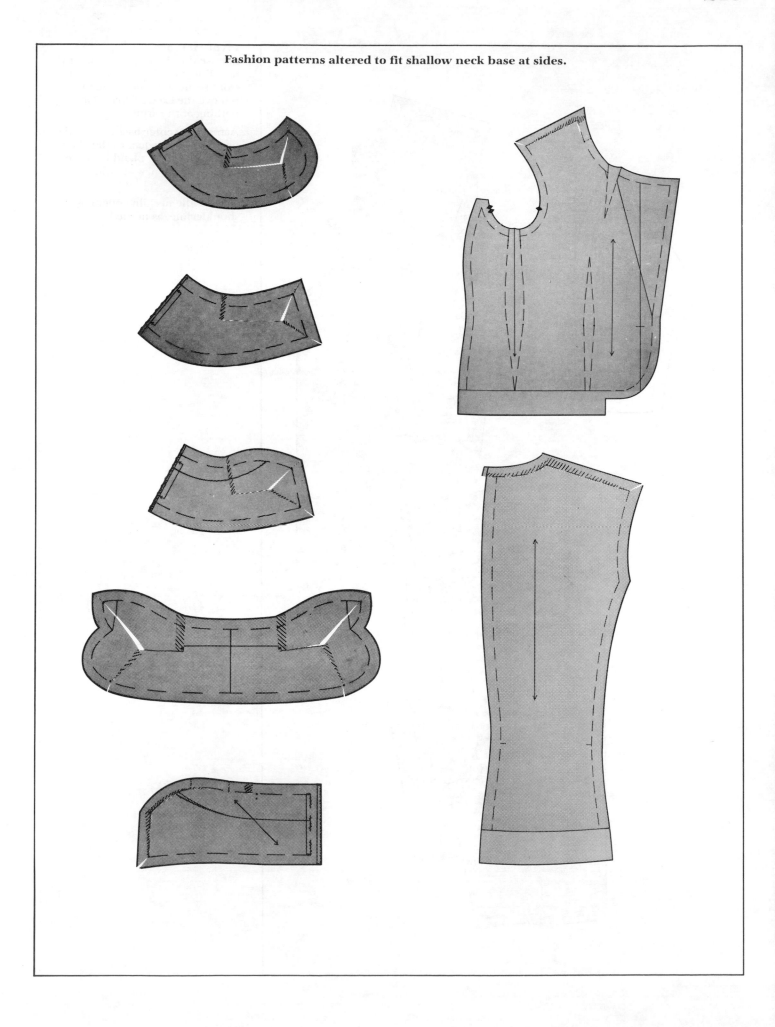

Fashion patterns altered to fit shallow neck base at sides.

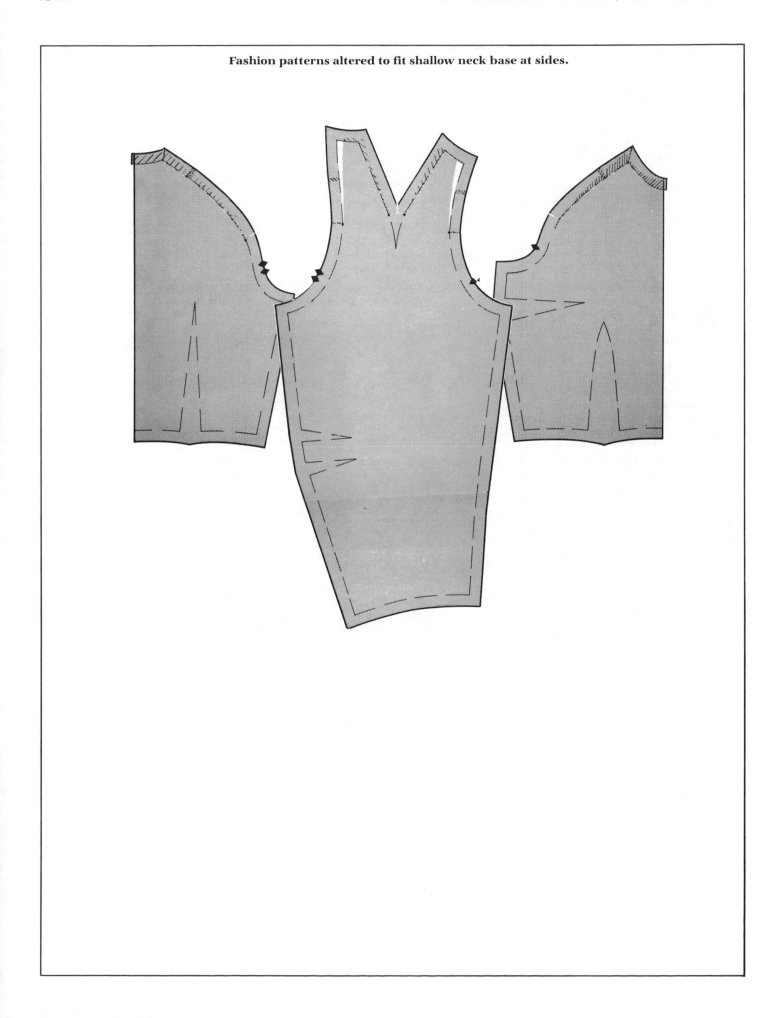

Fashion patterns altered to fit shallow neck base at sides.

BASIC FITTING THEORY

Figure Analysis
The neck circumference is larger than average because the neck muscles are heavier and the neckbones and concentration of other soft tissues may be larger. The muscles and soft tissues also may lack tone.

Fitting Analysis
When the closure is forced shut, the back neckline rises. The front neckline tightens uncomfortably and a circular wrinkle forms below it. The edges of the front armscyes may ripple, making them appear to be too large. The lower armscye areas on the front pull against the arm hinges and cause discomfort. The chest and blade fitting lines rise at the body centers.

Fabric Requirements for Proper Fit
The larger neck circumference requires a neckline opening that is wider at the sides and lower at the center front. The larger opening relieves the tightness so that fabric can lie smoothly against the neck. The chest and blade fitting lines become level.

GARMENT & PATTERN ALTERATIONS FOR SYMMETRICAL FIGURES

Change Required
Widen the back and front neckline; lower the front neckline.

Slash Method—fitting garment only
On the garment front, clip through the neckline seam allowance at ½ inch (1.2 cm) intervals across the center front area. Extend the cuts into the bodice area deep enough to relieve the tightness. Continue clipping the same depth around the entire front neckline. Clip the back neckline seam allowance as needed near each shoulder seam. Draw the new neck seamline along the line formed by the ends of the clips. Blend the new line into the original near the center back. If only the front is tight, see **37 Forward Neck**.

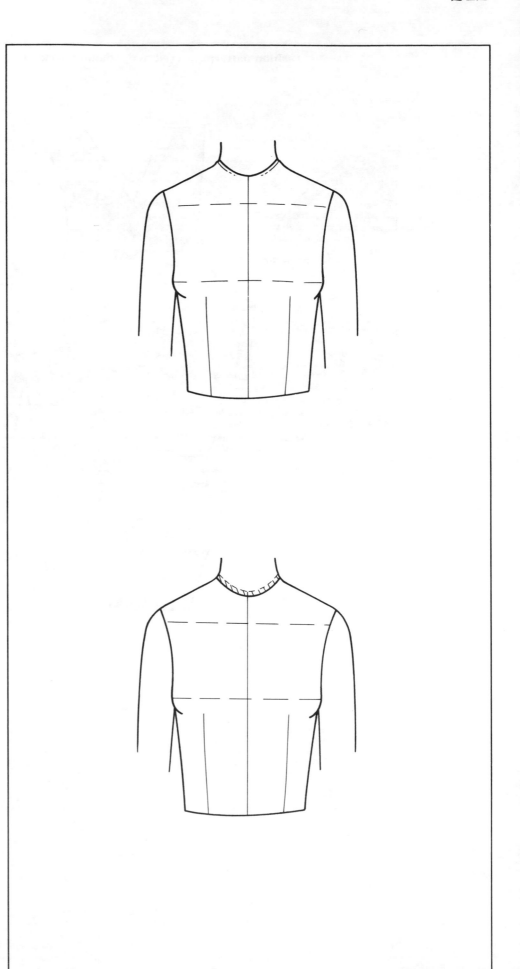

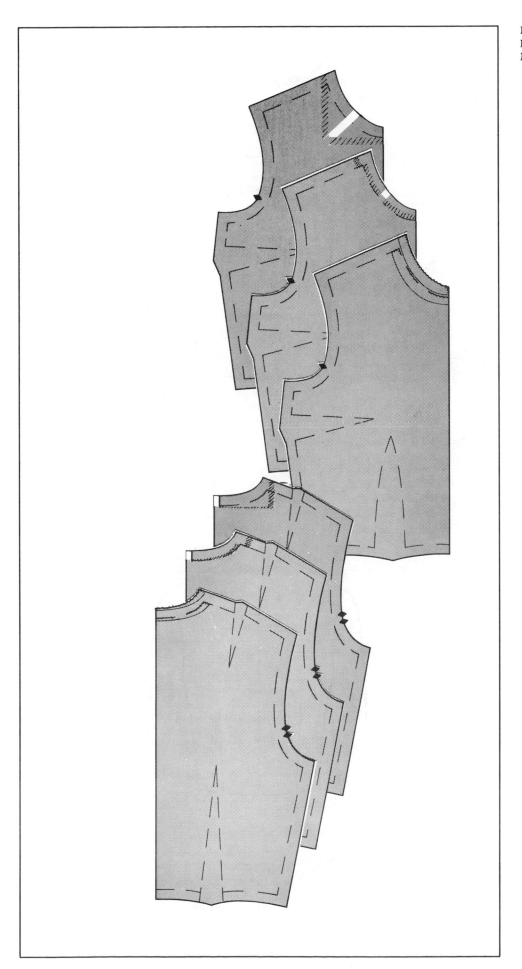

Pivot Method
Proceed as stated in the **Slash Method**.

BASIC FITTING THEORY

Figure Analysis
The neck circumference is smaller than average because the neck muscles are lighter, and the neck bones and concentration of other soft tissues may be smaller.

Fitting Analysis
The garment neckline area is smooth but does not reach the base of the neck at the sides or the body centers. There is poor proportion between the larger opening of the garment neckline and the smallness of the neck. The chest and blade fitting lines remain level.

Fabric Requirements for Proper Fit
The smaller neck circumference requires a neckline opening that is narrower at the sides and higher at the center front. The smaller opening aligns with the base of the neck and creates better proportions between the size of the neck opening and that of the neck.

GARMENT & PATTERN ALTERATIONS FOR SYMMETRICAL FIGURES

Change Required
Narrow the back and front neckline; raise the neckline as needed at the body contours.

Slash Method—fitting garment only
Leave the neckline seam allowance extended toward the neck or lay the front neckline over a fabric insert. Align the grain of both fabrics. Across the center front raise the seamline position the desired amount. Continue marking the new neckline along the base of the neck. At the shoulderline, begin to blend the new line into the original near the center back.

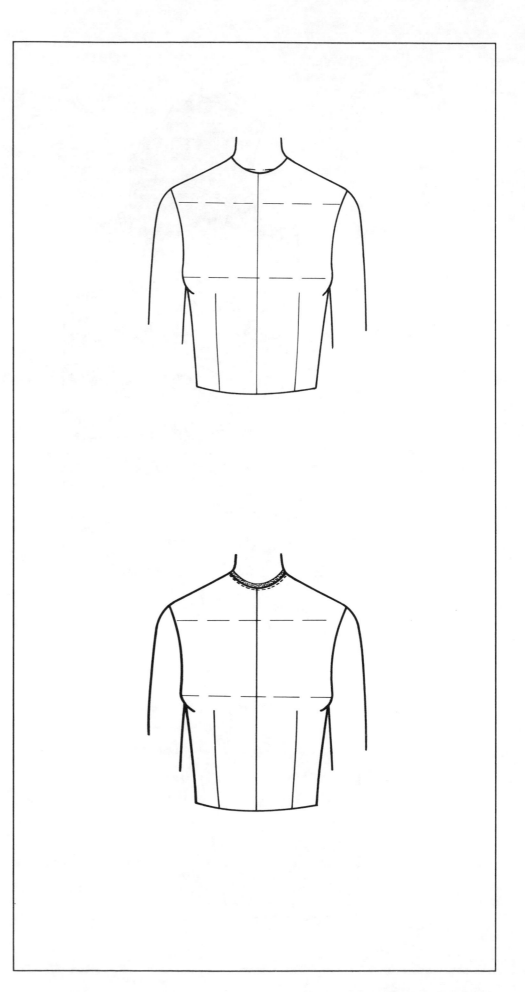

Pivot Method
Proceed as stated in the **Slash Method.**

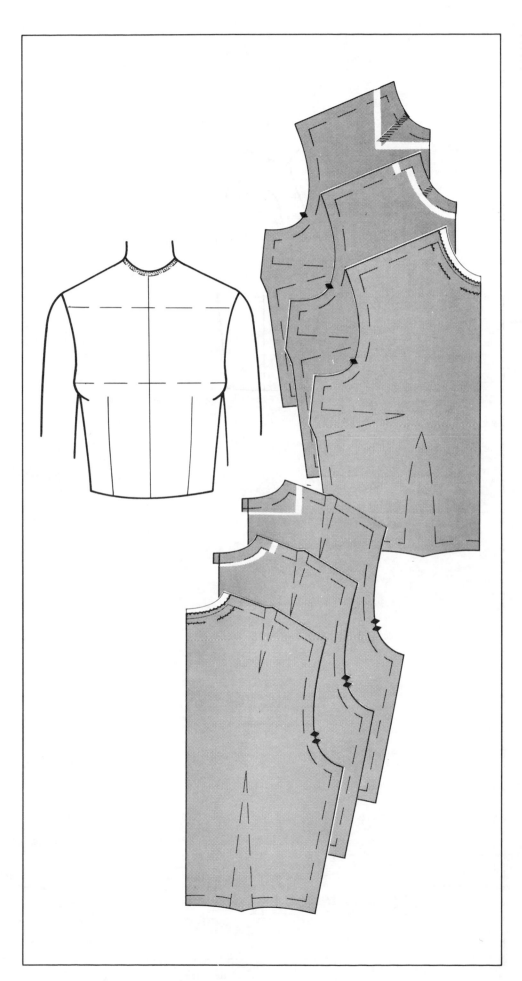

BASIC FITTING THEORY

Figure Analysis

The head may tilt forward more than average and rest in front of the central axis of the body. The forward thrust of the head sharpens the angle where the neck meets the chest. This increases the front neck depth and lengthens the upper center back area. The front neck depth also increases due to prominent neck tendons or excess soft body tissue.

Fitting Analysis

When a basic jewel neckline is worn, strain tightens the front neckline and forms a fold of fabric below it. The shoulderlines pull forward at the edges of the neck. The back neckline tightens or may rise. The blade fitting line rises across the center back. The chest fitting line remains level. A neckline worn open or designed lower at the center front does not require alteration.

Fabric Requirements for Proper Fit

The fuller front neck area requires a deeper front neckline. The length adjustments relieve the strain and permit the fabric to lie smoothly below the neckline so that they can align with the neck base. The blade fitting line becomes level.

GARMENT & PATTERN ALTERATIONS FOR SYMMETRICAL FIGURES

Change Required

Lower the front neckline.

Slash Method—fitting garment only

On the garment front, clip through the neckline seam allowance at ½ inch (1.2 cm) intervals across the center front area. Extend the cuts into the bodice area deep enough to relieve the tightness and to permit the shoulder seam to align with the shoulder. Continue with shorter clips toward the shoulderline as needed. Draw the new front neck seamline along the line formed by the ends of the clips. Blend into the original seamline near the shoulder.

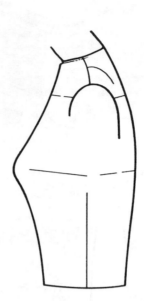

Pivot Method
Proceed as for the **Slash Method**.

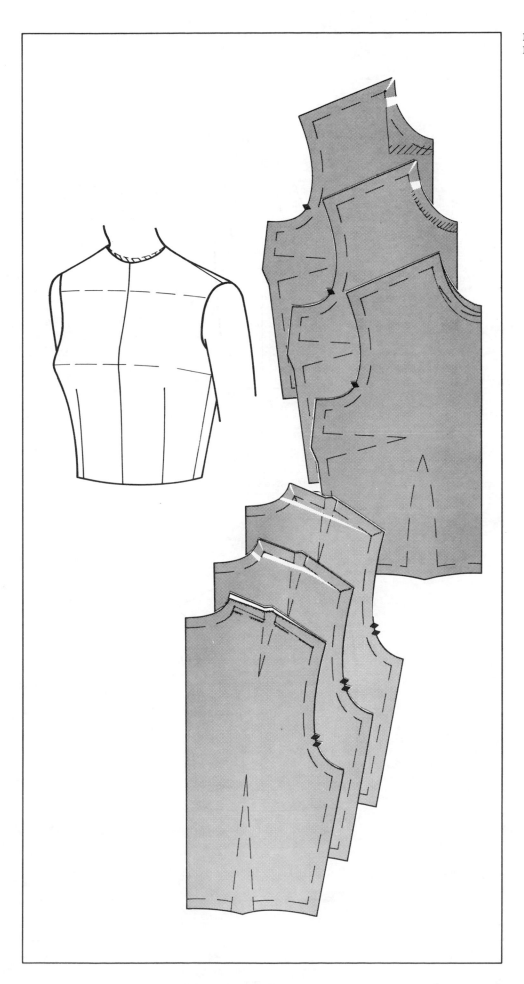

BASIC FITTING THEORY

Figure Analysis

An enlargement of the bone structure and other tissues develops high on the spine. The width and length of the upper center back area increases. This figure variation creates the illusion of rounded shoulders and usually is accompanied with a forward head position and/or a hollow chest.

Fitting Analysis

The garment pulls taut across the back of the neck. The edges of the back armscyes ripple. They appear to be too large. The strain tightens the front neckline and causes a fold of fabric to form below it. The blade fitting line and the back waistline rise at the body centers.

Fabric Requirements for Proper Fit

The fullness over the spine requires more fabric length and width at the upper center back area. Neckline darts are necessary to shape the fabric properly. The longer, more shaped garment area relieves the strain and permits both back and front to lie smoothly against the body. The chest and blade fitting lines and waistline become level.

GARMENT & PATTERN ALTERATIONS FOR SYMMETRICAL FIGURES

Change Required

Lengthen and widen the upper center back area.

Slash Method—fitting garment only

Slash through the back neck seam allowance at both mid-back areas. Cut at a slight diagonal toward the blade fitting line then continue over to the armscye seamlines. Insert fabric strips from each armscye to the blade line. Spread each set of cut edges evenly until the armscyes align with the body contour and the blade fitting line becomes level.

Slash from one shoulder dart tip to the other following the crossgrain. Insert a fabric strip. Lift the neckline section evenly until the neckline rises to a comfortable and attractive position. Taper to nothing at the dart tips.

Near the neckline slashes, form darts of equal widths to remove the excess fabric and create the shaping for the body contour.

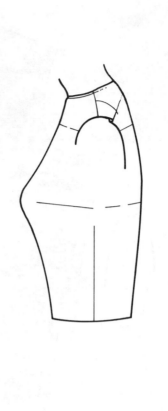

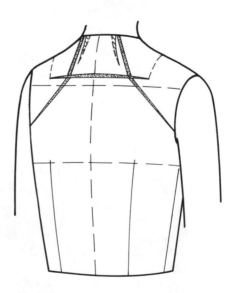

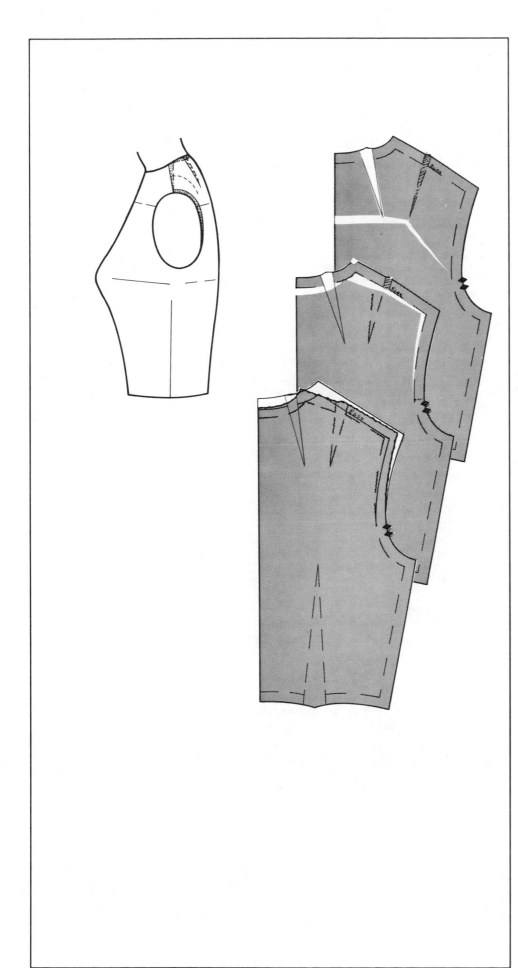

If the front neckline remains too high, follow the procedure for **37 Forward Neck**. If excess fabric length is present at the center front, see **48 Hollow Chest**.

Pivot Method

Release the back armscye, the shoulder seams and the back shoulder darts. Smooth the fabric over the blade areas until the blade fitting line becomes level. Retain part of the shoulder dart as ease, if needed. Lay the front shoulder seamline in place over the extended back shoulder seam allowances. The original armscye lines and necklines will no longer match but the two sets of lines should align similarly on each shoulder. Form new neck darts of equal widths to remove the excess fabric from the back neckline. Across the center back, draw a new neck seamline at an attractive and comfortable position. Blend smoothly into the front neckline at the shoulder. If the front neckline is too high, follow the procedure for figure variation **37 Forward Neck**.

shoulders

39 Broad Shoulders

40 Narrow Shoulders

41 Square Shoulders

42 Sloping Shoulders

43 Long Arm Joints (bodice)

44 Short Arm Joints (bodice)

45 Forward Arm Joints (bodice)

46 Prominent Collar Bones

BASIC FITTING THEORY

Figure Analysis

The collar bones are longer than average. The bone structure of the spine, collar bones, and shoulder joints may be heavier also. These factors increase the body width and its circumference at shoulder tip level. The arm structure is not affected.

Fitting Analysis

Horizontal wrinkles pull across the armscye seamlines. The sleeve caps pull upward and toward the body centers. The sleeve caps appear to be too tight and both the upper and lower sleeve areas appear to be too short. The ends of the chest and blade fitting lines rise.

Fabric Requirements for Proper Fit

The broadness of the shoulders requires longer shoulder seamlines on the garment. The added fabric width at the upper blade and chest areas permits the armscyes to align with the body contour and relieves the strain on the sleeves. They lower to the correct position on the arm and require no adjustment. The fitting lines become level.

GARMENT & PATTERN ALTERATIONS FOR SYMMETRICAL FIGURES

Change Required

Lengthen the shoulder seamlines.

Slash Method—fitting garment only

Release 2 inches (5 cm) of each shoulder seam at the armscye areas. Slash the opened shoulder seam near each armscye and continue diagonally down to the armscye seamline at the arm hinge areas. Insert fabric strips. To increase width, spread the cut edges equally at the shoulder until the armscye seamlines align with the crest of the shoulder curves. Taper to nothing at the armscye. True and restitch the shoulder seam using the original slope of the neckline portion as a guide.

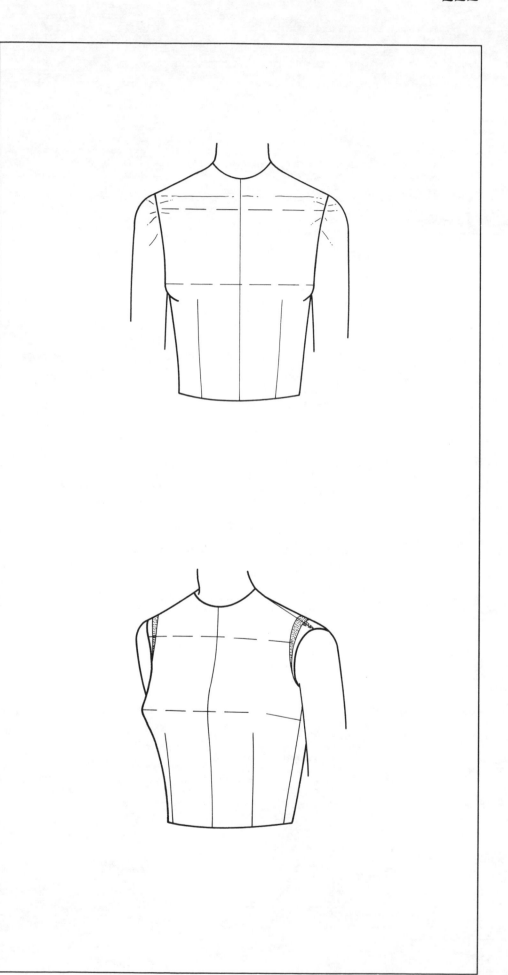

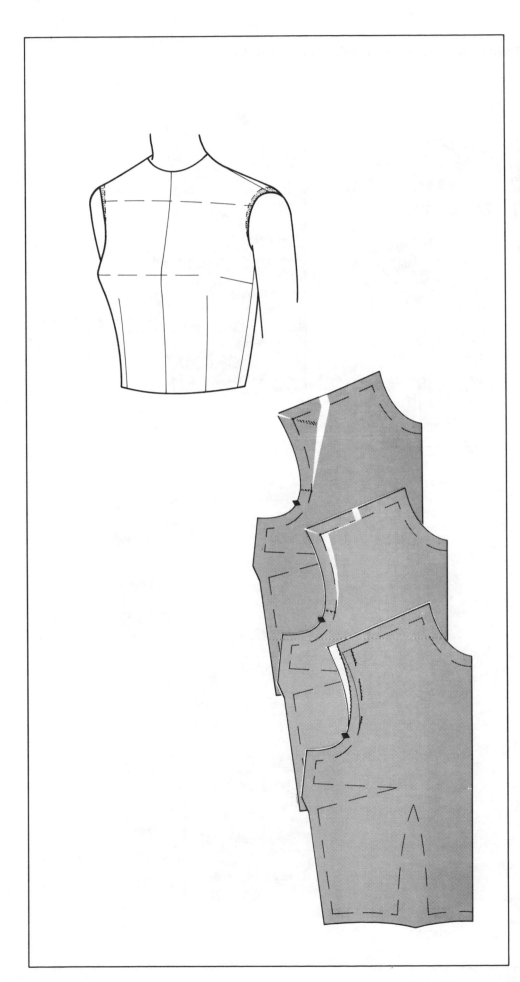

Pivot Method

If the sleeves are not attached, mark the new armscye seamlines from the shoulder to the arm hinge areas. Set in the sleeves along the new armscye seamlines.

If the sleeves are attached, release the sleeve caps down to the arm hinge areas at front and back. Turn under the sleeve cap seam allowance along the eased seamline. Move the sleeve cap outward along the shoulderline until the seamline is in a comfortable and attractive position. Pin the sleeve in place and stitch the armscye.

Fashion patterns altered to fit fit broad shoulders.

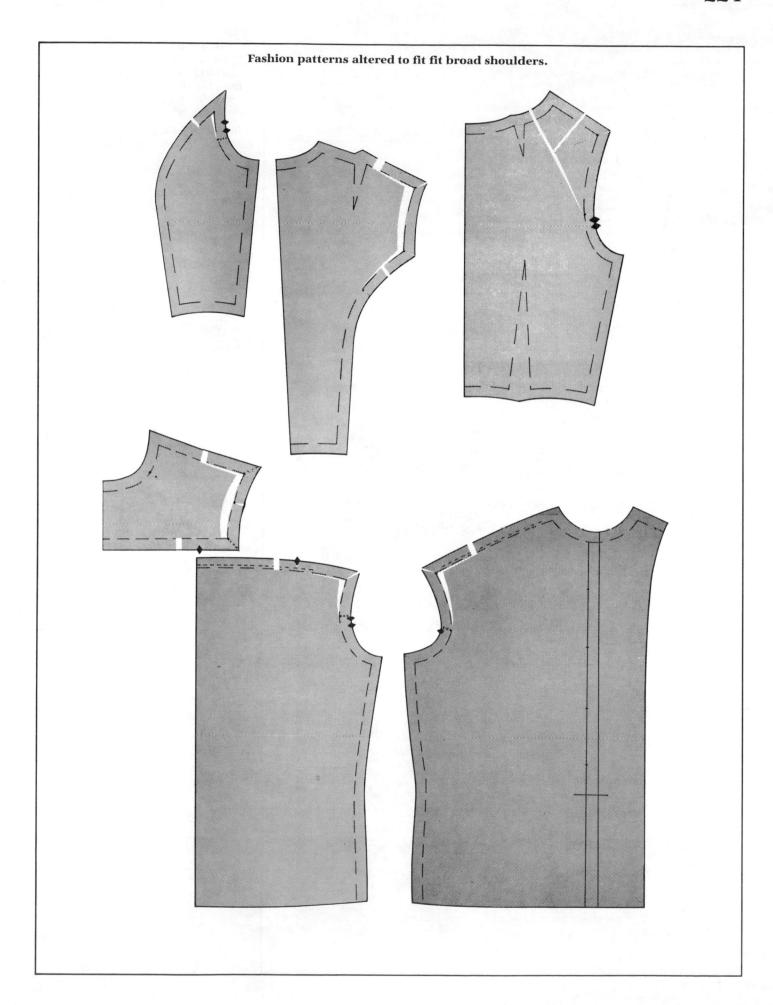

Fashion patterns altered to fit fit broad shoulders.

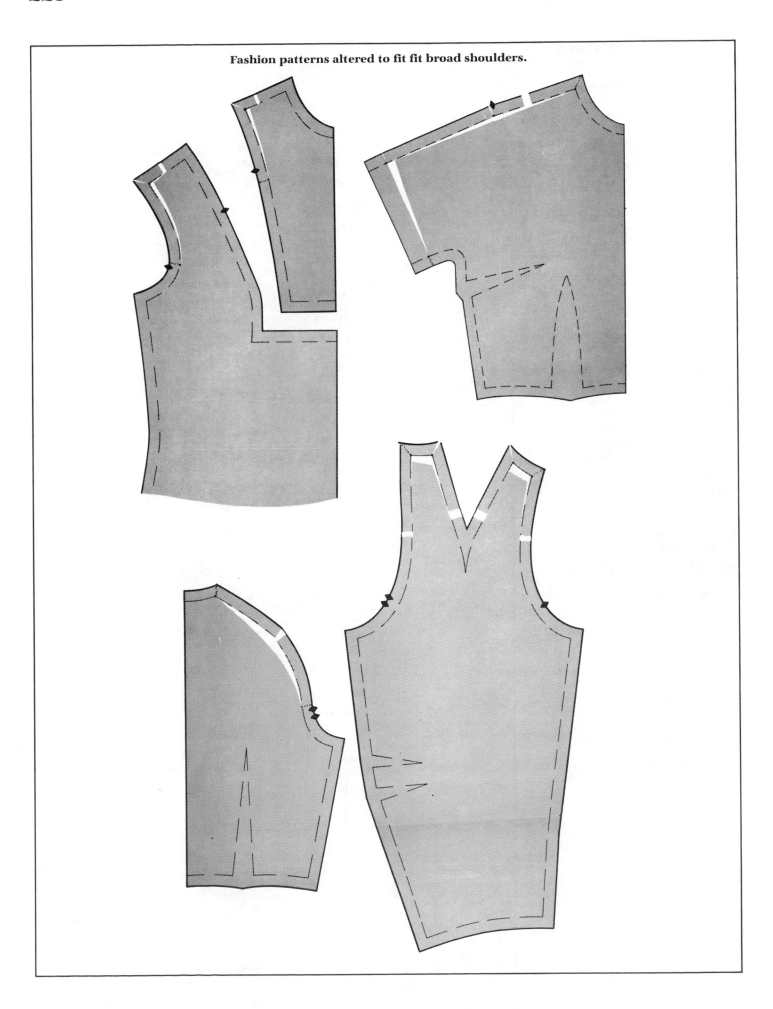

BASIC FITTING THEORY

Figure Analysis

The collar bones are shorter than average. The bone structure of the spine, collar bones, and shoulder joints may be lighter also. These factors decrease the body width and its circumference at shoulder tip level. The arm structure is not affected.

Fitting Analysis

The armscye seamlines drop off the crest of the shoulder curves and lie against the arms. The sleeve caps sag and appear to be too large. The garment fabric is loose at the chest edges. The front armscye cuts against the arm hinge. The ends of the chest and blade fitting lines droop.

Fabric Requirements for Proper Fit

The narrowness of the shoulders requires shorter shoulder seamlines on the garment. The reduced fabric width at the upper blade and chest areas permits the armscyes to align with the body contour. The sleeves rise to the correct position on the shoulder and require no adjustment. The fitting lines become level.

GARMENT & PATTERN ALTERATIONS FOR SYMMETRICAL FIGURES

Change Required

Shorten the shoulder seamlines.

Slash Method—fitting garment only

Release 2 inches (5 cm) of each shoulder seam at the armscye areas. Pin tucks of equal widths across the opened seam areas near each armscye seam. Adjust the width of the tucks until the armscye seamlines align with the crest of the shoulder curves. True and restitch the shoulder seam using the original slope of the neckline portion as a guide.

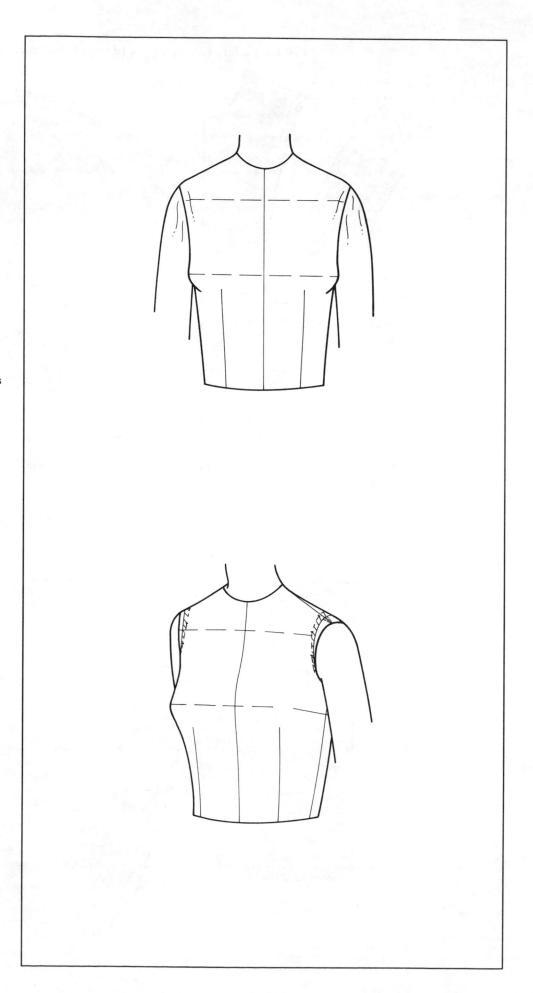

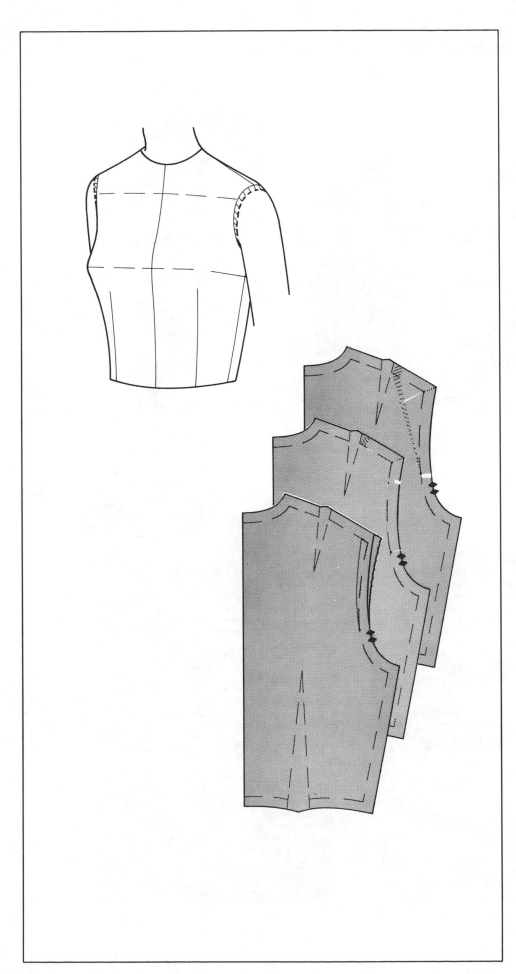

Pivot Method
If the sleeves are not attached, mark the new armscye seamlines from the shoulder to the arm hinge areas. Clip the widened seam allowances, as necessary. Set in the sleeves along the new armscye seamlines.

If the sleeves are attached, release the sleeve caps down to the arm hinge areas at the front and back. Turn under the sleeve cap seam allowance along the eased seamline. Move the sleeve inward along the shoulderline until the seamline is in a comfortable and attractive position. Pin the sleeve in place and stitch the armscye.

Fashion patterns altered to fit narrow shoulders.

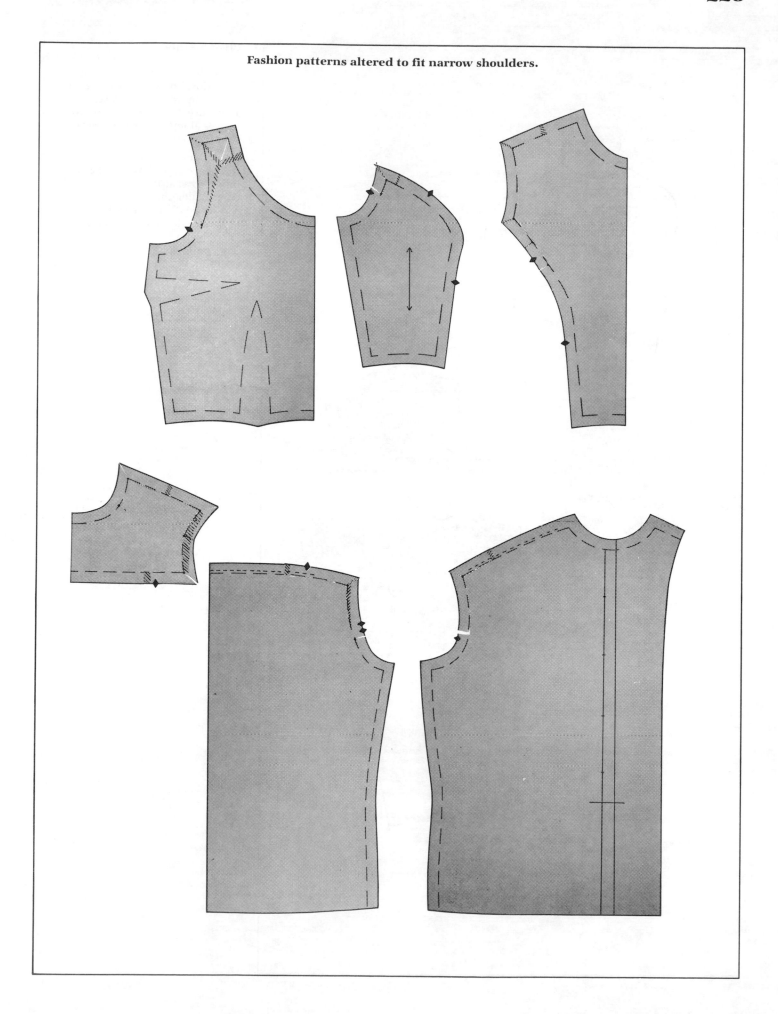

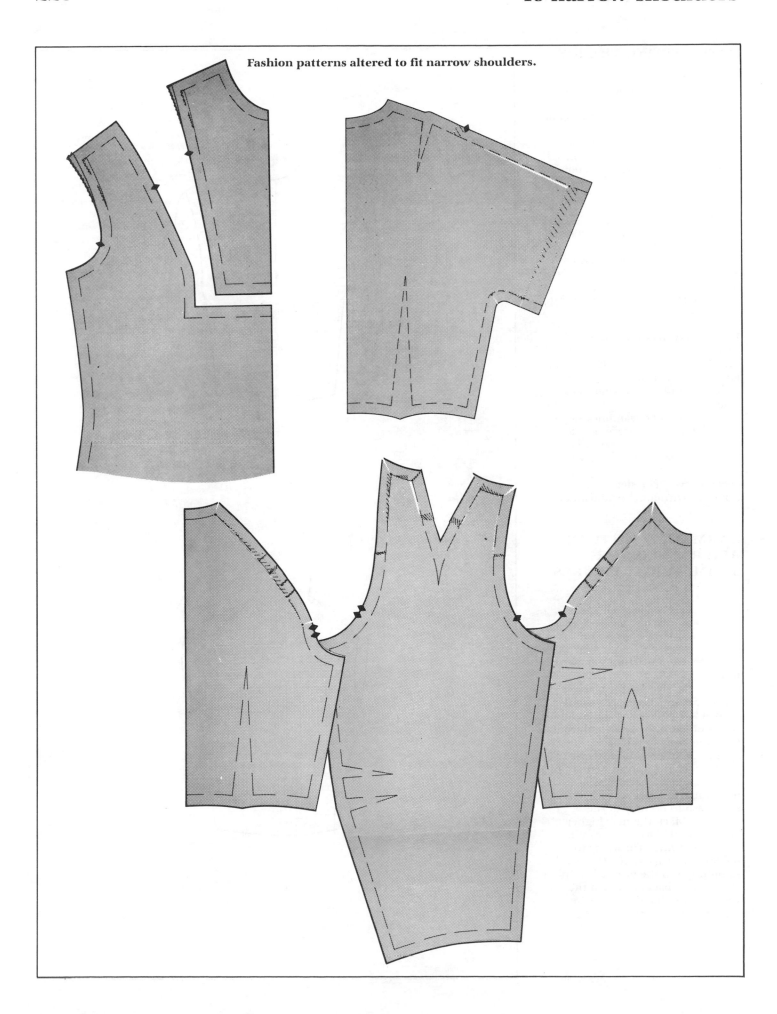

Fashion patterns altered to fit narrow shoulders.

BASIC FITTING THEORY

Figure Analysis

The collar bones slope less than average because they meet the vertical bone structure of the spine more nearly at 90-degree angles. The distance increases from the waist up to the base of the arm joints. The arm structure is not affected.

Fitting Analysis

The fabric pulls into tight diagonal wrinkles from the upper armscye area to the bust, the blade, and the biceps areas. The sleeves rise and appear to be too short. The ends of the chest and blade fitting lines rise. The centers of the cap fitting lines rise.

Fabric Requirements for Proper Fit

The higher position of the shoulder joint requires lifting the armscye farther from the waistline. As a result, the side seamlines lengthen and the shoulder seamlines slope less. The raised armscye position aligns with the body contours and relieves the strain at the neckline. The chest and blade fitting lines become level. The sleeves fit correctly without any adjustment.

GARMENT & PATTERN ALTERATIONS FOR SYMMETRICAL FIGURES

Change Required

Lengthen each side seam at the armscye to raise the armscye to a higher position.

Slash Method—fitting garment only

Remove the sleeves. Slash across the armscye seam allowances about ½ inch (1.2 cm) below the shoulder seams on both the back and front. Continue over to the neck seamlines. Insert fabric strips. To increase length, spread each set of cut edges equally at the armscye until the fabric lies smooth. Taper each slash to nothing at the neckline. Mark the new higher position of the armscye seamline across the underarm seams to restore the armscye depth. Blend smoothly into the original seamline at front and back. Reattach the sleeves using the new armscye seamline markings.

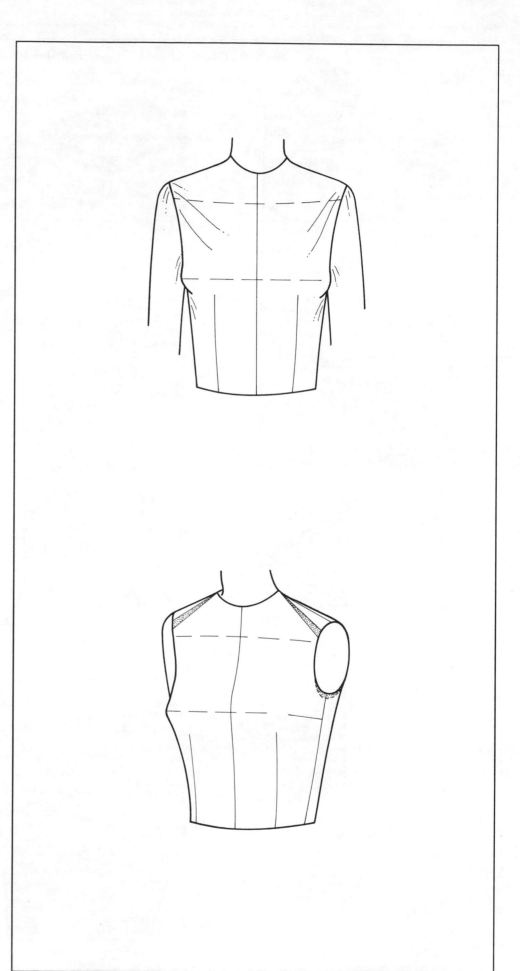

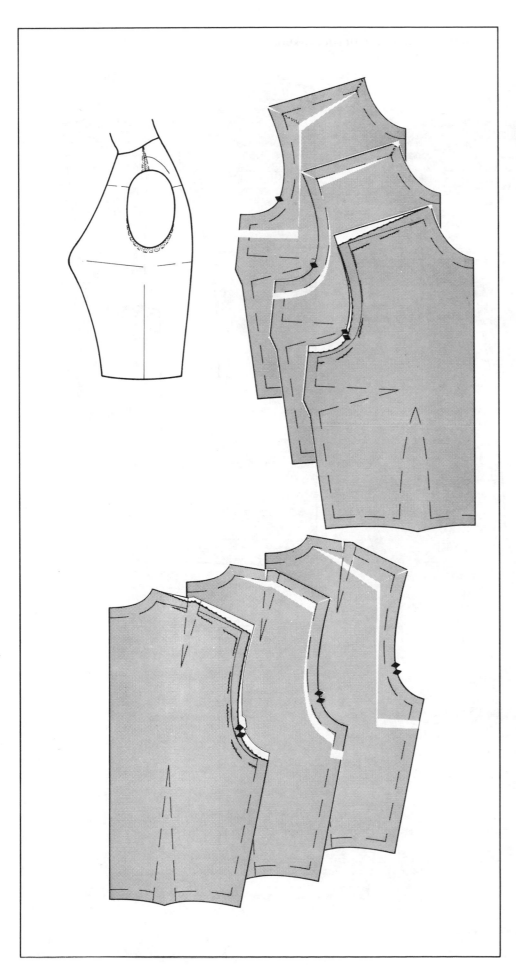

Pivot Method

Remove the sleeves. Release the shoulder seams. Let out the shoulder seam allowances equally at the armscyes on both the back and front until the fabric relaxes and the chest and blade fitting lines become level. Raise the lower armscye seamline position to restore the armscye depth. Blend into the original seamline at the arm hinge area. Attach the sleeves using the new armscye seamlines.

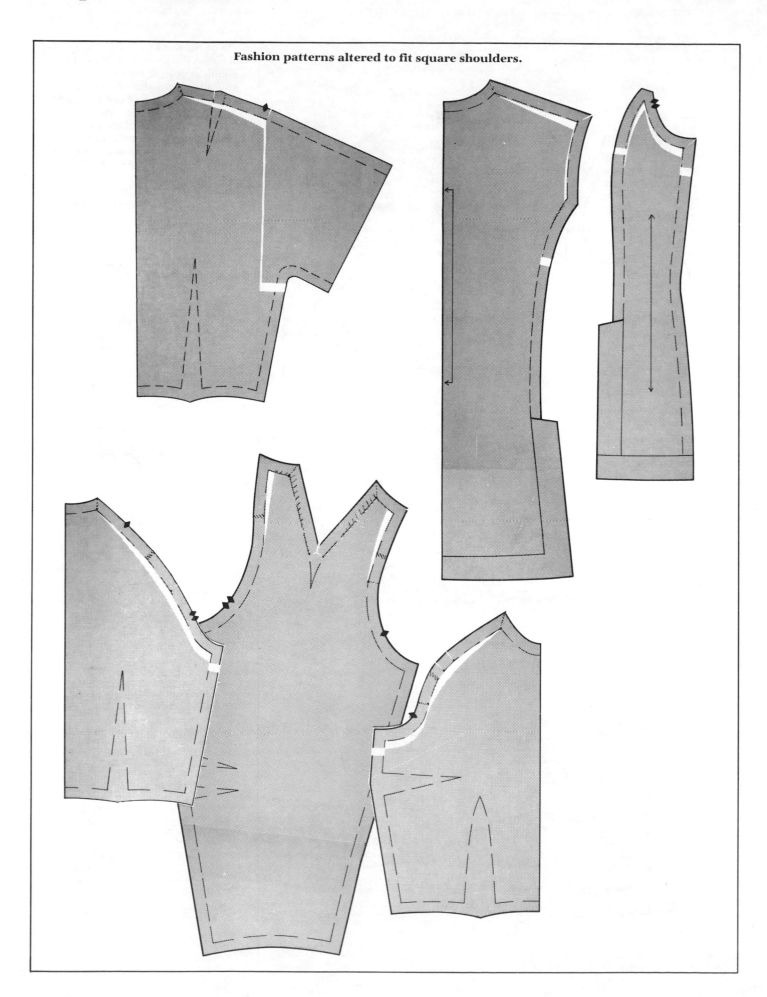

Fashion patterns altered to fit square shoulders.

Fashion patterns altered to fit square shoulders.

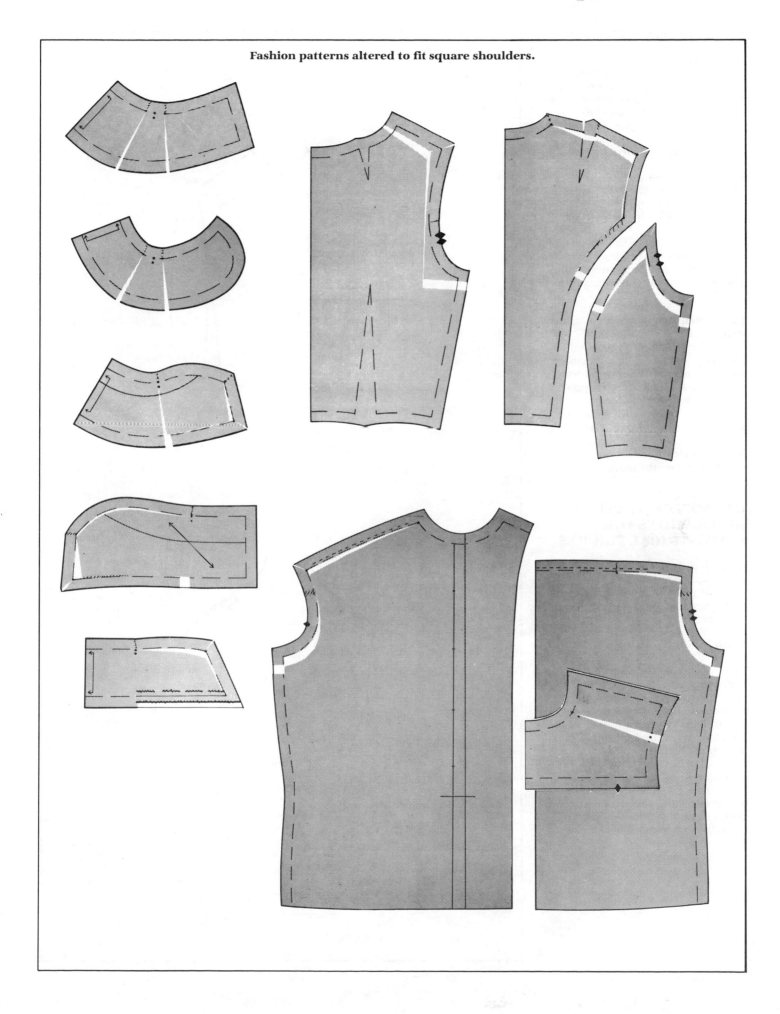

BASIC FITTING THEORY

Figure Analysis

The collar bones slope more than average because they meet the vertical bone structure of the spine at wider angles. The distance decreases from the waist up to the base of the arm joints. The arm structure is not affected.

Fitting Analysis

The sleeve caps sag off the crest of the shoulder and appear to be too large. The fabric along the armscyes sags into diagonal wrinkles from the neckline to the lower armscye areas. The ends of the chest and blade fitting lines droop. The centers of the cap fitting line also droop.

Fabric Requirements for Proper Fit

The lower position of the shoulder joint requires lowering the armscye closer to the waistline. As a result, the side seamlines shorten and the shoulder seamlines slope more. The lowered armscye position aligns with the body contours. The chest and blade fitting lines become level. The sleeves fit correctly without any adjustment.

GARMENT & PATTERN ALTERATIONS FOR SYMMETRICAL FIGURES

Change Required

Shorten each side seam at the armscye to drop the armscye to a lower position and increase the slope of the shoulder.

Slash Method—fitting garment only

Remove the sleeves. Clip the lower armscye seam allowance at ½ inch (1.2 cm) intervals to release the tension. Remove the excess armscye length equally with a tuck near the shoulder seams on both the back and front. Taper each tuck to nothing at the neckline. Mark the new lower position of the armscye seamline across the underarm seams to restore the armscye depth. Blend smoothly into the original seamline at front and back. Reattach the sleeves using the new armscye seamlines.

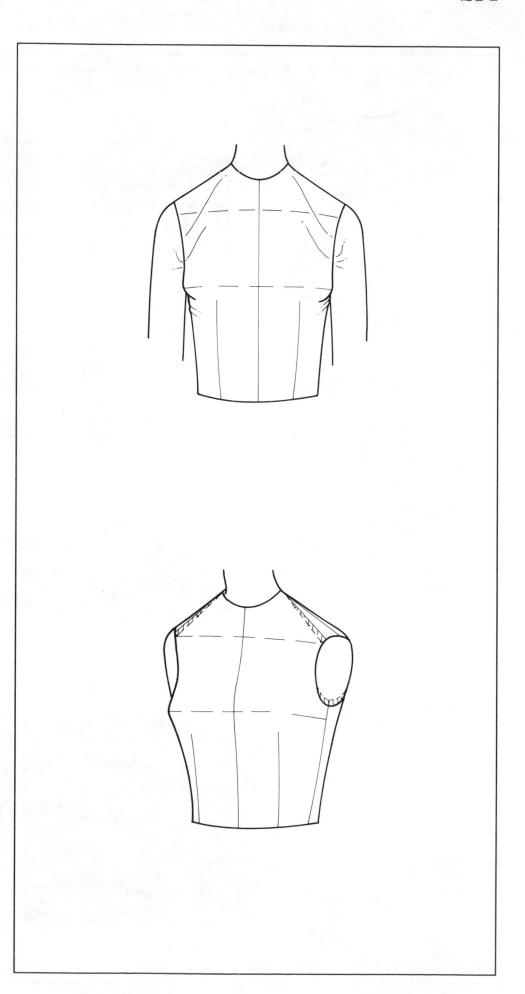

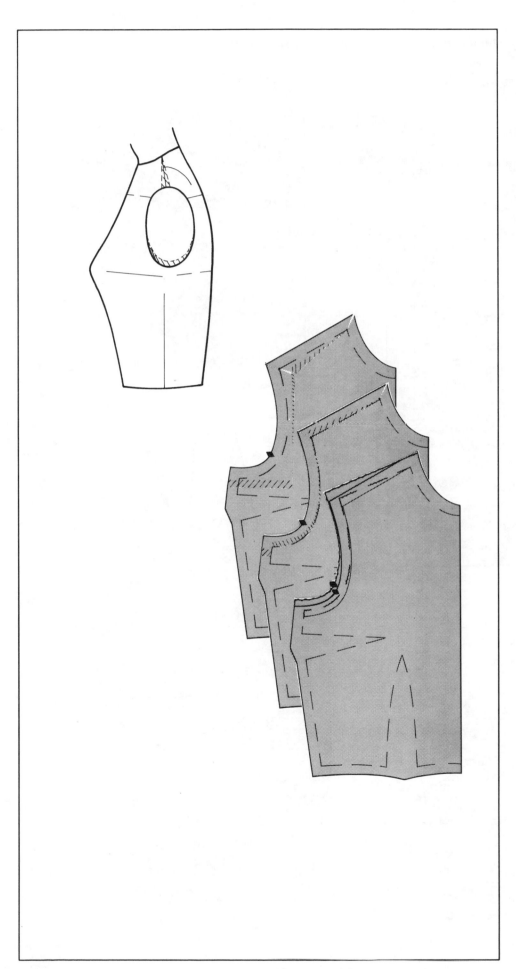

Pivot Method

Remove the sleeves. Clip the lower armscye seam allowances at ½ inch (1.2 cm) intervals to release the tension. Take in both the back and front shoulder seam areas equally at the armscye until the fabric is smooth and the chest and blade fitting lines become level. Taper to nothing at the neckline.

Mark the new lower position of the armscye seamline to restore the armscye depth. Blend into the original seamline at the arm hinge areas. Attach the sleeves using the new armscye seamlines.

Fashion patterns altered to fit sloping shoulders.

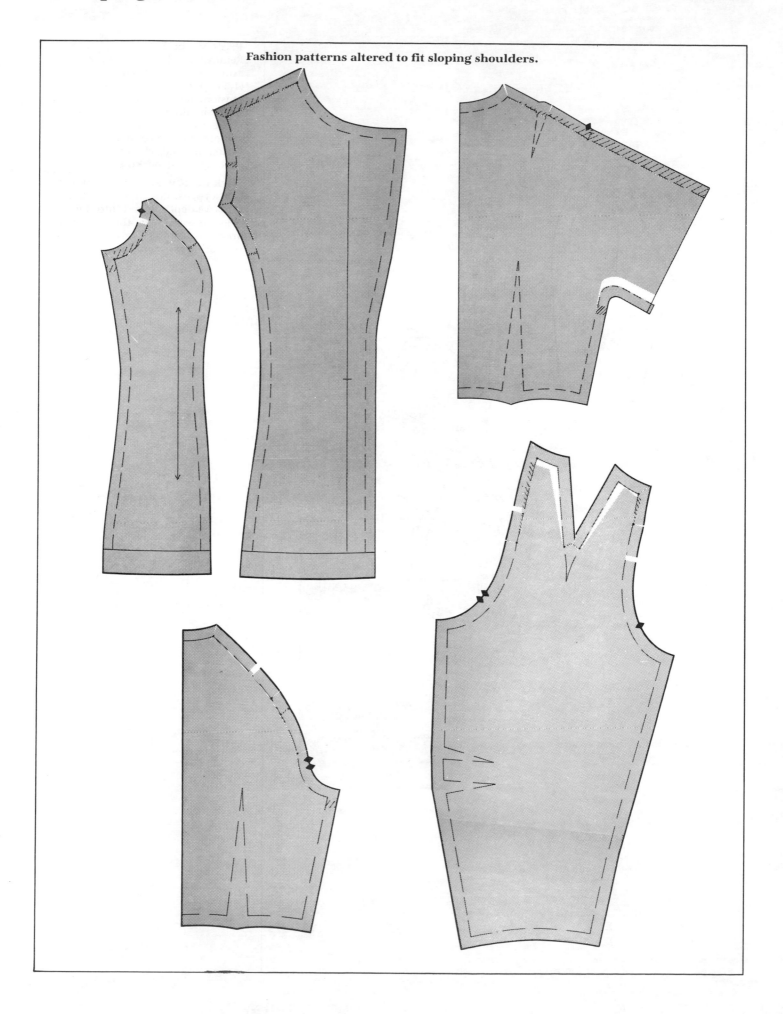

Fashion patterns altered to fit sloping shoulders.

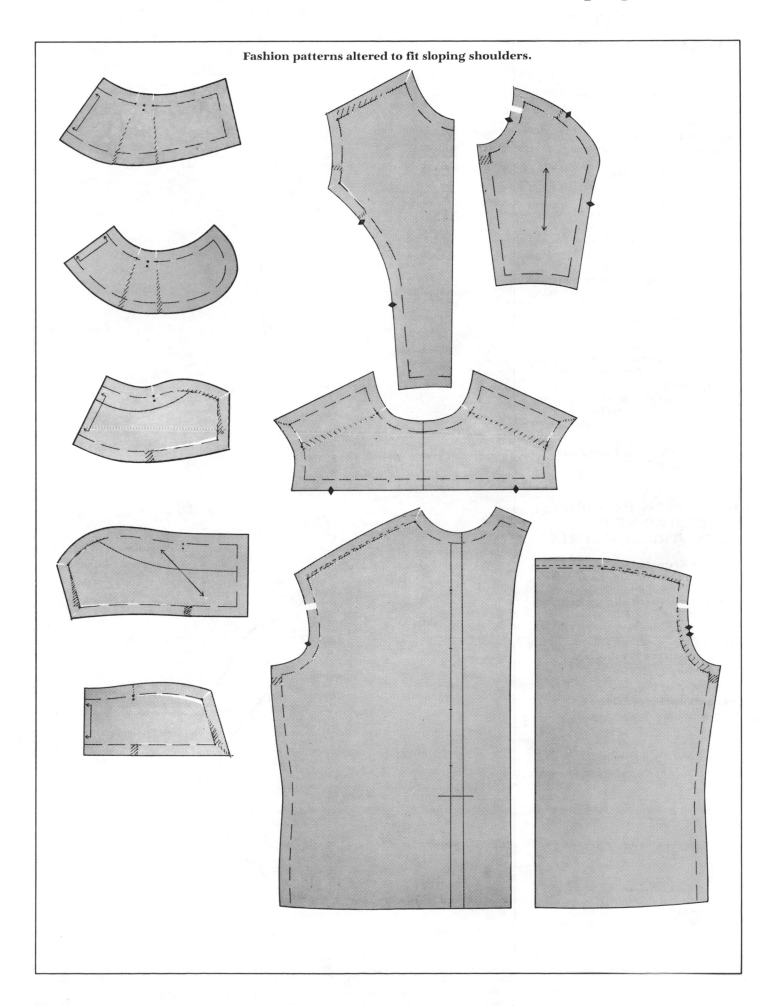

BASIC FITTING THEORY

Figure Analysis
The bones forming the joint structure may be longer than average or the "hinge" flesh separating the arm from the rib cage may form farther below the joint than average. Either factor increases the length from the shoulder to the scyeline.

Fitting Analysis
The lower armscye binds against the arm hinges. Diagonal wrinkles pull from the blade and chest areas to the underarms. A fold of fabric may form below the scyeline. The ends of the blade and chest fitting lines may pull downward.

Fabric Requirements for Proper Fit
The increased length of the shoulder joint area requires a longer armscye. This lowers the armscye seamline under the arm and shortens the side seamline. The armscye contour aligns in a comfortable position near the arm hinges. The sleeve cap height must be lengthened. See **73 Long Arm Joints (sleeves)**.

GARMENT & PATTERN ALTERATIONS FOR SYMMETRICAL FIGURES

Change Required
Lengthen the depth of the armscye.

Slash Method—fitting garment only
If sleeves are attached see **73 Long Arm Joints (sleeves)**. Follow this procedure to perfect the fit as illustrated.

When sleeves have not been attached use **Pivot Method** discussed below.

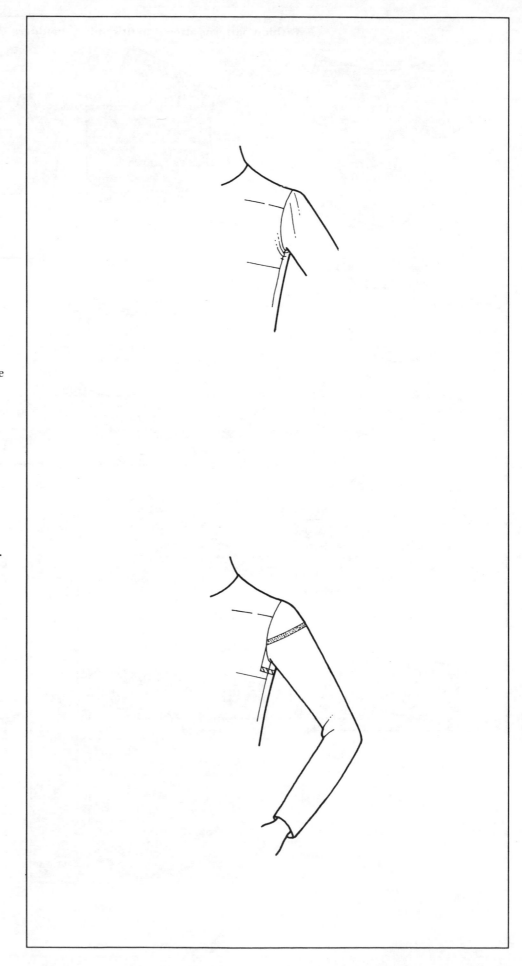

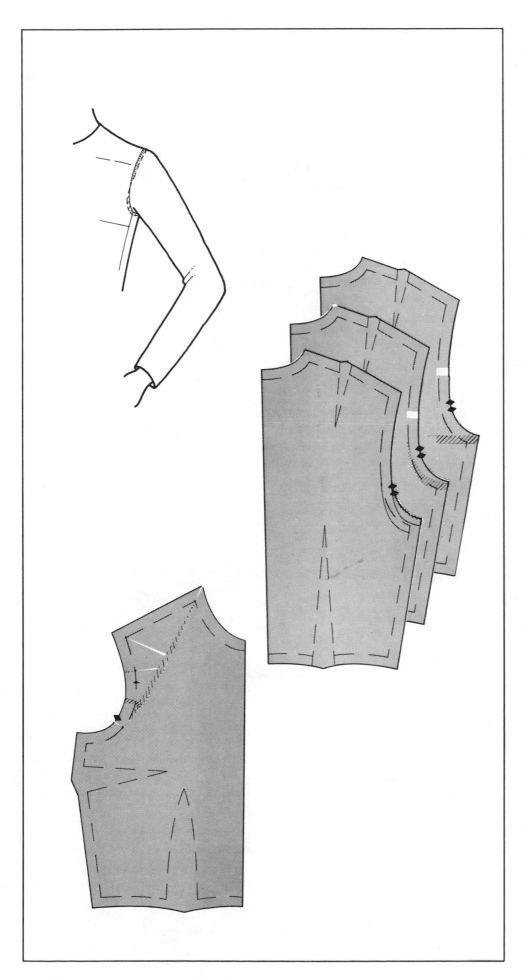

Pivot Method

Clip the seam allowance at ½ inch (1.2 cm) intervals across the underarm area to relieve the strain. Mark a new seamline below the original that will be a comfortable distance below the arm hinge. Across the side seams draw a line parallel to the original armscye seamline. Blend into the original seamline at the arm hinge areas on the front and back. Trim the excess fabric beyond the new seam allowance.

BASIC FITTING THEORY

Figure Analysis
The bones forming the joint structure may be shorter than average or the "hinge" flesh separating the arm from the rib cage may form nearer the joint than is average. Either factor decreases the length from the shoulder to the scyeline.

Fitting Analysis
The seamline at the lower armscye area is too far below the arm hinges. Lifting the arm pulls the sleeves tightly against the arm. The arms cannot be raised comfortably. The blade and chest fitting lines are not affected.

Fabric Requirements for Proper Fit
The decreased length of the shoulder joint area requires a shorter armscye. This raises the armscye seamline nearer the arm and lengthens the side seamline. The strain is relieved on the sleeve. The sleeve cap height must be shortened. See **74 Short Arm Joints (sleeves)**.

GARMENT & PATTERN ALTERATIONS FOR SYMMETRICAL FIGURES

Change Required
Shorten the depth of the armscye.

Slash Method—fitting garment only
If sleeves are attached see **74 Short Arm Joints (sleeves)**. Follow this procedure to perfect the fit as illustrated.

When sleeves have not been attached use **Pivot Method** discussed below.

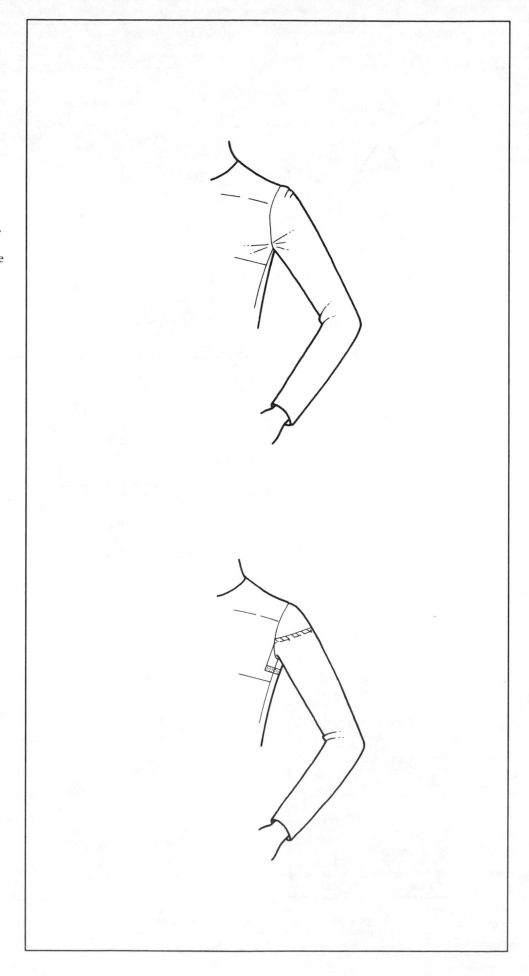

Pivot Method
At the underarm, mark a new
seamline above the original to lift
the armscye to a comfortable
position. Across the side seams
draw a line parallel to the original
armscye seamline. Blend into the
original seamline at the arm hinge
areas on the front and back.

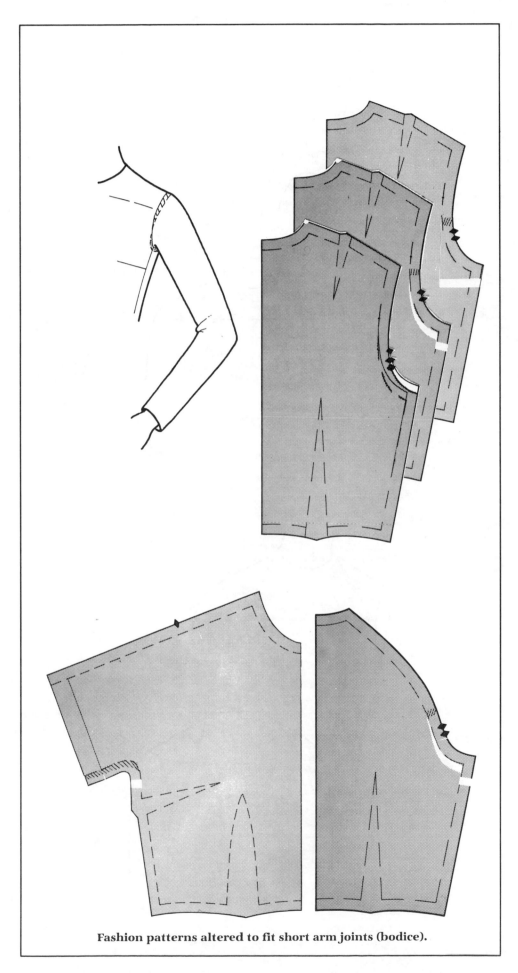

Fashion patterns altered to fit short arm joints (bodice).

BASIC FITTING THEORY

Figure Analysis

The collar bones bow forward more than average. This causes the arm joint to be more rounded in the front and flatter in the back; the chest becomes narrower and the blade area becomes broader. Thin muscles and smaller deposits of other soft tissues cause indented areas next to the front edges of the arm joints.

Fitting Analysis

At the armscye, the shoulder seams lie behind the shoulder tips. The garment front forms into vertical folds of fabric against the arm joints. The back armscye seams pull toward the blade areas. The front of the sleeve caps are taut near the front of the shoulder crest and loose at the back areas.

Fabric Requirements for Proper Fit

The forward curvature of the collar bones requires that the armscye ends of the shoulder seamlines be moved toward the front. This shortens the depth of the front armscye and lengthens the back armscye. The narrowness of the chest requires less fabric width in front of the armscyes. The broader upper back requires more garment width at the upper armscye areas. This figure variation affects the contour of the sleeve cap. See **77 Forward Arm Joints (sleeves)**.

GARMENT & PATTERN ALTERATIONS FOR SYMMETRICAL FIGURES

Change Required

Widen the blade area and raise the back shoulder seam at the armscye. Narrow the chest area and lower the front shoulder seam at the armscye.

Slash Method—fitting garment only

Release the sleeve above the arm hinge areas. Slash across the back armscye seam allowances at the arm hinge areas and cut diagonally toward the point of each neckline extension. Insert fabric strips. To increase armscye length, separate the cut edges at the armscye until the shoulderline is in the correct position. Across each front armscye seam allowance at the arm hinge areas, form a diagonal tuck to remove the excess fabric. Adjust the back and front changes until

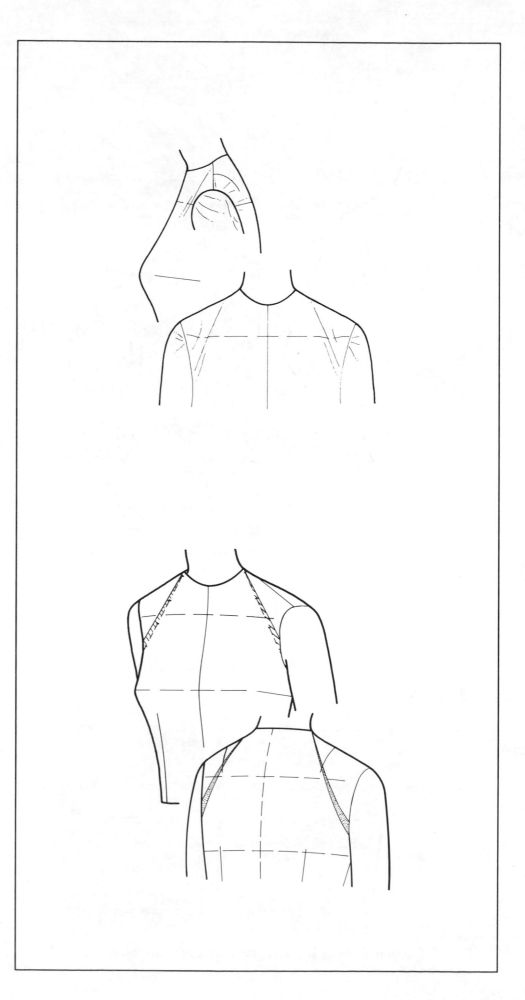

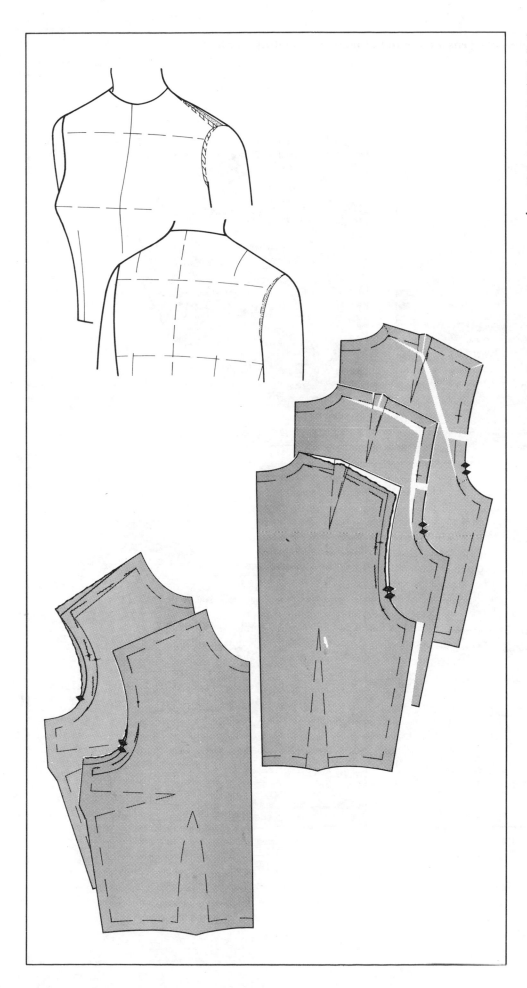

the shoulder seamlines divide the shoulder area evenly. Taper the tucks and slashes to nothing at the neckline extensions. Correct the back armscye distortions with a new, straighter seamline from the shoulder tip to the arm hinge area. Correct the front distortion with a curved line through the center of the distorion. Blend into the original seamline at the lower armscye. For the sleeve cap adjustment see **77 Forward Arm Joints (sleeves)**.

Pivot Method
Remove the sleeve cap above the arm hinge areas. Release the shoulder seams for the armscye to the neckline. Extend the seam allowance of the back shoulder toward the front. Turn under the front shoulder seam allowance at the armscye until the fold divides the shoulder and the arm evenly. Secure the fold to the back shoulder seam allowance. Clip the seam allowance of the front armscye at ½ inch (1.2 cm) intervals along the mid-chest area to relieve the strain. Draw a new, front armscye seamline even with the crease in the flesh at the arm hinge areas. Blend into the original at the shoulder and the lower armscye. Let out the back armscye seam allowance at the blade area to form a straighter line. Blend into the original seamlines at the shoulder and arm hinge area. For the sleeve cap adjustment see **77 Forward Arm Joints (sleeves)**.

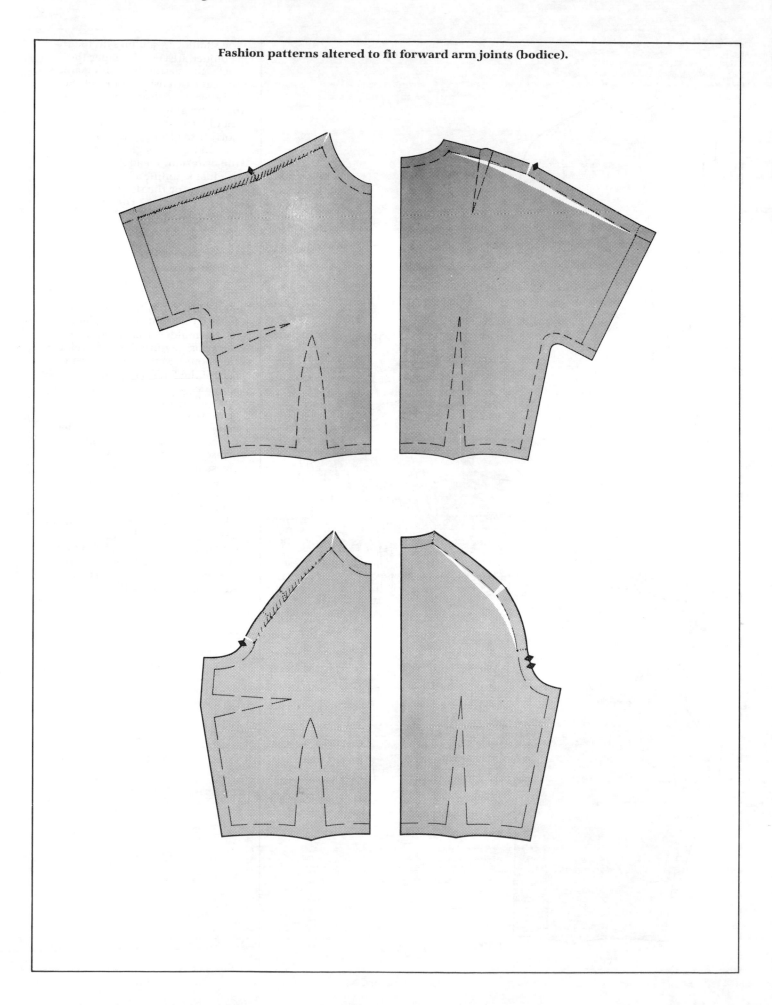

Fashion patterns altered to fit forward arm joints (bodice).

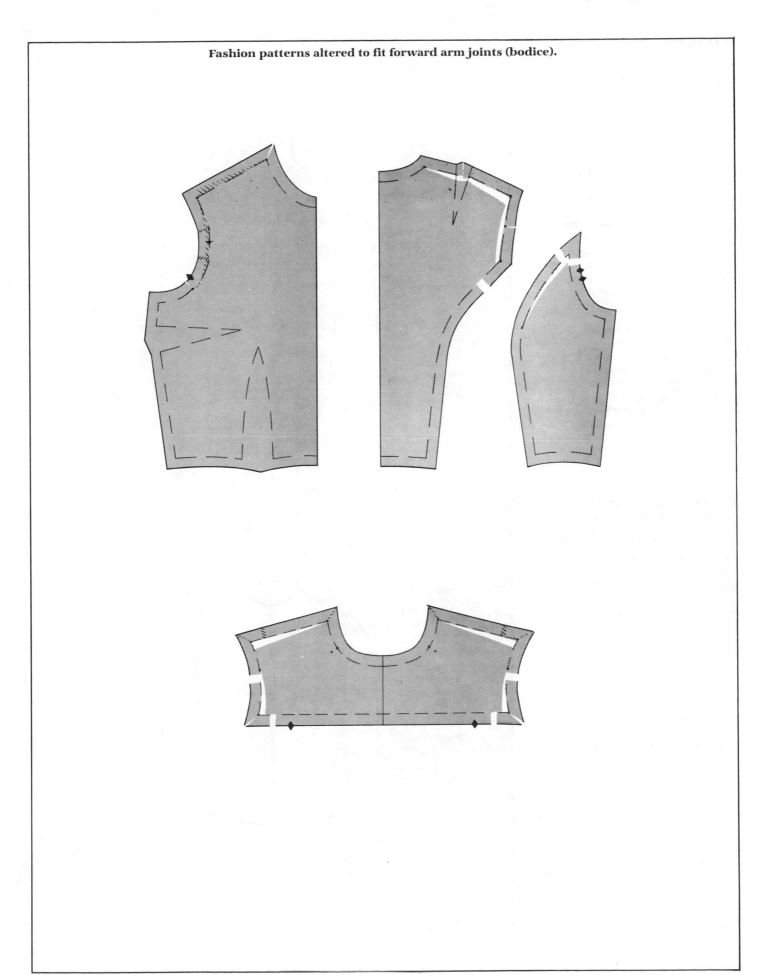

Fashion patterns altered to fit forward arm joints (bodice).

BASIC FITTING THEORY

Figure Analysis

The collar bone endings near the center front are larger than average. A bulged area forms at the base of the front neck area.

Fitting Analysis

The center front lines on a front closure do not meet. The fabric near the neckline is taut across the center front when the closure is forced to stay closed. If the figure variation is extreme, the strain pulls the vertical fitting lines toward each other at the upper chest area and the front armscye edges ripple. The neckline and chest fitting lines may rise at the center front.

Fabric Requirements for Proper Fit

The enlarged bone structure below the throat requires more fabric width at the upper center front area. The wider garment area relieves the strain and permits the neckline to close comfortably and to align with the base of the neck. The fitting lines become plumb and level.

GARMENT & PATTERN ALTERATIONS FOR SYMMETRICAL FIGURES

Change Required

Widen and lengthen the upper center front area.

Slash Method—fitting garment only

If the fitting garment has no center front seam, slash along the center front line from the neckline seam allowance to the waistline. Insert a fabric strip. To increase width, spread the cut edges enough at the neckline to relieve the strain and relax the vertical fitting lines. Draw a new center front line down the center of the fabric insert.

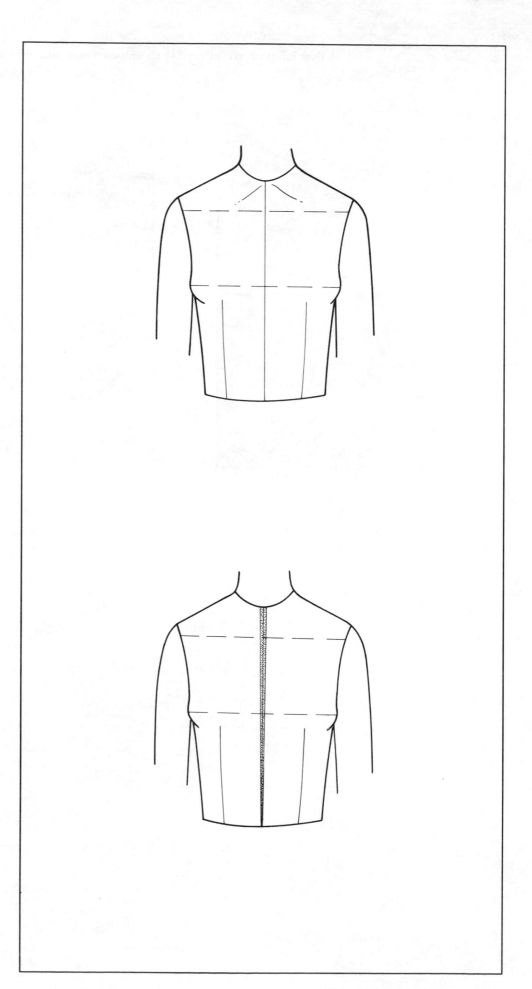

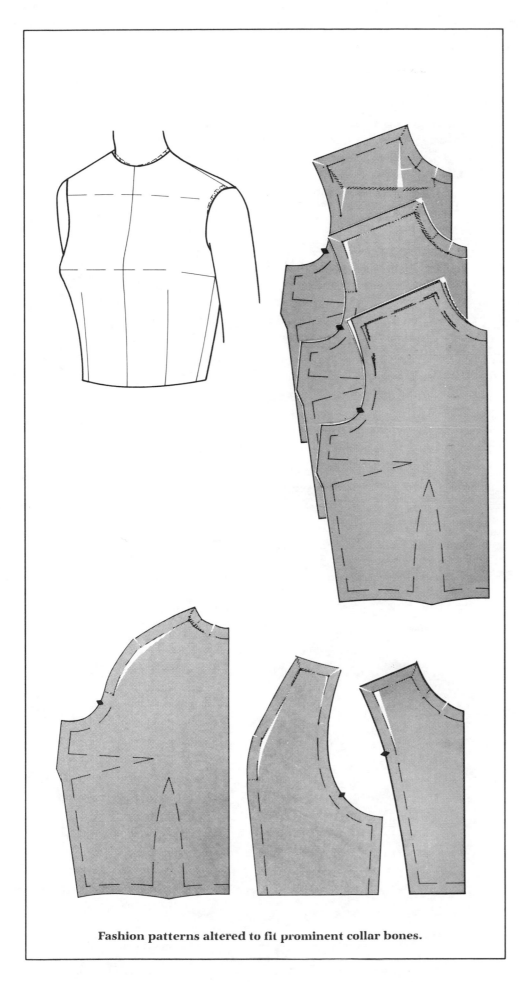

Fashion patterns altered to fit prominent collar bones.

Pivot Method

If the garment has a center front seamline, let out the seam allowances equally at the neckline to relieve the strain and to permit the center front lines to meet. Taper the new center front lines to nothing at the waistline.

If the garment does not have a center front seamline, release the shoulder seams and the front of the armscyes from the shoulders down to the point where the strain no longer pulls the sleeve away from the armscye. Fold the back shoulder seam allowance under along the shoulder seamline. Lay the fold onto the extended front seam allowances. The front neckline edges will move toward the neck. Clip as needed to remove strain at the neckline. Restitch the shoulder seams. Continue the back neckline and the armscye seamlines into the original seamlines on the front at the chest area.

rib cage

47 Prominent Sternum/Rounded Chest

48 Hollow Chest

49 Rounded Upper Back

50 Erect Upper Back

51 Prominent Shoulder Blades

52 Flat Shoulder Blades

53 Broad Chest/Upper Back

54 Narrow Chest/Upper Back

55 Wide Rib Cage

56 Narrow Rib Cage

57 Cylindrical-shaped Torso (rib cage)

58 Oval-shaped Torso (rib cage)

59 Long Upper Rib Cage

60 Short Upper Rib Cage

61 High Bust Position

62 Low or Pendulous Bust Position

63 Wide Bust Point Span

64 Prominent Bust

65 Large Bust

66 Small Bust

67 Flared Lower Ribs

68 Long Midriff

69 Short Midriff

70 Large Waist

71 Small Waist

BASIC FITTING THEORY

Figure Analysis

The upper portion of the sternum is larger than average and protrudes beyond the surface of the ribs. When a rounded chest is present, the chest wall curves outward along the upper center front. Both reasons for fullness increase the length from the neck to the scyeline area. The width across the chest may increase.

Fitting Analysis

The fabric is taut at the upper center front areas and pulls into diagonal wrinkles from the armscyes to the neckline. The armscyes on a sleeveless dress may ripple at the edges of the chest. The chest fitting line rises at the center.

Fabric Requirements for Proper Fit

The fullness at the center of the chest requires more fabric length at the upper center front area. The longer garment area relieves the strain at the neckline; the fabric relaxes and the chest fitting line becomes level. More width may be needed at chest level. The fabric will relax at the armscyes, and they will align correctly with the body contours.

GARMENT & PATTERN ALTERATIONS FOR SYMMETRICAL FIGURES

Change Required

Lengthen and widen the upper center front.

Slash Method—fitting garment only

Slash across the garment front from one armscye to the other 2 inches (5 cm) below the neckline; follow the crosswise grain. Insert a fabric strip. To increase length, spread the cut edges evenly until the chest fitting line is level. Taper to nothing at each armscye.

If the fabric is taut across the armscyes, follow the procedure for **Pivot Method.**

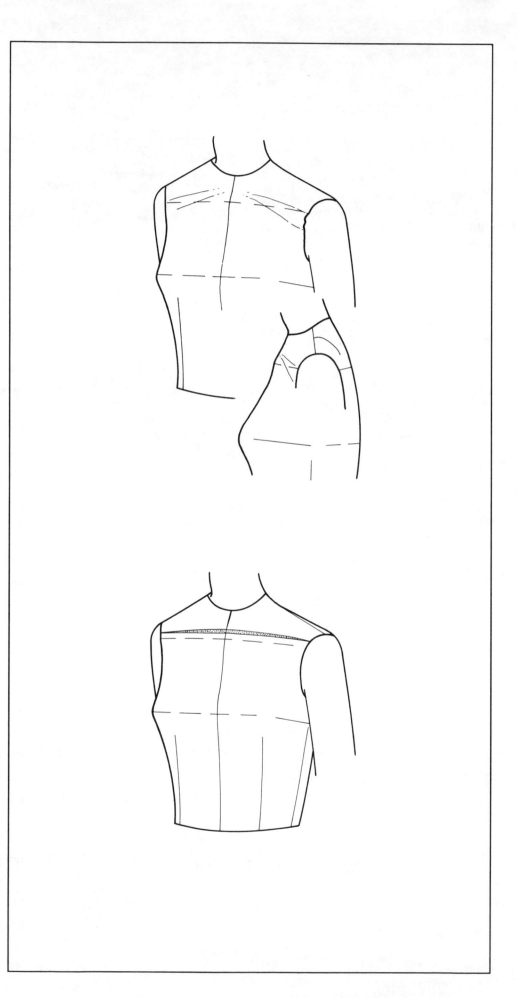

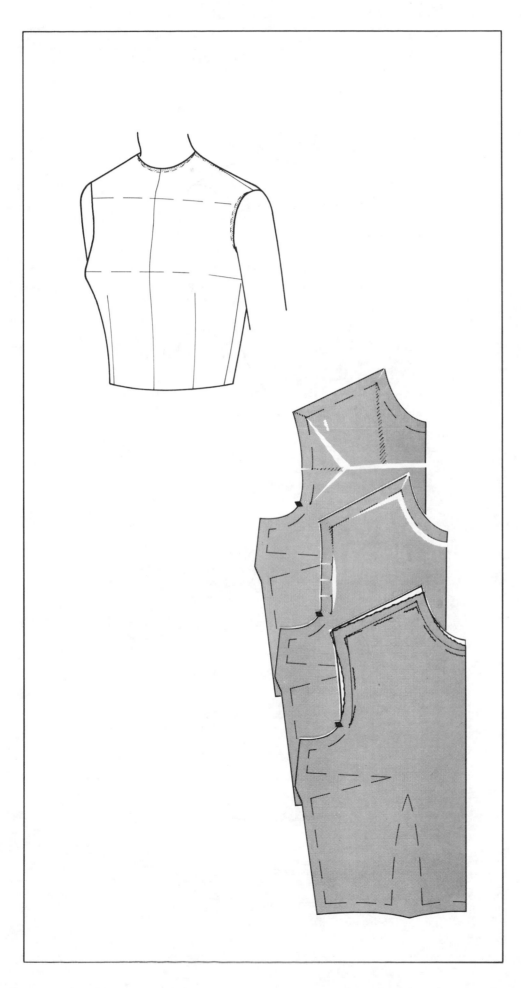

Pivot Method
Release the shoulder seams. To increase length, let out the front shoulder seam allowances equally at the neckline until the chest fitting line is level. Taper to nothing at each armscye. Raise the neck seamline across the center front area to restore the neckline circumference; blend into the original near each shoulder. Restitch the shoulder seams.

Check the armscye seamline positions. If they pull toward the center front, let out the armscye seam allowances equally across the chest area to form a straighter armscye line. Taper into the original seamline near each shoulder and arm hinge area. Attach the sleeves using the new armscye seamlines.

BASIC FITTING THEORY

Figure Analysis
The chest wall is flat or concave. The chest muscle development and soft tissue deposits are minimal. The arm joints appear to be larger than average; the bust curvature appears smaller and lower. The length decreases from the neck to the scyeline area. The width across the chest contour may increase between the shoulder tips. A hollow chest is often in combination with a rounded upper back. See **49 Rounded Upper Back.**

Fitting Analysis
The fabric sags into diagonal wrinkles from the shoulder tips to the center of the chest. The chest fitting line droops at the center front.

Fabric Requirements for Proper Fit
The shortness of the chest requires less fabric length at the upper center front area. This permits the garment to lie smoothly against the chest; the chest fitting line becomes level.

GARMENT & PATTERN ALTERATIONS FOR SYMMETRICAL FIGURES

Change Required
Shorten the upper center front area; widen the area at the shoulder tips.

Slash Method—fitting garment only
Below the front neck area, form a parallel tuck wide enough to remove the excess fabric and lift the chest fitting line to a level position. Follow the crosswise grain. Taper to nothing at each armscye.

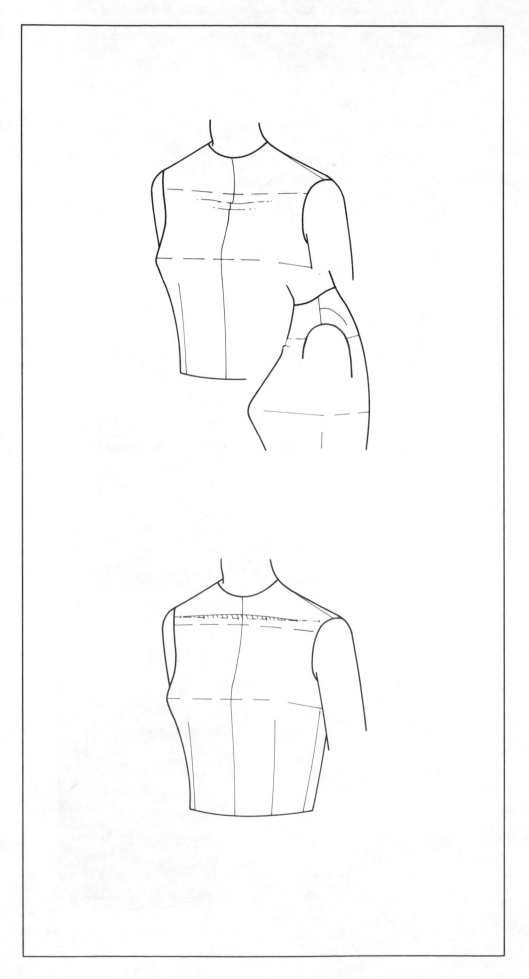

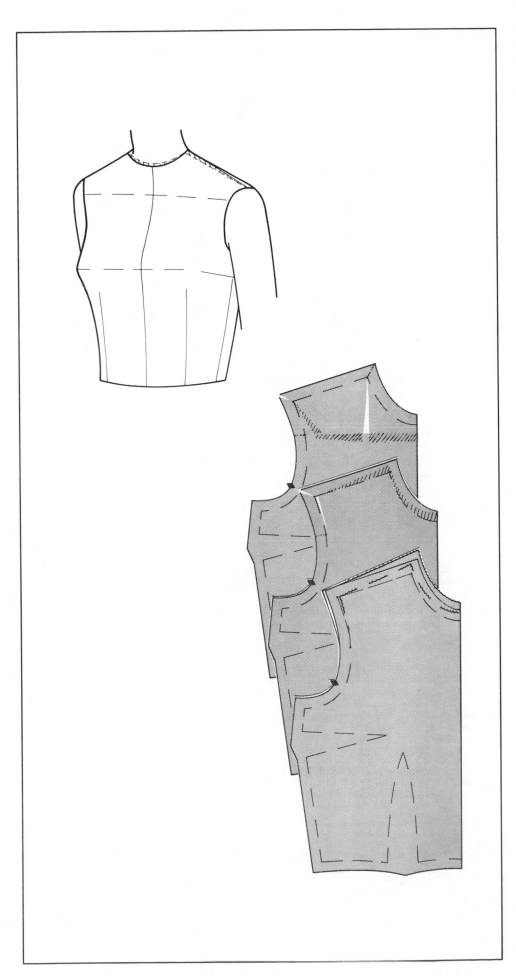

Pivot Method
Release the shoulder seams. Clip
the neck seam allowance across the
center front area. To decrease the
garment length, take up the front
shoulders equally at the neckline
until the chest fitting line is level;
taper to nothing at each armscye.
To restore the neckline, mark a
new neckline position across the
center front area. Blend into the
original near the shoulders. Stitch
the shoulder seams using the new
front shoulder seamlines.

BASIC FITTING THEORY

Figure Analysis

The upper portion of the spine curves outward more than average. The head may rest forward of the central body axis. The length increases from the neck to the mid-blade area. This figure variation is often in combination with a hollow chest. See **48 Hollow Chest.**

Fitting Analysis

The fabric is taut at the back neckline area. The strain pulls the neckline below the center of the neck vertebra. Diagonal wrinkles pull from the armscyes to the upper center back. Strain pulls the blade fitting line and waistline up at their centers. The front neckline may appear to be too tight.

Fabric Requirements for Proper Fit

The outward contour of the spine requires more fabric length and more fabric shaping at the upper center back area. This relieves the strain at the necklines; the blade fitting line and the waistline become level.

GARMENT & PATTERN ALTERATIONS FOR SYMMETRICAL FIGURES

Change Required

Lengthen the upper center back area.

Slash Method—fitting garment only

Slash across the garment back from one shoulder tip to the other. Follow the crosswise grain. Insert a fabric strip. To increase the garment length at the neckline area, spread the cut edges evenly until the blade fitting line is level. Taper to nothing at each armscye.

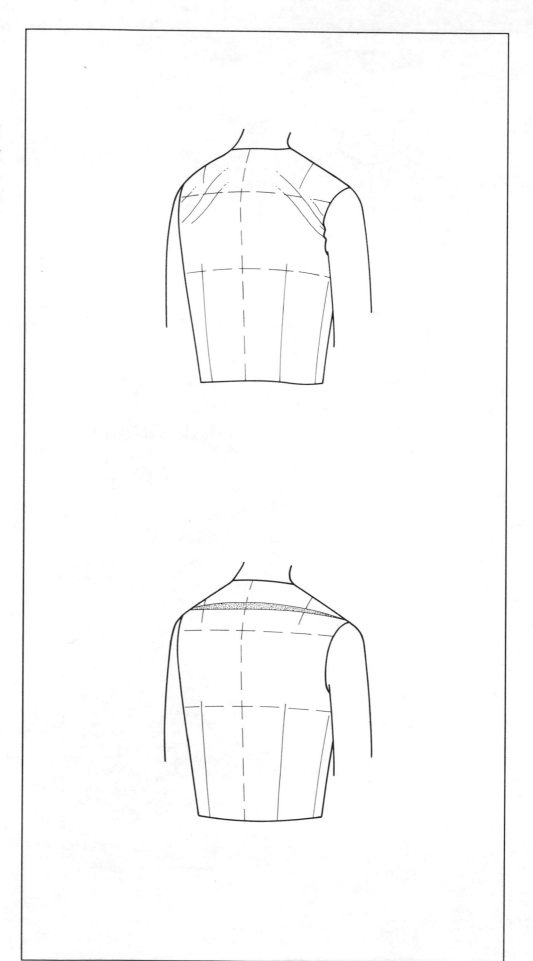

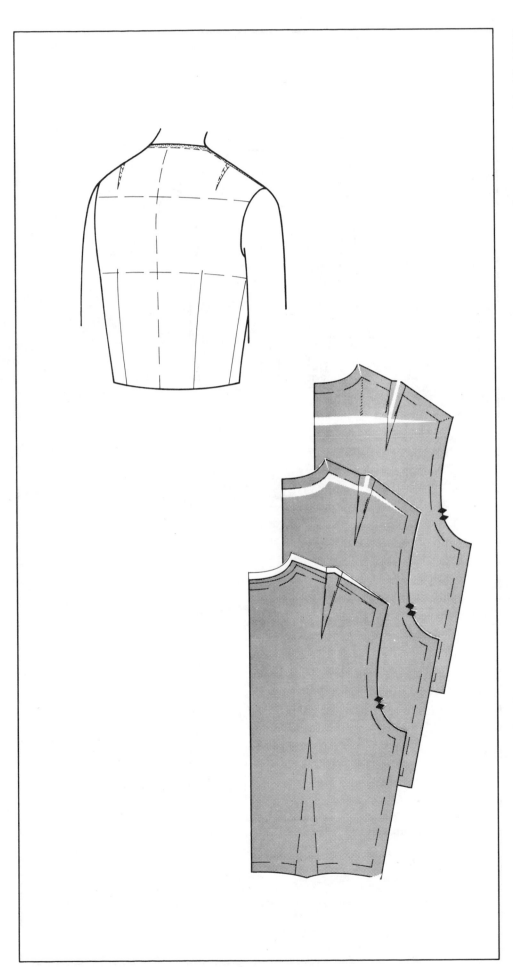

Pivot Method
Release the shoulder seams. Let out the back shoulder seam allowances equally at the neckline until the blade fitting line is level. Taper to nothing at the armscyes. This lengthens the shoulder seamline. Widen the shoulder darts to increase the garment shaping and to restore the shoulder seamline length. Draw new shoulder seamlines in straight lines across the widened darts. Mark a new back-neck seamline above the original at the center back equal to the adjustment of the shoulder seamlines. Stitch the shoulder seams using the new back shoulder seamlines.

BASIC FITTING THEORY

Figure Analysis
The upper portion of the spine curves less than average. The head may rest back of the central body axis. The length decreases from the neck to the mid-blade area. This figure variation may be a result of overly erect posture and is often in combination with a prominent bust or rounded chest. See **64 Prominent Bust** or **47 Prominent Sternum/Rounded Chest**

Fitting Analysis
The fabric is loose over the shoulder blades and sags into horizontal folds across the center back. The blade fitting line droops at the center back.

Fabric Requirements for Proper Fit
The straighter contour of the spine requires less fabric length and less shaping at the upper center back area. This permits the garment area to lie smoothly against the upper back; the blade fitting line becomes level.

GARMENT & PATTERN ALTERATIONS FOR SYMMETRICAL FIGURES

Change Required
Shorten the upper center back area.

Slash Method—fitting garment only
Form a parallel tuck wide enough to lift the blade fitting line to a level position. Follow the crosswise grain. Taper to nothing at each armscye.

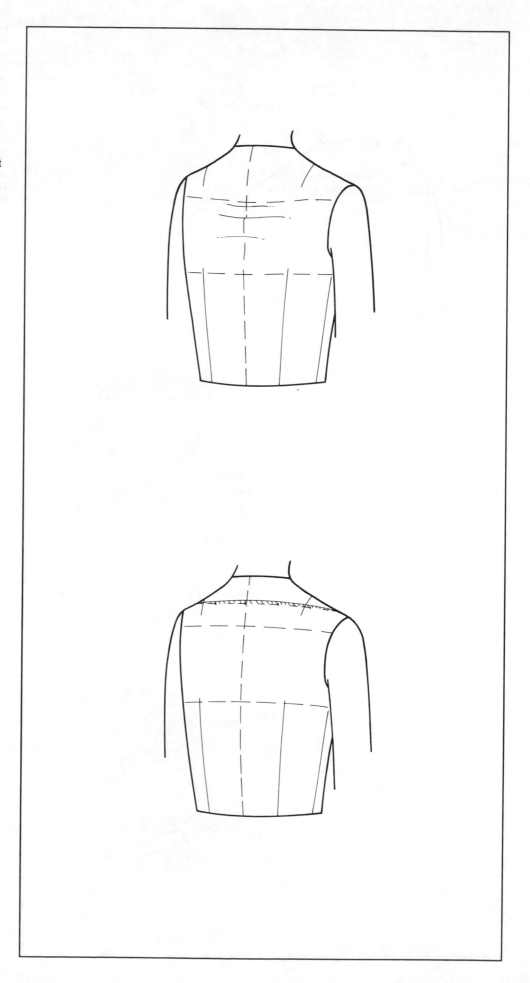

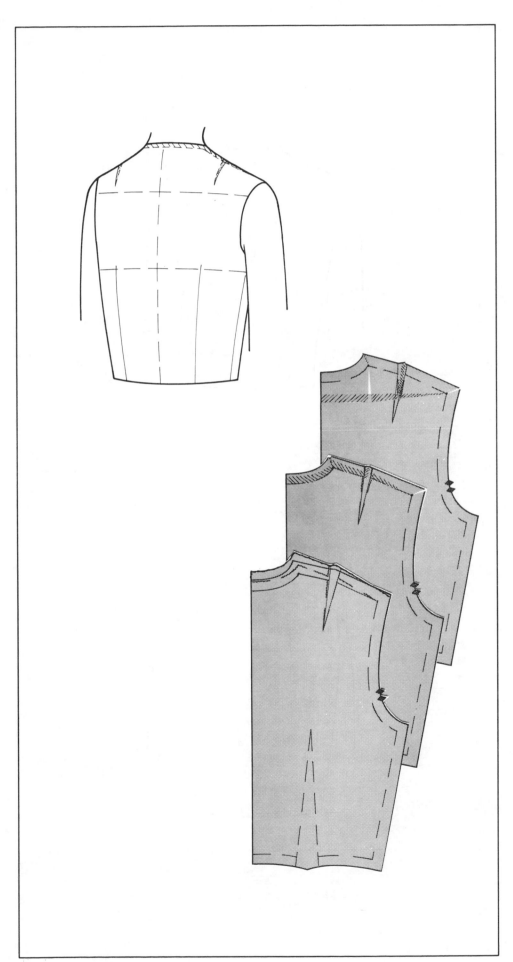

Pivot Method

Release the shoulder seams. Take up shoulder area equally at the back neckline until the blade fitting line is level. Let out the shoulder darts to restore the shoulder seam length. Draw each new shoulder seamline in a straight line across the narrowed dart. Taper to nothing at the armscyes.

Mark the lowered neck seamline across the center back equal to the adjustment at the shoulders. Blend into the original near each shoulder. Trim the excess width from the neckline contour. Stitch the shoulder seams using the new back shoulder seamlines.

BASIC FITTING THEORY

Figure Analysis

The shoulder blades are larger and protrude more than average. The upper back muscle development and soft tissue deposits may be minimal. The body is recessed along the upper area of the spine. The length and width increase from the center of each shoulder seamline to the blade line and from armscye to armscye, respectively. Asymmetrical figures may have one prominent and one flat blade.

Fitting Analysis

The angularity of the shoulder blades pulls tight horizontal wrinkles into the fabric between the blades. Sleeveless armscyes ripple. At each blade, diagonal wrinkles radiate toward the armscyes. The sleeve caps pull toward the back. The blade fitting line rises.

Fabric Requirements for Proper Fit

The fullness of the shoulder blades requires more fabric width and length and increases shaping. Wider darts result. This relieves the strain and permits the armscyes and sleeves to align properly over the arm joints. The blade fitting line becomes level. Adjustment of the armscye size and the sleeve is unnecessary.

GARMENT & PATTERN ALTERATIONS FOR SYMMETRICAL FIGURES

Change Required

Widen and lengthen the area over the blades.

Slash Method—fitting garment only

Slash diagonally from each neckline extension to the corresponding armscye at the arm hinge area. Insert fabric strips. To increase width and length, spread the cut edges equally at the dart tips to relax the fabric and restore the ease. Taper to nothing at the neckline and the armscyes.

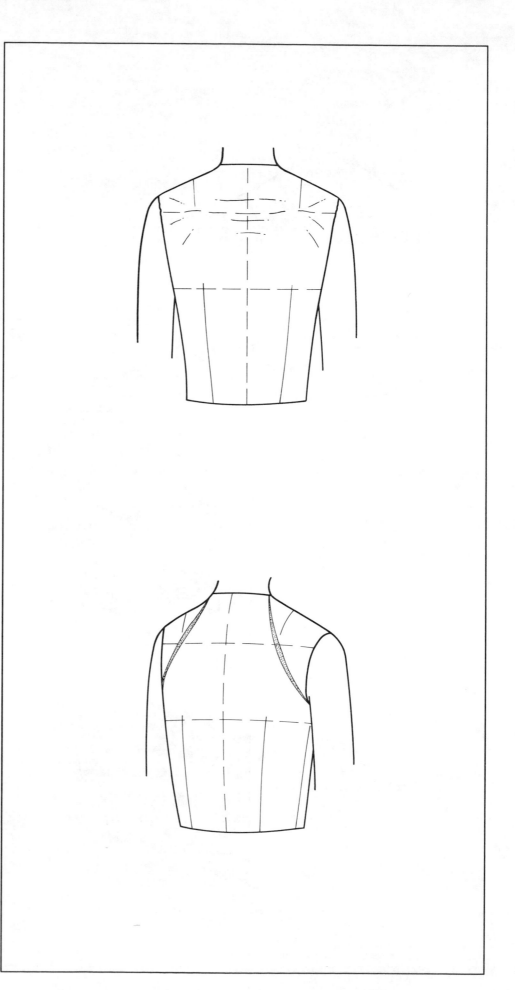

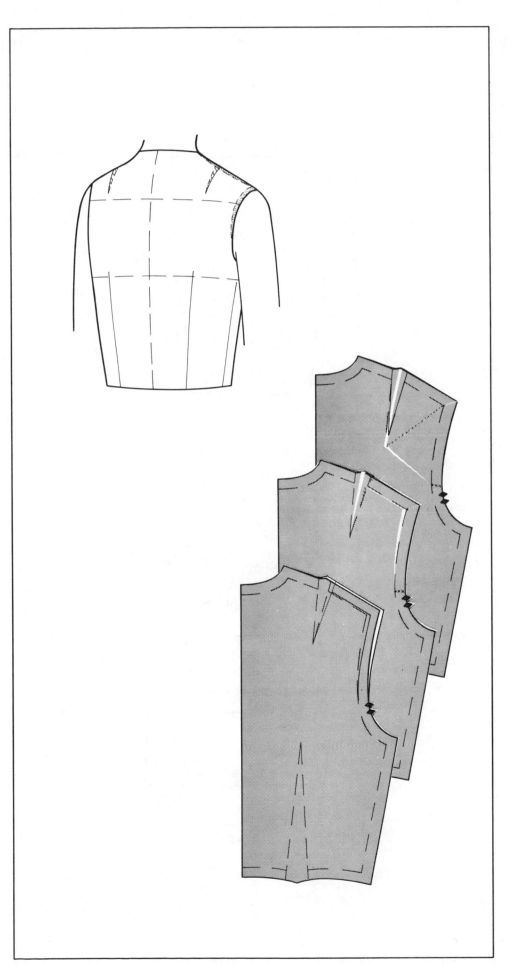

Pivot Method
Release the shoulder and the back armscye seams above the arm hinge areas. Widen the back darts equally until the garment is smooth but relaxed over the shoulder blades and at the armscye. Curve and lengthen the darts as needed. Let out the armscye seam allowances to restore the length of the shoulder seamlines. Blend the new armscye into the original at the arm hinge area. Draw each new shoulder seamline in a straight line across the stitched darts.

BASIC FITTING THEORY

Figure Analysis
The upper portions of the shoulder blades curve outward less than average; the back may appear to be erect. The width and length decrease from armscye to armscye and from the center of each shoulder seamline to the blade line, respectively. Asymmetrical figures may have one prominent and one flat blade.

Fitting Analysis
The fabric is loose over the shoulder blades and may form loose vertical wrinkles.

Fabric Requirements for Proper Fit
The less-curved contour of the shoulder blades requires less fabric width and length and dart shaping. The shoulder dart becomes narrower. The smaller garment area lies smoothly against the body.

GARMENT & PATTERN ALTERATIONS FOR SYMMETRICAL FIGURES

Change Required
Narrow and shorten the area over the blades.

Slash Method—fitting garment only
To remove the excess fabric at the tips of the back shoulder darts, form diagonal tucks of equal widths that point toward the neck and underarm. Adjust the tuck widths until the fabric lies smooth. Retain sufficient ease. Taper to nothing at the neckline and armscyes.

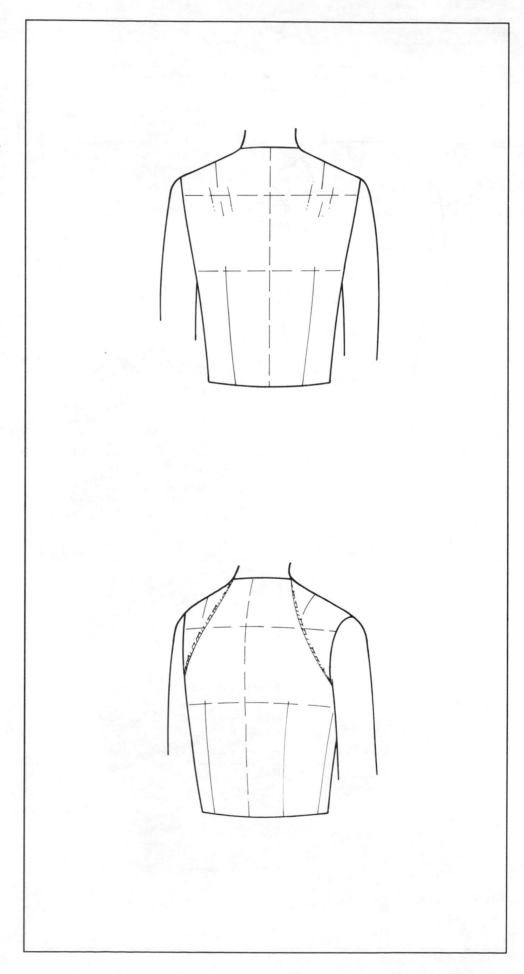

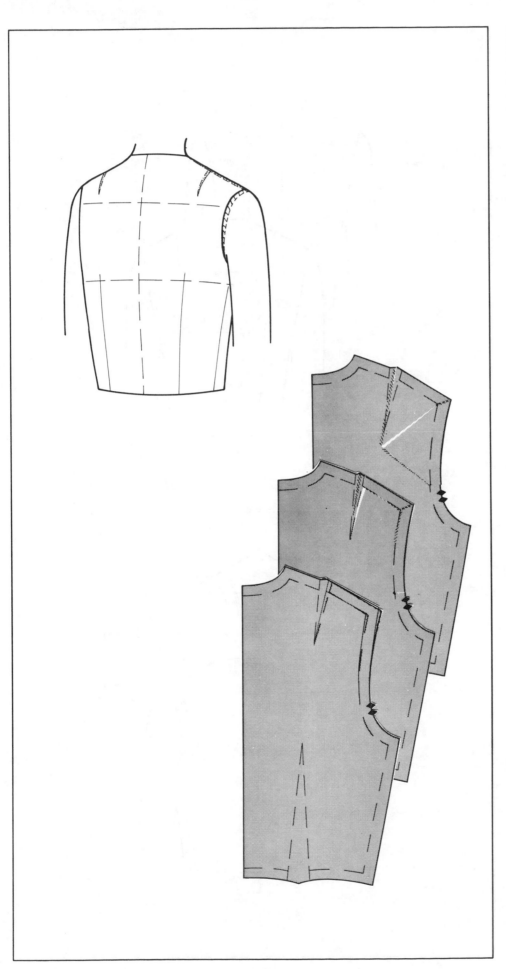

Pivot Method
Release the shoulder seams, the darts, and the back armscye seams above the arm hinge areas. Let out the darts equally until the garment is smooth but relaxed over the shoulder blades. Straighten and shorten the darts as needed. Draw new armscye seamlines in the garment area to restore the length of the shoulder seamlines. Blend the new armscye into the original at the arm hinge area. Draw each new shoulder seamline in a straight line across the stitched darts.

BASIC FITTING THEORY

Figure Analysis
The upper part of the rib cage is fuller than average. The chest or the upper back muscle development and deposits of soft tissues may be heavier. This increases the width between the arm joints. The structure of the arm joints and the arms are not affected.

Fitting Analysis
The fabric is taut from armscye to armscye and forms tight horizontal wrinkles. The sleeve pulls toward the body centers causing the armscye to cut against the arm hinge. The vertical fitting line on the sleeve cap bows toward the fullness. The chest and blade fitting lines remain level.

Fabric Requirements for Proper Fit
The increased chest or blade span requires more fabric width at the corresponding scyeline and armscyes. This relieves the strain at the underarm and chest (blade); the sleeves and armscyes relax and align without adjustment.

GARMENT & PATTERN ALTERATIONS FOR SYMMETRICAL FIGURES

Change Required
Widen the area across the chest or the blades.

Slash Method—fitting garment only
About 1 inch (2.5 cm) from each armscye, slash from the shoulderline to the scyeline along the lengthwise grain. Insert fabric strips. To increase width, separate the cut edges equally at the chest or blade line until the armscye lines move to comfortable and attractive positions. Taper to nothing at the shoulders and the scyeline.

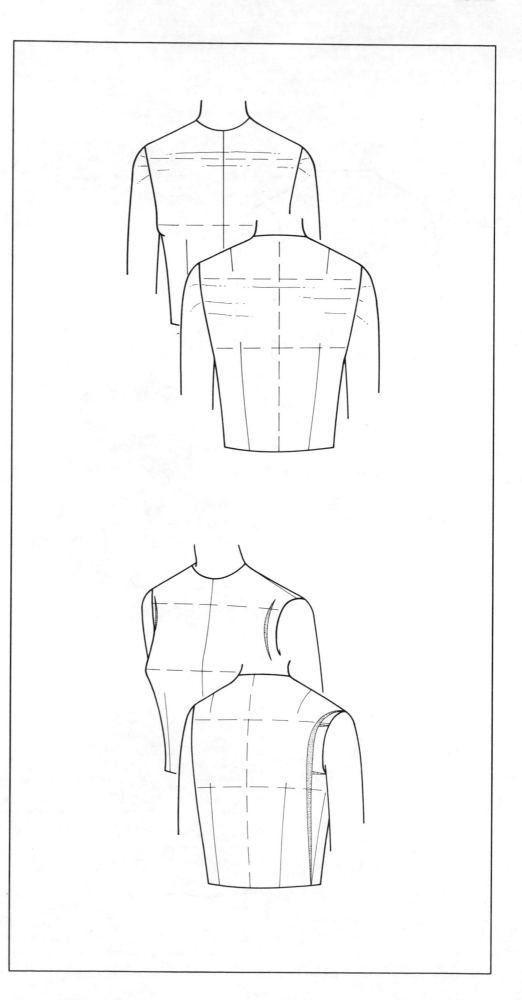

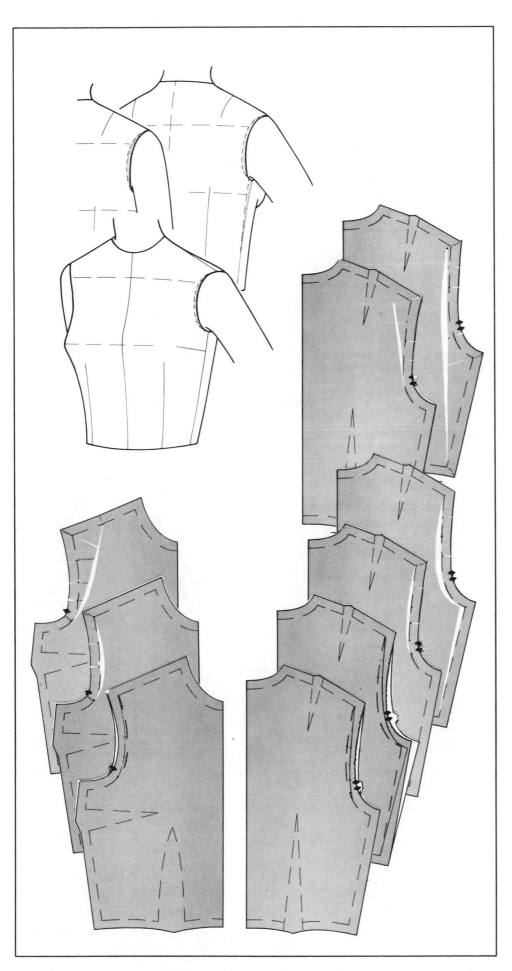

Pivot Method
Release the front of the sleeves. Mark the new armscye stitching lines in the seam allowance areas at the edges of the chest (blade) so that they lie in comfortable and attractive positions. Taper into the original seamlines near the shoulders and lower armscye curves. Attach the sleeves to the armscyes using the new armscye seamlines.

BASIC FITTING THEORY

Figure Analysis

The upper part of the rib cage is smaller than average. The chest or the upper back muscle development and deposits of soft tissues are minimal; the back may appear to be erect. The width decreases between the arm joints. The structure of the arm joints and the arms are not affected.

Fitting Analysis

The fabric is loose along the edges of the chest or the blades and the underarm areas. When the arms are moved forward, the front armscyes cut against the arm hinges. When the arms are lifted, the sleeves pull against the arm and restrict movement. The chest and blade fitting lines remain level.

Fabric Requirements for Proper Fit

The decreased chest or blade span requires less fabric width at the corresponding scyeline and armscyes. This permits the garment area to lie smoothly and comfortably against the rib cage. The sleeves align properly with the body contours without adjustment.

GARMENT & PATTERN ALTERATIONS FOR SYMMETRICAL FIGURES

Change Required

Narrow the area across the chest or the blade.

Slash Method—fitting garment only

About 1 inch (2.5 cm) from each armscye, form a vertical tuck to remove the excess fabric.

Adjust the widths equally until the garment area is smooth; retain sufficient ease at the blade line. Taper the ends of the tucks to nothing near the shoulders and the scyeline.

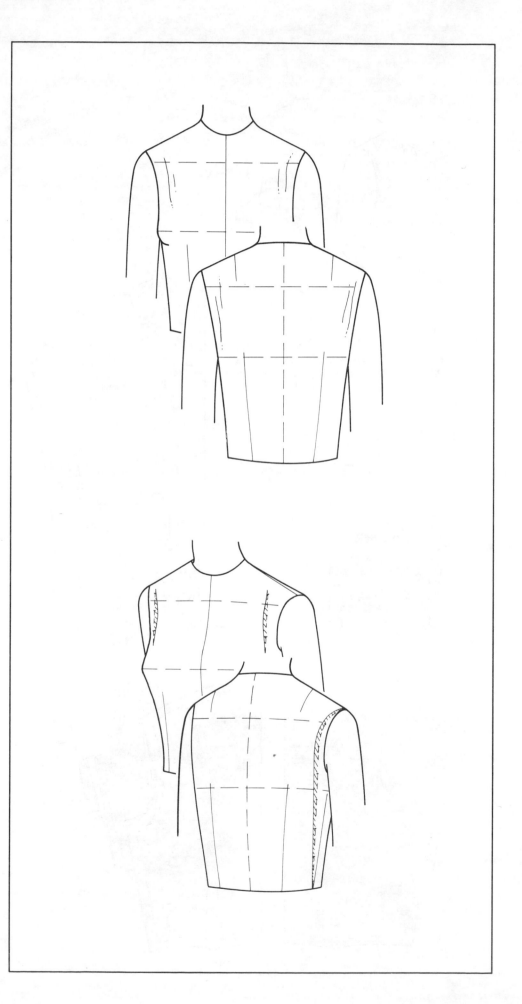

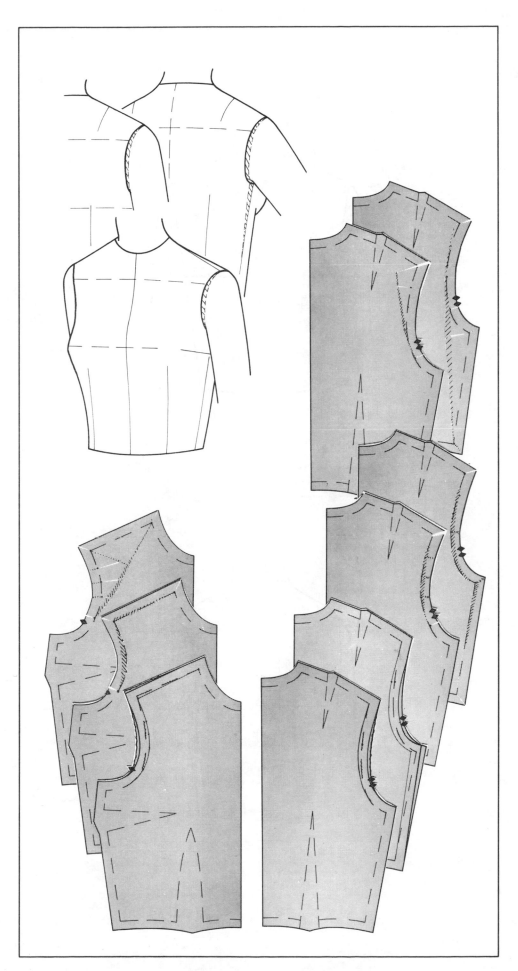

Pivot Method
Mark new armscye seamlines in the garment area at the edges of the chest (blade) so that they lie in comfortable and attractive positions. Taper into the original seamlines near the shoulder and the lower armscye curves. If the sleeves have been set in, release the front (back) areas from the shoulders to the underarm areas and proceed as stated above. Attach the sleeves to the armscyes using the new armscye seamlines.

BASIC FITTING THEORY

Figure Analysis

The midsection of the rib cage is fuller than average and increases the body circumference at the scye line. The side of the rib cage tapers more than average. This lengthens the side of the body between the base of the arm joints and the waist. The chest and blade fitting lines remain level. The structure of the arm joints and arms are not affected.

Fitting Analysis

The fabric is taut under each arm and forms tight wrinkles which follow the curves of the armscye seamlines. The tightness makes the armscyes appear to be too tight and the bust area of the garment appear too small.

Fabric Requirements for Proper Fit

The increased rib cage circumference requires more fabric width at the scyeline. This relieves the strain and restores the ease in the garment at the underarm areas. The armscyes align properly with the body contours. The adjustment may be required on the back or the front of the garment or on both areas.

GARMENT & PATTERN ALTERATIONS FOR SYMMETRICAL FIGURES

Change Required

Widen the area near the underarm extension.

Slash Method—fitting garment only

Slash from the mid-armscye to the waistline. Follow lengthwise grain. Insert fabric strips. To increase width, spread the cut edges equally at the scyeline to relieve the tension and restore the ease. Taper the end of each slash to nothing at the armscye and waistline.

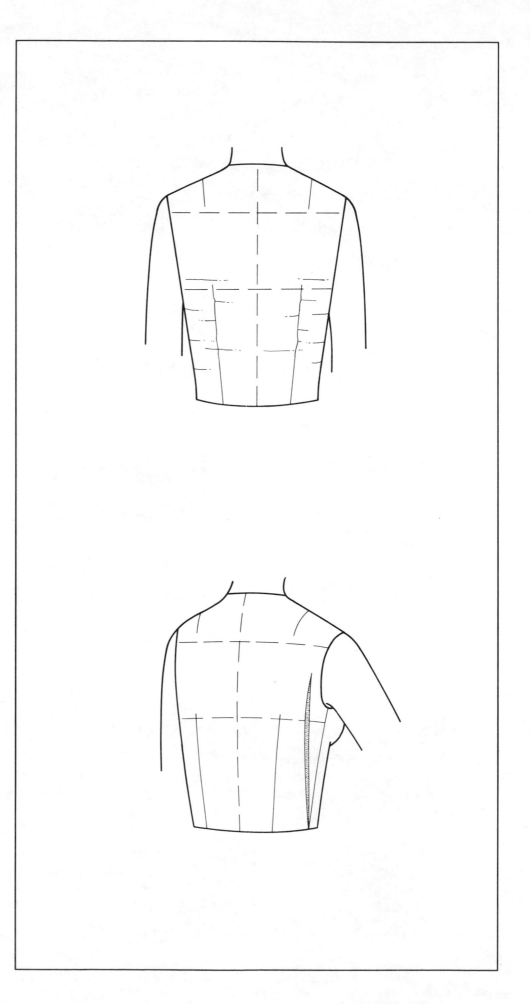

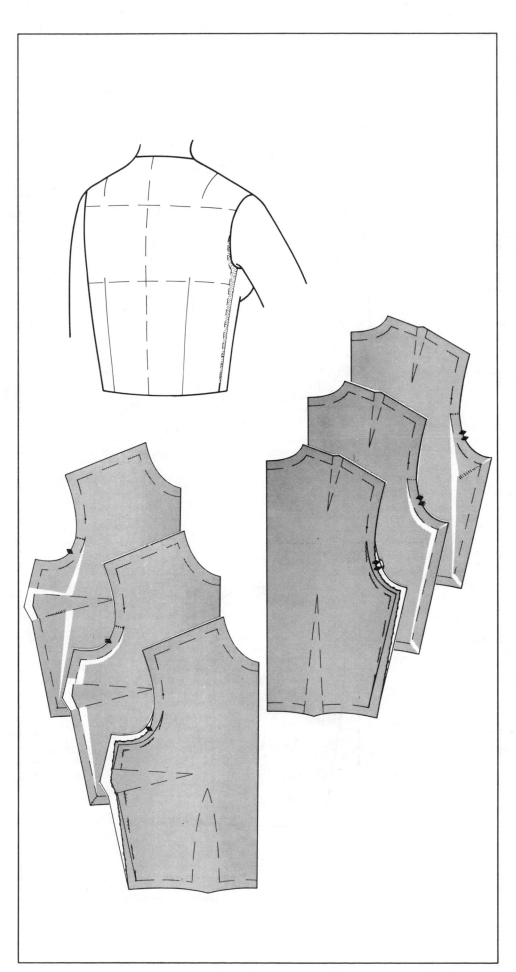

Pivot Method
Release the side seams and the lower armscye seams up to the corresponding blade or chest area. Let out the side seam allowances equally at the scyeline to relieve the tension and restore the ease. Restore the armscye seamline from the new side seam position to the original at the blade or chest area. Draw a new side seam in a straight line from the new position at the underarm to the original at the waistline. Repeat the procedure on the front as needed.

BASIC FITTING THEORY

Figure Analysis

The mid-section of the rib cage is narrower than average and decreases the body circumference at the scyeline. The upper torso area tapers less than average. This shortens the side of the body between the base of the arm joints and the waist. The chest and blade fitting lines remain level.

Fitting Analysis

The fabric near the lower armscye areas hangs in vertical folds near the armscyes on the front and back. The excess garment width inhibits arm movement; the front armscye cuts against the arm hinge. The sleeves appear to be too tight when the arms are lifted.

Fabric Requirements for Proper Fit

The decreased rib cage circumference requires less fabric width at the scyeline. This permits the armscyes to align with the body contour and the arm to move without constraint or discomfort. The adjustment may be required on the back or the front of the garment or on both areas.

GARMENT & PATTERN ALTERATIONS FOR SYMMETRICAL FIGURES

Change Required

Narrow the area near the underarm extension.

Slash Method—fitting garment only

Below the vertical portion of the armscyes, form vertical tucks of equal widths at the scyeline. Adjust the widths equally until the excess fabric is removed; retain sufficient ease. Taper the tucks to nothing at the armscye and the waistline.

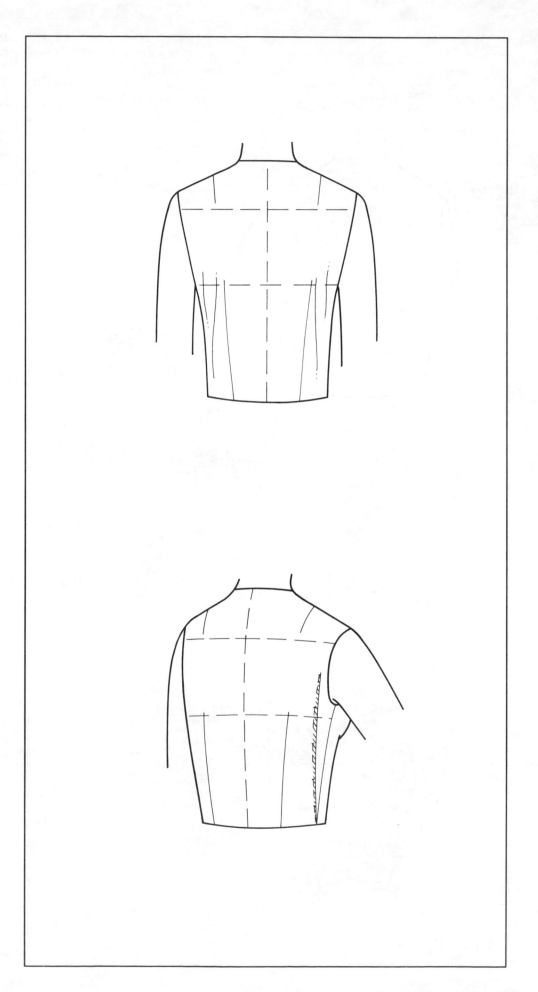

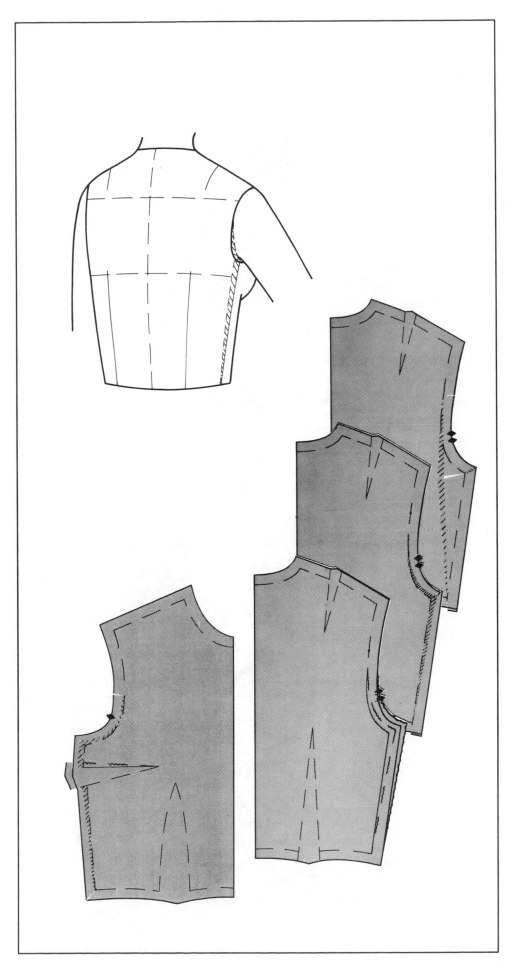

Pivot Method
Release the side seams and the lower armscye seams to the corresponding blade or chest area. At the scyeline, take in the sides garment areas equally until the excess fabric is removed; retain sufficient ease. Restore the armscye seamline from the new side seam position to the original at the blade or chest area. Draw a new side seam in a straight line from the new position at the underarm to the original at the waistline. Repeat the procedure on the front as needed.

BASIC FITTING THEORY

Figure Analysis
The shape of the rib cage is more round than average. The torso is deeper from the center front through to the center back. The bone structures forming the arm joints may be larger than average also. These factors increase the body depth from the front arm hinge to that at the back.

Fitting Analysis
The armscye cuts against the arm hinges. Diagonal wrinkles pull from the blade and chest areas to the underarm. A fold of fabric forms below the scyeline. Sleeves also pull at the underarm and may be too tight around the arm. The armscye seamlines pull toward the arm at the front and back.

Fabric Requirements for Proper Fit
The greater profile depth requires more fabric width at the underarm area on both the sleeve and the garment. More armscye length also may be required at the shoulder. The wider armscye extensions on the garment and the sleeve permit the fabric to relax underneath the arms and around the torso. The armscyes relax and align properly along the blade and chest.

GARMENT & PATTERN ALTERATIONS FOR SYMMETRICAL FIGURES

Change Required
Widen the armscye extension.

Slash Method—fitting garment only
Near each side seam, slash the garment from the armscye to the waistline on both the front and back. Insert fabric strips. To increase width, spread each set of cut edges equally at the scyeline to relax the fabric and restore the ease. Taper to nothing at the waistline. See **75 Large Shoulder Joints** and **80 Large Upper Arms** for the sleeve adjustment.

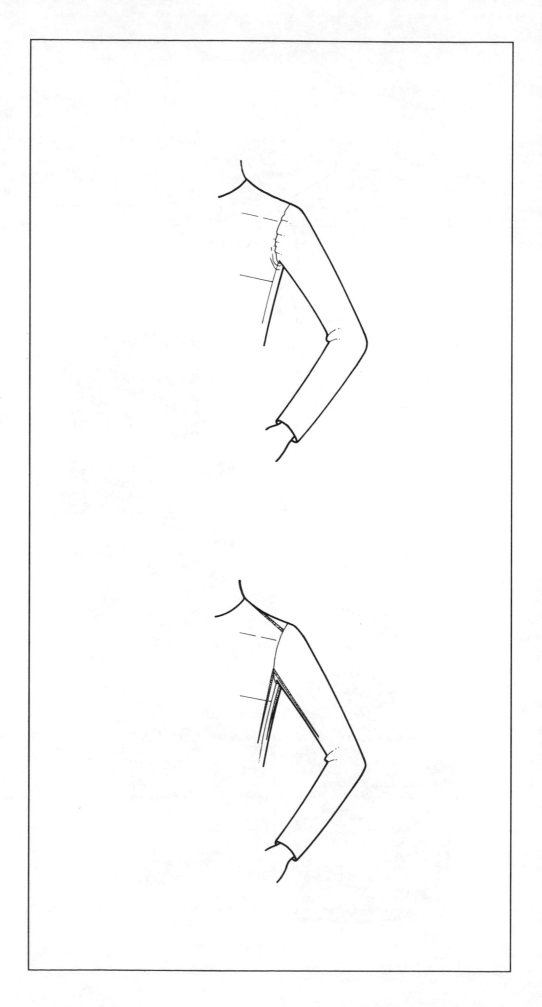

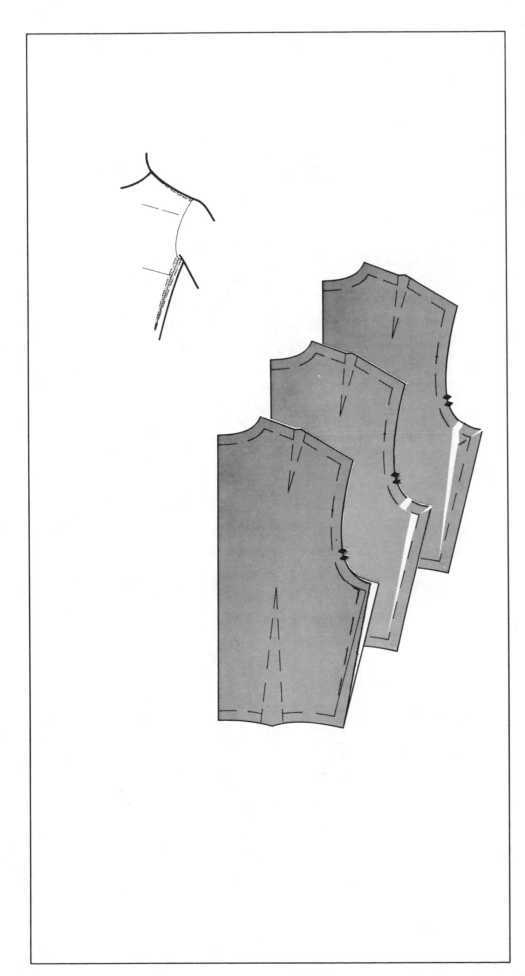

Pivot Method

Release the side seams and the lower armscye area if the sleeves are attached. At the scyeline, let out both front and back seam allowances equally to relax the fabric and restore the ease, Taper to nothing at the waistline. See **75 Large Shoulder Joints** and **80 Large Upper Arms** for the sleeve adjustment.

BASIC FITTING THEORY

Figure Analysis

The shape of the rib cage is more oval than average. The torso is narrower from the center front through to the center back. The bone structures forming the arm joints may be smaller than average also. These factors decrease the body depth from the front arm hinge to that at the back.

Fitting Analysis

The garment hangs in loose vertical folds near the underarm on both the front and the back. The sleeve appears to be too large. When the arms are raised, strain pulls the sleeves tightly against the arm, the arms cannot be raised comfortably.

Fabric Requirements for Proper Fit

The smaller profile depth requires less fabric width at the underarm area on both the sleeve and the garment. Less armscye length also may be required at the shoulder. The narrower armscye extensions on the garment and the sleeve bring the fabric closer to the body surface. The arms can be raised easily and comfortably.

GARMENT & PATTERN ALTERATIONS FOR SYMMETRICAL FIGURES

Change Required

Narrow the armscye extension.

Slash Method—fitting garment only

Near each side seam, form a vertical tuck at the scyeline on both front and back. Adjust the widths equally until the excess fabric is removed but the ease is retained. Taper the tucks to nothing at the waistline. See **76 Small Shoulder Joints** and **79 Thin Arms** for the sleeve adjustment.

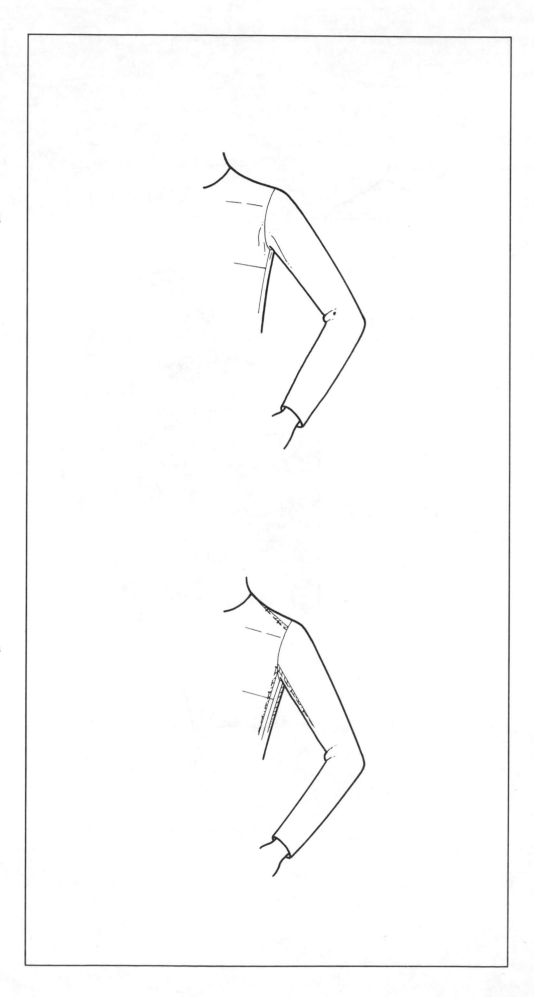

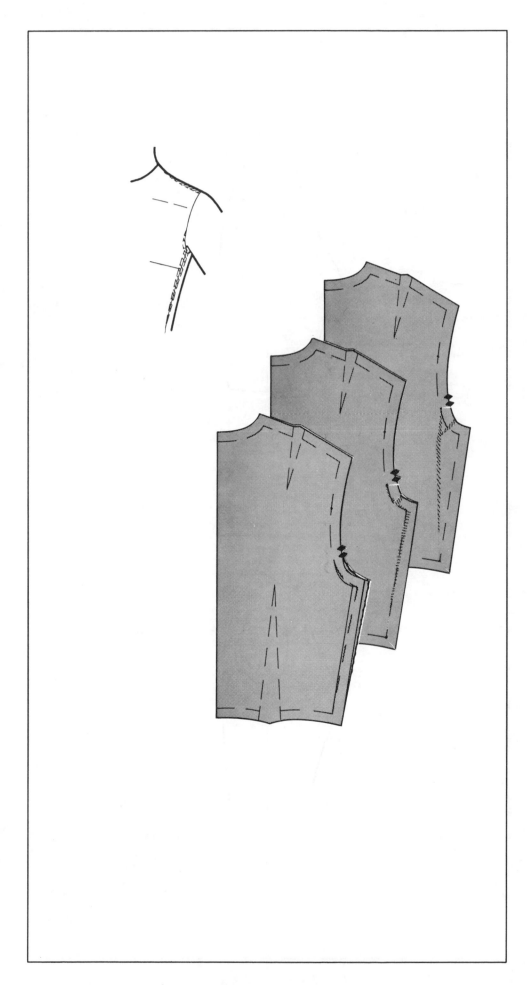

Pivot Method
Release the side seams and the lower armscye area if the sleeves are attached. At the scyeline, take in the garment areas equally until the excess fabric is removed; retain sufficient ease. Taper into the original at the waistline. See **76 Small Shoulder Joints** and **79 Thin Arms** for the sleeve adjustment.

BASIC FITTING THEORY

Figure Analysis

The bones forming the upper rib cage area are heavier than average. The spacing between the adjacent ribs may be greater. The length increases from the shoulder to the bustline. The length variation may affect the space between the arm hinge or the length of the arm joints.

Fitting Analysis

The fabric is taut between the shoulder seams and the waistline and may form tight vertical wrinkles. The darted area is too high and creates the illusion of a low bust position. The midriff and waistline rise onto the larger body areas and appear to be too small. The armscye may cut against the arm hinge. The chest and blade fitting lines remain level.

Fabric Requirements for Proper Fit

The longer rib cage areas require more fabric length between the shoulder seams and the bustline. This relieves the strain at the chest and upper back areas. The garment shaping, the midriff, and the waistline lower and align with the body contours.

GARMENT & PATTERN ALTERATIONS FOR SYMMETRICAL FIGURES

Change Required

Lengthen the appropriate area between the shoulder area and the bustline.

Slash Method—fitting garment only

If the armscye pulls against the arm hinge, cut across the front and back of the garment through the armscye. Follow crosswise grain. Insert fabric strips. Separate each set of cut edges evenly until the armscye seamline lowers to a comfortable position. The length adjustment may not be equal on both the front and back.

If the armscye length is correct but the garment shaping is too high, slash completely around the garment about 1 inch (2.5 cm) below the scyeline. Follow the crosswise grain. Insert a fabric strip. Spread the cut edges of the garment evenly until the garment shaping and the waistline align with the bust and waist, respectively.

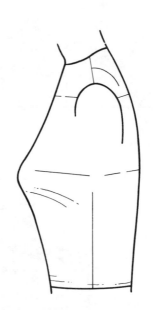

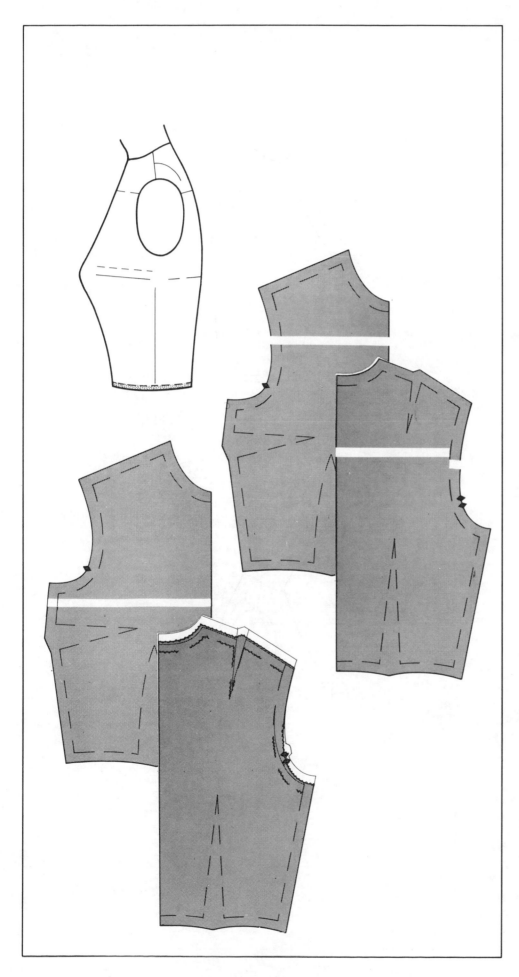

If the length of the armscye and the center front are correct but the garment shaping is too full and the center back is too short, lengthen only the back. Release the side seams across the side dart area. Release the side darts. Cut across the entire back area at the bustline. Insert a fabric strip. To gain the needed length, seperate the cut edges evenly until the strain is relieved and the waistline is level. Let out the dart width as needed. For additional front length, let out the front waistline seam evenly. True the sidé seams across the adjustments. See **66 Small Bust.**

Pivot Method
If the armscye cuts against the arm hinge, release the shoulder seams. Let out both the back and front seam allowances evenly on each shoulder area until the lower armscye seamline lowers to a comfortable position. Adjust the length change parallel to the original seamlines until the garment lies smooth but relaxes over the chest and blade areas.

Restore the depth of the back and front necklines. Raise the neckline seam at center front and center back equal to the length adjustment at the shoulders. Blend the new neckline into the original near the shoulder areas.

If the armscye length is correct but the garment shaping and the waistline are too high, release the side seam, the underarm dart, and the waistline seam. Move the underarm dart down until it aligns with the fullest part of the bust. Shorten both the back and front waistline darts equal to the side dart adjustment. Mark the new waistline parallel to the original. Restore the back and front waistline circumferences. Remark and stitch the new underarm seamlines.

On a princess-style garment, release the seams across the bust area. Reshape the side panel so that the greatest curvature is at the bustline. Correct the waistline as stated above.

If only the back is too short and the dart shaping is too large, release the side seams and the side darts. Narrow the darts until the shaping is correct. Trace the side seamlines in a straight line across the closed darts. Stitch the side seams. Mark the new back waistline even with that of the front. See **66 Small Bust.**

BASIC FITTING THEORY

Figure Analysis

The bones forming the upper rib cage area are lighter than average; the spacing between the adjacent ribs may be closer. The length decreases from the shoulder to the bustline. The length variation may affect the length of the joints or the space between the arm hinge and the bustline.

Fitting Analysis

The fabric sags into a loose horizontal fold at the bustline or near the waistline. The armscye may drop too far below the arm hinge. The darted area is too low and creates the illusion of a high bust position. The midriff lowers into the smaller body area and appears too large. The chest and blade fitting lines remain level.

Fabric Requirements for Proper Fit

The shorter rib cage area requires less fabric length between the shoulder seams and the bustline. This permits the garment area to lie smoothly against the chest and the upper back. The garment shaping, the midriff, and the waistline align with the body contours.

GARMENT & PATTERN ALTERATIONS FOR SYMMETRICAL FIGURES

Change Required

Shorten the appropriate area between the shoulder and the bustline.

Slash Method—fitting garment only

If the armscye drops too far below the arm hinge, make a parallel tuck across the garment at the chest and the blade lines. Follow the crosswise grain. Adjust the size of each tuck until the armscye seamline rises to a comfortable position. The length adjustment may not be equal on both the front and back.

If the armscye length is correct but the garment shaping is too low, form a parallel tuck completely around the garment about 1 inch (2.5 cm) below the scyeline. Follow the crosswise grain. Adjust the tuck width evenly to lift the underarm dart into the correct position.

If the armscye length and the center front length are correct but

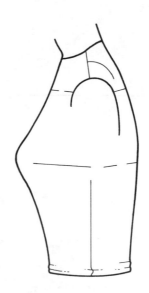

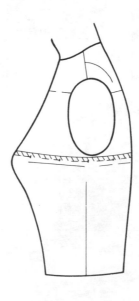

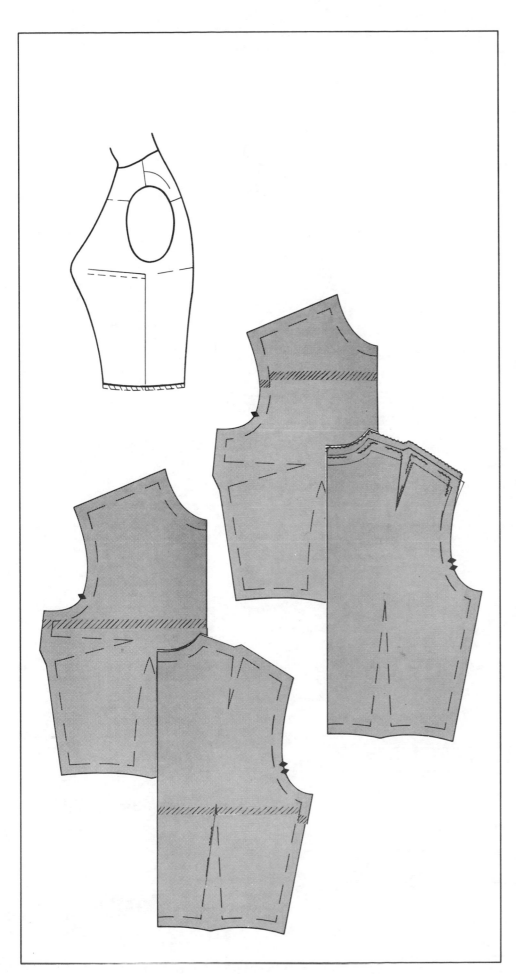

the garment shaping is too small, and the center back is too long, shorten only the back. Release the side seams. Make a parallel tuck completely across the back area at the bustline to remove the excess fabric length. Widen the dart equal to the length adjustment. True the side seams with straight lines across the adjustment. See **65 Large Bust**.

Pivot Method
If the armscye drops too far below the arm hinge, release the shoulder seams. Clip the front neck seam allowance across the center front area. Take up both the front and back shoulder seam areas evenly until the lower armscye seamline rises to a comfortable position. Adjust the length change parallel to the original seamlines until the garment lies smoothly but relaxed over the chest and blade areas.

Restore the depth of the front and back necklines. Lower the neckline seam at center front and center back equal to the length adjustment at the shoulders. Blend into the original at the shoulder areas.

If the armscye length is correct but the garment shaping and the waistline are too low, release the side seams, the underarm darts, and the waistline. Move the underarm darts up to align with the fullest part of the bust. Lengthen both the back and front waistline darts equal to the side dart adjustment. Mark the new waist seamline parallel to the original. Restore the back and front waistline circumferences. Remark and stitch the new underarm seamlines.

On a princess-style garment, release the seams across the bust area. Reshape the side panel so that the greatest curvature is at the bustline. Correct the waistline as stated above.

If only the back is too long but the dart shaping is too small, release the side seams and the side darts. Widen the darts until the shaping is correct. Mark a new, front side seam in a straight line across the closed dart. Stitch the side seams. Mark the new back waistline even with that of the front. See **65 Large Bust**.

BASIC FITTING THEORY

Figure Analysis

When associated with the youthful figure, the bust level is higher than that of the mature figure because the breast tissues are still firm, taut, and rounded. For other figures, the position of the bust contour is higher than average. Erect posture and bras with tight straps or firm support under the cups also raise the crest of the bust fullness. The distance from the shoulders to the bustline is shorter than average; the distance is greater from the bustline to the waist.

Fitting Analysis

The fabric is taut across the fullest area of the bust but is loose underneath the bust because the fabric shaping lies below the bust contour. The bust fitting line remains level.

Fabric Requirements for Proper Fit

The change in length above and below the crest of the bust requires raising the tip of the side dart and lengthening the front waist darts. The adjusted positions of the dart tips permit the fabric shaping to align properly with the bust contour.

GARMENT & PATTERN ALTERATIONS FOR SYMMETRICAL FIGURES

Change Required

Raise the tips of all the bust darts.

Slash Method—fitting garment only

Only the dart stitching line positions are affected. Use the procedure indicated for **Pivot Method.**

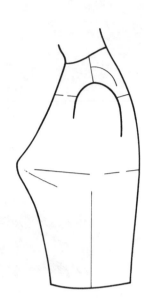

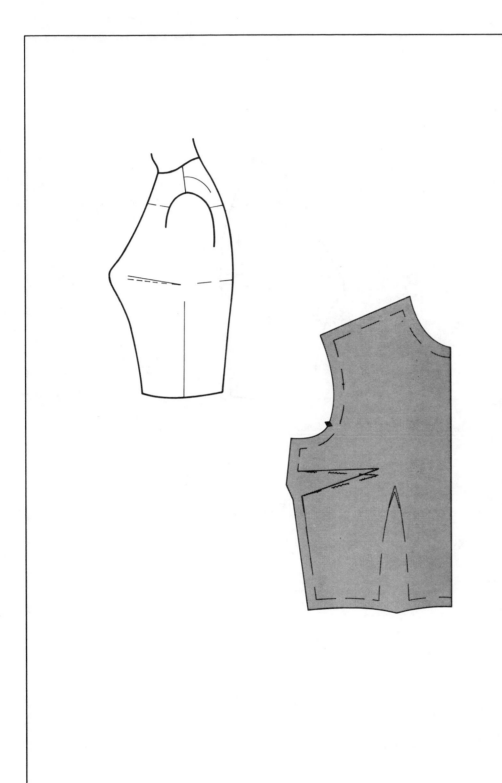

Pivot Method

Mark the position for the new underarm dart tips directly above those of the original darts. Release the side seams and the underarm darts. Form new dart center folds between the new dart tip mark and the place where the original fold meets the side seamline. Stitch each new dart straight from the new tip to the original dartline marking at the side seamline. The side edges will not match. True the distorted side seamline in a straight line across the closed dart. Draw from the original side seam markings at the armscye and waistline. Stitch the side seams.

Lengthen each waist dart by an amount equal to the adjustment at the underarm dart tip.

On princess-style garments, release the seamline across the bust area. Let out the seam allowance of the side panel at the bust level enough to relax the fabric and restore the ease. Take in the side panel below the bust level to remove the excess fabric. Blend smoothly into the original seamline above and below the bust area. Stitch the seams.

BASIC FITTING THEORY

Figure Analysis

When associated with the mature figure, the fullness of the breast tissues rests below the area of origin because the connective tissues have lost tone. For other figures, the position of the bust contour is lower than average. Slumped posture both emphasizes and contributes to a lowered bust contour. The distance from the shoulders to the bustline is greater than average, the distance is less from the bustline to the waistline. Properly fitted bras with adequate support minimize the variation and help to prevent further flaccidness of the supporting tissues.

Fitting Analysis

The fabric is taut across the fullest area of the bust but is loose above it because the fabric shaping is above the crest of the bust contour. Tight horizontal wrinkles pull across the waist dartlines. The bust fitting line remains level.

Fabric Requirements for Proper Fit

The change in length above and below the crest of the bust requires lowering the side darts and shortening the waistline darts to permit the fabric shaping to align properly with the bust contour.

GARMENT & PATTERN ALTERATIONS FOR SYMMETRICAL FIGURES

Change Required

Lower the side bust darts parallel to the original; lower the tips of the waistline darts.

Slash Method—fitting garment only

Only the dart stitching line positions are affected. Use the procedure indicated for **Pivot Method.**

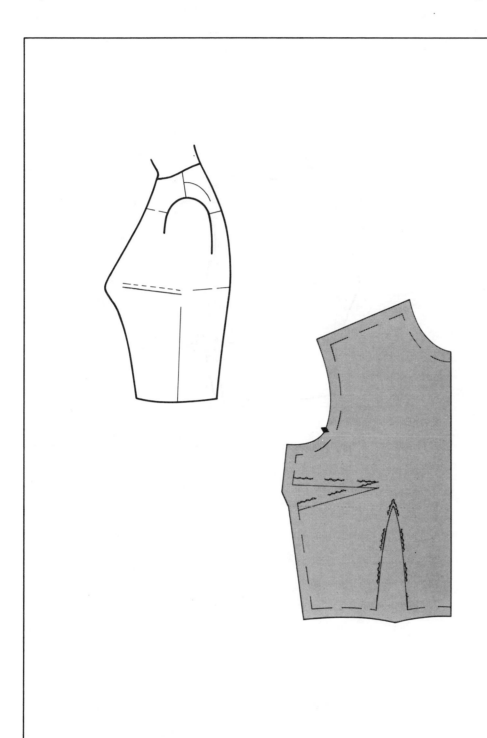

Pivot Method
Mark the position for new underarm dart tips directly below those of the original darts. Release the side seams across the underarm darts; release the underarm darts. To form the new center folds, begin at the new tip mark and fold the fabric parallel to the original folds. At the side seamlines, mark the dart width equal to the original width of the folded dart. Stitch the new darts. True the distorted, side seamline in a straight line across the closed dart. Stitch the side seams.

Release the waistline seam across the waistline darts. Shorten each waistline dart by an amount equal to the adjustment at the underarm dart tips. Retain the dart width. Stitch the new darts. Remove the original dart stitching. Stitch the waistline seam.

On princess-style garments, release the seamline across the bust area. At bust level, let out the side panel enough to relax the fabric and restore the ease. Take in the side panel enough above the bust level to remove the excess fabric. Blend smoothly into the original seamline above and below the bust area. Stitch the seams.

BASIC FITTING THEORY

Figure Analysis

The breast contours develop further from the sternum than average. This increases the span between the bust points and decreases the measurement from the bust points to the sides of the body.

Fitting Analysis

The waistline dart tips point toward the center edges of the bust; therefore, the fabric shaping is too near the center front. Horizontal wrinkles may form across the center front at bust level. The underarm dartlines extend onto the bust curvature instead of ending along the side edges of the curves. This causes tight, vertical wrinkles to pull across these dartlines. The bust fitting line remains level.

Fabric Requirements for Proper Fit

The wider space between the bust points requires that the waist dart tips end farther from the center front. The proportion of the figure may require either changing the slope of the waist darts or moving the entire dart farther from the center front. The narrowness of the side areas requires shorter underarm darts.

GARMENT & PATTERN ALTERATIONS FOR SYMMETRICAL FIGURES

Change Required

Reposition the waistline darts to align the dart tips with the bust points; shorten the underarm darts.

Slash Method—fitting garment only

Only the dart stitching line positions are affected. Use the procedure indicated for **Pivot Method.**

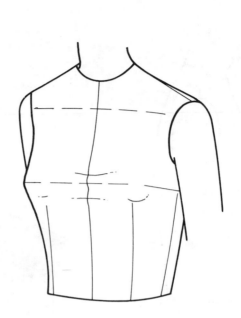

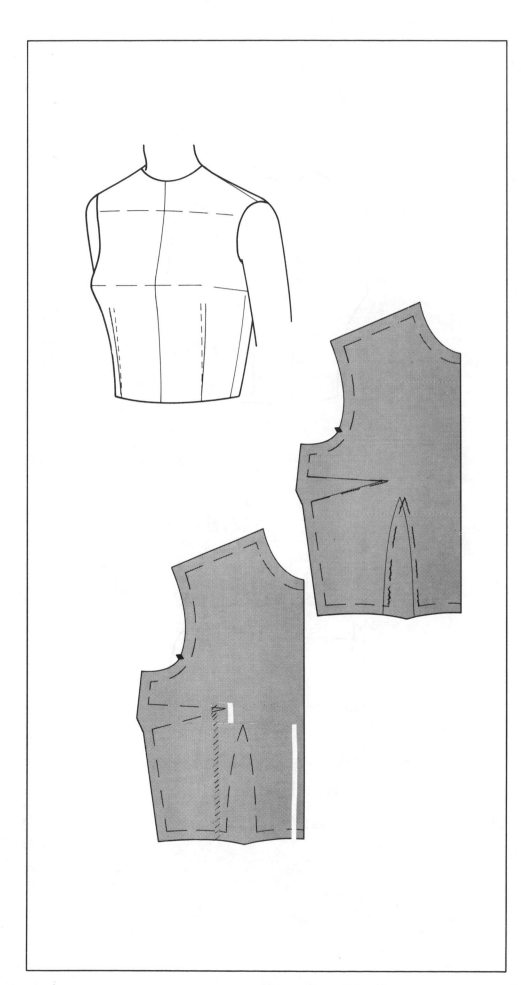

Pivot Method

Mark the new dart tip positions in the correct location toward the side of the original dart tips. Release the waist and side seamlines across the dart areas. Release the waistline darts.

For each waistline dart, form a new center fold from the new tip mark to the place where the original center fold meets the waistline. Stitch the new darts from the tip to the waistline. The waistline edges will no longer be even. The entire dart position may be moved toward the side instead.

Shorten the underarm darts. Retain the original center folds and stitch straight from the new tip mark to the original dart stitching lines at the side seam.

True the side seamlines with a straight line across the closed darts. Stitch the side seams and the waist seam.

BASIC FITTING THEORY

Figure Analysis
The person assumes an erect stance with an upward, forward thrust to the rib cage. The breast tissues form a lifted, conical contour. The bust contour may be prominent regardless of the amount of development (cup size). If the cup size is a "C" or larger the front measurements at bust level increase in length, width, and depth.

Fitting Analysis
The fabric is taut across the fullest area of the bust because the fabric shaping is too low. If the cup size is a "C" or larger, the front of the garment is too short and too narrow. Diagonal wrinkles radiate from the bust curves to the garment edges. Buttoned front closures gap at bust level. The bust fitting line rises across the center front area. The lower edges of an unfastened, front closure overlap. The waist and hemlines on loosely fitted garments rise at center front.

Fabric Requirements for Proper Fit
The lift of the bust contour requires raising the front dart tip positions. Figures with a cup size larger than a "B" require more width and length at bust level. Wider, longer darts result. The adjusted garment area lies smooth but relaxed and aligns appropriately with the body contours. The lower edges of the garment become level and the closure edges lie plumb.

GARMENT & PATTERN ALTERATIONS FOR SYMMETRICAL FIGURES

Change Required
Widen and lengthen the front at the bustline as necessary; lengthen the front darts.

Slash Method—fitting garment only
To add width, slash the garment front from the armscye to the waistline near each side seam. Insert fabric strips. Separate each set of cut edges evenly to relax the fabric and restore the ease at the bustline. True the armscye seamline across the adjustment. Restore the armscye size with a dart in each lower armscye area. Taper to nothing at the underarm dart tips.

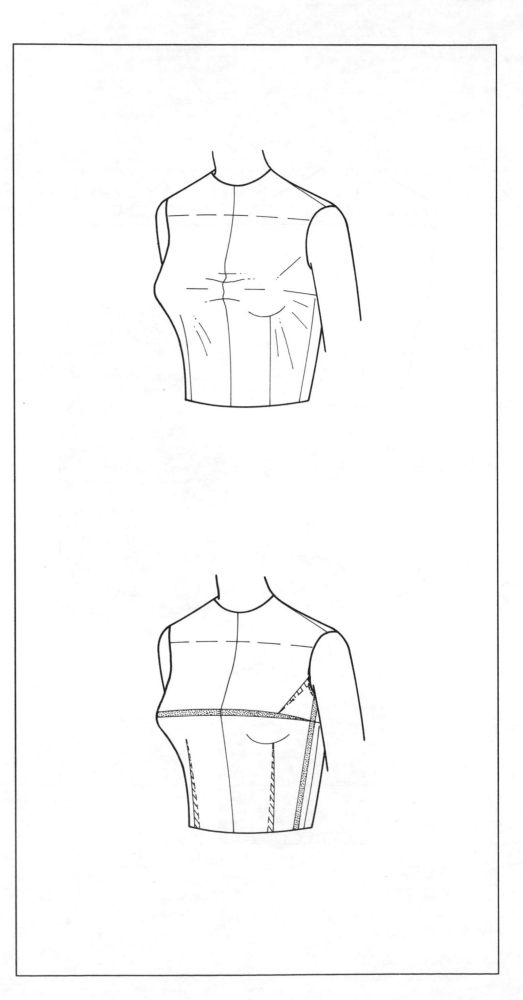

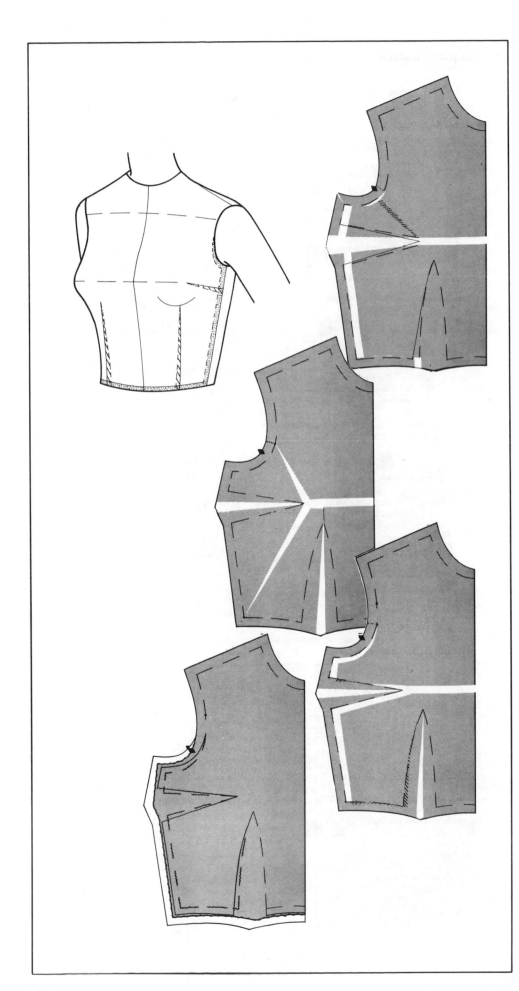

To add length, slash across the front just below the underarm dartlines. Follow crosswise grain. Insert fabric strips. Between the waist dart tips, separate the cut edges evenly until the waistline becomes level. Taper to nothing at the side seams. Mark the new position for waist dart tips if they require lengthening.

To restore the waistline size, release the waistline from the dart to the side insert; remove the waist dart stitching. Widen each dart at the *side dartline* to absorb the width adjustment at the side seam. Move the dart tip toward the side equal to one-half this amount. Stitch the new darts from the tip to the waistline.

True the distorted seamline contour in the lower armscye area and across the waist dart areas. Stitch the waistline.

Pivot Method
Adjust for width first. Release the side seams. Let out the front seam allowances equally at the bustline as needed to relax the fabric and restore the ease over the bust. Mark the new side seamline position at each underarm dart.

Widen the underarm darts equally until the fabric lies smooth but relaxed at the edge of the bust area. Retain the original dart center folds.

Draw each new side seamline parallel to the original from the waistline through the armscye seam allowance. Restore the length of the side seamline by measuring equal distances into the armscye and waistline seam allowances. Mark the ends of the seamline at the waistline and armscyes.

Draw new armscye seamlines from the original seamline at the arm hinge area to the end of the new side seamline.

To restore the waistline size, release the front waistline and the waistline darts. Widen each waist dart at the *side dartline* to absorb the width adjustment at the side seam. Move the dart tip toward the side equal to one-half the dart width adjustment. Stitch the darts. Draw the new waistline parallel to the original at the center front and side seam areas and in a smooth curve across the darts. Stitch the side seamlines and the waistline seam.

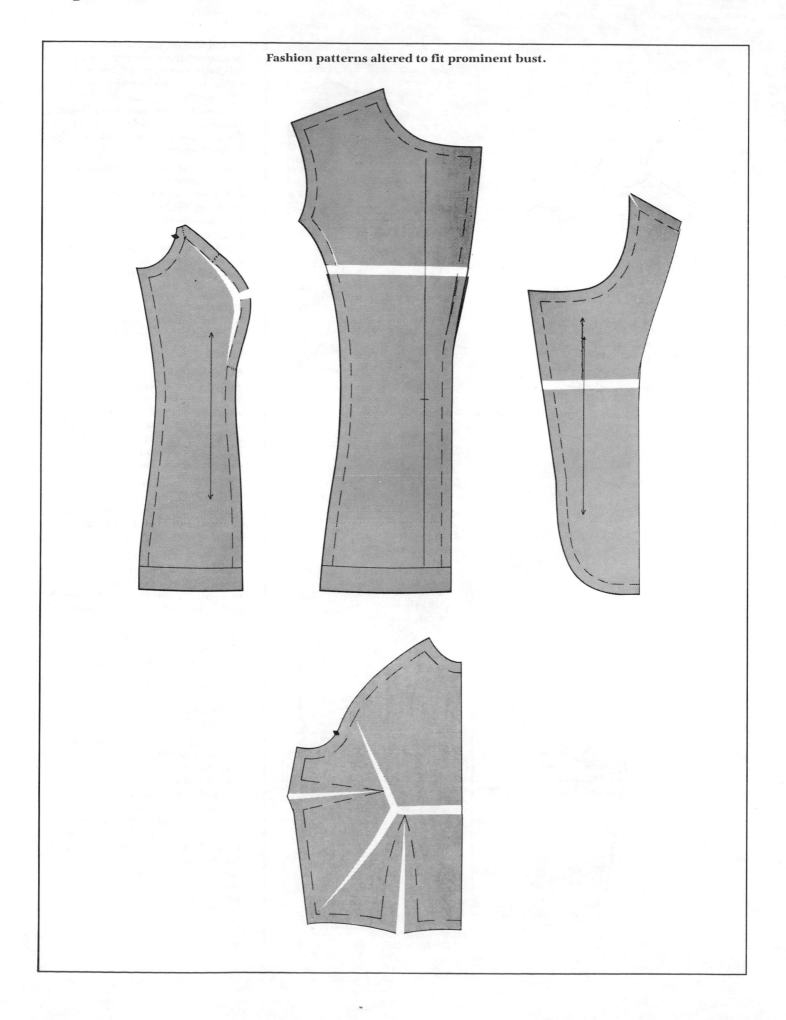

Fashion patterns altered to fit prominent bust.

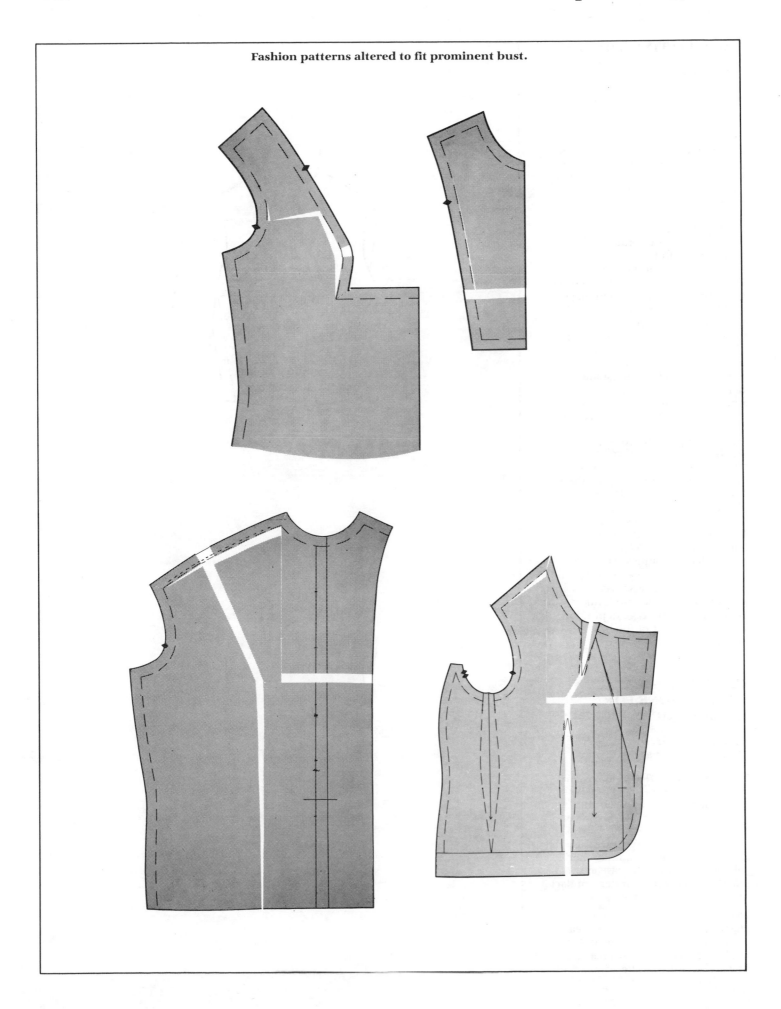

Fashion patterns altered to fit prominent bust.

BASIC FITTING THEORY

Figure Analysis

The bust development is larger than the average which is a "B"; cup; the circumference at the bust-line is greater. There is no relationship between the development of muscle and frame size and that of the bust. However, if excess fatty tissues develop, these may accumulate in the breast tissues also.

Fitting Analysis

The fabric is taut at the bustline; this attracts undue attention to the amount of bust development. Diagonal wrinkles radiate from the bust curves to the garment edges and the center front. Deep ripples form at the armscyes making them appear too large. Buttoned, front closures gap at bust level. The underarm dart pulls onto the bust curvature, the front waist and hemlines raise the lower edges of unfastened, front closures overlap. The bust fitting line remains level.

Fabric Requirements for Proper Fit

The larger bust circumference requires more fabric width at the bustline. Wider front darts result. The larger garment area and the fuller shaping relaxes over the bust. The lower edges of the garment become level. The center front edges lie plumb. The armscye size does not increase although the shape changes. The size is determined by the arm joint structure and rib cage depth, not the development of the breast tissues.

GARMENT & PATTERN ALTERATIONS FOR SYMMETRICAL FIGURES

Change Required

Widen the front at the bustline.

Slash Method—fitting garment only

Near each side seam, slash the garment front from the armscye to the waistline. Insert fabric strips. To increase width, separate each set of cut edges evenly to relax the fabric and restore the ease at the bustline. Mark new underarm dart tip positions, if necessary.

Restore the armscye size with a dart in each lower armscye area. Taper to nothing at the new underarm dart tip positions. True the armscye across the adjustment.

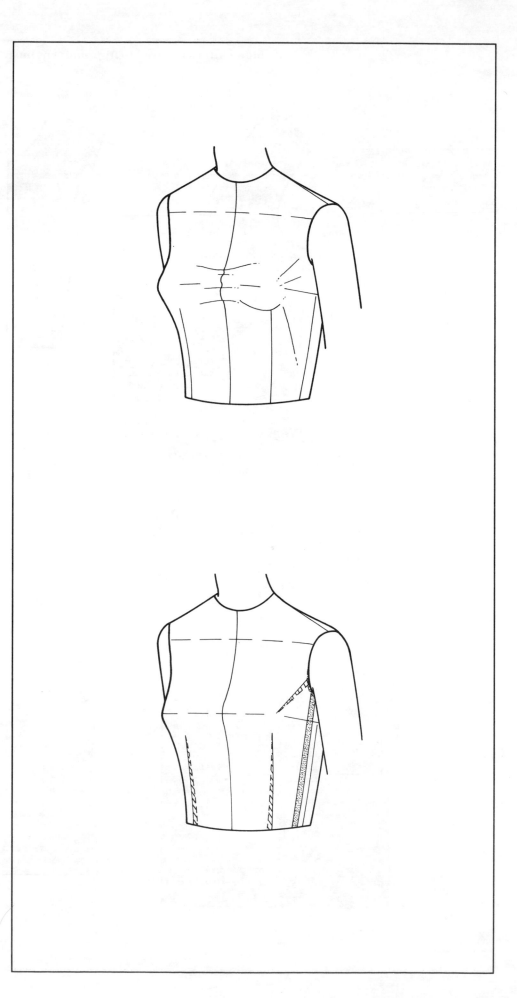

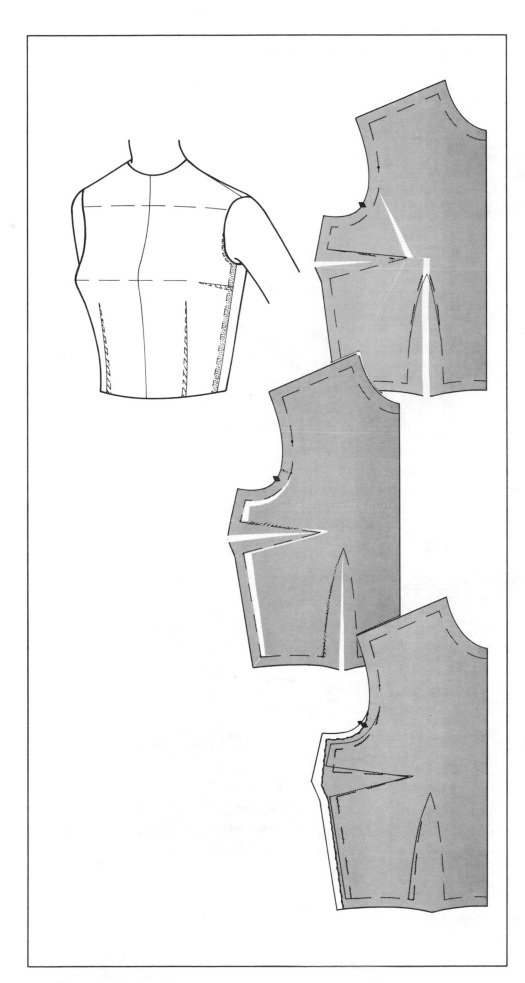

To restore the waistline size, release the waistline from each dart to the side seam. Remove the dart stitching. Widen each dart at the *side dartline* to absorb the width gained at the side seam area. Move the dart tip toward the side equal to one-half this amount. Stitch the darts. True the waistline across the dart areas. Stitch the waistline.

For a "C" and larger cup size, often the center front length is correct but the center back is too long. Shorten only the back. Release the side seams. Make a parallel tuck completely across the back area at the bustline to remove the excess fabric length. Widen the dart equal to the length adjustment. True side seams in straight lines across the adjustments.

Pivot Method

Adjust for width first. Release the side seams. Let out the front seam allowances equally at the bustline as needed to relax the fabric and restore the ease over the bust. Mark the new side seamline position at the underarm dart.

Release the underarm darts and widen them equally at the *upper dartline* until the fabric lies smooth but relaxed at the edge of the bust area.

Draw each new side seamline in a straight line parallel to the original from the waistline to the armscye seam allowances. Restore the length of the side seamline by measuring from the waistline into the armscye. Mark the ends of the seamlines at the armscyes.

Draw new armscye seamlines from the original seamline at the arm hinge area to the end of the new side seamline.

To restore the waistline size, release the front waistline and the waistline dart. Widen each waistline dart at the *side dartline* to absorb the width adjustment at the side seam. Move the dart tip toward the side equal to one-half the dart width adjustment. Stitch the darts. True the waistline across the adjusted darts. Stitch the side seamlines and the waistline seam.

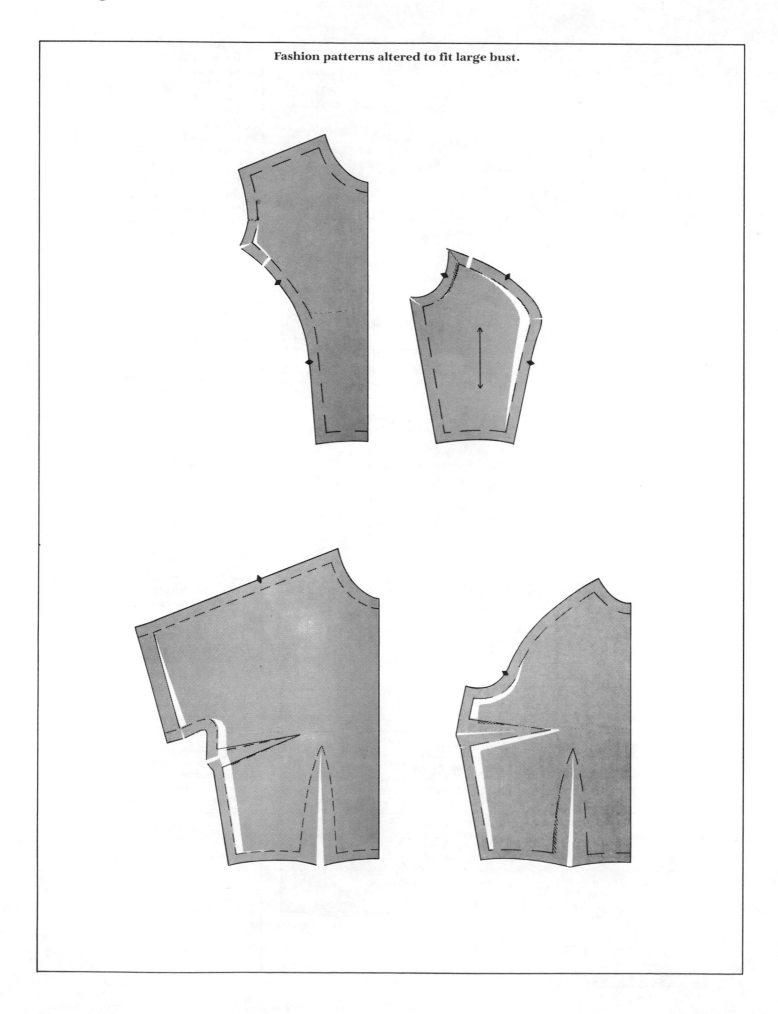

Fashion patterns altered to fit large bust.

Fashion patterns altered to fit large bust.

BASIC FITTING THEORY

Figure Analysis

The bust development is less than the average which is a "B" cup; the circumference at the bustline is smaller. There is no relationship between the development of muscle and frame size and that of the bust.

Fitting Analysis

The garment is too loose at the bustline. This attracts undue attention to the smallness of the contour. Loose vertical folds form across the underarm dart. The bust fitting line may droop at the center. A loose horizontal fold may form underneath the bust area. The lower edges of unfastened, front closures spread apart; the front waist and hemlines droop. Choosing to wear a padded "B" cup bra may eliminate the need for garment adjustment.

Fabric Requirements for Proper Fit

The smaller bust circumference requires less fabric width at the bustline. Less length may be needed along the center front area at the bust level. Narrower darts result. The smaller garment area lies smoothly against the body. The bust fitting line and lower edges of the garment become level. The edges of the front closure lie plumb. The armscye size does not decrease although the shape will change. Its size is determined by the arm joint structure and rib cage depth, not the development of the breast tissues.

GARMENT & PATTERN ALTERATIONS FOR SYMMETRICAL FIGURES

Change Required

Narrow the front at the bustline; shorten the front, if necessary.

Slash Method—fitting garment only

Near each side seam form a vertical parallel tuck on the garment front. Adjust the tuck widths equally until the fabric is smooth but relaxed at the bustline. Continue the tucks an even width to the armscye and the waistline. Mark new underarm dart tip positions, if necessary.

To restore the armscye size, slash through the lower armscye area. Continue to the new tip of each underarm dart. Insert fabric strips.

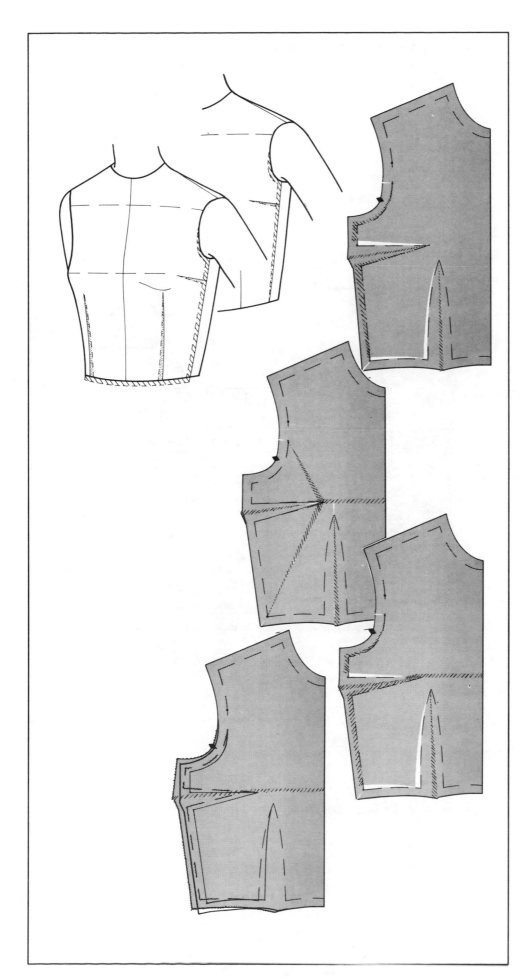

Separate each set of cut edges equally at the armscye to gain an amount of width equal to the adjustment at the side seam area. True the armscye across the adjustment.

To restore the waistline size, release the waistline across the darts. Release the waist darts. Let out each dart at the *side dartline* equal to the amount of width adjustment at the side seam area. Move the dart tip toward the front equal to one-half this amount. Stitch the darts.

If the center front area is too long over the bust, form a horizontal tuck at the bustline. Keep the tuck parallel across the center front of the garment. Taper the tuck to nothing along the dartline at the side seam, adjust the tuck width until the fabric is smooth but relaxed at the bustline and the waistline aligns with the waist contour.

Pivot Method
Adjust for width first. Release the side seams. Take in the side seam areas equally at the bustline to remove the excess fabric. Retain sufficient ease over the bust. Mark the new side seamline position at the underarm dart.

To correct the length, release the underarm darts. Narrow both darts equally at the *upper dartlines* until the fabric lies smooth but relaxed at the armscye areas. Draw each new side seamline in a straight line parallel to the original from the waistline to the armscye seamlines.

To restore the waistline size, release the front waistline and the waistline darts. Narrow each waistline dart at the *side dartlines* to let out the width taken up at the side seam. Move the dart tip toward the center equal to one-half the dart width adjustment. Stitch the darts. Raise the waistline seam if needed. Shorten the back an equal amount. True the waistline across the adjusted darts. Restore the length of each side seamline by measuring from the new waistline toward the armscye. Mark the end of each seamline at the armscye areas.

Draw new armscye seamlines from the original seamline at the arm hinge area to the end of the new side seamline. Stitch the side seamlines and the waistline seam.

Fashion patterns altered to fit small bust.

Fashion patterns altered to fit small bust.

BASIC FITTING THEORY

Figure Analysis
The front of the rib cage slopes outward excessively from the chest to the lower edge. The lower rib contour protrudes more than is average and increases the torso circumference at that level. The area over the diaphragm may be recessed.

Fitting Analysis
The garment is taut across the lower edge of the rib cage and at the center front the fabric forms tight horizontal wrinkles. The strain causes the waist dartlines to curve toward each other.

Fabric Requirements for Proper Fit
The fullness at the lower edge of the rib cage requires more fabric width at the midfront areas. The waist darts are sewn in straight rather than curved lines. The increase in garment width relieves the strain and relaxes the fabric.

GARMENT & PATTERN ALTERATIONS FOR SYMMETRICAL FIGURES

Change Required
Release width from the front waistline darts.

Slash Method—fitting garment only
This method is not appropriate because only the dartline contours can be adjusted. Use the procedure stated in **Pivot Method.**

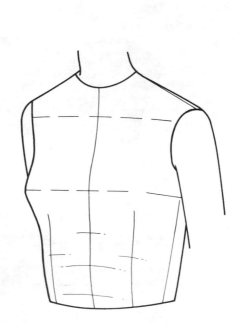

Pivot Method
Release the waist seam across the front waistline darts. Put on the garment and let out both darts until the darts and the fabric relax. Stitch the darts and the waistline.

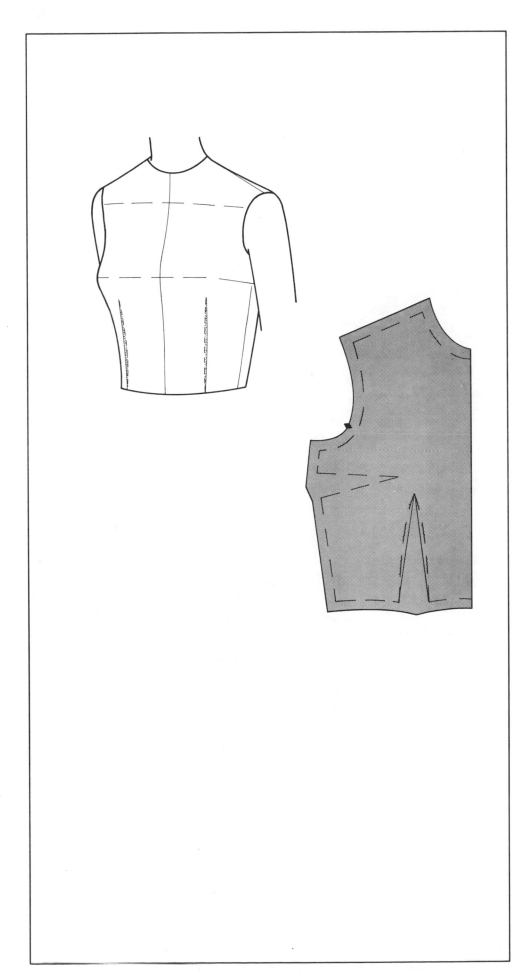

BASIC FITTING THEORY

Figure Analysis

The lower ribs and vertabrae may be heavier than average. The spacing between the ribs may be greater or the spine may be longer than average in the area between the waist and the lower rib cage. These factors increase the body length between the waist and the bust and blade areas.

Fitting Analysis

The garment is taut at the waistline and the fabric forms tight horizontal wrinkles because the garment waistline lies above the waist level of the body. The higher position of the waistline on a jacket and other semi-fitted garments in which the bodice and skirt are cut in one may create unattractive body proportions.

Fabric Requirements for Proper Fit

The longer midriff area requires more fabric length between the waistline and the lower edges of the bust and blade contours. The longer garment area permits the fabric to relax. The waistline aligns with the contour of the body at the waist.

GARMENT & PATTERN ALTERATIONS FOR SYMMETRICAL FIGURES

Change Required

Lengthen the midriff.

Slash Method—fitting garment only

Slash around the entire garment near the waistline. Insert fabric strips. To increase length, separate the cut edges evenly around the garment until the waistline aligns with the waist contour.

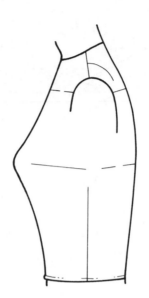

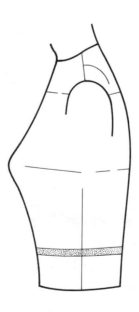

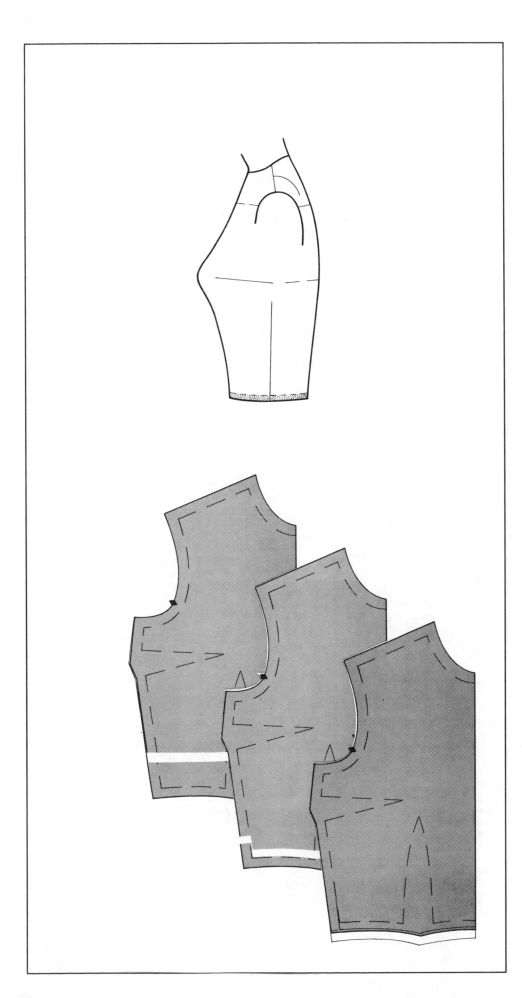

Pivot Method
Release the entire waistline and side seams. Mark the correct waistline position in the seam allowance across the center front. Continue the new waist seamline parallel to the original completely around the garment. Extend each end of the back and front waistlines equally into the side seam allowances to restore the waistline measurements. Mark each new side seamline from the original at the armscyes to the mark on the new waistline. Stitch the side seams and the waist seam.

BASIC FITTING THEORY

Figure Analysis

The lower ribs and vertabrae may be lighter than average. The spacing between the ribs may be less or the spine may be shorter than average in the area between the waist and the lower rib cage. These factors decrease the body length between the waist and the bust and blade areas.

Fitting Analysis

The fabric sags around the waistline area and forms into a loose horizontal fold at the waistline. The lower position of the waistline on jackets and other semi-fitted garments in which the bodice and skirt are cut in one will drop below the waist level and may create unattractive body proportions.

Fabric Requirements for Proper Fit

The shorter midriff area requires less fabric length between the waistline and the lower edges of the bust and blade contours. The shorter midriff area of the garment fits smoothly against the body. The waistline of loosely fitted garments aligns with the contour of the body at the waist.

GARMENT & PATTERN ALTERATIONS FOR SYMMETRICAL FIGURES

Change Required

Shorten the midriff.

Slash Method—fitting garment only

Form a parallel tuck near the waistline completely around the garment. Adjust the width of the tuck until the waistline seam aligns with the waist contour.

When stitching the tuck, place the waistline area of the garment uppermost on the machine.

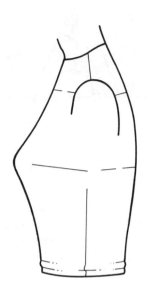

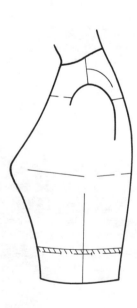

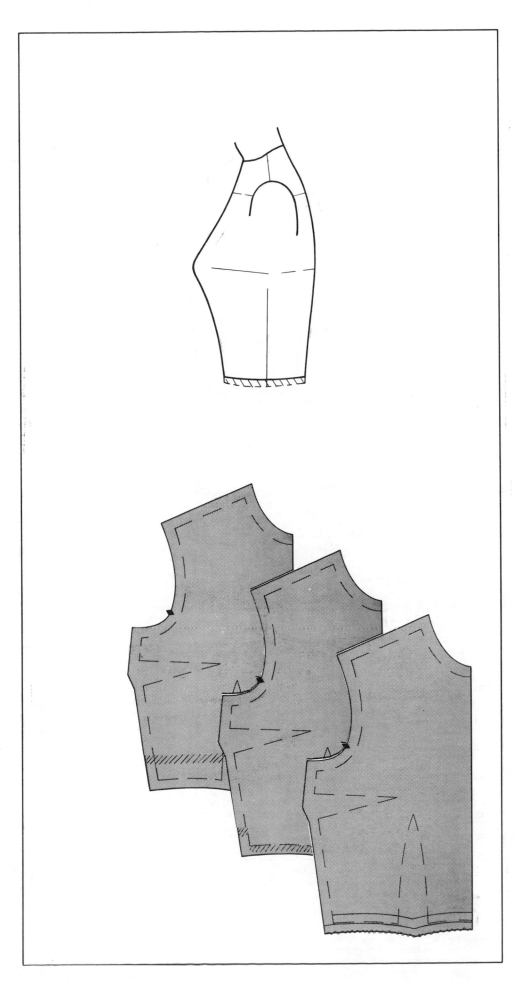

Pivot Method
Release the entire waistline and
side seams. Mark the correct
waistline position across the center
front. Continue the new waist
seamline parallel to the original
completely around the garment.
Mark the ends of the new waist
seamline at the side seam areas to
restore the waistline
measurements. Mark each new side
seamline from the original at the
armscyes to the mark on the new
waistline. Stitch the side seams and
the waist seam.

BASIC FITTING THEORY

Figure Analysis

The body indents very little at the waist either because the muscles lack tone, the posture is slumped or the deposits of soft tissues are larger than average in that area. The circumference of the waist is more nearly equal to that of the rib cage and the hips. The sides of the body are straighter and measure slightly shorter than average from the base of the arm joints to the waist.

Fitting Analysis

The fabric pulls into taut horizontal wrinkles near the waist. This may cause the garment waistline to rise. As a result, the bodice may appear to be too long. The lengthwise ease cannot distribute itself properly below the bust level.

Fabric Requirements for Proper Fit

The larger waist circumference requires more fabric width at the waistline. The wider garment area relaxes. The waistline lowers and aligns with the contour of the body.

GARMENT & PATTERN ALTERATIONS FOR SYMMETRICAL FIGURES

Change Required

Widen the side seam area at the waistline.

Slash Method—fitting garment only

Near the side seams, slash through the waistline on the back and front of the garment. Continue cutting to the armscye seamlines. Insert fabric strips. To increase width, separate each set of cut edges equally at the waistline to relax the garment and restore the ease. Taper to nothing at the armscye.

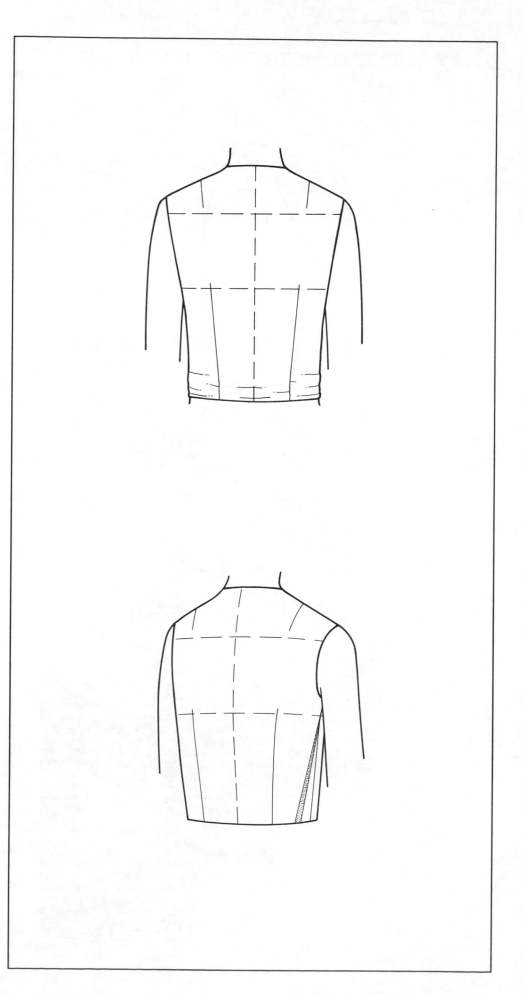

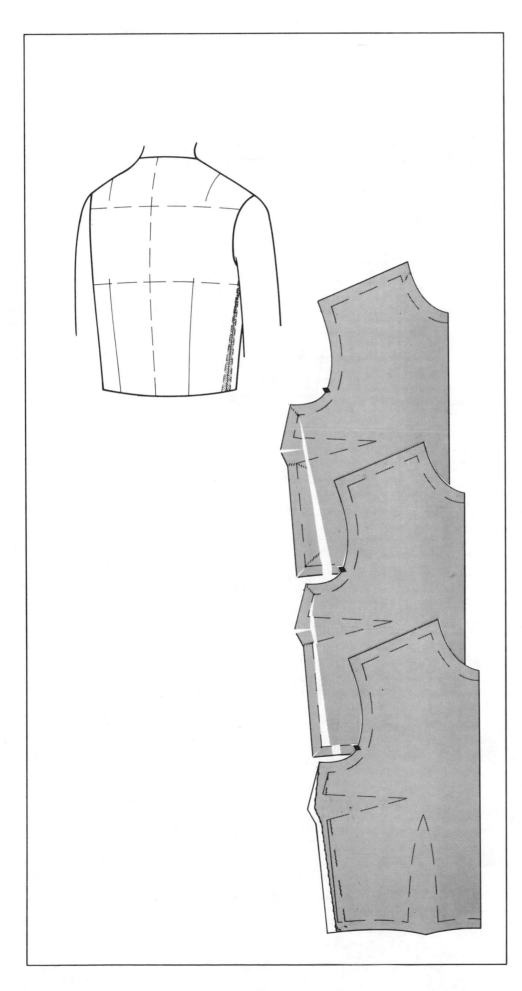

Pivot Method
Release the side seams. Let out
equal amounts on the front and
back at the waistline on both side
seams to relax the fabric and
restore the ease. Taper each new
side seamline straight from the
original at the armscye to the new
waistline position. Stitch the new
side seams.

BASIC FITTING THEORY

Figure Analysis
The body indents more than average at the waist either because the muscles are more taut, the posture is overly erect, or the deposits of soft tissues are smaller than average. The circumference of the waist is noticeably less than that of the rib cage or the hips. The indentation at the waist defines the "hourglass" figure type. The sides of the body are more sloped and measure slightly longer than average from the base of the arm joints to the waist.

Fitting Analysis
The garment is baggy around the waist area. The fabric at the waistline forms loose vertical folds.

Fabric Requirements for Proper Fit
The smaller waist circumference requires less fabric width at the waistline. The narrower garment area lies closer to the body.

GARMENT & PATTERN ALTERATIONS FOR SYMMETRICAL FIGURES

Change Required
Narrow the side area at the waistline.

Slash Method—fitting garment only
Form tucks of equal width through the waistline on the back and front near the side seams. Adjust the tucks equally until the excess fabric is removed and the ease is retained. Taper each tuck to nothing at the armscye seamline.

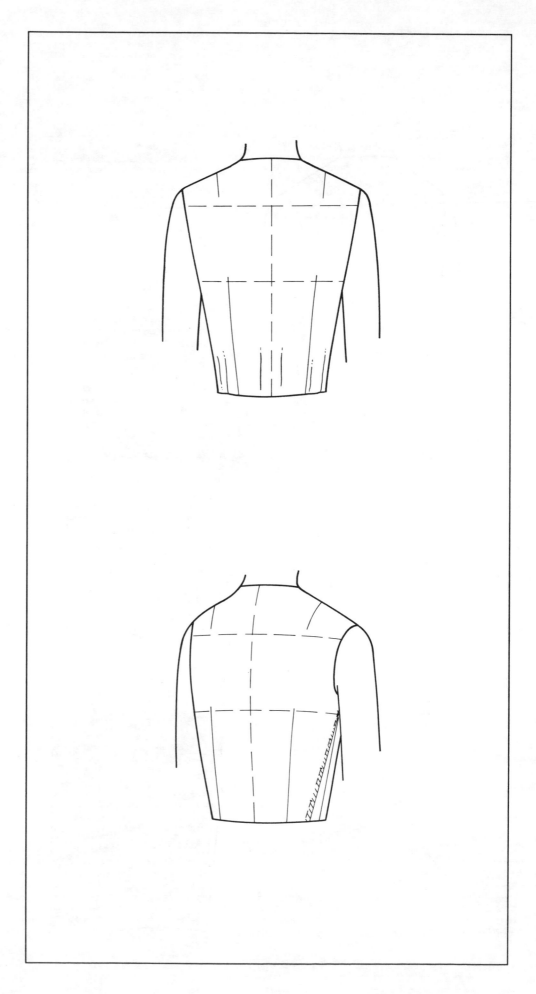

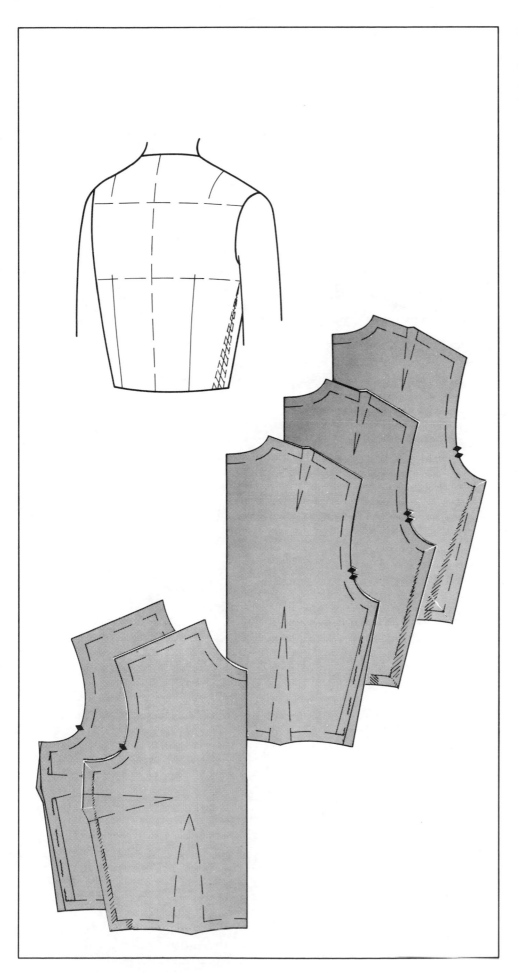

Pivot Method
Release the side seams. Take in
equal amounts on the front and
back at the waistline on both side
seams until the fabric is smooth
and the ease is retained. Taper each
new side seamline straight from the
original at the armscye to the new
waistline position.

arms

72 Arm Length Variations

73 Long Arm Joints (sleeves)

74 Short Arm Joints (sleeves)

75 Large Shoulder Joints

76 Small Shoulder Joints

77 Forward Arm Joints (sleeves)

78 Large Arms

79 Thin Arms

80 Large Upper Arms

81 Large Elbows

82 Large Forearms

83 Inward Rotation of the Elbow

84 Large Wrists

85 Small Wrists

BASIC FITTING THEORY

Figure Analysis

The elbow position determines upper and lower length variations. The lengths of the upper and lower arm bone areas develop independently. Several length variations may be observed. The total length of the arms may be average, but the upper area may be shorter and the lower area longer or vice-versa. The total length may be shorter or longer than average, the length variation may occur in the upper arm, the lower arm or both.

Fitting Analysis

The center of the darted or eased area of the sleeve should align with the elbow point. When the dart shaping rises above the elbow, the narrower, lower sleeve area lies over the elbow and restricts mobility. When the shaping drops below the elbow level, the larger, upper sleeve area lies over the elbow; the sleeve may appear to be too big. When the hemline of a long sleeve lies above the wristbone, the sleeve is uncomfortably short; the wrist and hand may appear too long and thin. When the hemline lies below the wristbone, the sleeves drag; the hands appear short and stubby.

Fabric Requirements for Proper Fit

A longer upper arm area requires more fabric length between the scyeline and the elbow line—a shorter upper arm area requires less fabric length. A longer, lower arm area requires more fabric length below the elbow—the shorter, lower arm area requires less fabric length. When both the upper and lower arm areas vary from average, fabric length changes are required both above and below the elbow line.

Aligning the center of the darted area with the elbow permits comfortable elbow movement. Aligning the hemline with the wristbone creates attractive and comfortable proportions between the lower arm and sleeve areas.

GARMENT & PATTERN ALTERATIONS FOR SYMMETRICAL FIGURES

Change Required

Adjust the lengths of the upper and lower sleeve areas so that the elbow line crosses the elbow point and the wristline is attractively near the wristbone.

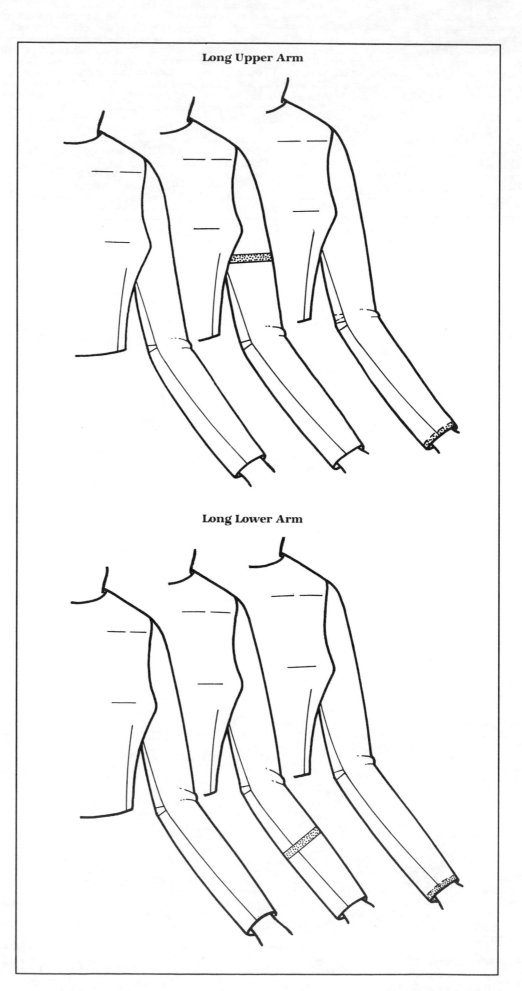

Long Upper Arm

Long Lower Arm

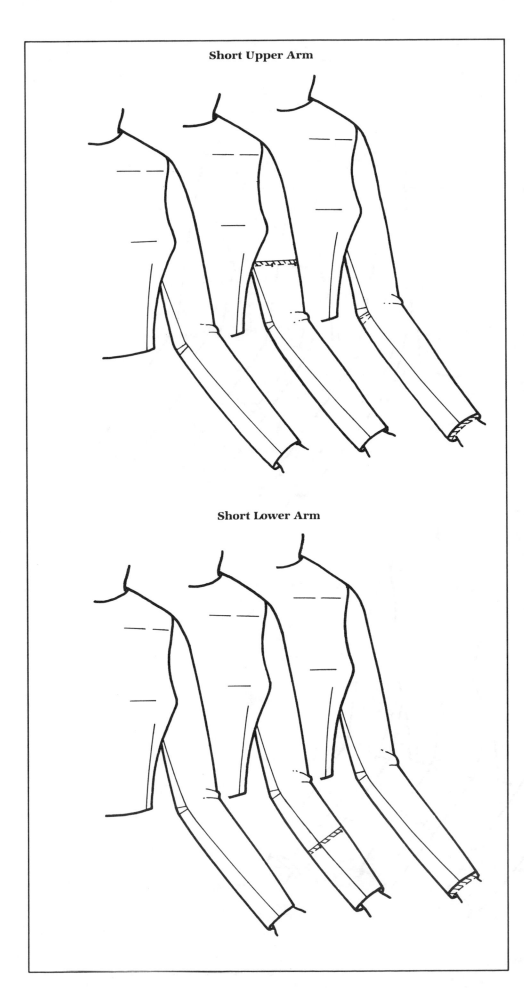

Short Upper Arm

Short Lower Arm

Slash Method—fitting garment only

Align the center front and center back of the body centers. Fold both arms simultaneously across the front of the body. Mark the position of each elbow point on the corresponding sleeve.

If the elbow position is above the center of the darted area, remove the excess length with a parallel tuck around the upper sleeve area. Follow the crosswise grain. Adjust the tuck width until the center of the darted area aligns with the elbow point. If the elbow position is below the center of the darted area, slash and spread the upper sleeve area evenly over a fabric insert to gain the necessary length. Follow crosswise grain.

Check the wristline position when both arms are relaxed. If the wristline lies too far above the wristbone, slash and spread the lower area evenly over a fabric insert to gain the necessary length. Cut parallel to the wristline. If the wristline lies below the wristbone, remove the excess length with a parallel tuck around the lower sleeve area. Make the tuck parallel to the wristline.

Pivot Method

Align the center front and center back of the bodice with the body centers. Fold both arms simultaneously across the front of the body. Mark the position of each elbow point on the corresponding sleeve. Relax both arms. Mark the position of each wristbone on the corresponding sleeve or if the sleeve is too short, make a note of the additional length needed.

If the elbow position is above or below the center of the darted area, release the sleeve underarm seams across the darts and raise or lower the dart markings to align the center of the darted area with the elbow mark. Stitch the new darts and the underarm seam areas if the wrist length requires no change.

If the wristbone mark lies above or below the hemline, take up or let out the hem to align the finished hemline with the wristbone mark. Mark the new hemline parallel to the original.

To restore the wristline circumference, fold one lower sleeve area along the seam. Flatten the sleeve. Divide the original wrist measurement by two. Measure from the fold toward the seam on both sleeves. Mark the ends of the adjusted wristline. True the underarm seamlines. Stitch each new seamline in a straight line from the elbow level to the end of the new wristline.

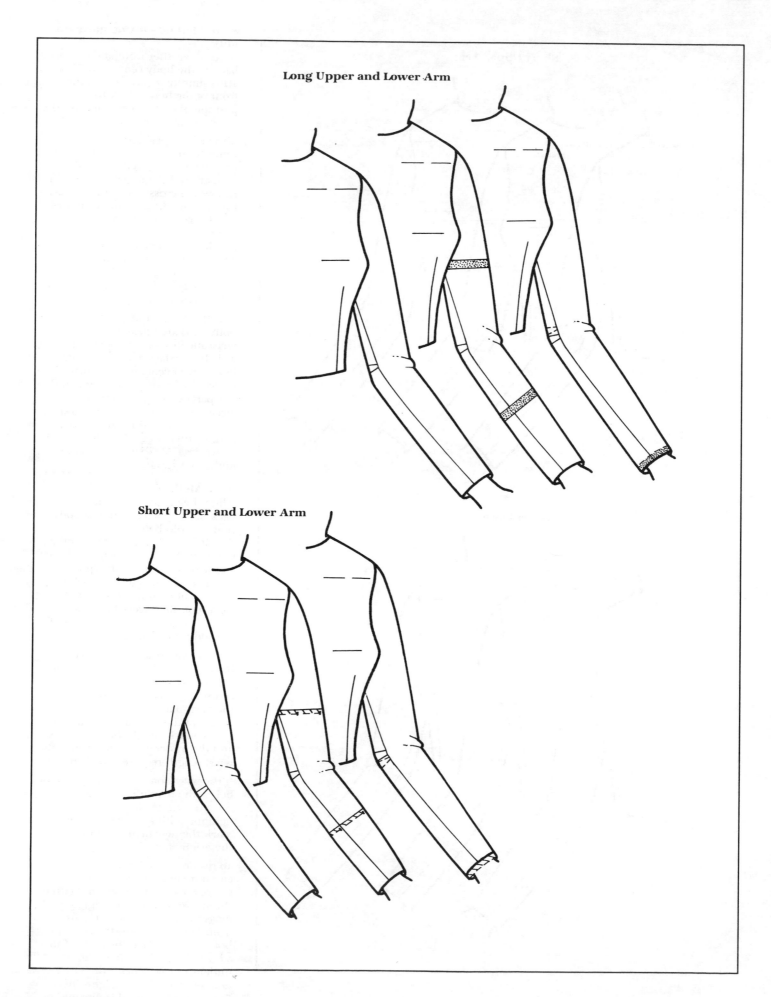

Long Upper and Lower Arm

Short Upper and Lower Arm

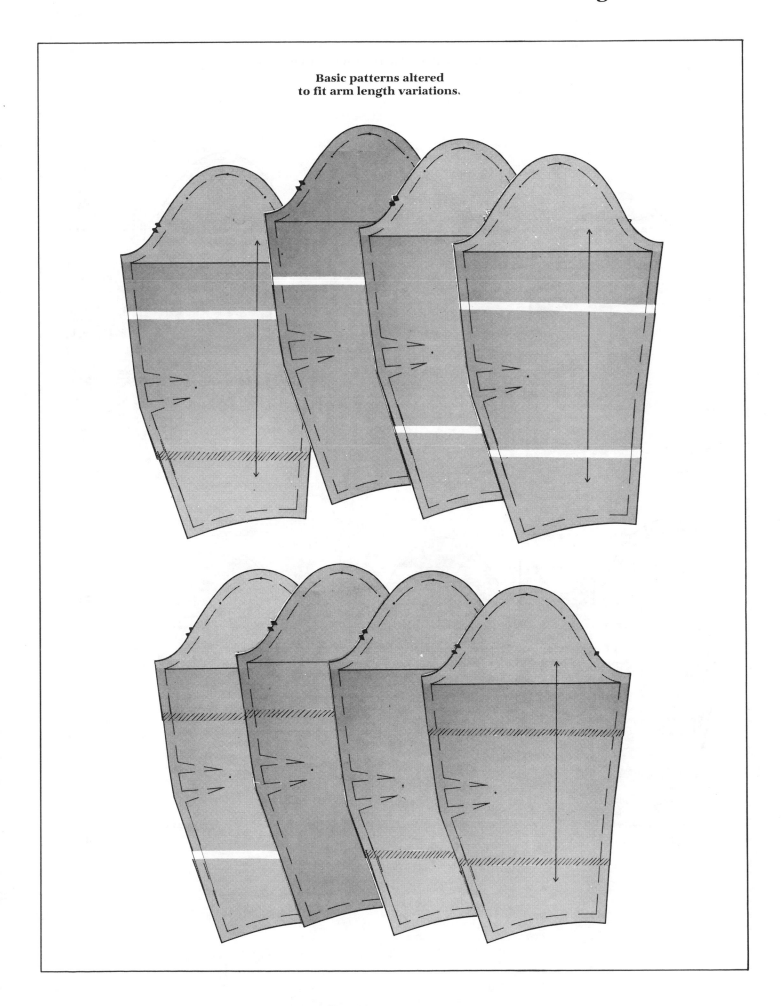

**Basic patterns altered
to fit arm length variations.**

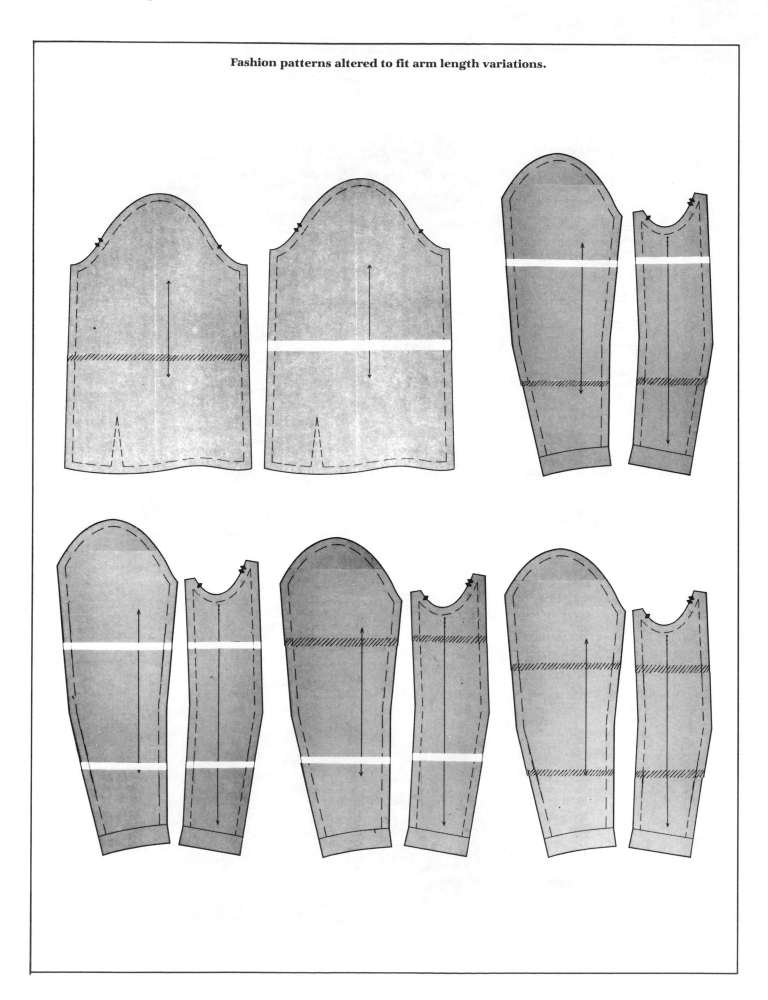

Fashion patterns altered to fit arm length variations.

BASIC FITTING THEORY

Figure Analysis
The bones forming the joint structure may be longer than average or the "hinge" flesh separating the arm from the rib cage may form farther than average below the joint. Either factor increases the length from the shoulder to the scyeline.

Fitting Analysis
Diagonal wrinkles radiate from the top of the sleeve cap toward the armscye seams at both the back and front. The horizontal, cap fitting line curves upward at the center. The lower armscye area cuts against the arm hinges and wrinkles form in both the garment and sleeve. The elbow dart shaping rises above the elbow level. On a short sleeve, the hemline extends outward from the arm; the sleeve appears to be too wide.

Fabric Requirements for Proper Fit
The increased length of the shoulder joint requires a longer sleeve cap and armscye. The increased length relieves the strain at the top of the sleeve and underarm. The fabric relaxes and the sleeve shaping aligns with the elbow. The cap fitting line becomes level. To adjust the armscye depth on the garment, see **59 Long Upper Rib Cage.**

GARMENT & PATTERN ALTERATIONS FOR SYMMETRICAL FIGURES

Change Required
Lengthen the sleeve cap.

Slash Method—fitting garment only
If the garment armscye has been corrected, lengthen the sleeve cap *before* attaching the sleeve to the garment. Follow **Pivot Method.**

If the sleeves are attached and the armscye is too short, adjust the sleeve cap height and the garment armscye length simultaneously. Cut across the sleeve cap about halfway between the arm hinge area and the top of the cap. Where the sleeve slash meets the back and front armscye, cut downward into the garment. Follow the lengthwise grain to a point 1 inch (2.5 cm) below the scyeline. Cut across the underarm area between the vertical slashes. Lap the garment edges *below* the armscye until the

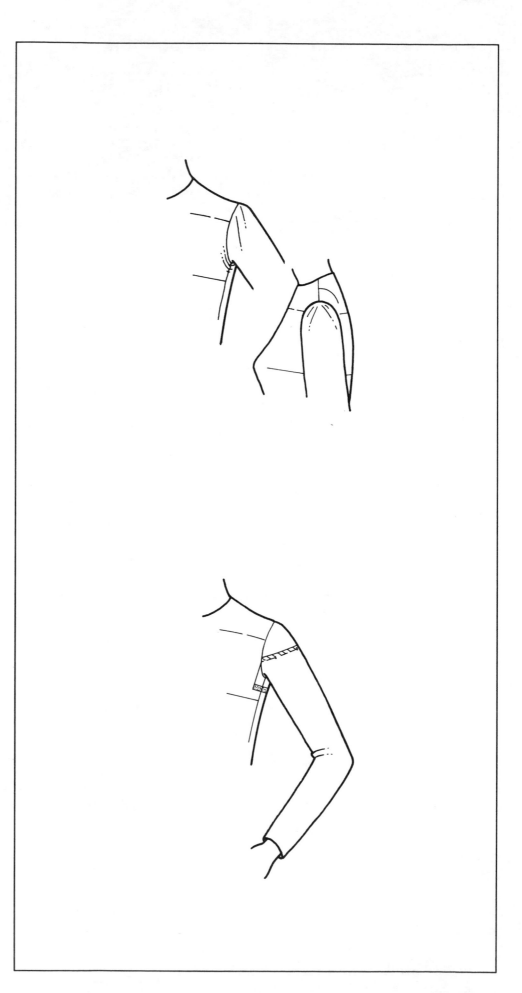

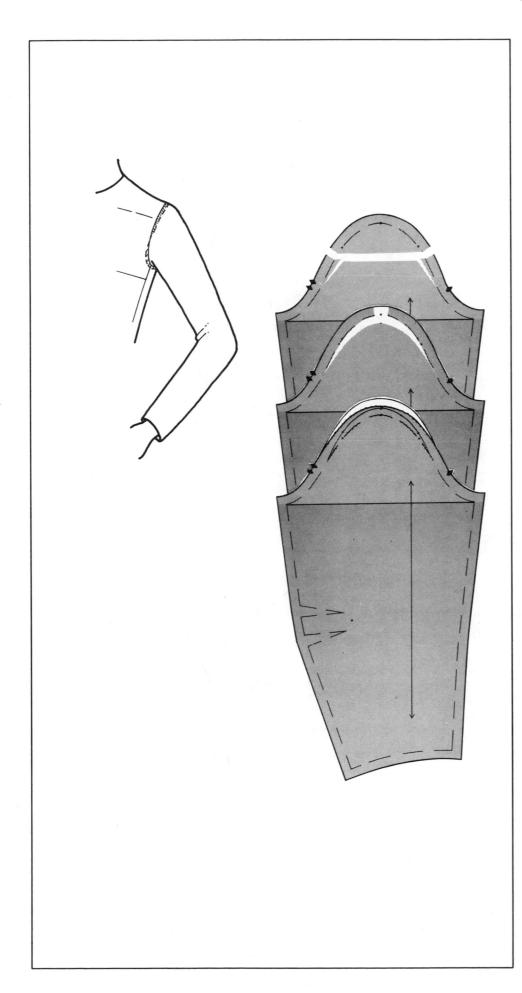

armscye seamline is in a comfortable position. Stitch across the lapped fabric. Insert a fabric strip under the slashed area of each sleeve. Separate the cut edges equal to the width of the lapped area at the underarm. Join the vertical slashes with multi-stitch zig-zagging or reinforce with fabric strips.

This procedure may drop the dart shaping below the elbow position. To correct the length, make a parallel tuck completely around the sleeve above the elbow line. If only the cap requires length, see **Pivot Method.**

Pivot Method

If the garment armscye depth has been corrected, lengthen the sleeve cap *before* attaching the sleeves. Across the top of the cap, mark above the seamline at the center to let out an amount equal to the length adjustment of the garment. Blend into the original seamline at the front and back of the armscye. Raise the sleeve balance marks equal to the cap height adjustment. Attach the sleeves to the garment using the new markings.

If the sleeves are attached and only the cap requires an alteration in length, remove only the upper part of the sleeves. Let out the sleeve cap seam allowance as needed for the arm joint. Blend into the original seamline at the balance marks. Stitch the sleeve to the garment.

If the sleeves are attached and both the cap and the armscye require an alteration in length, lower the armscye seamline across the underarm area. Draw a line parallel to the original seamline *below* the original armscye seamline to indicate the correct amount of adjustment. Blend into the original seamline at the arm hinge areas. Trim the widened seam allowances.

BASIC FITTING THEORY

Figure Analysis
The bones forming the joint structure may be shorter than average or the "hinge" flesh separating the arm from the rib cage may form closer to the joint than is average. Either factor decreases the length from the shoulder to the scyeline.

Fitting Analysis
The seamline at the lower armscye area lies too far below the arm hinges. Lifting the arm creates strain on the sleeve and makes it appear too narrow and too tight. The arm cannot be raised comfortably or very high. The cap fitting lines are not affected.

Fabric Requirements for Proper Fit
The decreased length of the shoulder joint requires a shorter sleeve cap and armscye. The decreased length brings the armscye seamline closer to the arm hinge and relieves the strain on the garment and sleeve. The arm may be raised comfortably and easily. To adjust the armscye depth on the garment, see **60 Short Upper Rib Cage.**

GARMENT & PATTERN ALTERATIONS FOR SYMMETRICAL FIGURES

Change Required
Shorten the sleeve cap.

Slash Method—fitting garment only
If the garment armscye has been corrected, shorten the sleeve cap *before* attaching the sleeve to the garment. Follow **Pivot Method.**

If the sleeves are attached and the armscye is too long, adjust the sleeve cap height and the garment armscye length simultaneously. Cut across the sleeve cap about halfway between the arm hinge area and the top of the cap. Where the sleeve slash meets the back and front armscye, cut downward into the garment. Follow the lengthwise grain to a point 1 inch (2.5 cm) below the scyeline. Cut across the underarm area between the vertical slashes. Lap the cut edges of the sleeve until the lower armscye seamline rises to a comfortable position. Insert a fabric strip across the underarm area. Separate the cut edges evenly equal to the width of the sleeve adjustment and stitch.

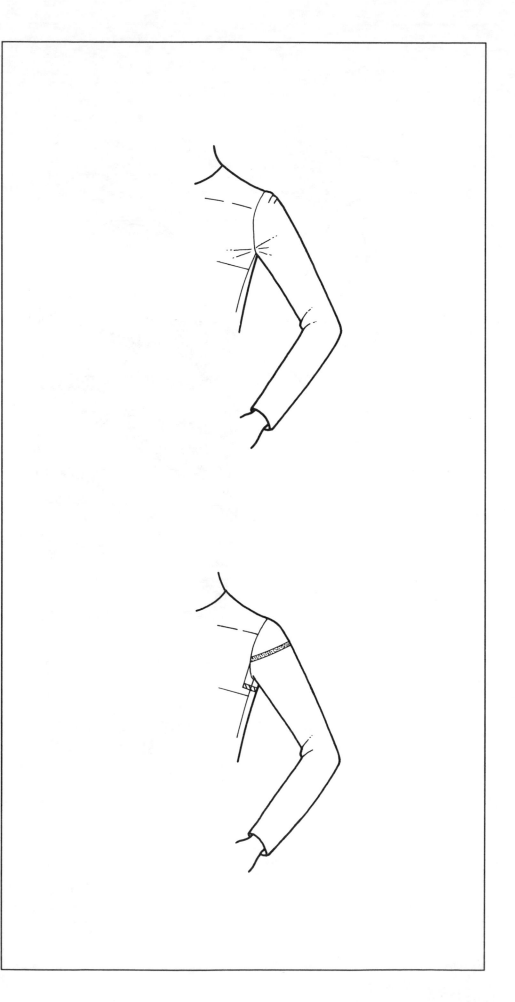

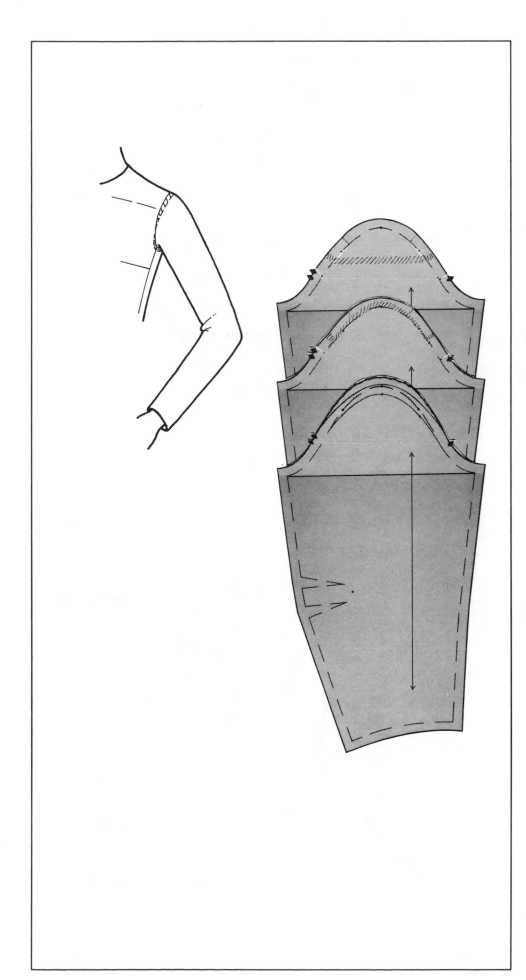

Join the vertical slashes with multi-stitch zigzagging or reinforce with fabric strips. This procedure may raise the dart shaping above the elbow position.

To correct the length, slash completely around the sleeve above the elbow line. Separate the cut edges evenly over a fabric insert until the length is correct.

Pivot Method

If the garment armscye depth has been corrected, shorten the sleeve cap before attaching the sleeves to the garment. Across the top of the cap, mark below the center of the seamline to take up an amount equal to the length adjustment of the garment. Blend into the original seamline at the front and back of the armscye. Lower the sleeve balance marks equal to the cap height adjustment. Attach the sleeves to the garment using the new markings.

If the sleeves are attached and the sleeve length is correct, raise the lower armscye seamline closer to the arm hinges. Mark across the underarm seam area *above* the original armscye seamline to indicate the correct amount of adjustment. Blend the new seamline into the original at the arm hinge areas. Remove the original stitching.

If the sleeves are attached and the lower armscye needs no adjustment but the top of the cap is too loose, release the seam across the top of the cap. Take in the cap seamline enough across the top of the cap to remove the excess fabric. Blend into the original seamline at the front and back. Stitch the sleeve to the garment.

BASIC FITTING THEORY

Figure Analysis
The bones forming the joint structure are larger than average. The surrounding muscles and other tissues may be heavier. These factors increase the circumference of the shoulder joint. A more cylindrical rib cage may accompany this figure variation.

Fitting Analysis
The armscye tightens against the joint. Tight horizontal wrinkles form across the armscye seams. Arm movement is uncomfortable.

If the sleeves are over-eased or the garment is eased to the sleeve, a similar appearance and discomfort is created because either factor reduces the size of the armscye; reset the sleeve properly.

Fabric Requirements for Proper Fit
The larger joint circumference requires a sleeve cap with more width above the arm hinge. When this variation is in combination with a cylindrical torso, wider armscye extensions are required on the garment and the sleeve. See **57 Cylindrical-shaped Torso (rib cage)** and **80 Large Upper Arms.**

GARMENT & PATTERN ALTERATIONS FOR SYMMETRICAL FIGURES

Change Required
Widen the upper sleeve cap area.

Slash Method—fitting garment only
Before attaching the sleeves adjust the cap to correspond to the change made in the garment. See **Pivot Method.**

If the sleeves are attached, release the armscye seam across the shoulder area. Increase the armscye length by slashing from the armscye to but not through the neckline near the shoulder seamline. Insert fabric strips and spread each set of cut edges equally until the fabric relaxes.

Slash the sleeve cap vertically through the center down to the capline. Insert a fabric strip. Spread the cut edges to equal the shoulder adjustment. Taper to nothing at the capline. Stitch the sleeve across the top. If the underarm area is tight see **57 Cylindrical-shaped Torso (rib cage)** and **80 Large Upper Arms.**

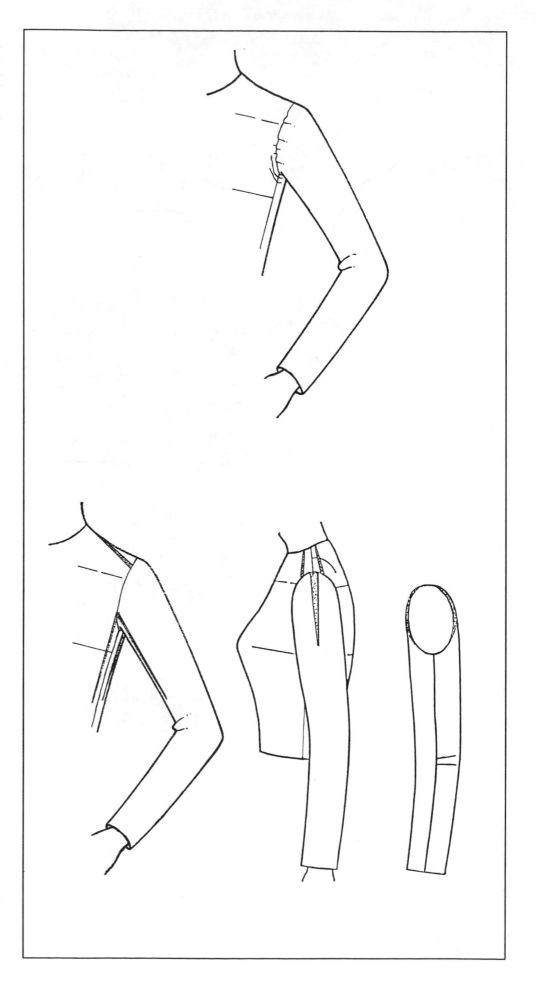

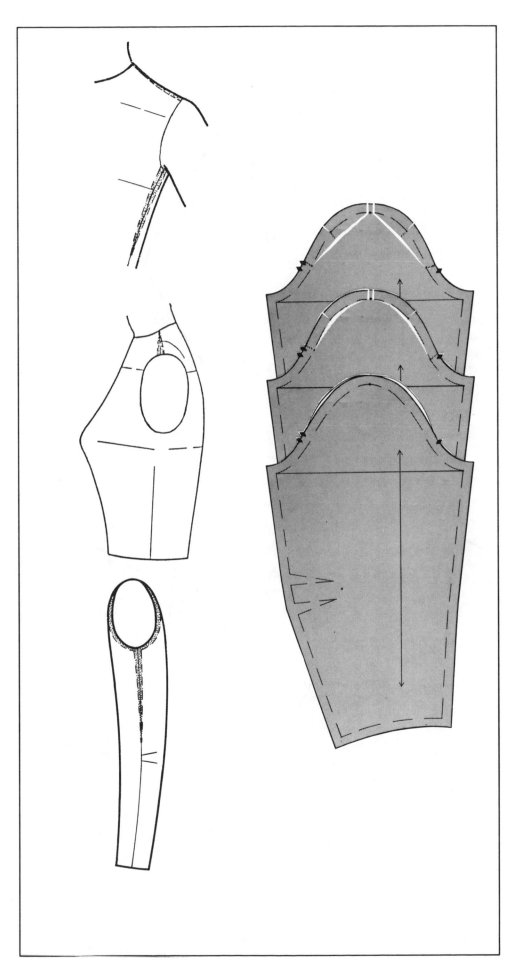

Pivot Method

Before attaching the sleeves increase each side of the cap halfway between the notch and shoulder an amount equal to the change made in the garment. Blend into the original seamline at the shoulder mark and notches.

If the sleeves are attached and lack cap ease, release the armscye seam from the notch to within ½ inch (1.2 cm) of the shoulder. Increase each side of the sleeve cap until the sleeve lies smooth across the upper cap and the ease has been restored. Blend into the original at shoulder and arm hinge.

If the garment was not fitted properly, increase the armscye length at the shoulder seam and taper to nothing at the neckline. Adjust sleeves as directed above. When the underarm area is tight see **57 Cylindrical-shaped Torso (rib cage)** and **80 Large Upper Arms.**

BASIC FITTING THEORY

Figure Analysis

The bones forming the joint structure are smaller than average. The surrounding muscles and other tissues may be lighter. These factors decrease the circumference of the shoulder joint. A more oval rib cage may accompany this figure variation.

Fitting Analysis

The sleeve cap is too wide at the sides. The fabric forms loose vertical folds at the armscye.

Fabric Requirements for Proper Fit

The smaller joint circumference requires a sleeve cap with less width above the arm hinge. When this variation is in combination with an oval rib cage, narrow armscye extensions are required on the garment and sleeve. See **58 Oval-shaped Torso (rib cage)** and **79 Thin Arms.**

GARMENT & PATTERN ALTERATIONS FOR SYMMETRICAL FIGURES

Change Required

Narrow the upper sleeve cap area.

Slash Method—fitting garment only

Before attaching the sleeves adjust the cap to correspond to the shoulder area. Remove the excess armscye length equally with a tuck near the shoulder on both back and front. Taper to nothing at the neckline. At the top of the sleeve cap, form a lengthwise tuck equal to the amount removed at the shoulder. Taper to nothing at the capline. Stitch the sleeve across the top. If there is excess width at the underarm see **58 Oval-shaped Torso (rib cage)** and **79 Thin Arms.**

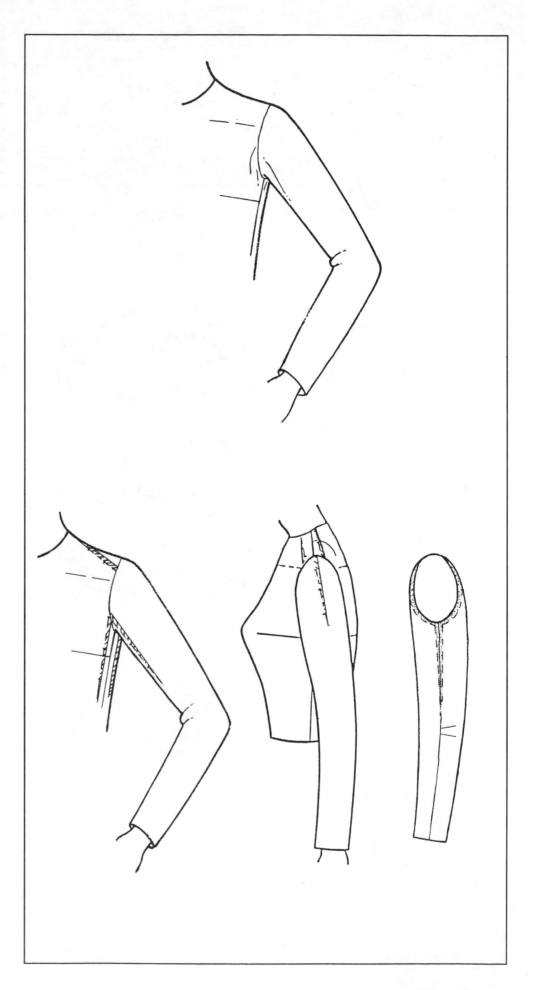

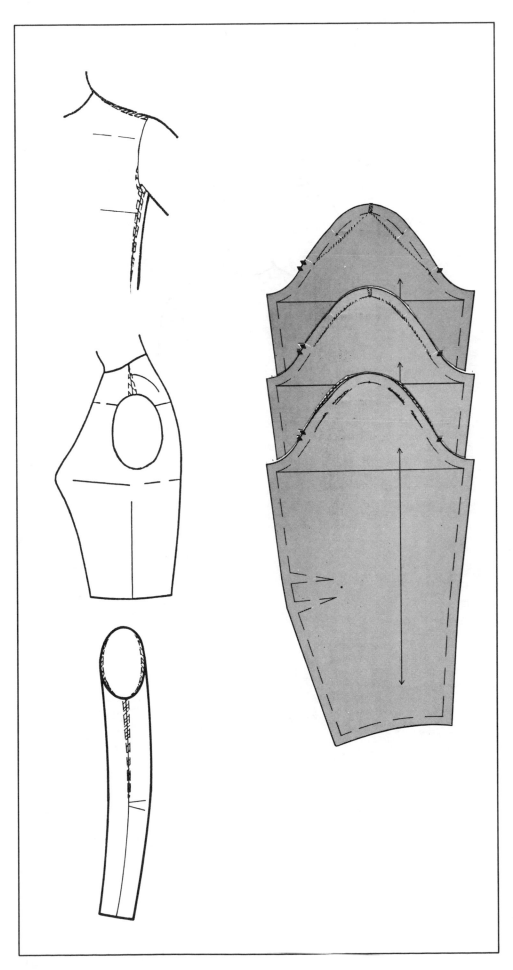

Pivot Method

Before attaching the sleeves decrease each side of the cap halfway between the notch and shoulder an amount equal to the change made in the garment. Blend into the original seamline at the shoulder mark and notches.

If the sleeves are attached and have excess ease, release the armscye seam from the notch to within ½ inch (1.2 cm) of the shoulder. Decrease each side of the sleeve cap until the sleeve lies smooth across the upper cap. Blend into the original at shoulder and arm hinge.

If the garment was not fitted properly, remove the excess armscye length at the shoulder seam and taper to nothing at the neckline. Adjust sleeves as directed above. When there is excess width at the underarm see **58 Oval-shaped Torso (rib cage)** and **79 Thin Arms.**

BASIC FITTING THEORY

Figure Analysis

The bones forming the shoulder-line bow forward and cause the shoulder joints to lie in front of the central body axis. The joint is noticeably rounded in the front; the back is more sloped. When the arms are relaxed, the elbow may lie more toward the back to counterbalance the forward position of the joint.

Fitting Analysis

The front of the sleeve cap is taut near the crest of the joint. The strain causes diagonal wrinkles to radiate toward the back of the sleeve. The back of the cap is loose along the upper armscye area. The horizontal cap fitting line rises at the front of the sleeve. The lengthwise cap fitting line bows forward over the center of the joint.

Fabric Requirements for Proper Fit

The shape of the shoulder joint requires a corresponding change in the shape of the sleeve cap. The curve near the top of the cap must be made rounder at the front to relieve the strain and more sloped at the back to remove the excess fabric. The cap fitting lines become level and plumb. This figure variation also affects the shape of the armscye. See **45 Forward Arm Joints (bodice)**.

GARMENT & PATTERN ALTERATIONS FOR SYMMETRICAL FIGURES

Change Required

Widen the upper front cap area; narrow the central back cap area.

Slash Method—fitting garment only

Only the edges of the cap are affected. See **Pivot Method.**

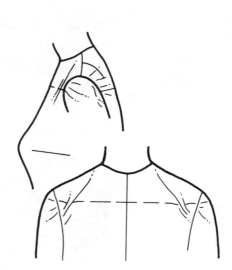

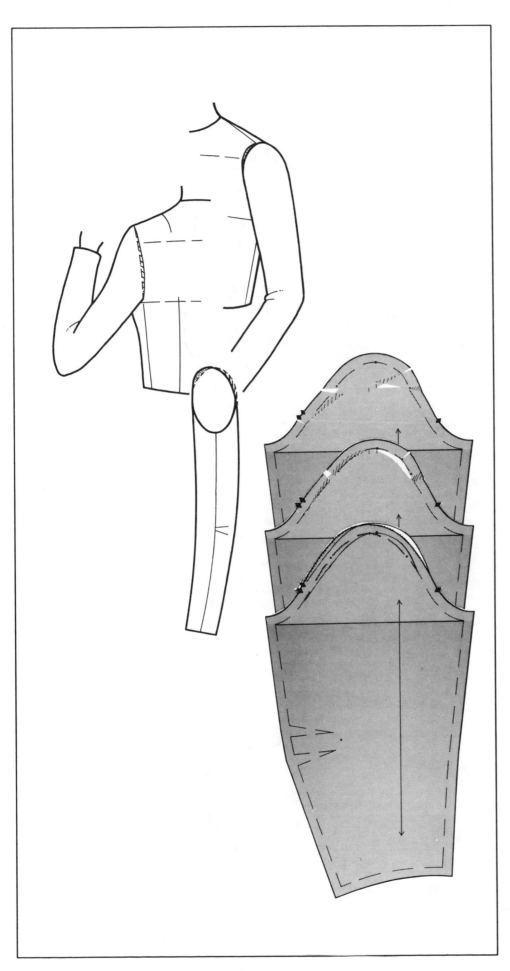

Pivot Method

Release the front area of the sleeve cap from the shoulder mark to the arm joint area. Let out the cap seam allowance near the curve of the joint until the fabric relaxes and the fitting lines become level and plumb. Turn under the remaining seam allowance and align the fold with the adjusted armscye line on the bodice.

Release the back cap area from the shoulder mark to the arm hinge area. Fold the arms in front of the body. Take in the cap area until the looseness is removed. Align the fold with the adjusted armscye line. Mark the new shoulder and balance points on the sleeves.

BASIC FITTING THEORY

Figure Analysis

The bone and muscle development is heavier than average. The arm joints may be larger also. These factors increase the arm circumference at any point along the entire arm.

Fitting Analysis

The entire sleeve pulls taut around the arm. Tight horizontal wrinkles form across the armscye seamlines and the sleeves. The strained fabric pulls both the front and back armscye seamlines toward the arm and prevents the elbow from bending comfortably. Both the upper and lower sleeves areas may appear to be too short. The tightness emphasizes the largeness of the arms.

Fabric Requirements for Proper Fit

The larger arm girth requires more fabric width from the capline to the wristline. This variation also may affect the size of the armscye. See **14 Cylindrical-shaped Torso (hip area)** and **75 Large Shoulder Joints.** The increased width relieves the strain on both the garment and the sleeves. The fabric slides freely over the arm; the elbows bend easily. The larger sleeve creates a more pleasing proportion between the arm and the sleeve. The arms can be raised without pulling the garment.

GARMENT & PATTERN ALTERATIONS FOR SYMMETRICAL FIGURES

Change Required

Widen the entire sleeve.

Slash Method—fitting garment only

If the garment armscye was increased at the underarm or the shoulder, adjust the sleeve width to correspond to this alteration *before* attaching sleeves to the garment. Follow the **Pivot Method.**

If the sleeves are attached and the armscye size is correct, adjust only the sleeve. Release the top of the cap and slash from the cap edge to the wrist. Follow the lengthwise grain. Insert fabric strips. Separate the cut edges equally at the scyeline until the ease and comfort are restored and the arm moves freely. Taper as needed at the top of the cap and at the wrist.

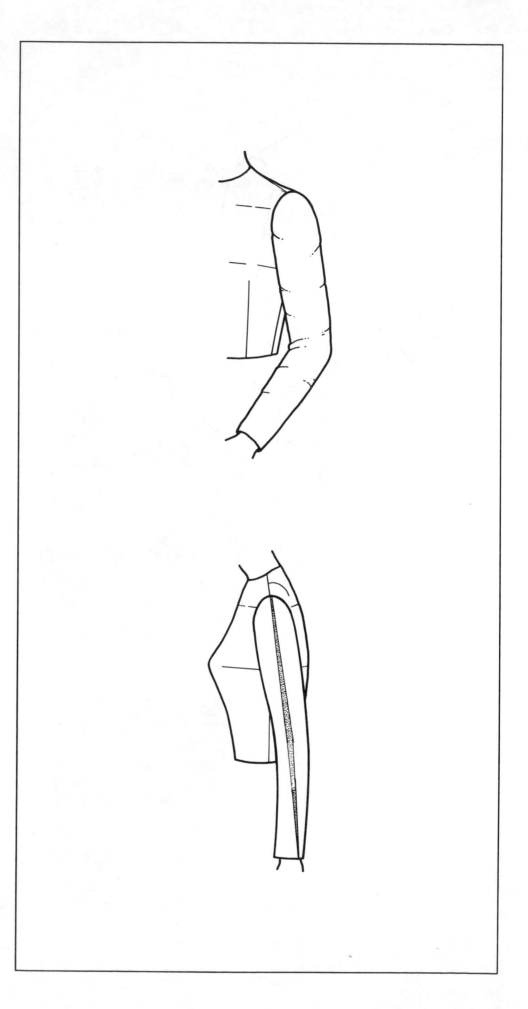

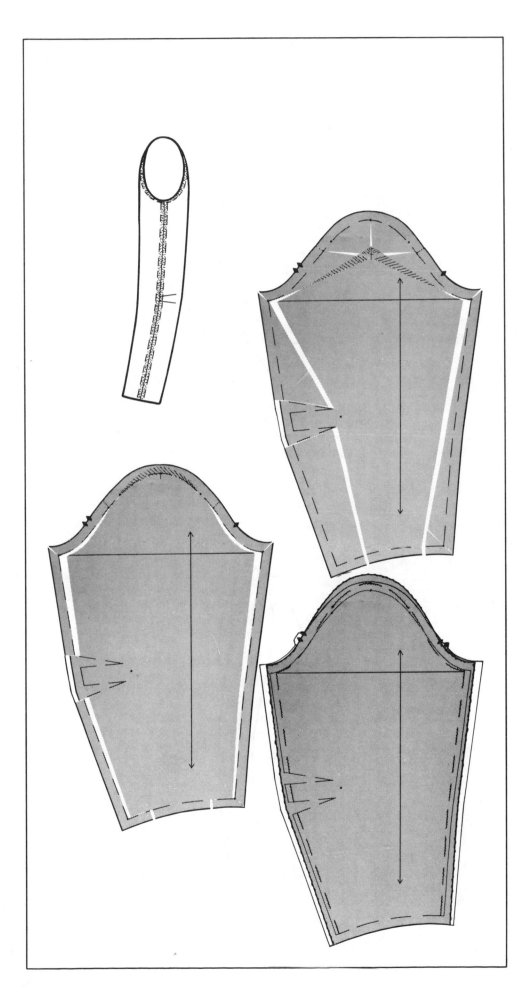

As an alternative procedure, keep the insert parallel along the entire sleeve length. Form a tuck in the insert at the top of the cap and the wrist to remove the excess width of the insert. Taper each to nothing at the scyeline and the elbow respectively.

These procedures shorten and widen the cap. If more cap height is needed to restore the sleeve armscye size, raise the cap seamline across the shoulder area.

Pivot Method

If the garment armscye was increased at the underarm or the shoulder, adjust the sleeve width evenly to correspond to this alteration *before* attaching sleeves to the garment.

If the sleeves are attached and the armscye size is correct, adjust only the sleeve. Remove the sleeves. Release the underarm seam and the darts. Let out the underarm seam allowances equally at the scyeline to restore the ease and comfort and to permit the arm to move freely. Taper toward the original at the wrist as needed. Restore the width and length of the darts.

To restore the sleeve armscye size, decrease the cap height equal to one-half the total width adjustment. Widen each side of the cap equal to one-fourth of the total width increase. Blend into the original near the top of the cap and near the ends of the armscye extensions.

BASIC FITTING THEORY

Figure Analysis
The bone and muscle development is lighter than average. The arm joints may be smaller also. The concentration of soft tissues is minimal. These factors decrease the circumference of the arm at any point along the entire arm.

Fitting Analysis
The fabric of the sleeves hangs in loose vertical folds from the capline to the wristline. The looseness gives a baggy appearance to the sleeve and emphasizes the thinness of the arm.

Fabric Requirements for Proper Fit
The smaller arm girth requires less fabric width from the capline to the wristline. This variation also may affect the size of the armscye. See **58 Oval-shaped Torso (rib cage)** and **76 Small Shoulder Joints**. The decreased width brings the fabric closer to the arm surface and creates a more pleasing proportion between the arm and sleeve.

GARMENT & PATTERN ALTERATIONS FOR SYMMETRICAL FIGURES

Change Required
Narrow the entire sleeve.

Slash Method—fitting garment only
If the garment armscye was decreased at the underarm or the shoulder, adjust the sleeve width to correspond to this alteration *before* attaching sleeves to the garment. Follow **Pivot Method**.

If the sleeves are attached and the armscye size is correct, adjust only the sleeves. Release the top of the cap. Form a tuck along the lengthwise center of the sleeve to remove the excess fabric and retain the ease. Taper the tuck to a narrower width, as needed, at the top of the cap and at the wrist.

This procedure lengthens and narrows the sleeve cap. If less cap height is needed, lower the cap seamline across the shoulder area.

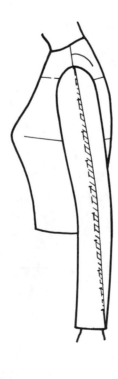

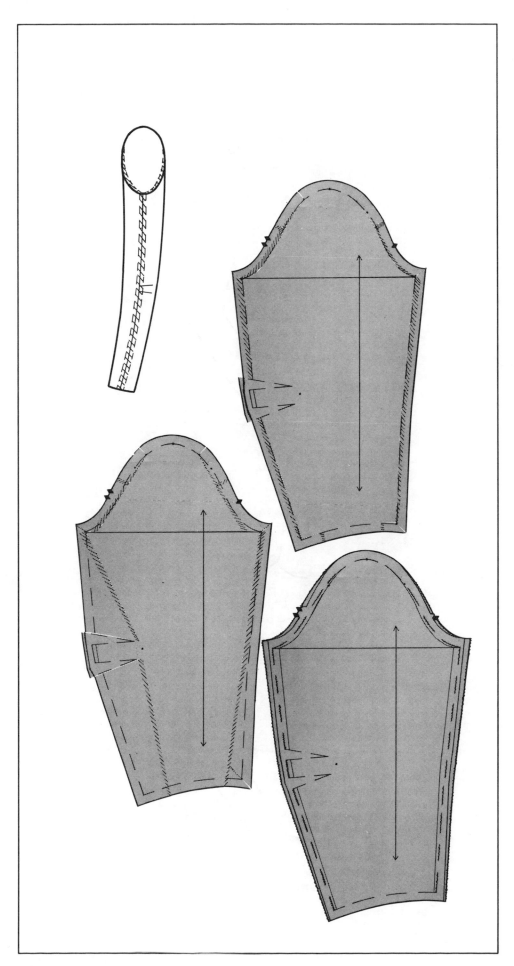

Pivot Method

If the garment armscye was decreased at the underarm or the shoulder, adjust the sleeve width to correspond to this alteration *before* attaching sleeves to the garment.

If the sleeves are attached and the armscye size is correct, adjust only the sleeve. Remove the sleeves. Release the underarm seams and the darts. Take up enough of the sleeve at each underarm seam to remove the excess looseness. Mark parallel to the original seamline from the scyeline to the elbow line. Taper toward the original at the wrist as needed. Restore the width and length of the darts. To restore the sleeve armscye size, increase the cap height equal to one-half the total width adjustment. Narrow each side of the cap equal to one-fourth of the total width decrease. Blend into the original near the top of the cap and near the ends of the armscye extensions.

BASIC FITTING THEORY

Figure Analysis

Heavier muscle development, bone, and excess soft tissue affects only the upper arm area. The arm joint may be larger, also. The fullness may be evenly distributed or may occur mostly at the front, the back, or underneath. It may be at the biceps area only or continue to the elbow. When the connective tissue deteriorates and the muscles lose tone, the soft tissues sag when the arm is lifted.

Fitting Analysis

The sleeve is taut from the capline to the elbow line. Horizontal wrinkles form around the upper sleeve area. The strain across the armscye pulls the entire seamline toward the arm and may pull the sleeve shaping above the elbow tip. The tightness restricts arm mobility and the sleeve may appear to be too short.

Fabric Requirements for Proper Fit

The larger arm girth requires more sleeve width at the capline and perhaps at the elbow level. This figure variation also may require a larger armscye. See **57 Cylindrical-shaped Torso (rib cage)** and **75 Large Shoulder Joints.** The added width relieves the strain on both the garment and the sleeve; each aligns properly with the body structure. The sleeve slides freely over the upper arm area.

GARMENT & PATTERN ALTERATIONS FOR SYMMETRICAL FIGURES

Change Required

Widen the sleeve at the capline.

Slash Method—fitting garment only

If the garment armscye was increased at the underarm or the shoulder, adjust the upper sleeve width to correspond to this alteration *before* attaching sleeves to the garment. Follow **Pivot Method.**

If the sleeves are attached and the armscye size is correct, adjust only the sleeves. Release the top of the cap and slash from the cap edge to the elbow line over the affected area. Follow the lengthwise grain. Insert fabric strips. Separate the cut edges enough at the capline to relax the fabric and restore the ease. Taper as needed at the top of the

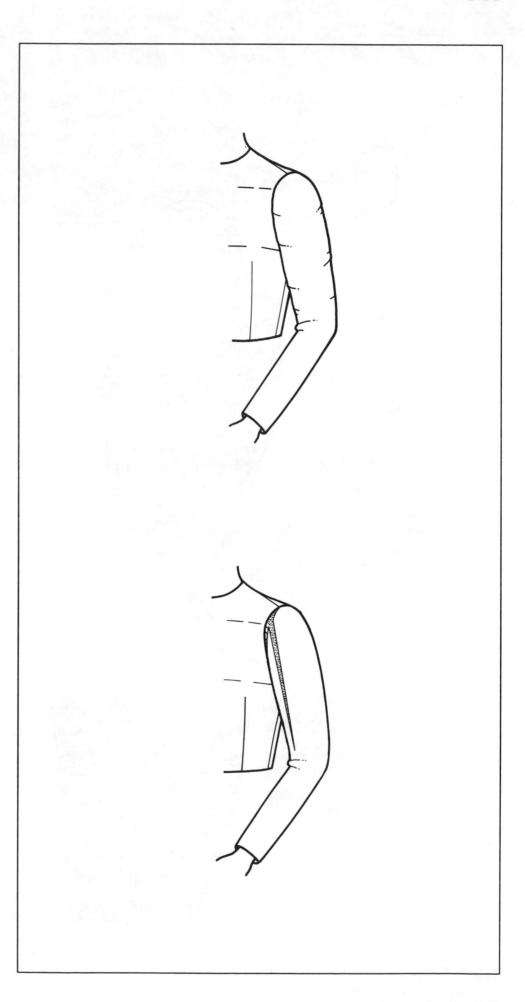

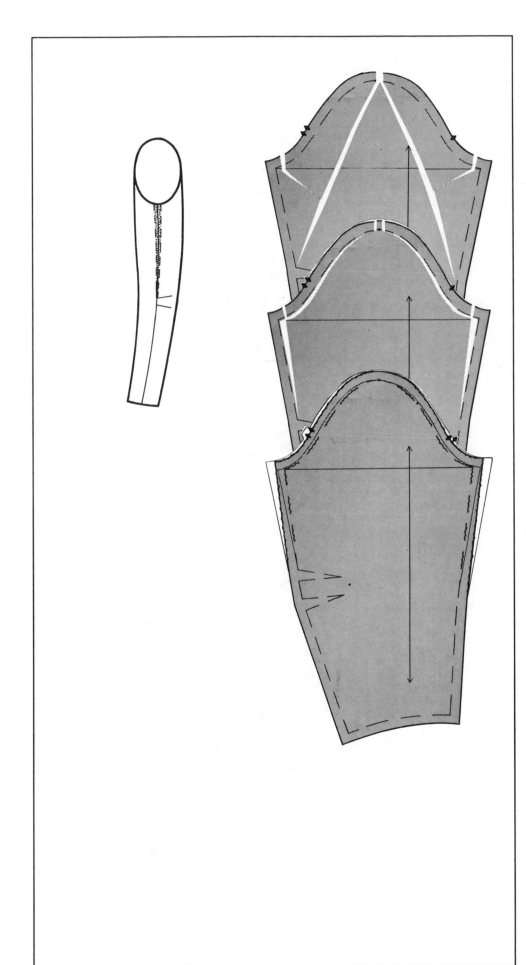

cap and to nothing at the elbow line. This procedure may change the cap height.

If more cap height is needed, raise the cap seamline across the affected area.

If the adjustment was made at the center of the cap, check the distribution of fabric ease around the arm. If uneven, release the sleeves and rotate each as needed to balance the ease over the arm fullness.

Pivot Method

If the garment armscye was increased at the underarm or the shoulder, adjust the sleeve width evenly to correspond *before* attaching it to the garment.

If the sleeves are attached and the armscye size is correct, adjust only the sleeves. Remove the sleeves. Release the underarm seams from the capline to the elbow position. Let out the underarm seam allowance equally at the scyeline to increase the circumference enough to restore the ease and comfort and to permit the arm to move freely. Taper into the original at the elbow as needed.

To restore the sleeve armscye size, widen each side of the cap equal to one-fourth of the total width increase. Decrease the cap height equal to one-half the total width adjustment. Blend into the original near the top of the cap and near the ends of the armscye extensions.

If the arm fullness is at the back area only, remove the sleeves and release the underarm seams. Let out the back underarm seam allowance as needed to restore the ease. Widen the back cap area equal to one-half of the width adjustment. True the cap seamline. If the arm fullness is at the front area only, reverse this procedure.

BASIC FITTING THEORY

Figure Analysis
The bone and ligament structures forming the elbow joint are heavier than average. Excess soft tissues may concentrate at the elbow area. If the elbow does not straighten as much as average when the arm is relaxed, the semi-bent joint will maintain a larger circumference around the elbow area.

Fitting Analysis
The sleeve pulls taut around the elbow and inhibits elbow movement. Diagonal wrinkles radiate toward the front of the sleeve. A horizontal wrinkle pulls across the sleeve front of the elbow area. The strain causes the wristline to rise; the sleeve appears to be too short and the wrist opening too small.

Fabric Requirements for Proper Fit
The larger elbow girth requires more fabric width and length over the elbow area. Longer, wider darts result. The increased shaping and larger sleeve area relieve the strain. The fabric relaxes and slides freely as the arm is moved. The wristline lowers to an attractive and comfortable level at the wristbone.

GARMENT & PATTERN ALTERATIONS FOR SYMMETRICAL FIGURES

Change Required
Widen and lengthen the sleeve at the elbow area.

Slash Method—fitting garment only
Fold the arms against the front of the body. Mark the position of the elbow tip on each sleeve. On the back of the sleeve, slash from the end of the armscye extension diagonally over to the elbow mark; continue diagonally back to the end of the wristline. Insert fabric strips. Separate the cut edges at the elbow level enough to restore the ease and to permit the sleeve to slide freely over the elbow. Taper to nothing at the scyeline and wristline.

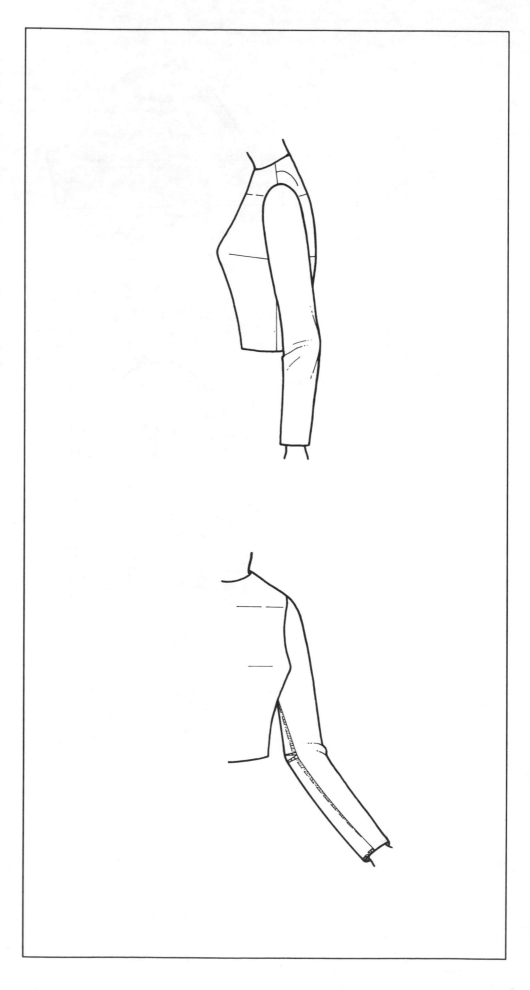

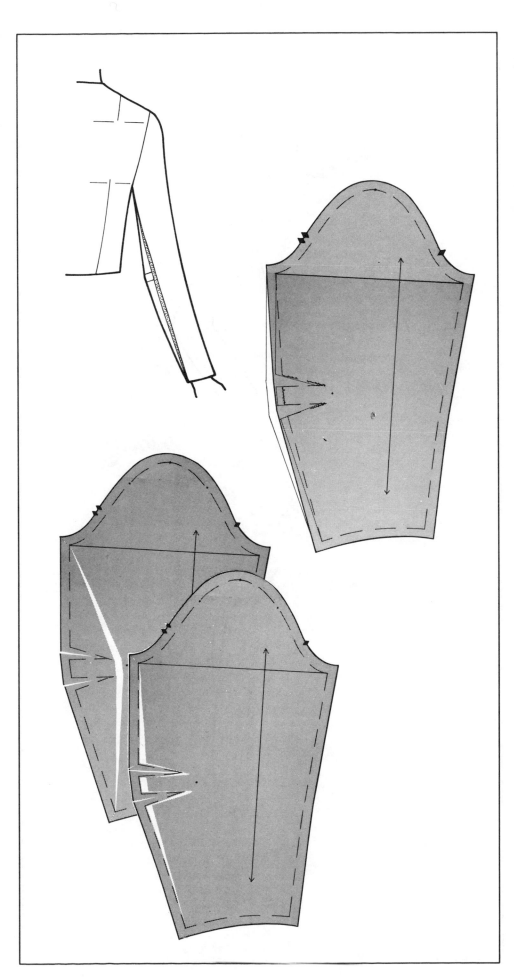

Pivot Method
Release the underarm seams and the darts on both sleeves. Let out the back seam allowance at the elbow level enough to relax the fabric and restore the ease for free elbow movement. Blend into the original at the capline and wristline. Wider dart bases result. Extend the new back seamline into the wrist seam allowance area as necessary to restore the length of the seamline. Taper the new wristline from the length adjustment at the back into the original near the front.

BASIC FITTING THEORY

Figure Analysis
The heavier bone, muscle development, and concentration of soft tissues are larger than average at the forearm area. These factors increase its circumference.

Fitting Analysis
The lower sleeve area pulls taut around the arm below the elbow and forms tight horizontal wrinkles in the fabric. The strained fabric pulls the darted area downward and prevents the arm from bending freely. The sleeve area above the elbow may pull into tight vertical wrinkles.

Fabric Requirements for Proper Fit
The larger forearm girth requires more fabric width below the elbow area. The increased circumference relieves the strain. The fabric relaxes and slides freely along the entire arm. The sleeve shaping aligns with the elbow point; the elbow bends easily and comfortably.

GARMENT & PATTERN ALTERATIONS FOR SYMMETRICAL FIGURES

Change Required
Widen the lower sleeve area.

Slash Method—fitting garment only
Slash from the back quarter position at the wristline up to the capline. Slash parallel to the underarm seam. Insert fabric strips. Separate the cut edges evenly along the lower sleeve area enough to permit the sleeve to slide freely over the arm. Taper to nothing at the capline.

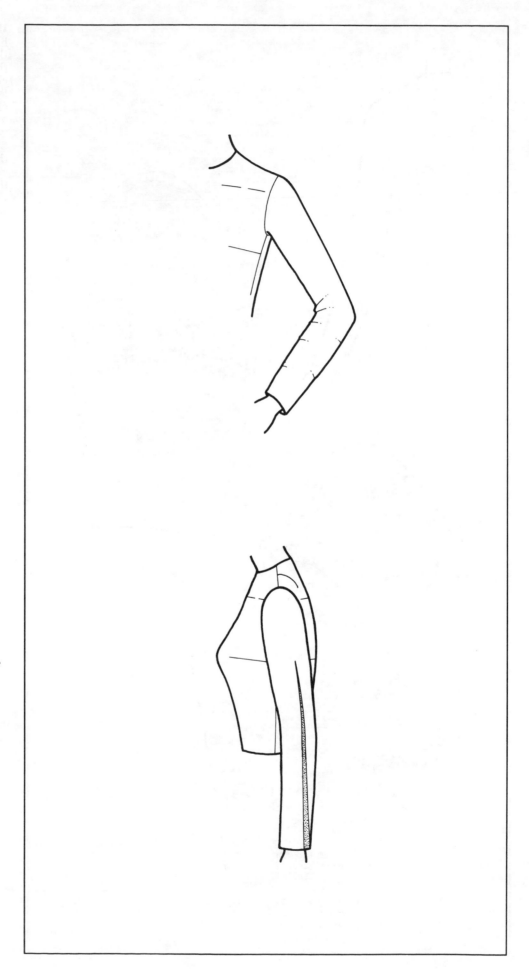

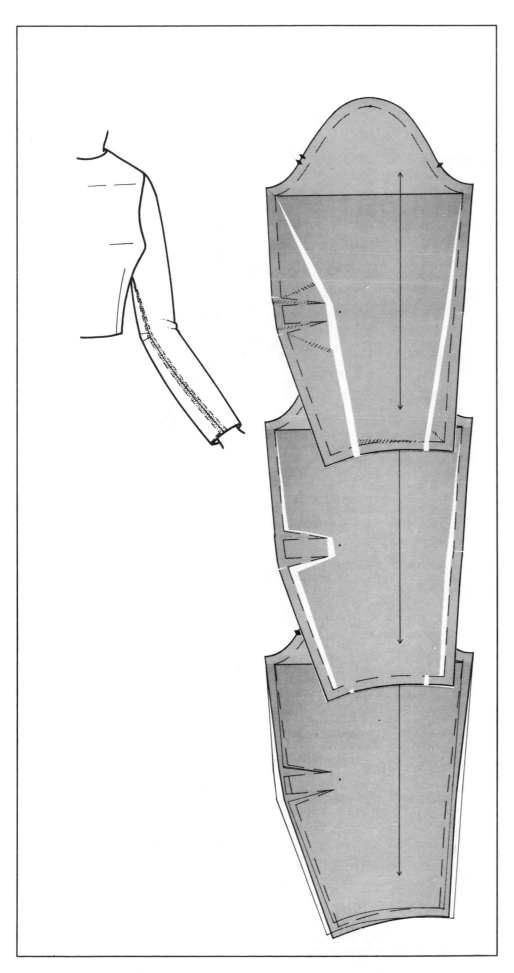

Pivot Method
Release the underarm seams and
the darts on both sleeves. Let out
front and back seam allowances
evenly along the forearm enough to
restore the ease and permit the
sleeve to slide freely over the arm.
Taper to nothing at the capline.
Narrow the darts. Shorten the new
back seamline at the wrist to
restore the length. Blend the new
wristline into the original near the
front seamlines.

BASIC FITTING THEORY

Figure Analysis
When the arms are relaxed, palms forward, the arm curves toward the body more than average at the elbow. The hand extends farther from the body.

Fitting Analysis
A long sleeve twists when the arms are relaxed. The underarm seam of the sleeve aligns with the base of the thumb instead of at the center of the inside wrist area. The sleeve pulls taut across the elbow. The finished sleeve edge pulls up at the prominent wristbone.

Fabric Requirements for Proper Fit
The greater inward curvature at the elbow joint requires increasing the fabric length and width over the elbow area and repositioning the underarm seam at the wristline. These adjustments result in wider, longer elbow darts and more curved underarm seamlines. The wider darts increase the fabric shaping to accommodate the more curved arm structure at the elbow.

GARMENT & PATTERN ALTERATIONS FOR SYMMETRICAL FIGURES

Change Required
Lengthen and widen the elbow area; reposition the underarm seam toward the back at the wristline.

Slash Method—fitting garment only
Mark the seam position so it aligns with the center of the inside wrist. Remove the sleeves. Release the underarm stitching from the wrist past the darted area. At the elbow level, slash across the sleeve from the back to the front stitching line. Insert strips of fabric. At the back, spread the cut edges an amount equal to the adjustment at the front wristline. Taper to nothing at the front edge. Let out the back seam at the dart area until the fabric relaxes over the elbow. Increase the darts equally to restore the underarm length. Stitch the new darts and the underarm seams.

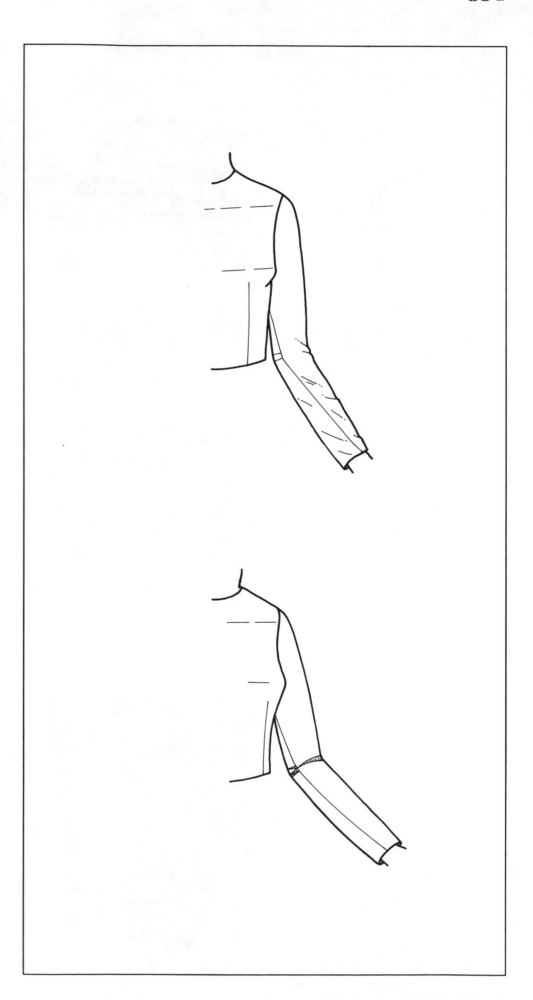

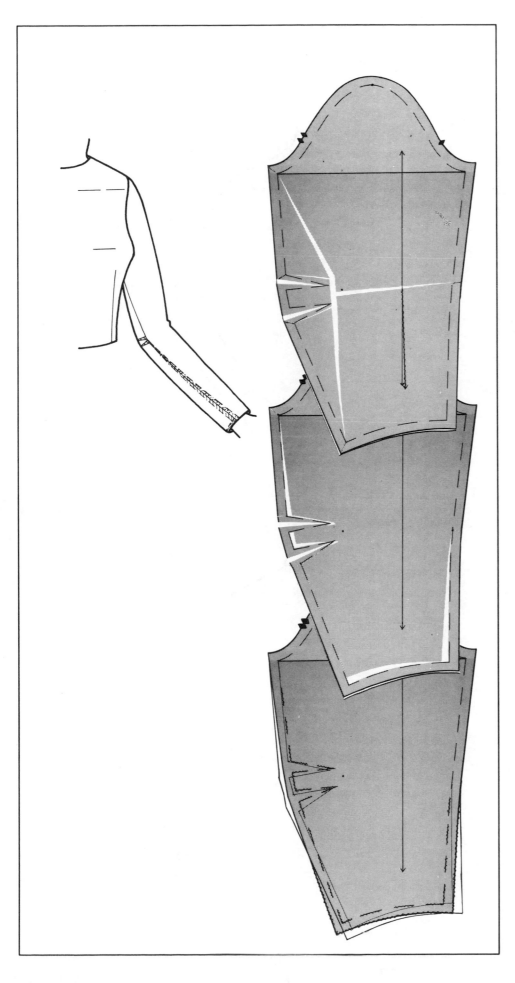

Pivot Method

Mark the position as it aligns with the center of the inside wrist. Remove the sleeves. Release the underarm seam from the wrist past the darted area. At the wrist, let out the front seam by an amount equal to the marked adjustment. Taper to nothing at the elbow. Increase the darts equal to the forward adjustment made at the wrist. Divide the increase evenly between the darts. Adjust the width at the elbow until the fabric relaxes over the joint.

Restore the wrist circumference and the underarm seam length. Close the darts. Begin at the new back underarm seamline at the elbow line. Taper to nothing at the capline. Take in the back seam width at the wrist until the adjustment is equal to the increase made at the front wrist. Begin at the elbow line and draw into the hem mark the end of the seamline. Blend the new hemline into the original at the front wrist. If there is not sufficient hem width remaining to finish the edge, face the edge.

BASIC FITTING THEORY

Figure Analysis

The bone and ligament structures forming the wrist joints are heavier than average. Soft body tissues may concentrate along the wrist area. The larger bone structure and tissue deposits increase the circumference of the wrist.

Fitting Analysis

The sleeve lacks sufficient ease at the wristline. The fabric may pull taut around the wrist area. When the arm is bent the sleeve slides upward and binds against the arm. After straightening the arm, the wristline remains too high and becomes annoying.

Fabric Requirements for Proper Fit

The larger girth of the wrist requires more fabric width at the wristline. To prevent enlarging the sleeve at the elbow, part of the elbow darting may be transferred to the wristline and released.

GARMENT & PATTERN ALTERATIONS FOR SYMMETRICAL FIGURES

Change Required

Widen the sleeve at the wristline.

Slash Method—fitting garment only

Mark the back quarter of the sleeve at the wristline. Slash from the wrist to the tips of the elbow dart. Cut parallel to the underarm seam. Insert fabric strips. Separate the cut edges equally at the wristline until the sleeve moves freely and the wristline lowers and aligns with the wristbone when the bent arm is straightened. Taper to nothing at the elbow mark. This procedure transfers part of the elbow darting to the wrist edge.

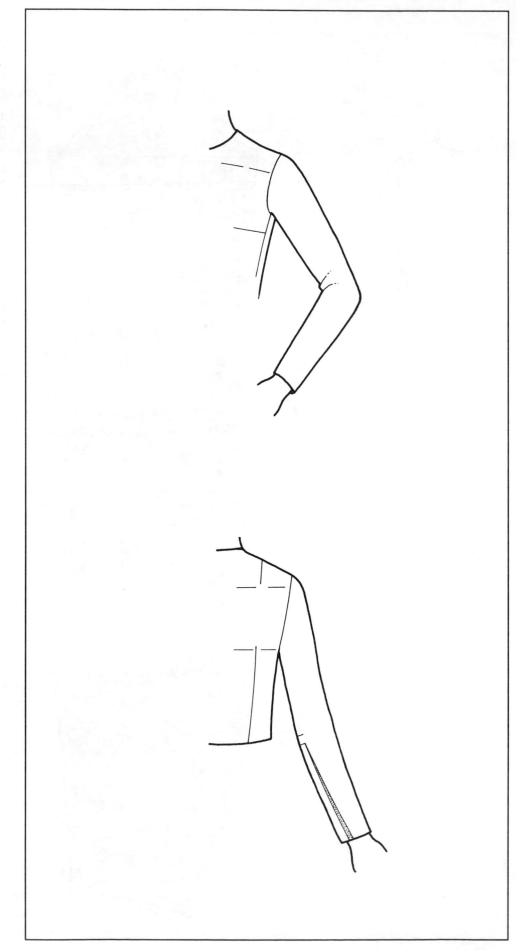

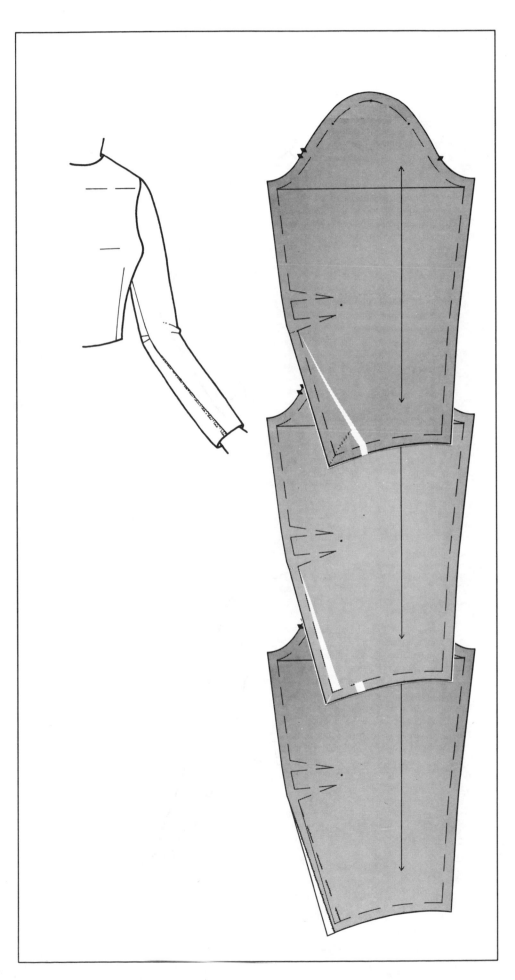

Pivot Method
Release the underarm seam from the wrist to the elbow line. Let out the back seam allowance at the wristline until the sleeve lowers and aligns with the wrist when the bent arm is straightened. Blend into the original at the elbow line.

When the variation is extreme or a looser fitting sleeve is desired, see **82 Large Forearms.**

BASIC FITTING THEORY

Figure Analysis

The bone and ligament structures forming the wrist joints are lighter than average. Deposits of soft body tissue are minimal. The smaller bone structure and tissue deposits decrease the circumference of the wrist.

Fitting Analysis

The wristline of the sleeve is too loose to be attractive. The too-large wrist opening creates an illusion of a too-narrow sleeve area at elbow level.

Fabric Requirements for Proper Fit

The smaller girth of the wrist requires less fabric width at the wristline. To prevent narrowing the sleeve at the elbow, some of the wristline width may be transferred into the elbow darting. The widths of the existing darts may be increased or an additional dart may be formed.

GARMENT & PATTERN ALTERATIONS FOR SYMMETRICAL FIGURES

Change Required

Narrow the sleeve at the wristline.

Slash Method—fitting garment only

Form a tuck along the back quarter of the wristline. Adjust the width to remove the excess looseness and retain the ease. The sleeve should lower and align with the wrist when the bent arm is straightened. Taper the tuck to nothing at the elbow tip. This procedure increases the amount of darting at the elbow.

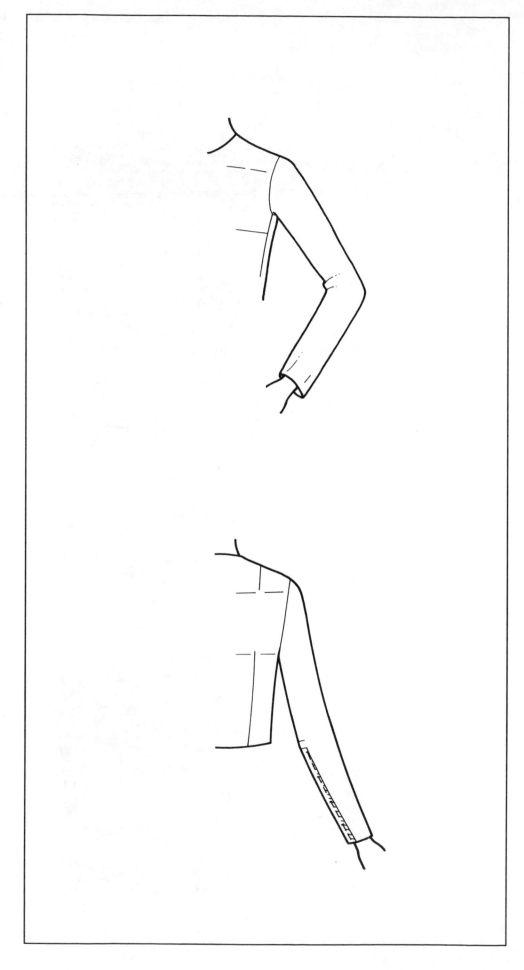

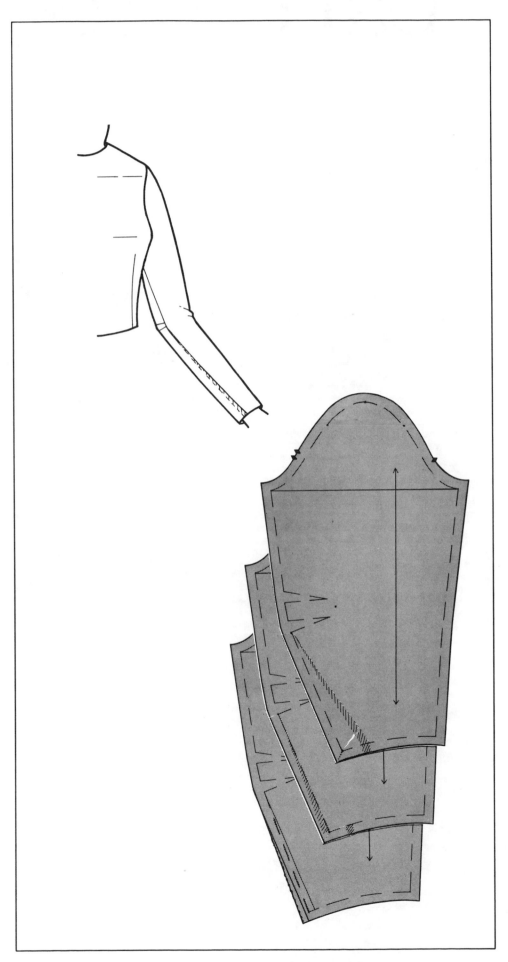

Pivot Method
Release the underarm seam from the wrist to the elbow line. Take up the back sleeve area at the wrist to remove the excess looseness. Retain the ease. Blend the new seamline into the original at the elbow area.

part three

Body Measurement + Ease	Back		Front		Body conformation or other observations
LOWER TORSO & LEG	R	L	R	L	
1. Center Length		X	X		
2. Inseam Length		X	X		
3. Knee Position		X	X		
4. Side Seam Length		X	X		
5. Hip Depth		X	X		
6. Crotch length + 1½″ (3.8 cm)		X	X		
7. Waist Circumference + 1″ (2.5 cm)					
8. Hip Circumference + 2″ (5 cm)					
*9. Thigh Circumference + 1″ (2.5 cm)		X	X		
*10. Knee Circumference + 1″ (2.5 cm)		X	X		
*11. Calf Circumference + 1″ (2.5 cm)		X	X		
*12. Instep Circumference + 1″ (2.5 cm)		X	X		
UPPER TORSO & ARM					
13. Center Length + ¼″ (0.6 cm)		X	X		
14. Full Bodice Length + ¼″ (0.6 cm)					
15. Blade & Bust Height					
16. Side Seam Length		X	X		
17. Shoulder Tip Width + ¼″ (0.6 cm)		X	X		
18. Shoulder Slope					
*19. Chest Length & Bust Contour		X	X		
20. Shoulder Length		X	X		
21. Across Blade or Chest					
22. Center to Blade & Bust Tip					
23. Full Bodice Width + ¾″ (2 cm)					
24. Waist Circumference + 1″ (2.5 cm) (same as above)					
25. Underarm Length		X	X		
26. Elbow Position		X	X		
27. Overarm length + ½″ (1.3 cm)		X	X		
28. Bicep Circumference + 1½″ (3.8 cm)		X	X		
29. Elbow Circumference		X	X		
30. Wrist Circumference + 1″ (2.5 cm)		X	X		
*31. Hand Circumference		X	X		

*Optional measurements
Bust, Waist and Hip Measurements = Pattern Size _____   Center Back Length = Pattern Type _____

Fitting and pattern alteration are simplified when one thinks in terms of where a change is required and how much change is involved to accommodate a figure variation. Use the following illustrations for recording changes in your personal fitting garment and pattern. Each short line on the interior of a pattern piece or around the perimeter indicates the location of a possible figure variation. The pattern pieces are in quarter scale.

1. At each location of a personal fitting adjustment, draw an arrow on the line. Indicate the direction the change should be made to increase or decrease, raise or lower the area.
2. At each arrow, record the amount of the adjustment. Use *full scale* measurements. Use a " + " or a " − " to indicate the result of the change.
3. Draw the new cutting line in red.

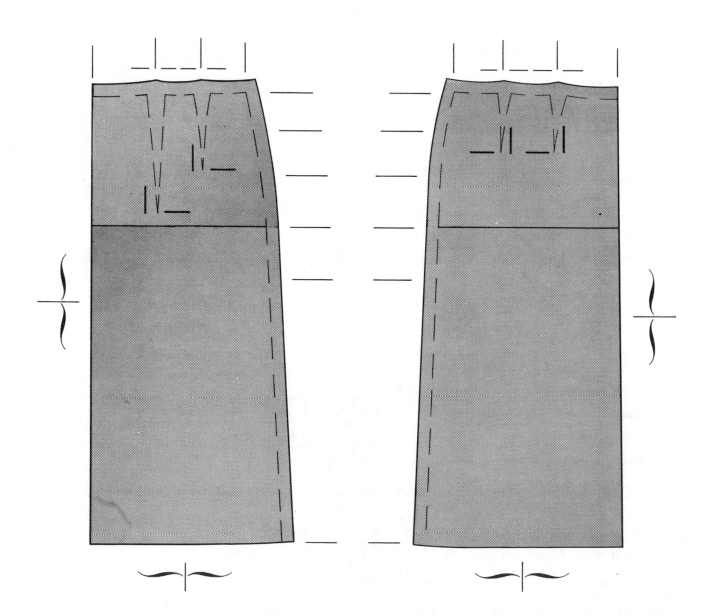

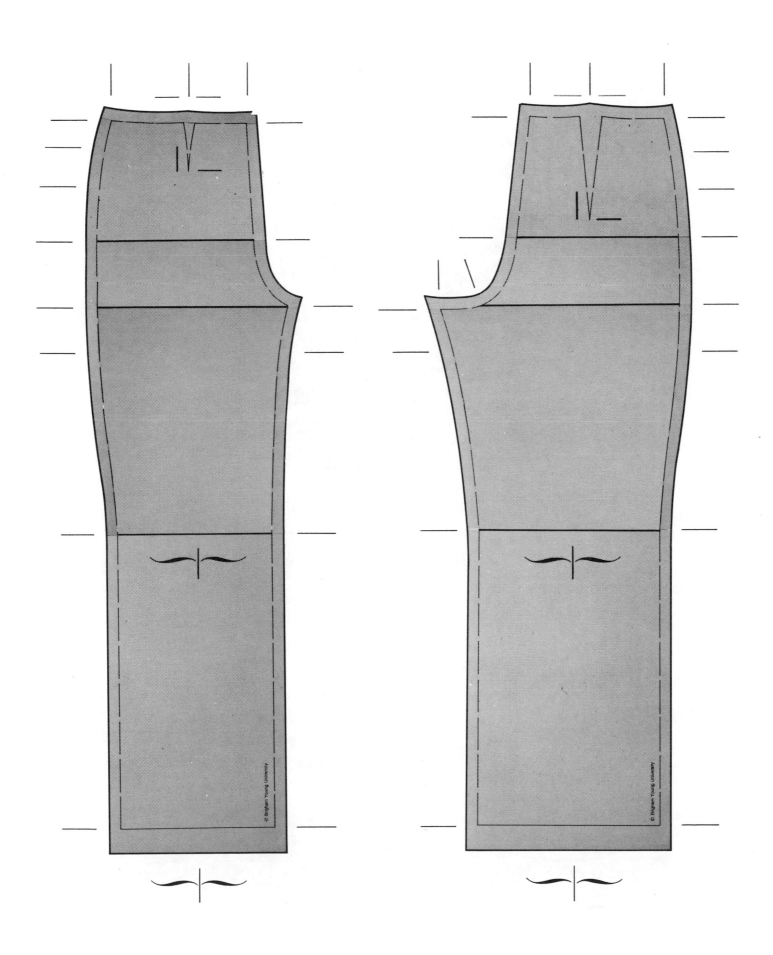

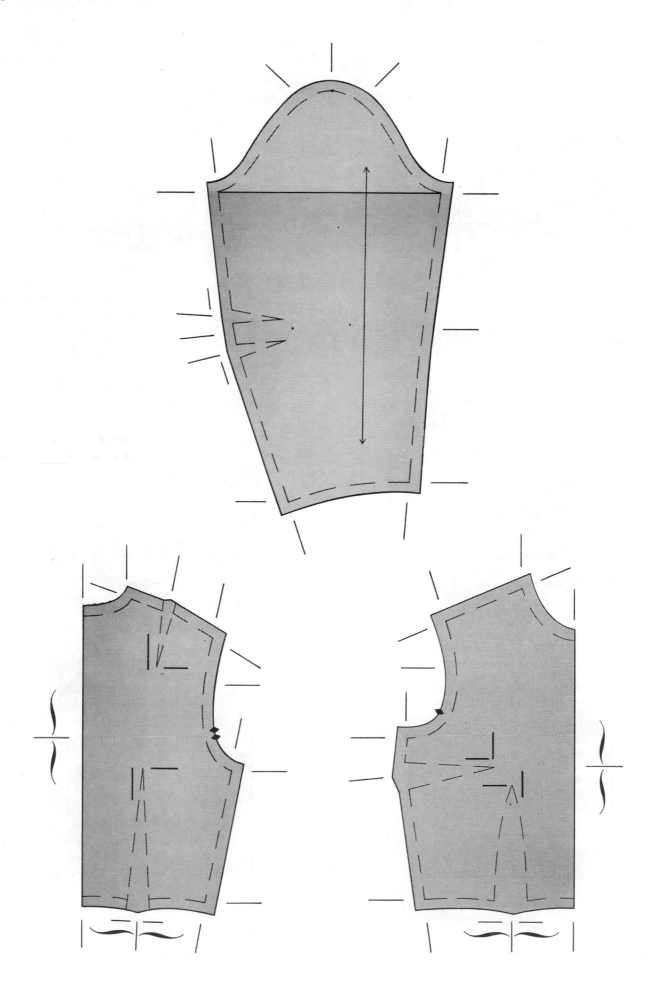